Fruits Basket

Volume 3

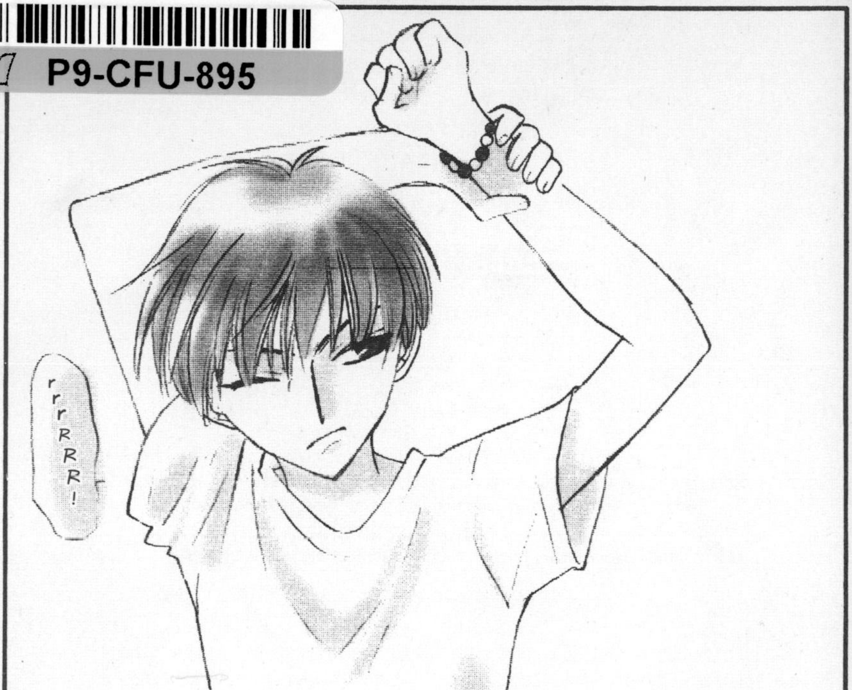
rrrRRR!

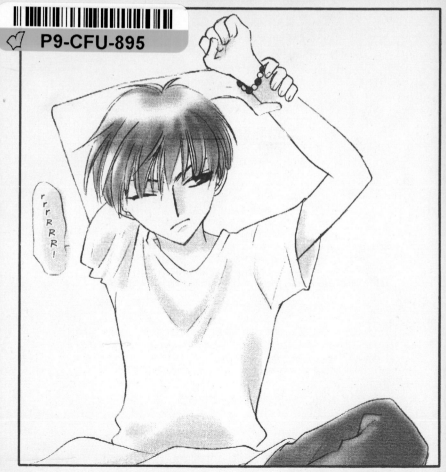

Natsuki Takaya

Translators - Alethea Nibley and Athena Nibley
Associate Editor - Kelly Sue DeConnick
Retouch and Lettering - Deron Bennett
Cover Designer - Gary Shum

Editor - Jake Forbes
Digital Imaging Manager - Chris Buford
Pre-Press Manager - Antonio DePietro
Production Managers - Jennifer Miller & Mutsumi Miyazaki
Art Director - Matt Alford
Managing Editor - Jill Freshney
VP of Production - Ron Klamert
President & C.O.O. - John Parker
Publisher & C.E.O. - Stuart Levy

E-mail: info@TOKYOPOP.com
Come visit us online at www.TOKYOPOP.com

A TOKYOPOP® Manga

TOKYOPOP Inc.
5900 Wilshire Blvd. Suite 2000
Los Angeles, CA 90036

Fruits Basket Vol. 3

FRUITS BASKET Vol. 3 by Natsuki Takaya

ISBN: 1-59182-605-5

First TOKYOPOP printing: June 2004

20 19 18 17 16 15 14 13 12

Printed in the USA

Fruits Basket™

Table of Contents

Tohru Honda

The ever-optimistic hero of our story. Recently orphaned, Tohru has taken up residence in Shigure Sohma's house, along with Yuki and Kyo. She's the only person outside of the Sohma family who knows about their Zodiac curse.

Yuki Sohma

At school he's known as Prince Charming. Polite and soft-spoken, he's the polar opposite of Kyo. Yuki is possessed by the spirit of the Rat.

Kyo Sohma

Just as the Cat of legend (whose spirit possesses him) was left out of the Zodiac, Kyo is ostracized by the Sohma family. His greatest wish in life is to defeat Yuki in battle and win his rightful place in the Zodiac.

Hatori Sohma

The family doctor of the Sohma clan and one of the Juunichi (his symbol is the dragon, which manifests as a seahorse). When Akito wills it, he erases the memories of those who stumble upon the family's secret. Hatori once had to erase the memories of the woman he loved, and ever since has been firmly against letting anyone else know the secret--even Tohru.

Fruits Basket Characters

Shigure Sohma

The enigmatic Shigure keeps a house outside of the Sohma estate where he lives with Yuki, Kyo and Tohru. He may act perverted at times, but he has a good heart. His Zodiac spirit is the Dog.

Kagura Sohma

Stubborn and jealous as her zodiac symbol, the boar, Kagura is determined to marry Kyo...even if she kills him in the process.

Hanajima & Arisa

The two best friends a girl could hope for. They always look out for Tohru, but they don't know about her new living arrangements...yet.

Akito Sohma

The mysterious leader of the Sohma clan, the other family members treat him with equal measures of fear and reverence. Tohru has never met him.

Momiji Sohma

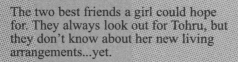

Playful and carefree as the Rabbit he turns into, Momiji is the youngest member of the Sohma family that Tohru has met. He's half German and half Japanese, and switches casually between the two languages. His father owns the building where Tohru works.

STORY SO FAR...

Hello. I'm Tohru Honda, and I have come to know a terrible secret. After the death of my mother, I was living by myself in a tent when the Sohma family took me in. I soon learned that the Sohma family lives with a curse! Each family member is possessed by the vengeful spirit of an animal from the Chinese Zodiac. Whenever one of them becomes weak or is hugged by a member of the opposite sex, they change into their Zodiac animal!

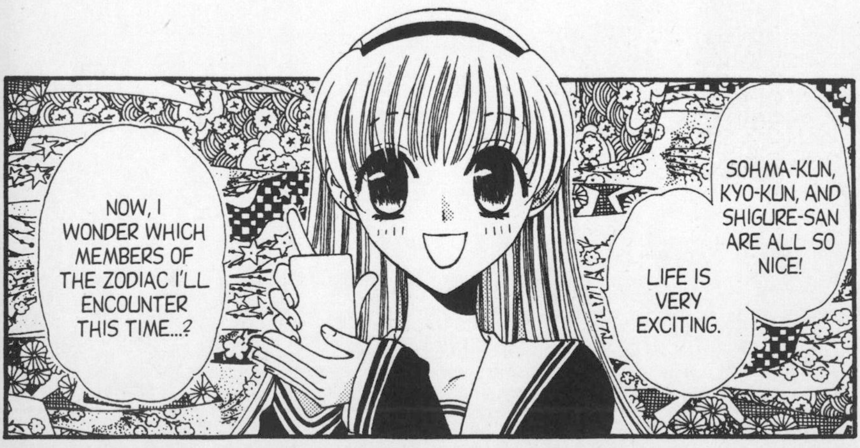
SOHMA-KUN, KYO-KUN, AND SHIGURE-SAN ARE ALL SO NICE!
LIFE IS VERY EXCITING.
NOW, I WONDER WHICH MEMBERS OF THE ZODIAC I'LL ENCOUNTER THIS TIME...?

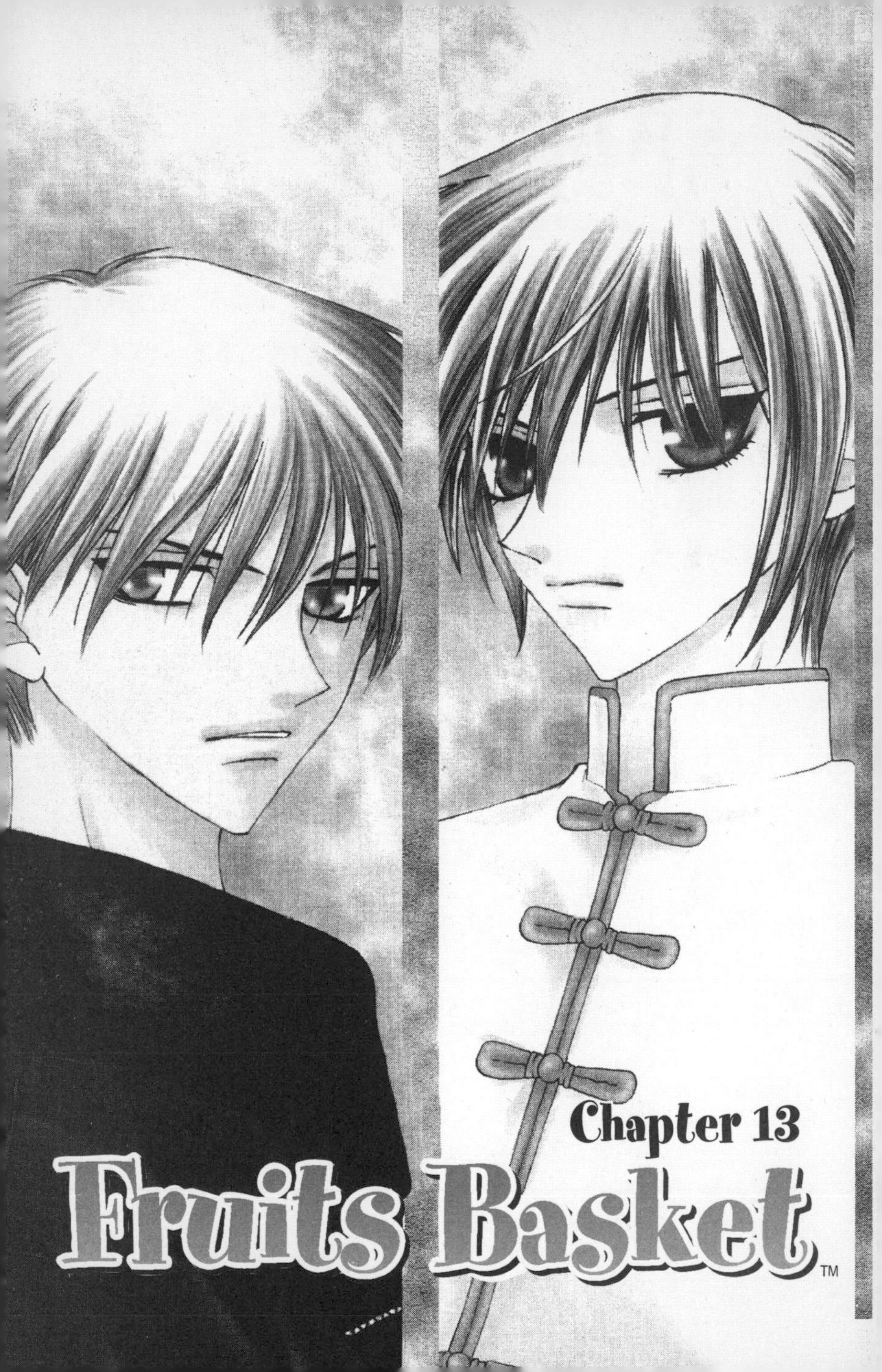
Chapter 13
Fruits Basket™

Omake Theater: The End of the World!

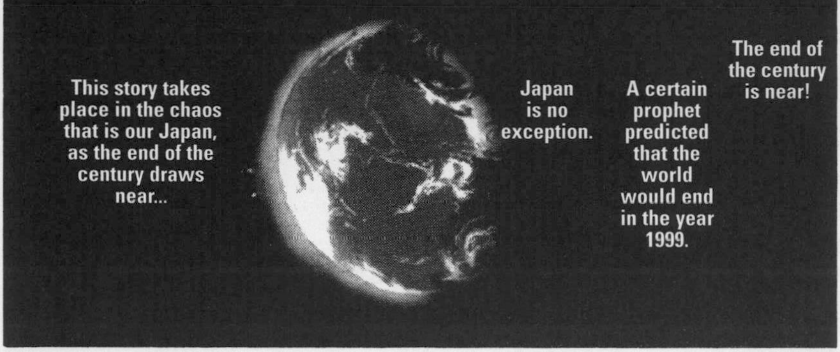
The end of the century is near!
A certain prophet predicted that the world would end in the year 1999.
Japan is no exception.
This story takes place in the chaos that is our Japan, as the end of the century draws near...

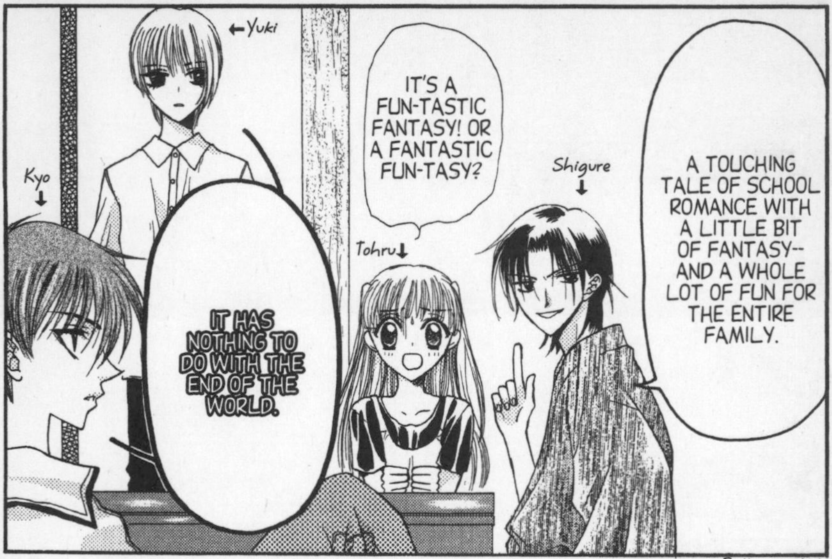
A TOUCHING TALE OF SCHOOL ROMANCE WITH A LITTLE BIT OF FANTASY--AND A WHOLE LOT OF FUN FOR THE ENTIRE FAMILY.
Shigure ↓
IT'S A FUN-TASTIC FANTASY! OR A FANTASTIC FUN-TASY?
Tohru ↓
←Yuki
IT HAS NOTHING TO DO WITH THE END OF THE WORLD.
Kyo ↓

Pretty accurate ↑

ULTRA SPECIAL BLAH BLAH BLAH 1

You may notice Yuki and Kyo have matured a bit in this volume. They're also getting taller. (The tallest character in Furuba is Hatori, in case anyone is keeping track!)

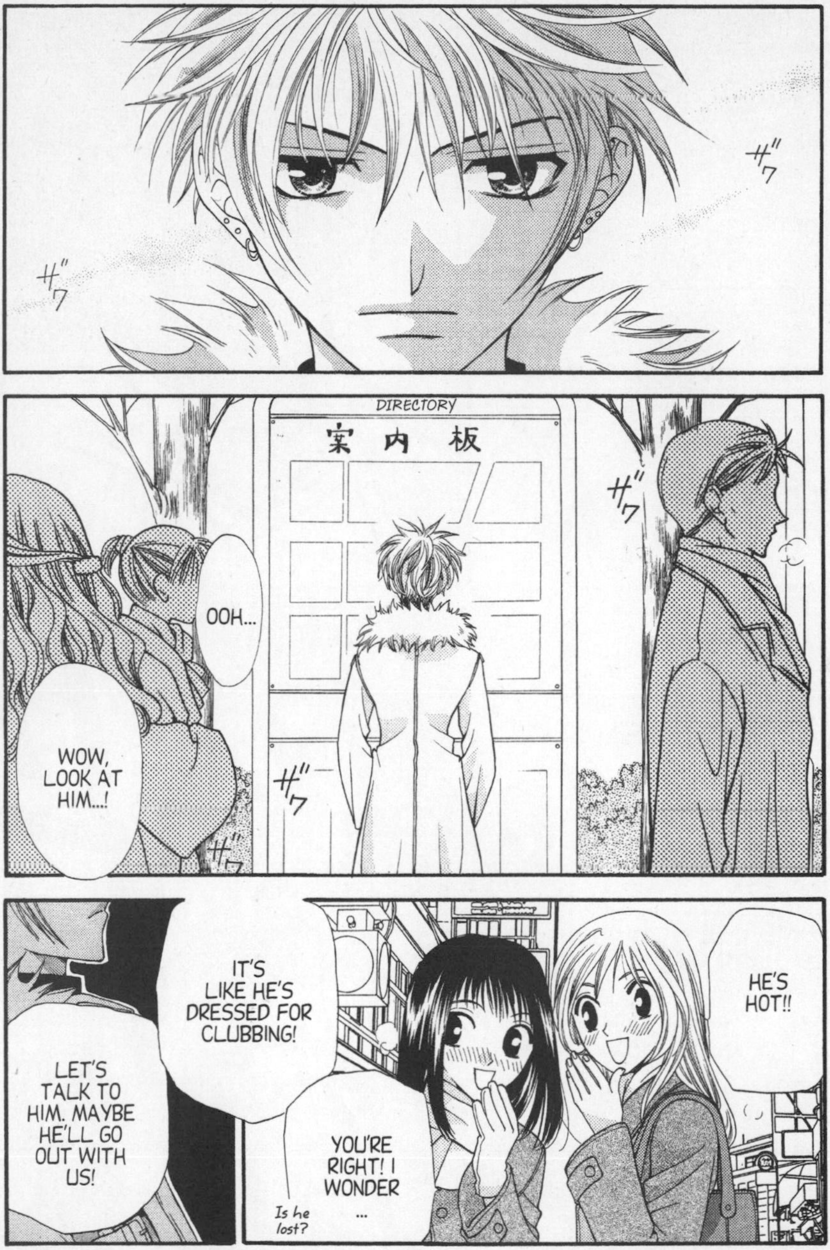
ザワ
ザワ
DIRECTORY
案内板
ザワ
OOH...
ザワ
WOW, LOOK AT HIM...!
ザワ
HE'S HOT!!
IT'S LIKE HE'S DRESSED FOR CLUBBING!
YOU'RE RIGHT! I WONDER ...
Is he lost?
LET'S TALK TO HIM. MAYBE HE'LL GO OUT WITH US!

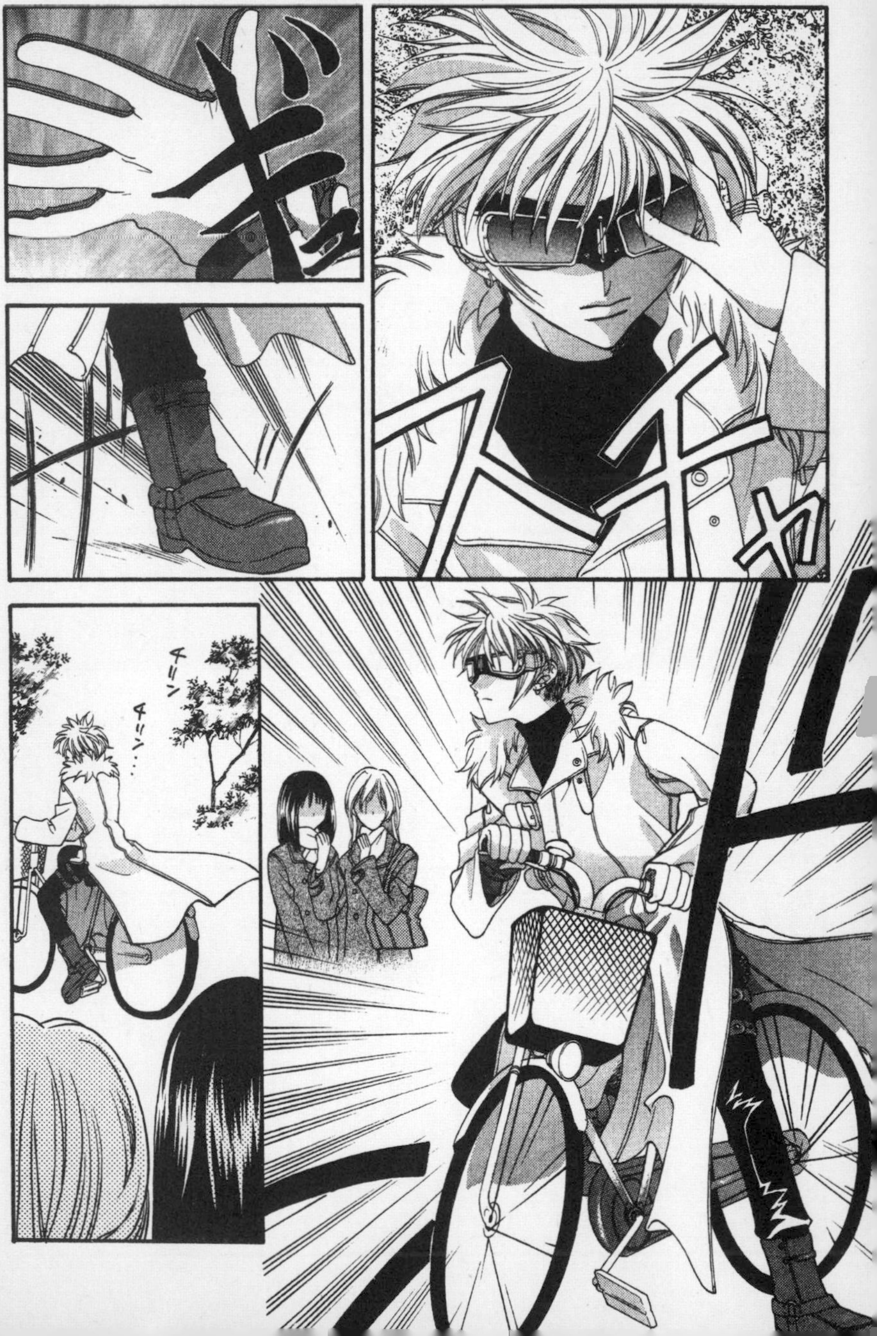
スチャ
ギ
ド
チリン
チリン…

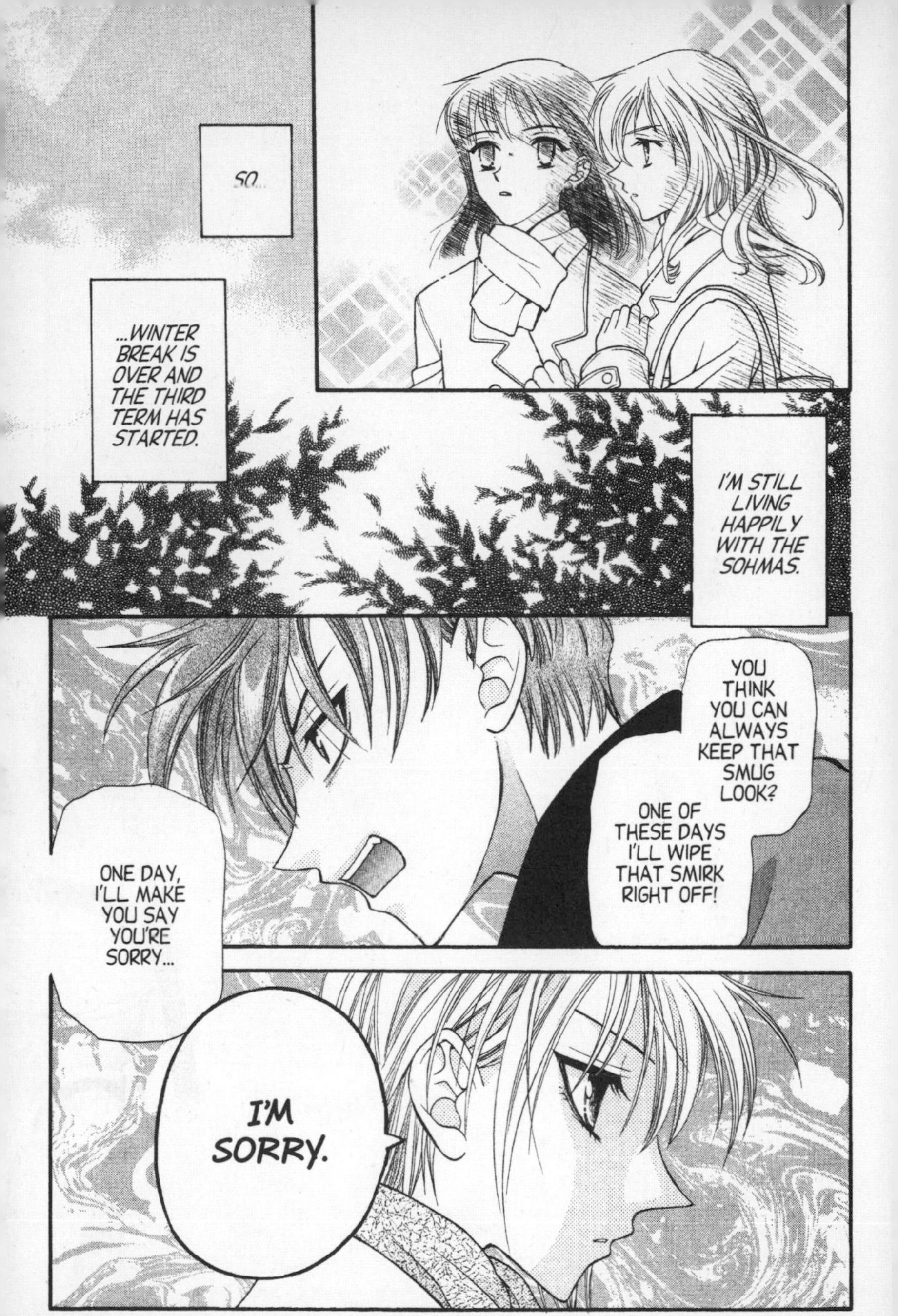
SO...
...WINTER BREAK IS OVER AND THE THIRD TERM HAS STARTED.
I'M STILL LIVING HAPPILY WITH THE SOHMAS.
YOU THINK YOU CAN ALWAYS KEEP THAT SMUG LOOK?
ONE OF THESE DAYS I'LL WIPE THAT SMIRK RIGHT OFF!
ONE DAY, I'LL MAKE YOU SAY YOU'RE SORRY...
I'M SORRY.

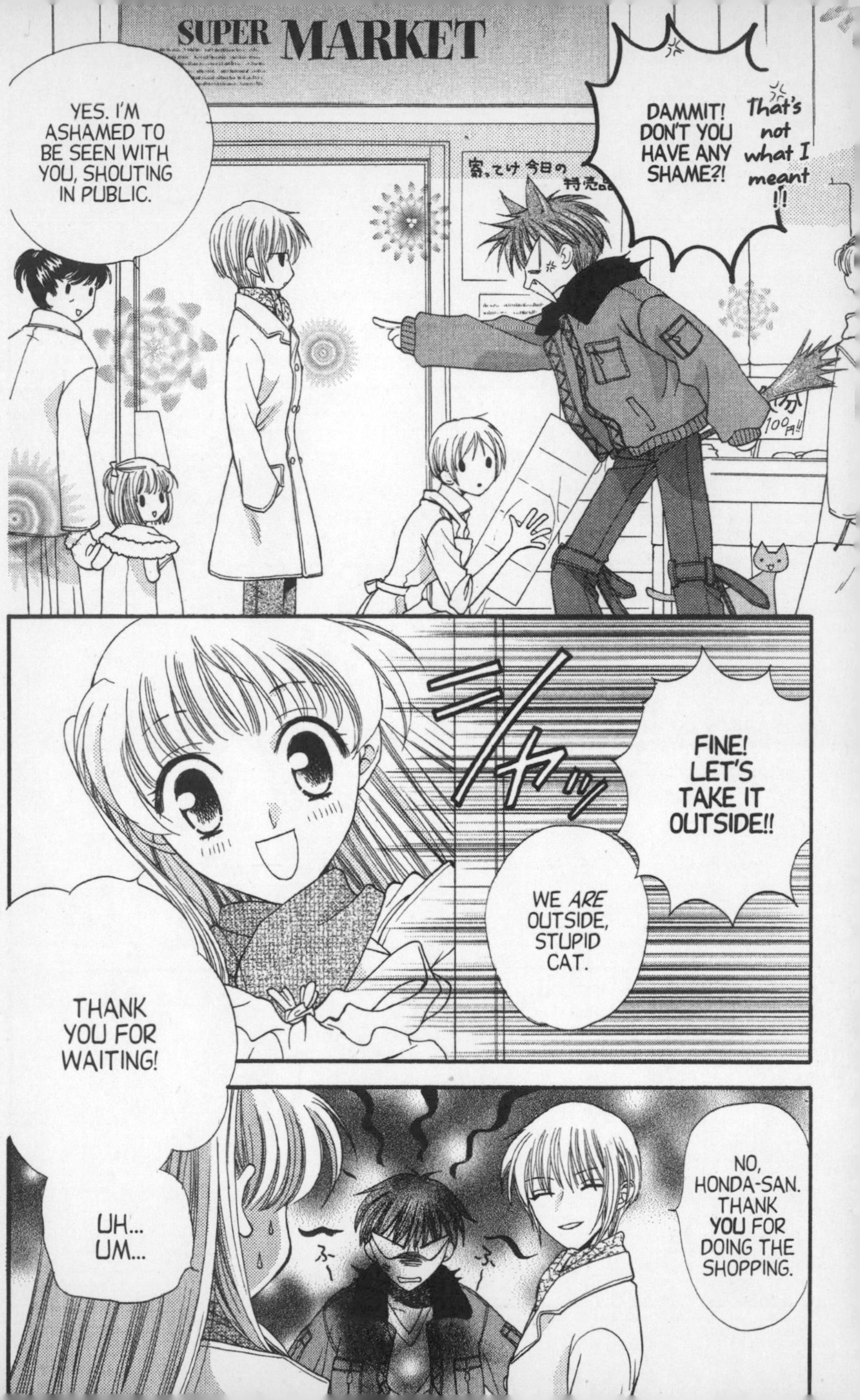
SUPER MARKET
DAMMIT! DON'T YOU HAVE ANY SHAME?!
That's not what I meant!!
YES. I'M ASHAMED TO BE SEEN WITH YOU, SHOUTING IN PUBLIC.
FINE! LET'S TAKE IT OUTSIDE!!
WE *ARE* OUTSIDE, STUPID CAT.
THANK YOU FOR WAITING!
NO, HONDA-SAN. THANK YOU FOR DOING THE SHOPPING.
UH... UM...

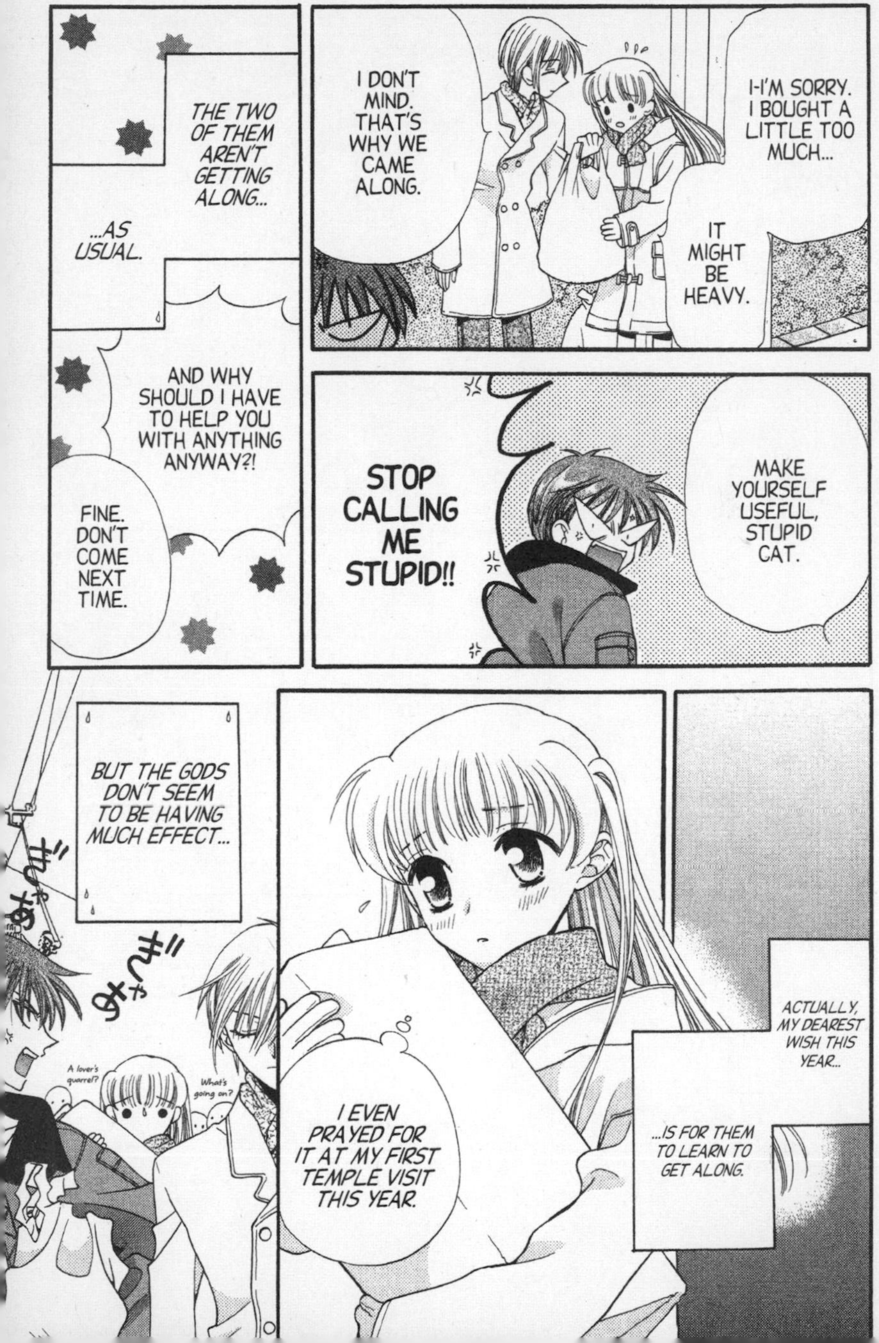
I-I'M SORRY. I BOUGHT A LITTLE TOO MUCH...
IT MIGHT BE HEAVY.
I DON'T MIND. THAT'S WHY WE CAME ALONG.
THE TWO OF THEM AREN'T GETTING ALONG...
...AS USUAL.
MAKE YOURSELF USEFUL, STUPID CAT.
STOP CALLING ME STUPID!!
AND WHY SHOULD I HAVE TO HELP YOU WITH ANYTHING ANYWAY?!
FINE. DON'T COME NEXT TIME.
ACTUALLY, MY DEAREST WISH THIS YEAR...
...IS FOR THEM TO LEARN TO GET ALONG.
I EVEN PRAYED FOR IT AT MY FIRST TEMPLE VISIT THIS YEAR.
BUT THE GODS DON'T SEEM TO BE HAVING MUCH EFFECT...
A lover's quarrel?
What's going on?

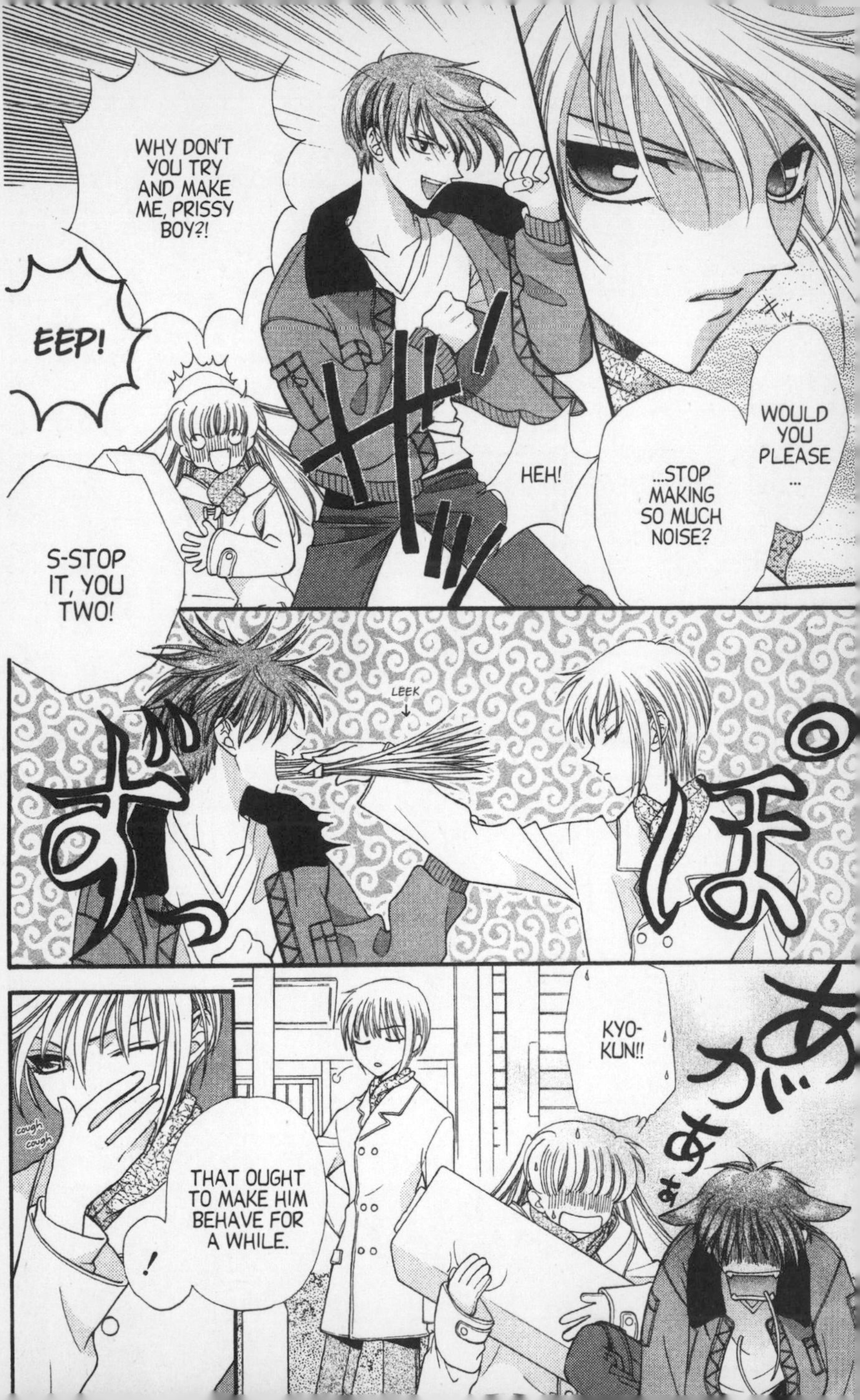
WOULD YOU PLEASE ...
...STOP MAKING SO MUCH NOISE?
HEH!
WHY DON'T YOU TRY AND MAKE ME, PRISSY BOY?!
EEP!
S-STOP IT, YOU TWO!
LEEK
KYO-KUN!!
THAT OUGHT TO MAKE HIM BEHAVE FOR A WHILE.
!
cough cough

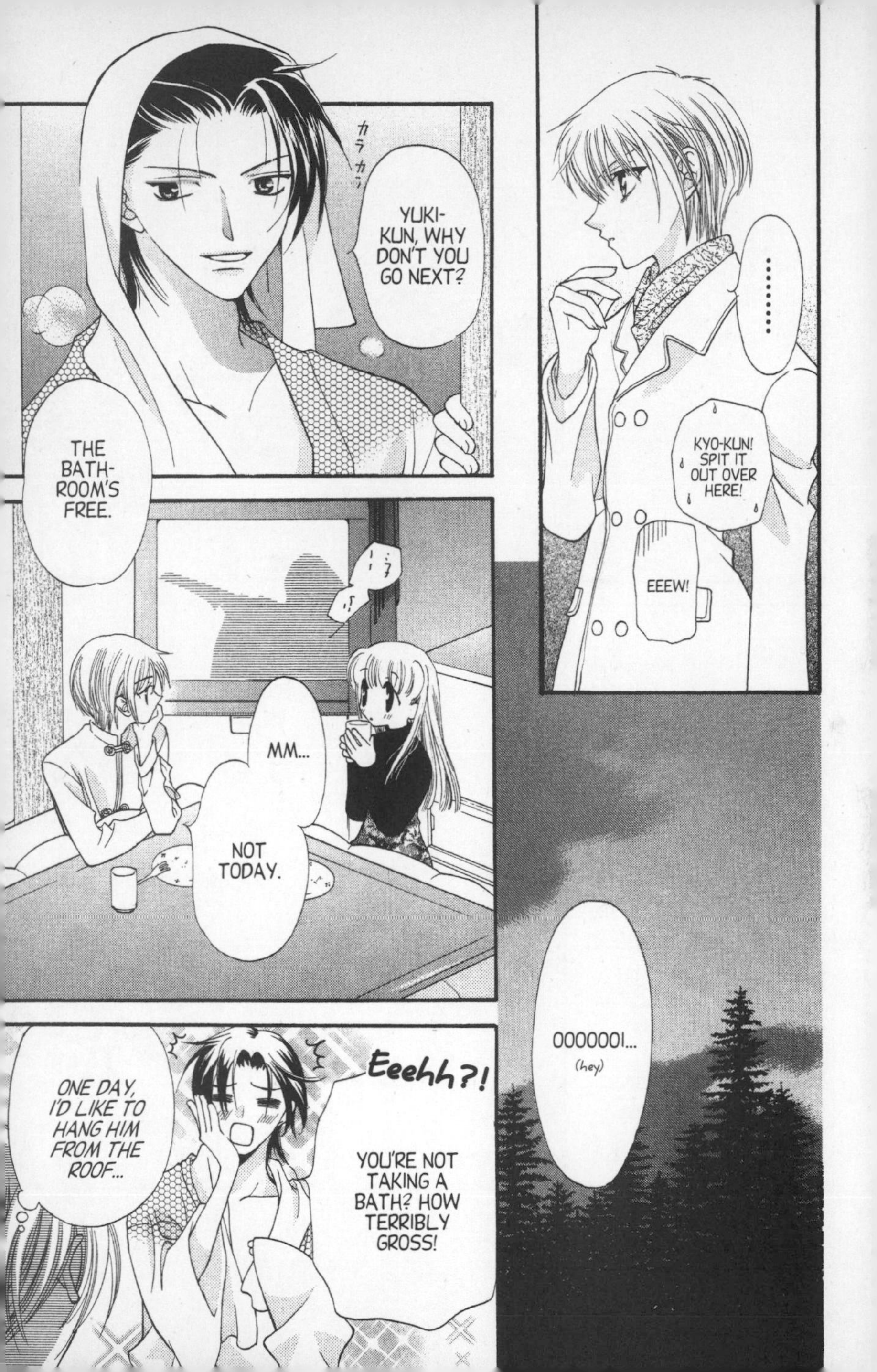
......
KYO-KUN! SPIT IT OUT OVER HERE!
EEEW!
OOOOOOI...
(hey)
カラ カラ
YUKI-KUN, WHY DON'T YOU GO NEXT?
THE BATH-ROOM'S FREE.
MM...
NOT TODAY.
Eeehh?!
YOU'RE NOT TAKING A BATH? HOW TERRIBLY GROSS!
ONE DAY, I'D LIKE TO HANG HIM FROM THE ROOF...

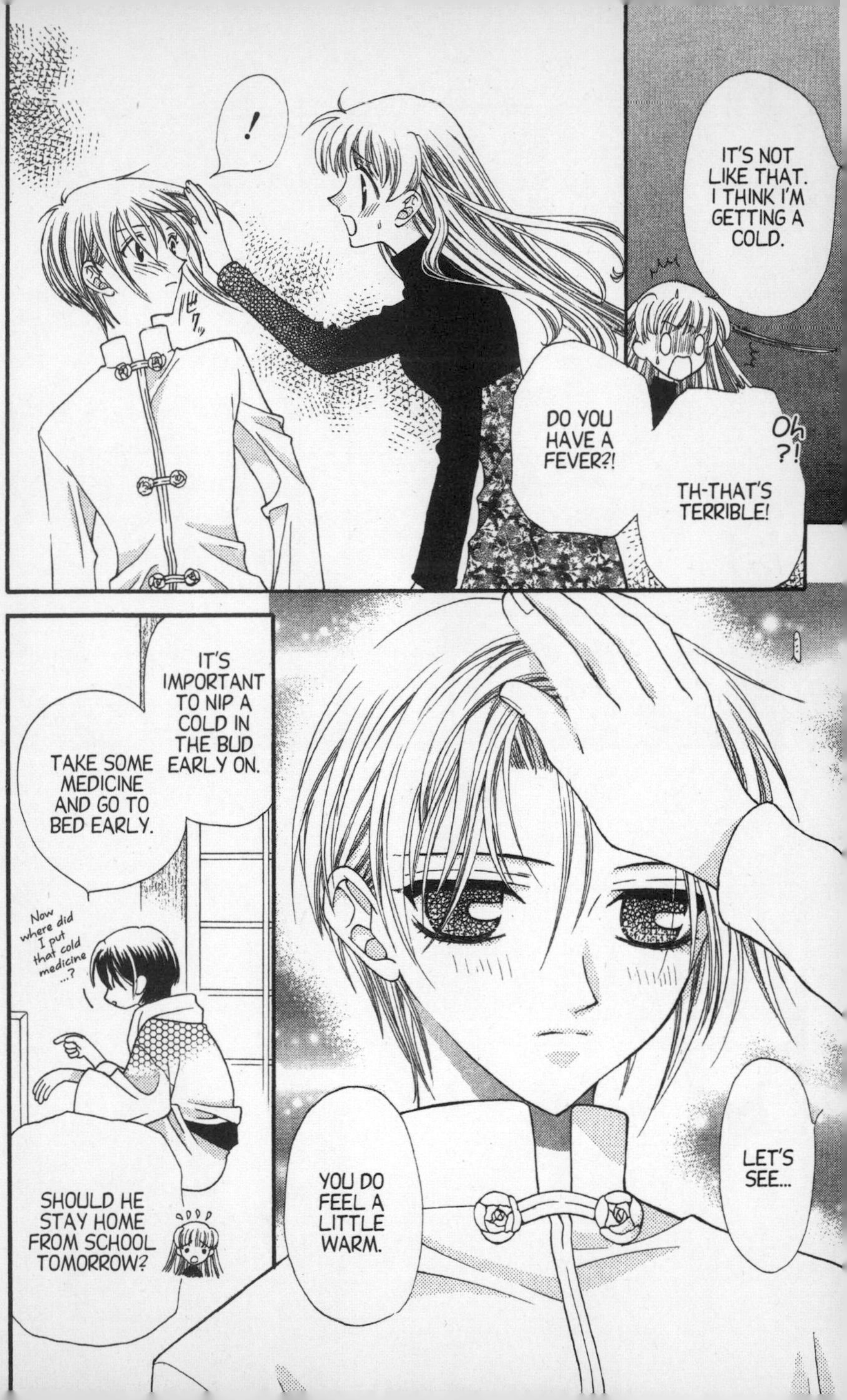
IT'S NOT LIKE THAT. I THINK I'M GETTING A COLD.
Oh?!
TH-THAT'S TERRIBLE!
DO YOU HAVE A FEVER?!
!
...
LET'S SEE...
YOU DO FEEL A LITTLE WARM.
IT'S IMPORTANT TO NIP A COLD IN THE BUD EARLY ON.
TAKE SOME MEDICINE AND GO TO BED EARLY.
Now where did I put that cold medicine ...?
SHOULD HE STAY HOME FROM SCHOOL TOMORROW?

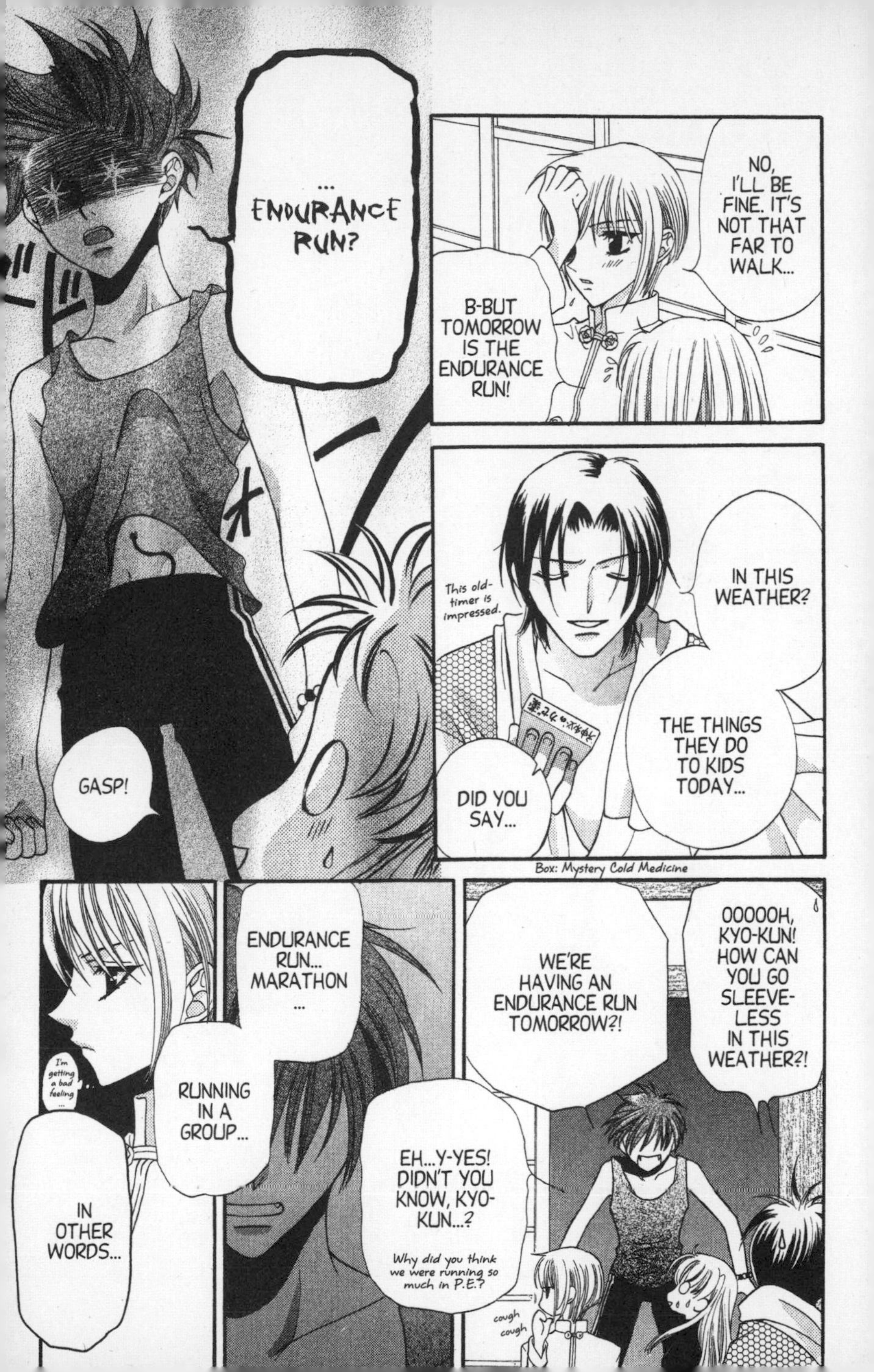
NO, I'LL BE FINE. IT'S NOT THAT FAR TO WALK...
B-BUT TOMORROW IS THE ENDURANCE RUN!
IN THIS WEATHER?
This old-timer is impressed.
THE THINGS THEY DO TO KIDS TODAY...
DID YOU SAY...
Box: Mystery Cold Medicine
... ENDURANCE RUN?
GASP!
OOOOOH, KYO-KUN! HOW CAN YOU GO SLEEVELESS IN THIS WEATHER?!
WE'RE HAVING AN ENDURANCE RUN TOMORROW?!
EH...Y-YES! DIDN'T YOU KNOW, KYO-KUN...?
Why did you think we were running so much in P.E.?
cough cough
ENDURANCE RUN... MARATHON ...
RUNNING IN A GROUP...
I'm getting a bad feeling...
IN OTHER WORDS...

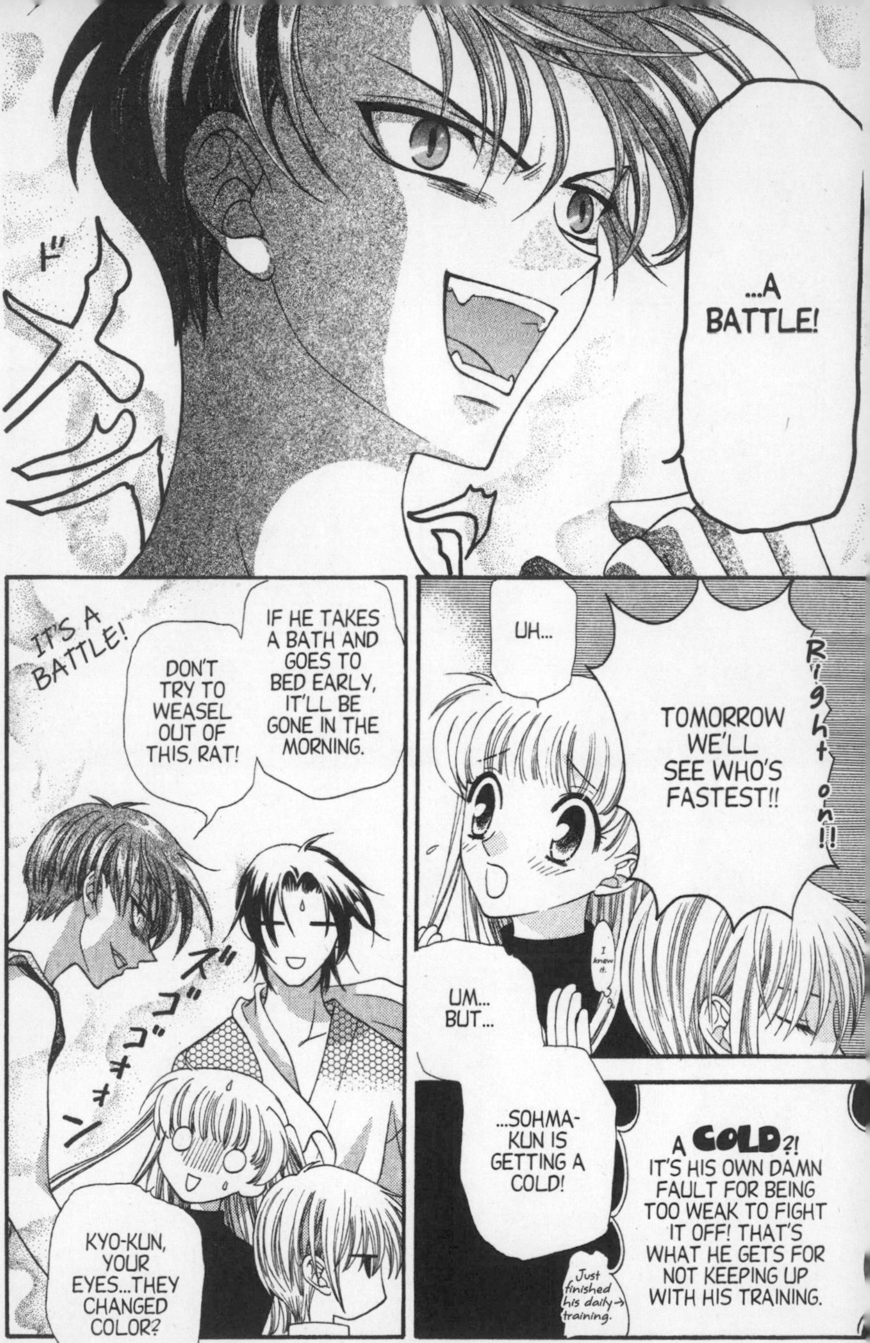
...A BATTLE!
UH...
TOMORROW WE'LL SEE WHO'S FASTEST!!
Right on!!
I knew it.
UM... BUT...
...SOHMA-KUN IS GETTING A COLD!
A COLD?! IT'S HIS OWN DAMN FAULT FOR BEING TOO WEAK TO FIGHT IT OFF! THAT'S WHAT HE GETS FOR NOT KEEPING UP WITH HIS TRAINING.
Just finished his daily training.
IT'S A BATTLE!
IF HE TAKES A BATH AND GOES TO BED EARLY, IT'LL BE GONE IN THE MORNING.
DON'T TRY TO WEASEL OUT OF THIS, RAT!
KYO-KUN, YOUR EYES...THEY CHANGED COLOR?

Fruits Basket 3 Part 1:

Hello! Nice to meet you! I'm Natsuki Takaya. Furuba Volume 3 already! (No, really-- didn't it happen fast?) The cover features Kyon-Kyon, just like I promised. If you're wondering why Kyo doesn't wear a necktie, it's because he can't breathe with anything around his neck. He doesn't even like clothes with tight collars. (That doesn't mean he'll never wear them. It just means he prefers not to wear them.) He's a cat who doesn't like collars. (Get it?)

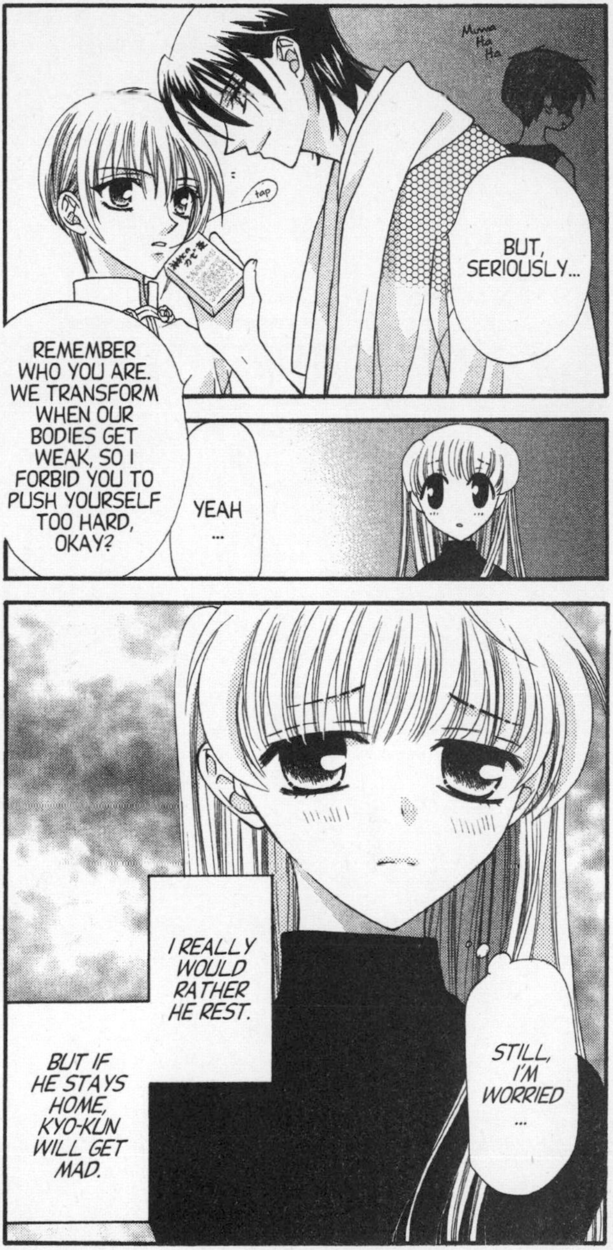
Mwa Ha Ha
BUT, SERIOUSLY...
tap
REMEMBER WHO YOU ARE. WE TRANSFORM WHEN OUR BODIES GET WEAK, SO I FORBID YOU TO PUSH YOURSELF TOO HARD, OKAY?
YEAH ...
STILL, I'M WORRIED ...
I REALLY WOULD RATHER HE REST.
BUT IF HE STAYS HOME, KYO-KUN WILL GET MAD.

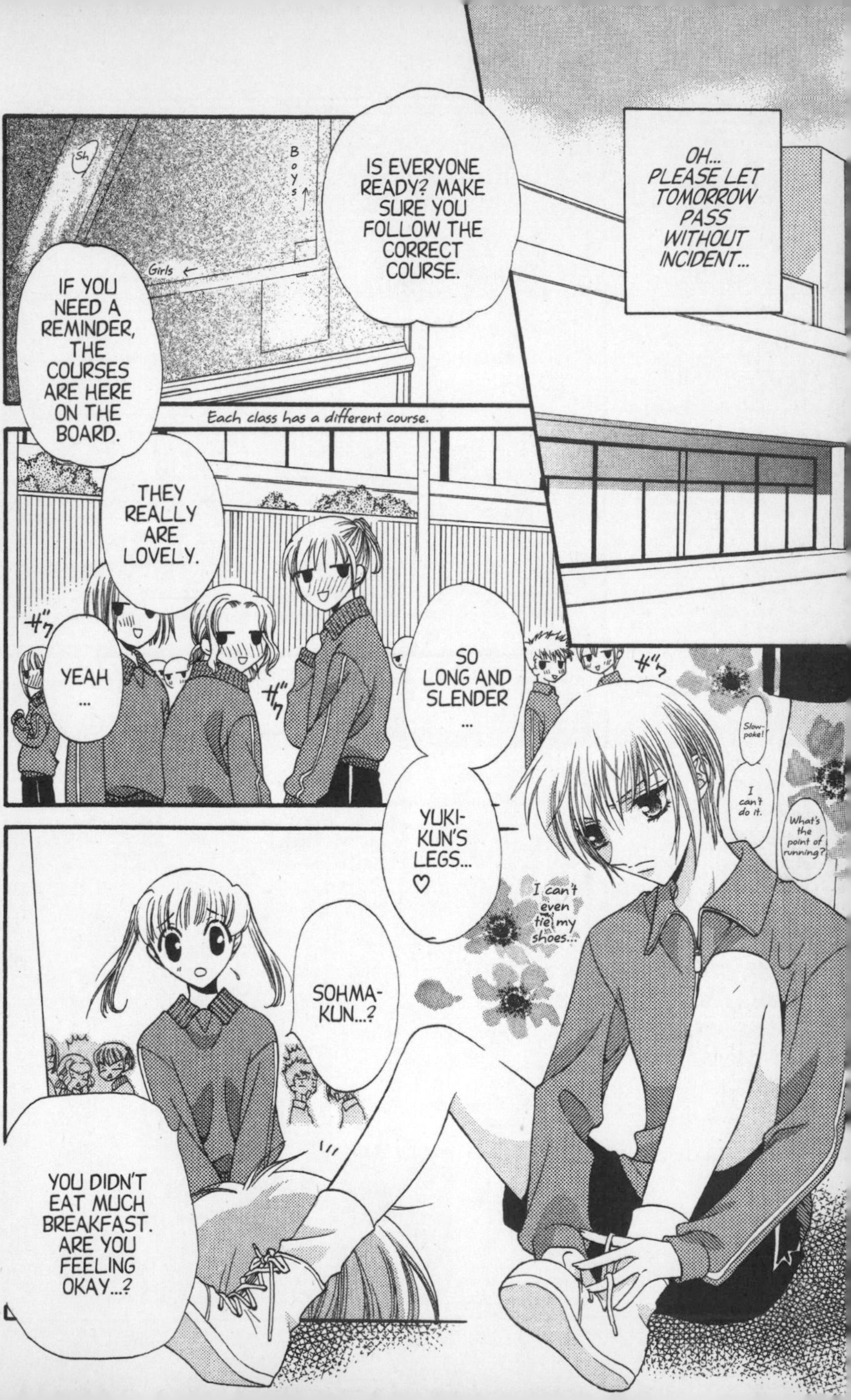
OH... PLEASE LET TOMORROW PASS WITHOUT INCIDENT...
IS EVERYONE READY? MAKE SURE YOU FOLLOW THE CORRECT COURSE.
Sh
Boys ↑
Girls ←
IF YOU NEED A REMINDER, THE COURSES ARE HERE ON THE BOARD.
Each class has a different course.
THEY REALLY ARE LOVELY.
YEAH ...
SO LONG AND SLENDER ...
YUKI-KUN'S LEGS... ♡
Slow-poke!
I can't do it.
What's the point of running?
I can't even tie my shoes...
SOHMA-KUN...?
YOU DIDN'T EAT MUCH BREAKFAST. ARE YOU FEELING OKAY...?

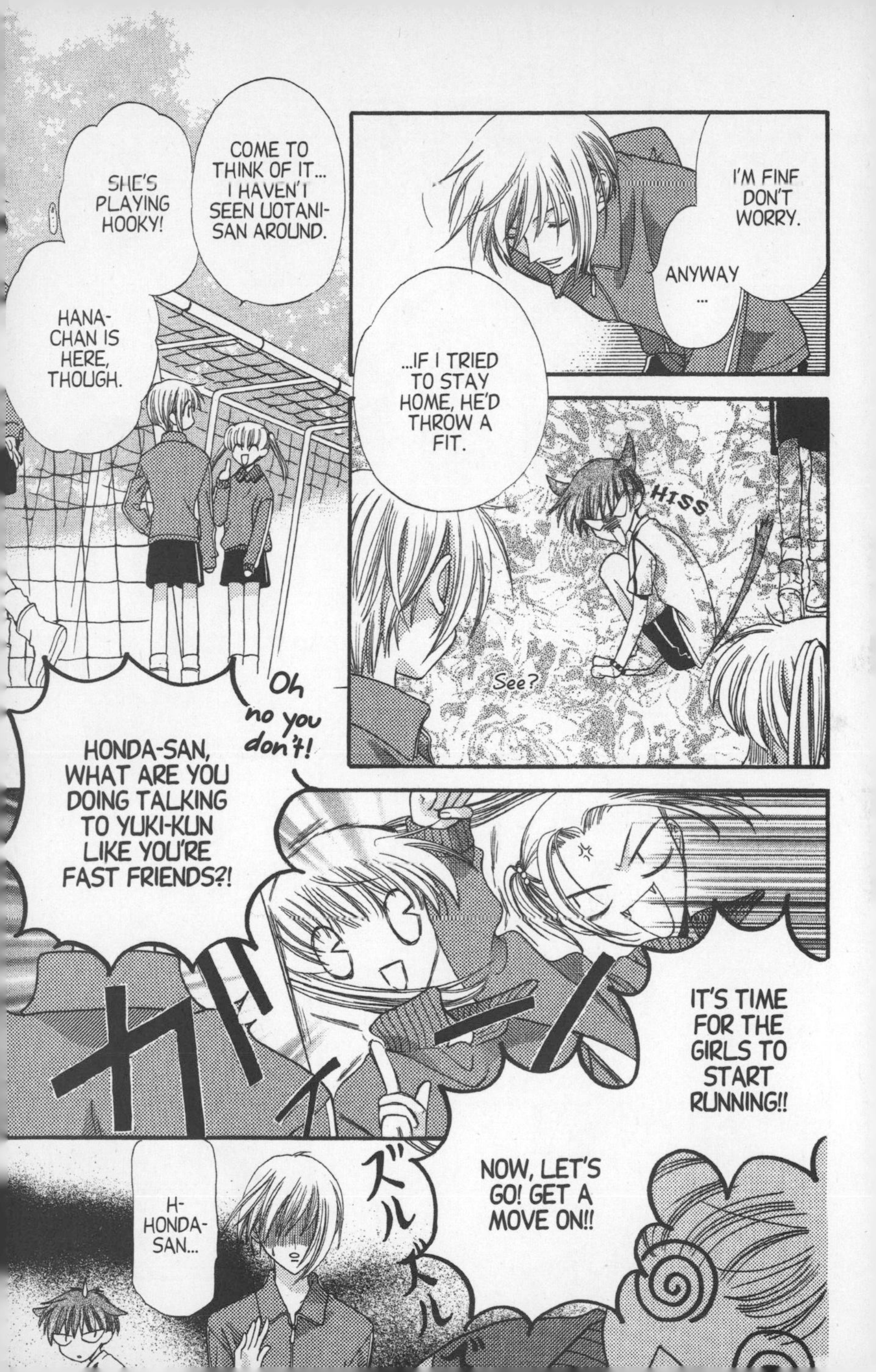
I'M FINF DON'T WORRY.
ANYWAY ...
...IF I TRIED TO STAY HOME, HE'D THROW A FIT.
HISS
See?
COME TO THINK OF IT... I HAVEN'T SEEN UOTANI-SAN AROUND.
SHE'S PLAYING HOOKY!
HANA-CHAN IS HERE, THOUGH.
Oh no you don't!
HONDA-SAN, WHAT ARE YOU DOING TALKING TO YUKI-KUN LIKE YOU'RE FAST FRIENDS?!
IT'S TIME FOR THE GIRLS TO START RUNNING!!
NOW, LET'S GO! GET A MOVE ON!!
H-HONDA-SAN...

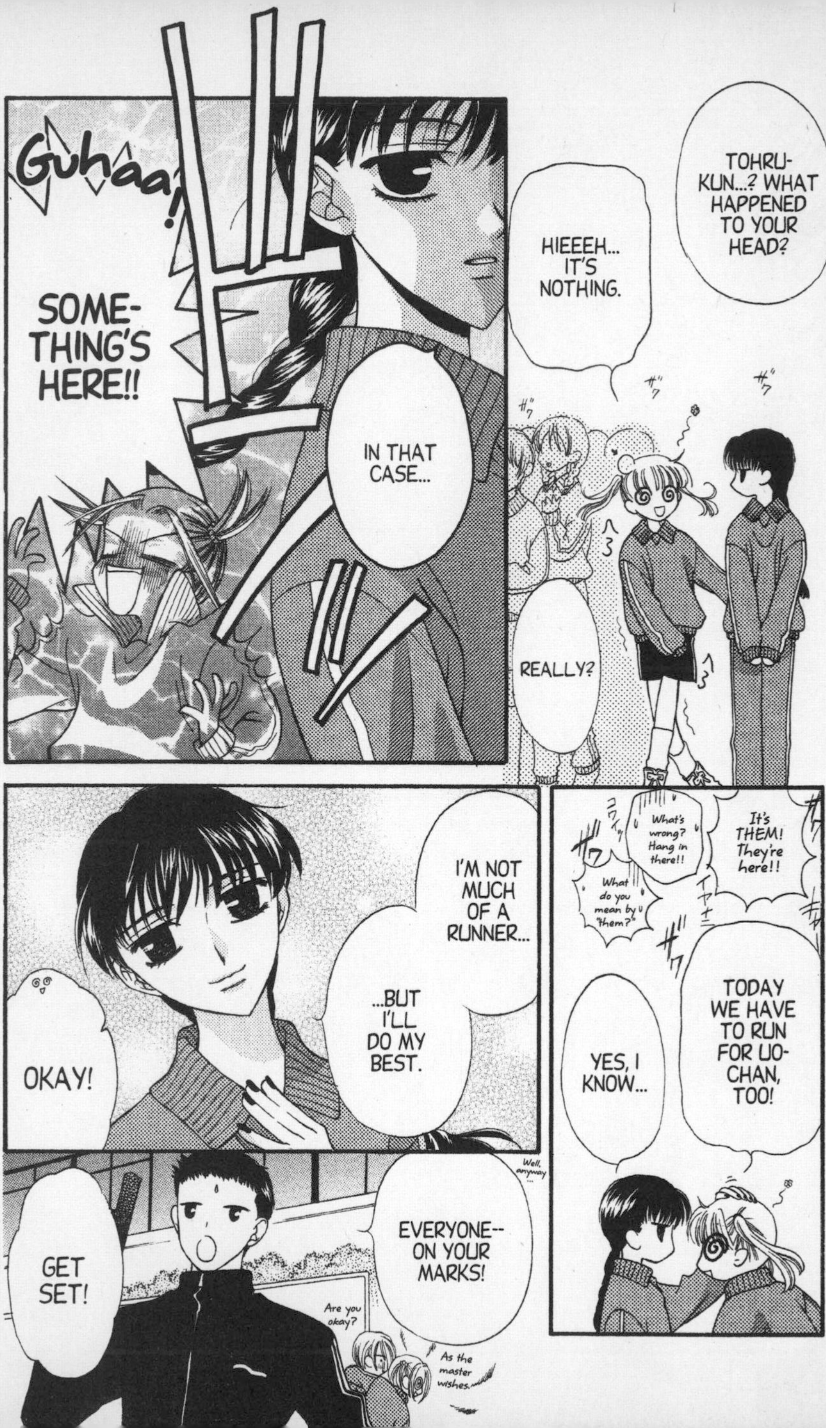
TOHRU-KUN...? WHAT HAPPENED TO YOUR HEAD?
HIEEEH... IT'S NOTHING.
REALLY?
IN THAT CASE...
Guhaa!
SOME-THING'S HERE!!
It's THEM! They're here!!
What's wrong? Hang in there!!
What do you mean by "them?"
TODAY WE HAVE TO RUN FOR UO-CHAN, TOO!
YES, I KNOW...
Well, anyway...
I'M NOT MUCH OF A RUNNER...
...BUT I'LL DO MY BEST.
OKAY!
EVERYONE-- ON YOUR MARKS!
GET SET!
Are you okay?
As the master wishes.

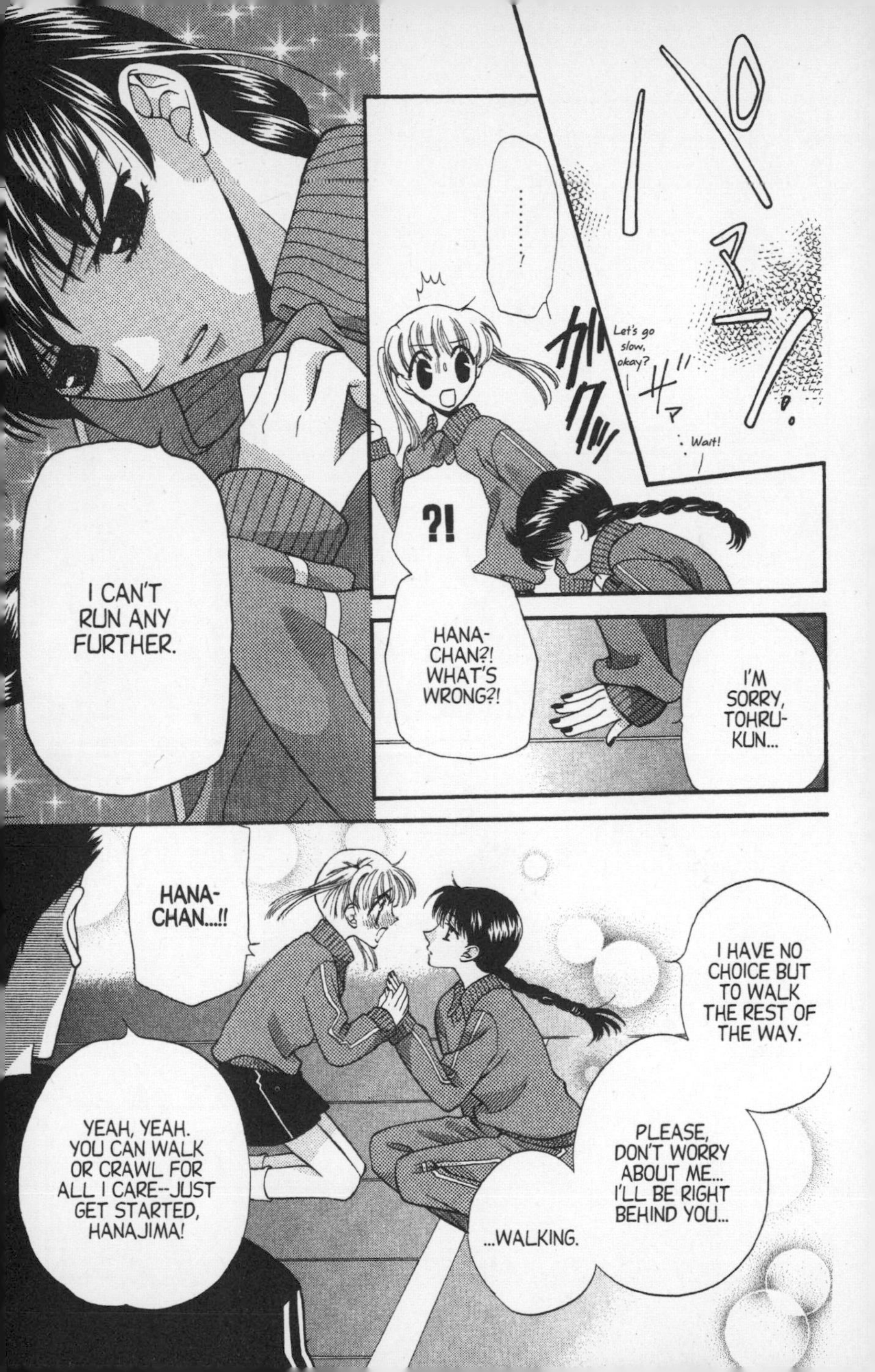
Let's go slow, okay?!
Wait!
......!
?!
I'M SORRY, TOHRU-KUN...
HANA-CHAN?! WHAT'S WRONG?!
I CAN'T RUN ANY FURTHER.
I HAVE NO CHOICE BUT TO WALK THE REST OF THE WAY.
HANA-CHAN...!!
PLEASE, DON'T WORRY ABOUT ME... I'LL BE RIGHT BEHIND YOU...
...WALKING.
YEAH, YEAH. YOU CAN WALK OR CRAWL FOR ALL I CARE--JUST GET STARTED, HANAJIMA!

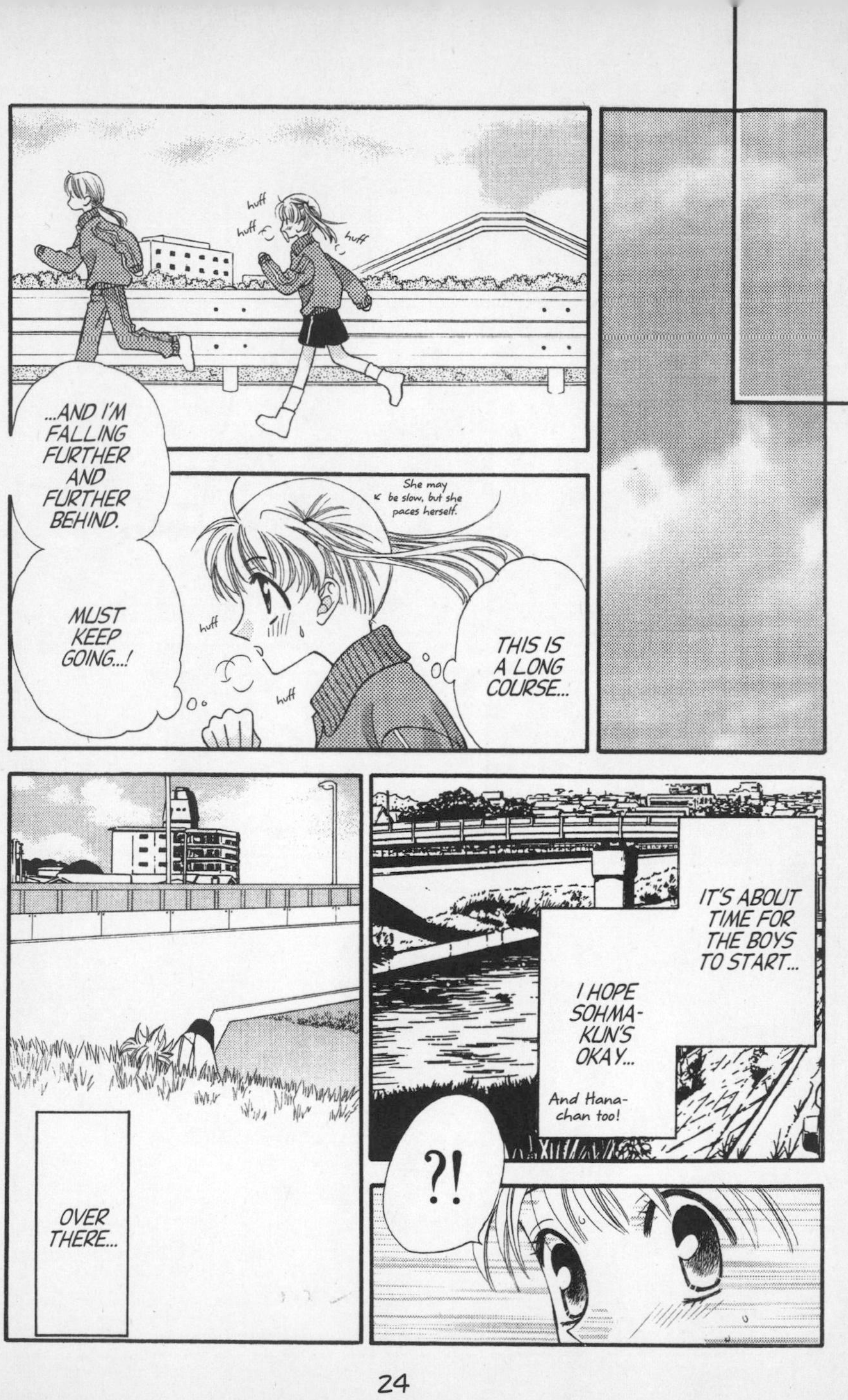
huff
huff
huff
...AND I'M FALLING FURTHER AND FURTHER BEHIND.
She may be slow, but she paces herself.
THIS IS A LONG COURSE...
huff
huff
MUST KEEP GOING...!
IT'S ABOUT TIME FOR THE BOYS TO START...
I HOPE SOHMA-KUN'S OKAY...
And Hana-chan too!
?!
OVER THERE...

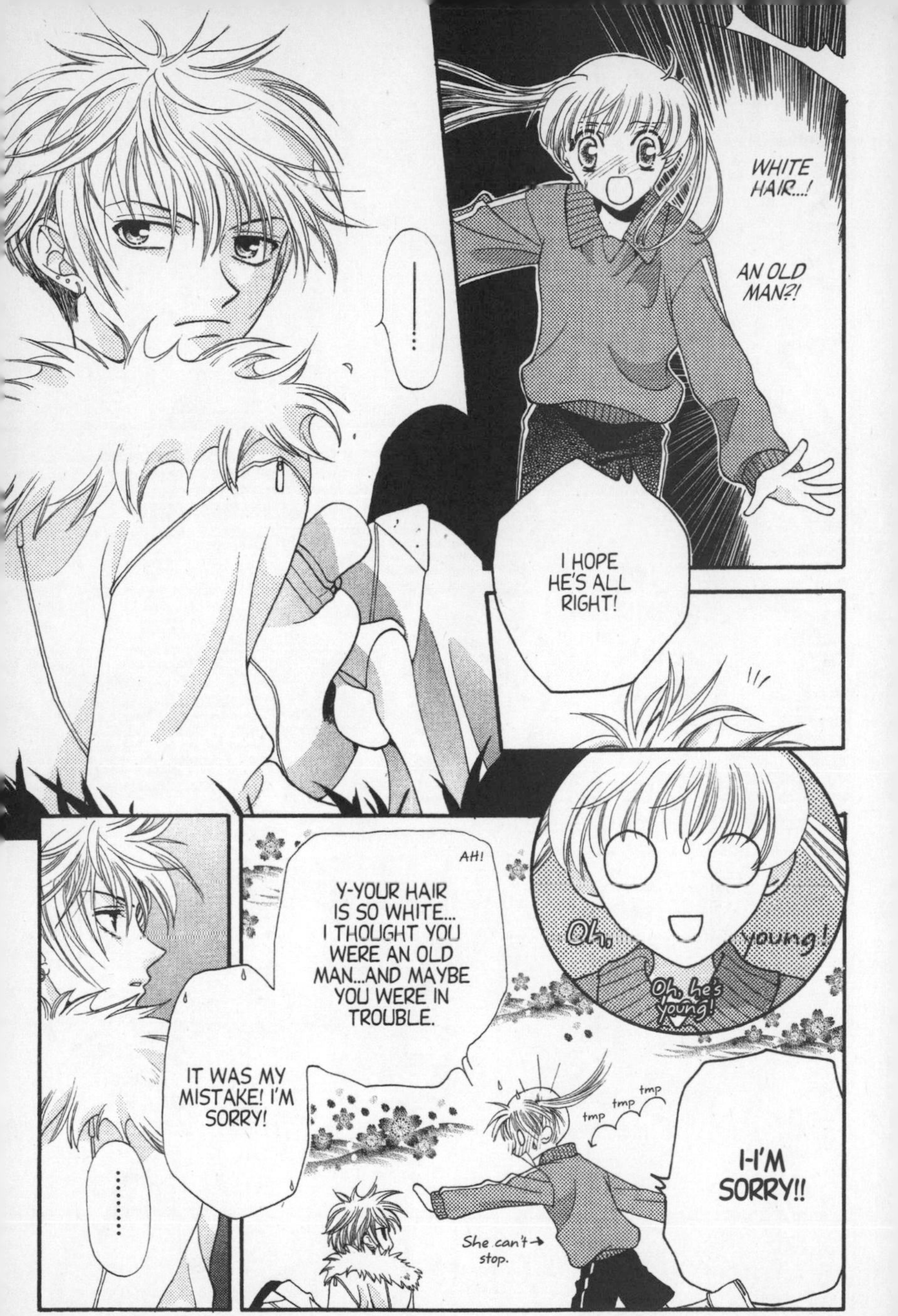
WHITE HAIR...!
AN OLD MAN?!
I HOPE HE'S ALL RIGHT!
Oh, he's young!
......!
I-I'M SORRY!!
tmp tmp tmp
She can't stop.
AH!
Y-YOUR HAIR IS SO WHITE... I THOUGHT YOU WERE AN OLD MAN...AND MAYBE YOU WERE IN TROUBLE.
IT WAS MY MISTAKE! I'M SORRY!
......

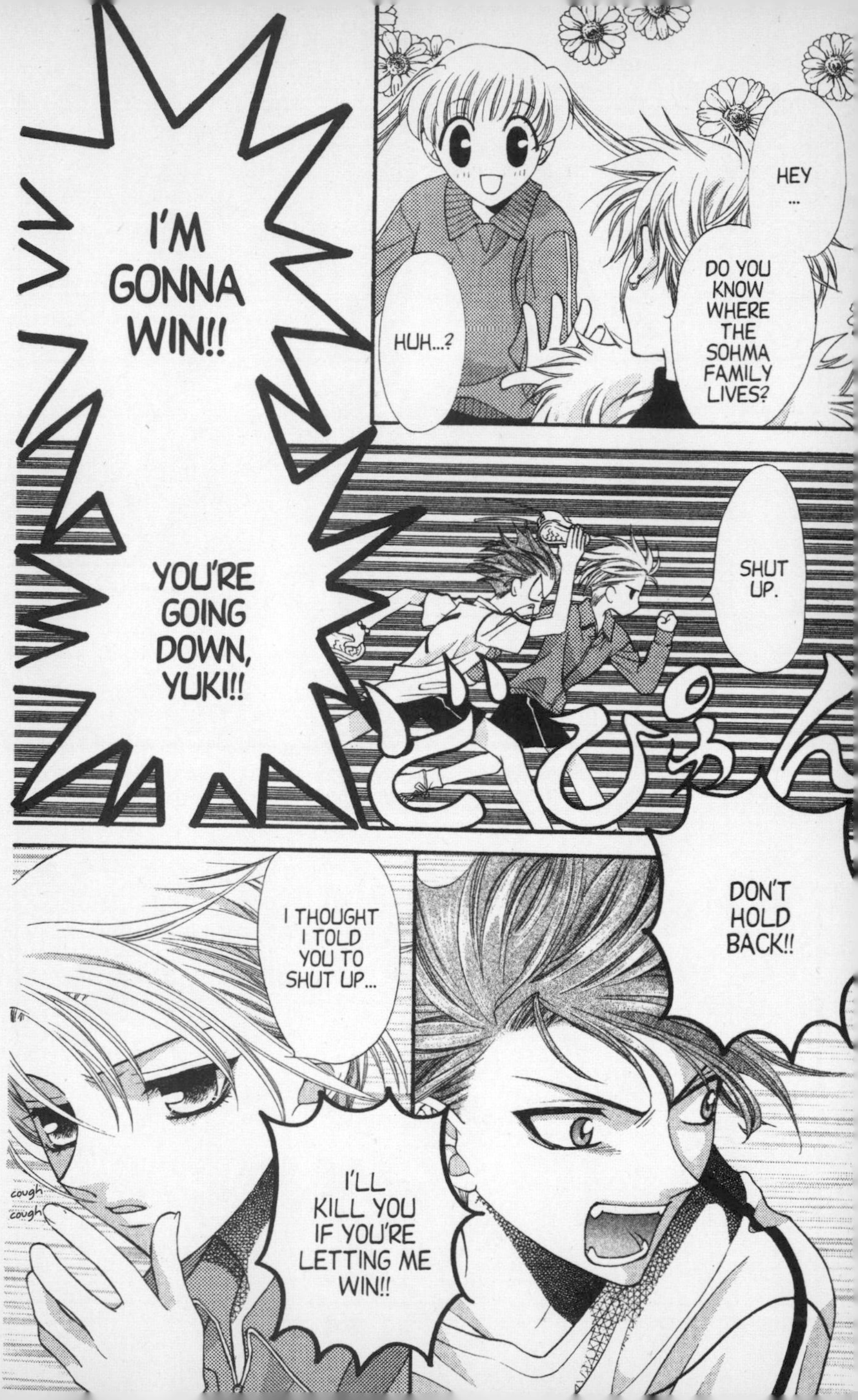
HEY ...
DO YOU KNOW WHERE THE SOHMA FAMILY LIVES?
HUH...?
SHUT UP.
どぴゅん
I'M GONNA WIN!!
YOU'RE GOING DOWN, YUKI!!
DON'T HOLD BACK!!
I'LL KILL YOU IF YOU'RE LETTING ME WIN!!
I THOUGHT I TOLD YOU TO SHUT UP...
cough
cough

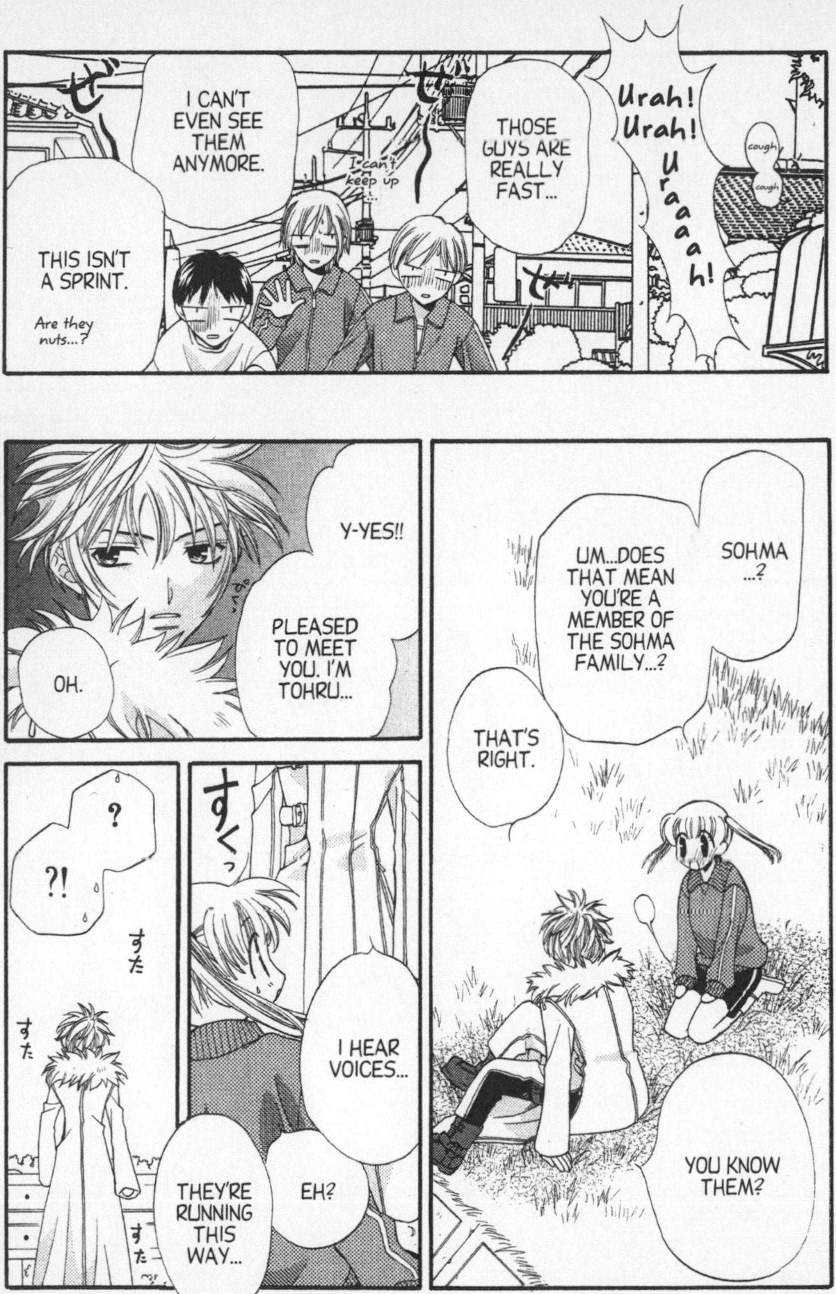
Urah! Urah! Uraaaah!
cough
cough
THOSE GUYS ARE REALLY FAST...
I can't keep up...
I CAN'T EVEN SEE THEM ANYMORE.
THIS ISN'T A SPRINT.
Are they nuts...?
SOHMA ...?
UM...DOES THAT MEAN YOU'RE A MEMBER OF THE SOHMA FAMILY...?
THAT'S RIGHT.
YOU KNOW THEM?
Y-YES!!
PLEASED TO MEET YOU. I'M TOHRU...
OH.
すくっ
I HEAR VOICES...
EH?
THEY'RE RUNNING THIS WAY...
?
?!
すた
すた
すた

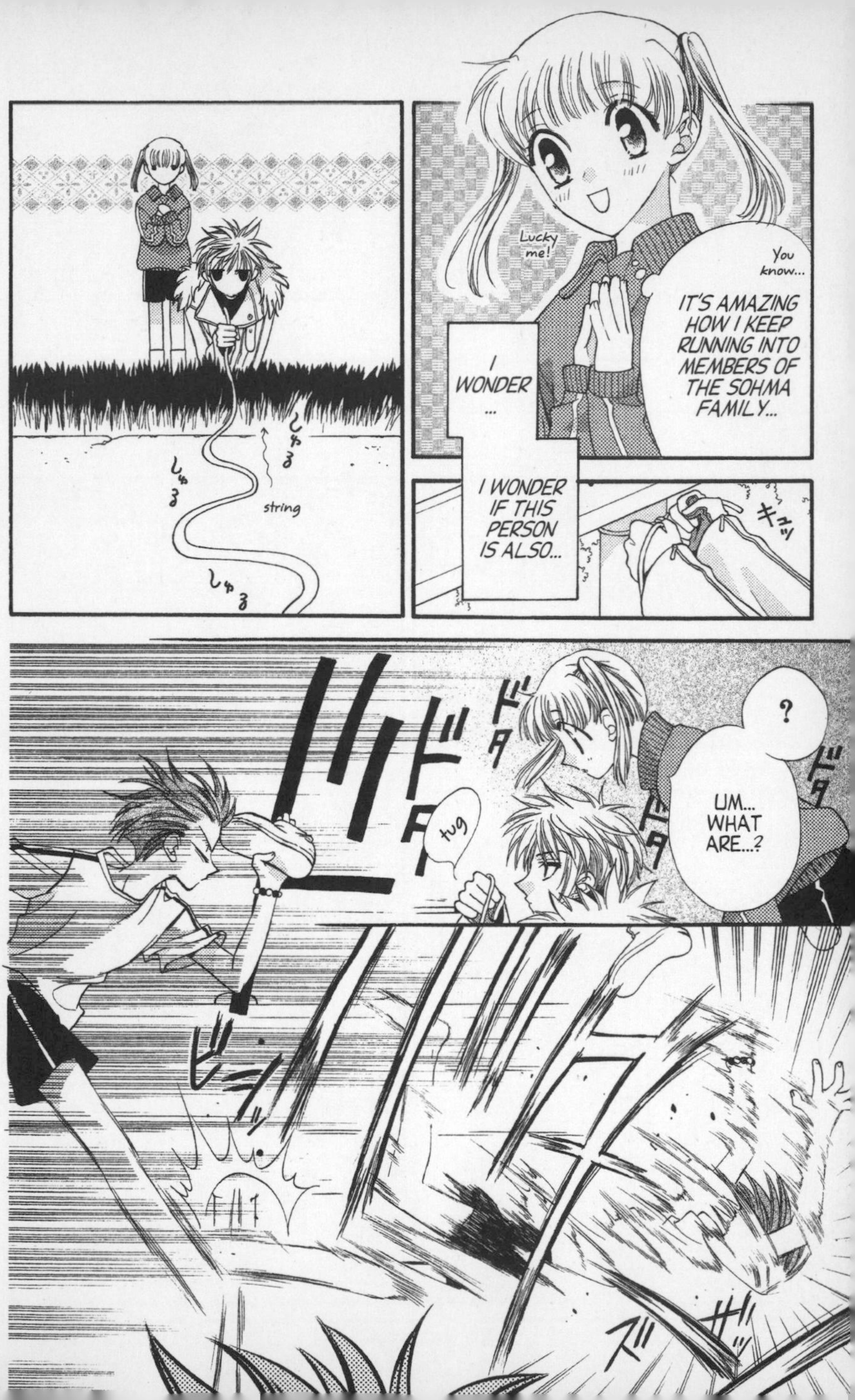
Lucky me!
You know...
IT'S AMAZING HOW I KEEP RUNNING INTO MEMBERS OF THE SOHMA FAMILY...
I WONDER...
I WONDER IF THIS PERSON IS ALSO...
string
?
UM... WHAT ARE...?
tug

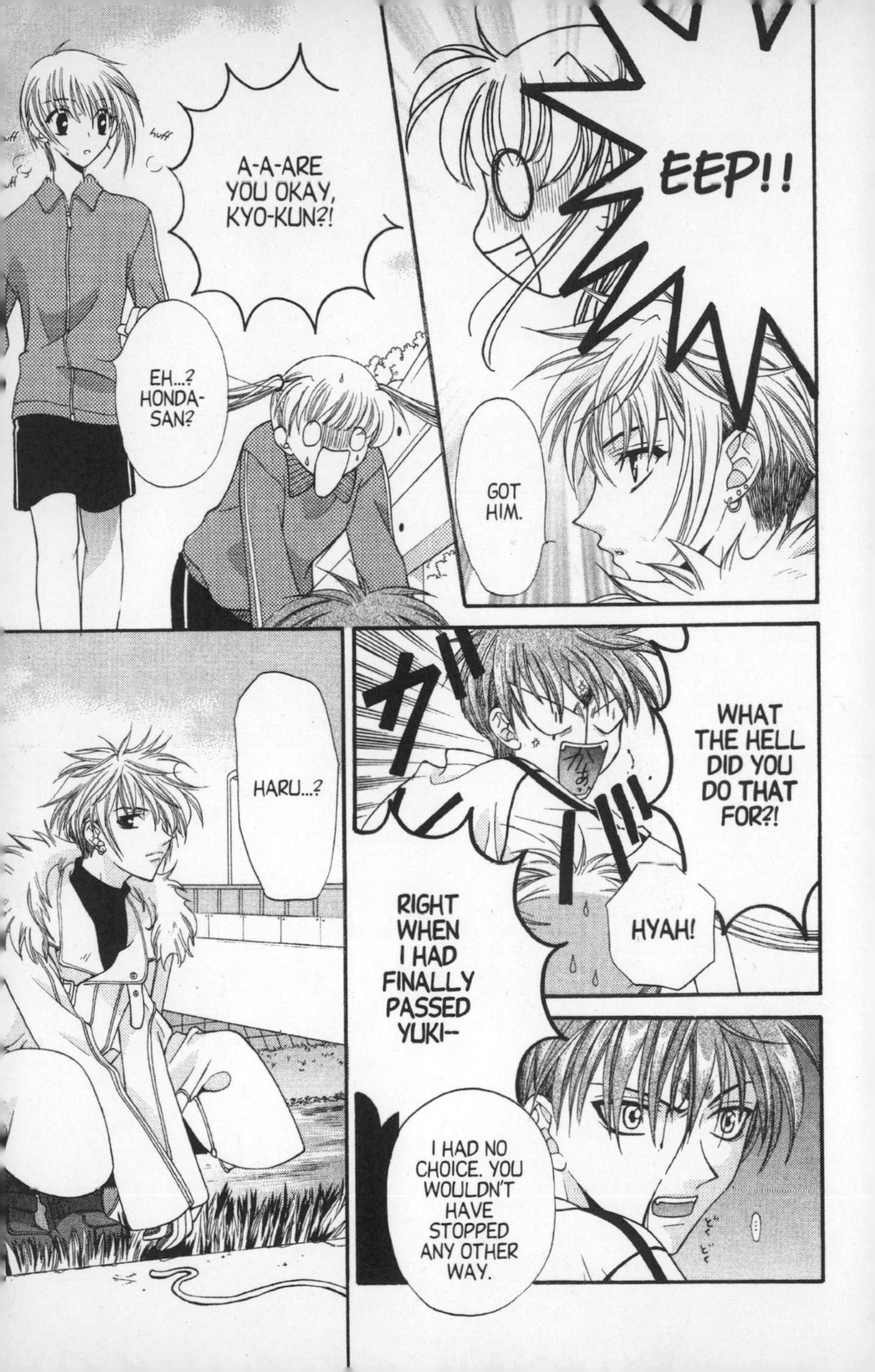
EEP!!
GOT HIM.
A-A-ARE YOU OKAY, KYO-KUN?!
huff huff
EH...? HONDA-SAN?
WHAT THE HELL DID YOU DO THAT FOR?!
RIGHT WHEN I HAD FINALLY PASSED YUKI--
HYAH!
I HAD NO CHOICE. YOU WOULDN'T HAVE STOPPED ANY OTHER WAY.
HARU...?

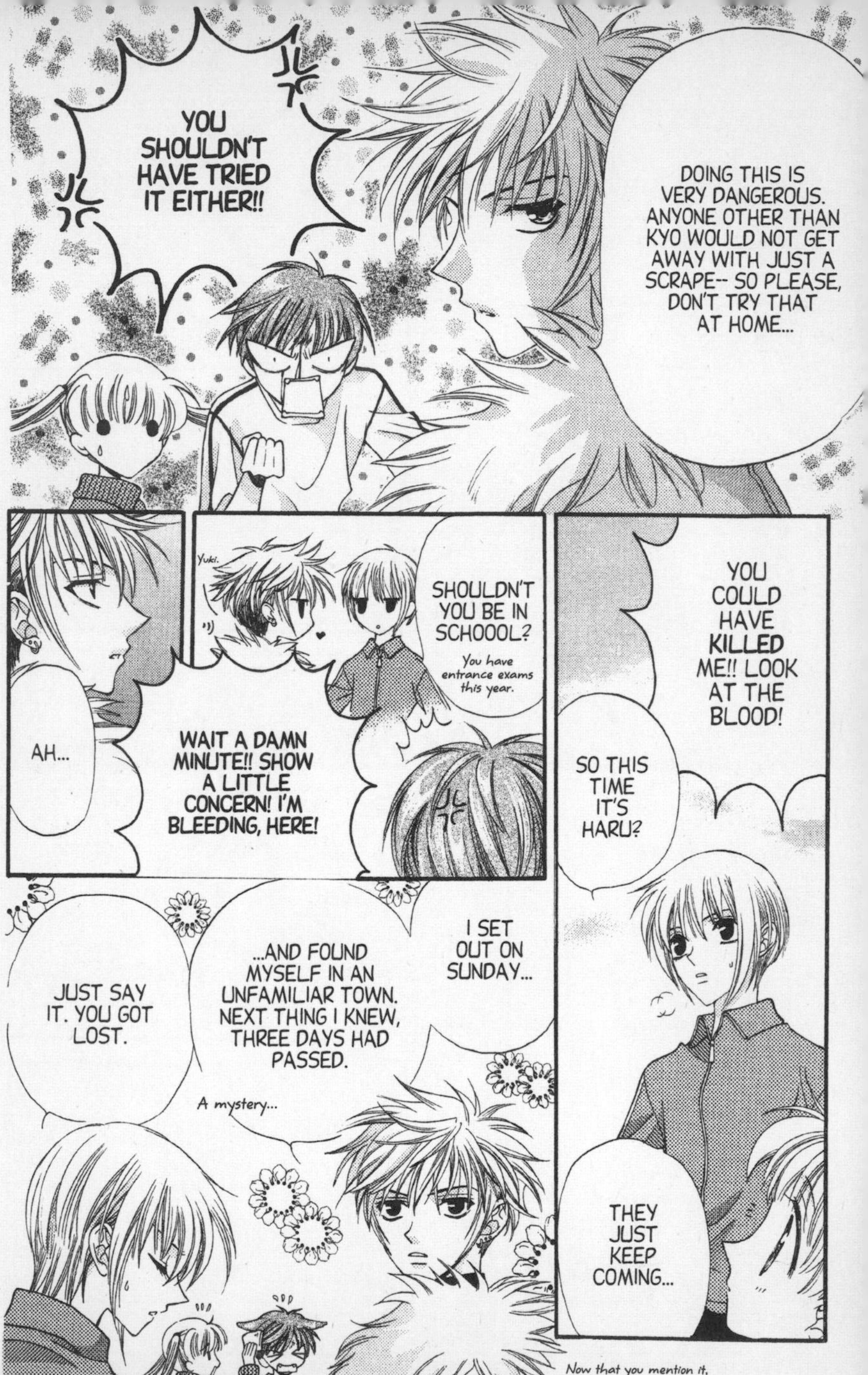
DOING THIS IS VERY DANGEROUS. ANYONE OTHER THAN KYO WOULD NOT GET AWAY WITH JUST A SCRAPE-- SO PLEASE, DON'T TRY THAT AT HOME...
YOU SHOULDN'T HAVE TRIED IT EITHER!!
YOU COULD HAVE KILLED ME!! LOOK AT THE BLOOD!
SO THIS TIME IT'S HARU?
THEY JUST KEEP COMING...
Yuki.
SHOULDN'T YOU BE IN SCHOOOL?
You have entrance exams this year.
WAIT A DAMN MINUTE!! SHOW A LITTLE CONCERN! I'M BLEEDING, HERE!
AH...
I SET OUT ON SUNDAY...
...AND FOUND MYSELF IN AN UNFAMILIAR TOWN. NEXT THING I KNEW, THREE DAYS HAD PASSED.
A mystery...
JUST SAY IT. YOU GOT LOST.
Now that you mention it, where's his bicycle?

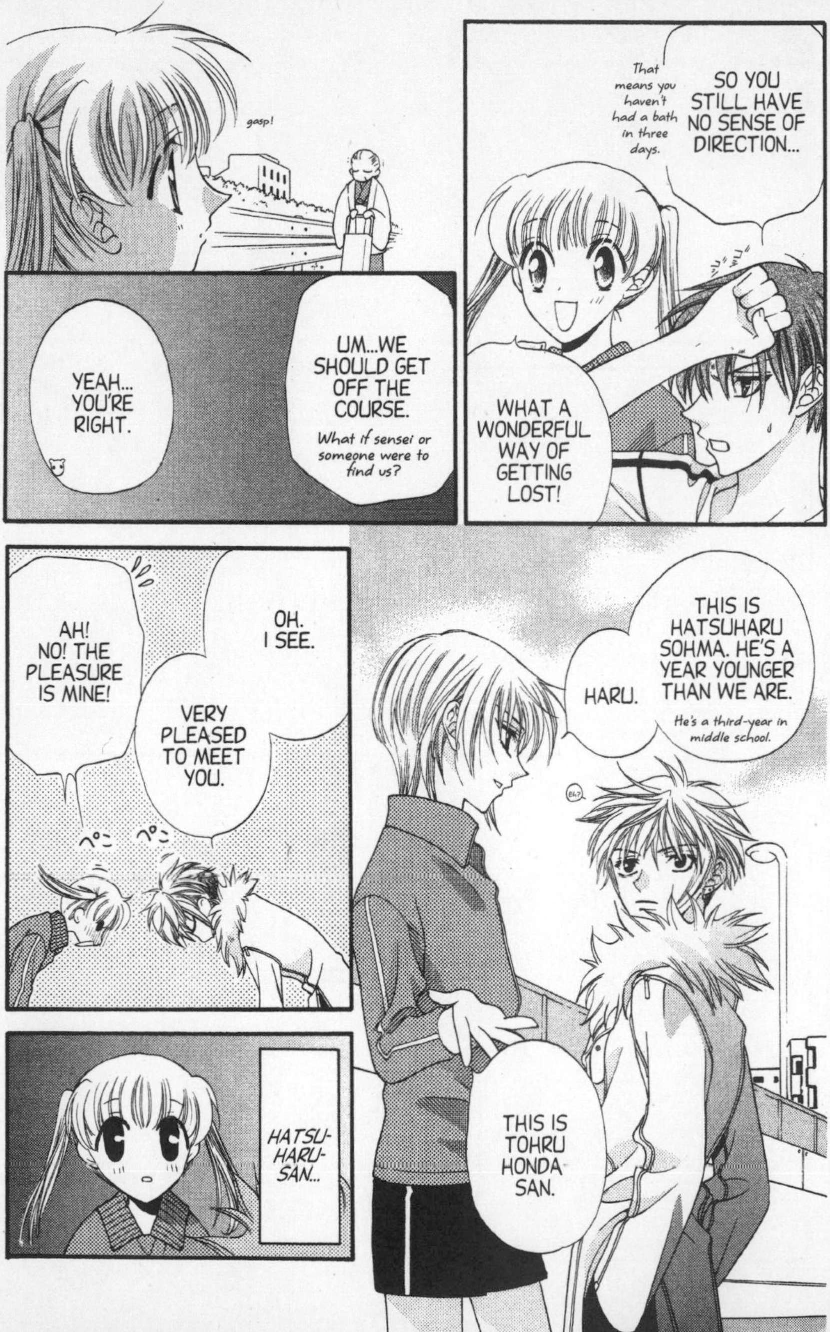
SO YOU STILL HAVE NO SENSE OF DIRECTION...
That means you haven't had a bath in three days.
WHAT A WONDERFUL WAY OF GETTING LOST!
gasp!
UM...WE SHOULD GET OFF THE COURSE.
What if sensei or someone were to find us?
YEAH... YOU'RE RIGHT.
THIS IS HATSUHARU SOHMA. HE'S A YEAR YOUNGER THAN WE ARE.
He's a third-year in middle school.
HARU.
Eh?
THIS IS TOHRU HONDA-SAN.
OH. I SEE.
VERY PLEASED TO MEET YOU.
AH! NO! THE PLEASURE IS MINE!
ぺこ ぺこ
HATSU-HARU-SAN...

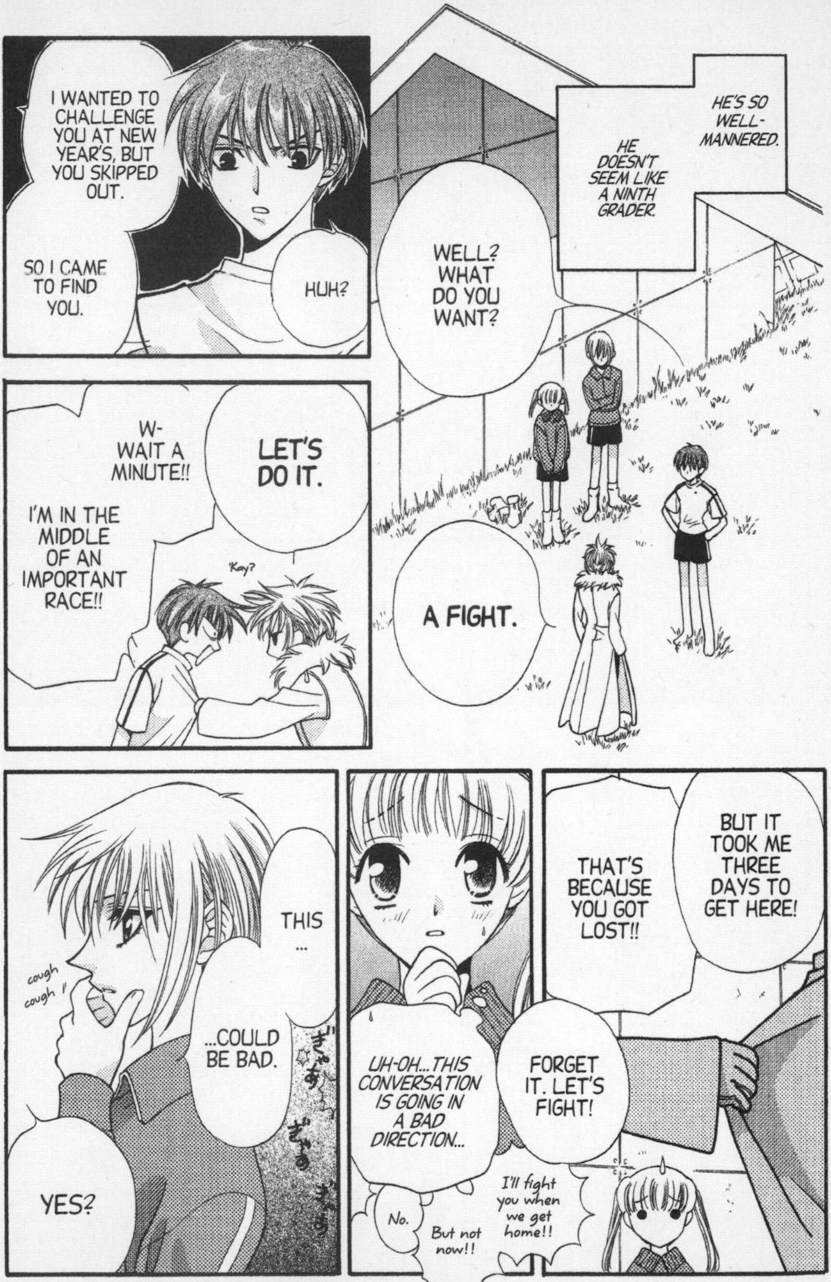
HE'S SO WELL-MANNERED.
HE DOESN'T SEEM LIKE A NINTH GRADER.
WELL? WHAT DO YOU WANT?
I WANTED TO CHALLENGE YOU AT NEW YEAR'S, BUT YOU SKIPPED OUT.
SO I CAME TO FIND YOU.
HUH?
A FIGHT.
LET'S DO IT.
W-WAIT A MINUTE!!
I'M IN THE MIDDLE OF AN IMPORTANT RACE!!
'Kay?
BUT IT TOOK ME THREE DAYS TO GET HERE!
THAT'S BECAUSE YOU GOT LOST!!
FORGET IT. LET'S FIGHT!
UH-OH...THIS CONVERSATION IS GOING IN A BAD DIRECTION...
I'll fight you when we get home!!
But not now!!
No.
THIS ...
...COULD BE BAD.
cough cough
YES?
ぎゃあ
ぎゃあ

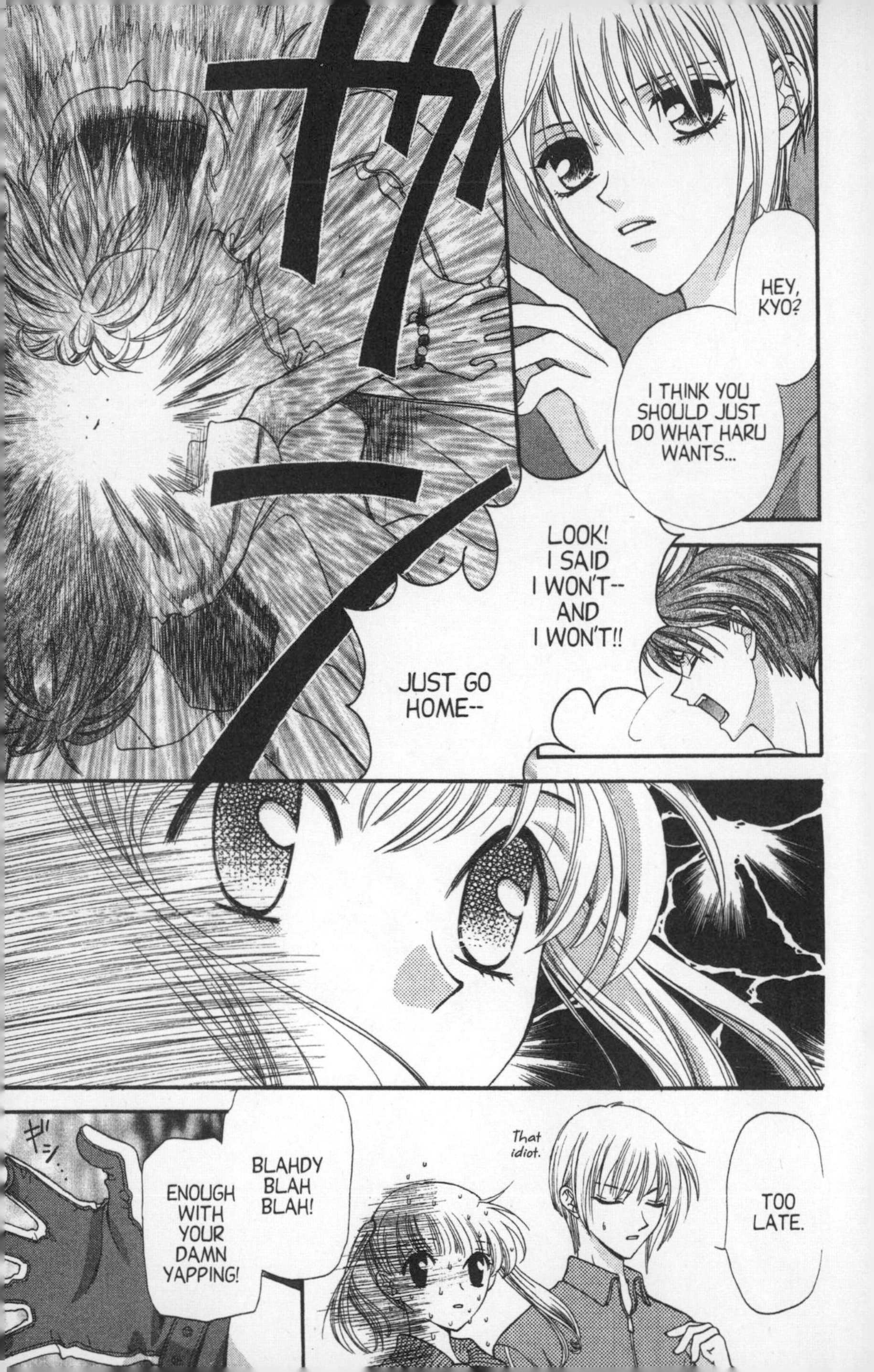
HEY, KYO?
I THINK YOU SHOULD JUST DO WHAT HARU WANTS...
LOOK! I SAID I WON'T-- AND I WON'T!!
JUST GO HOME--
TOO LATE.
That idiot.
BLAHDY BLAH BLAH!
ENOUGH WITH YOUR DAMN YAPPING!

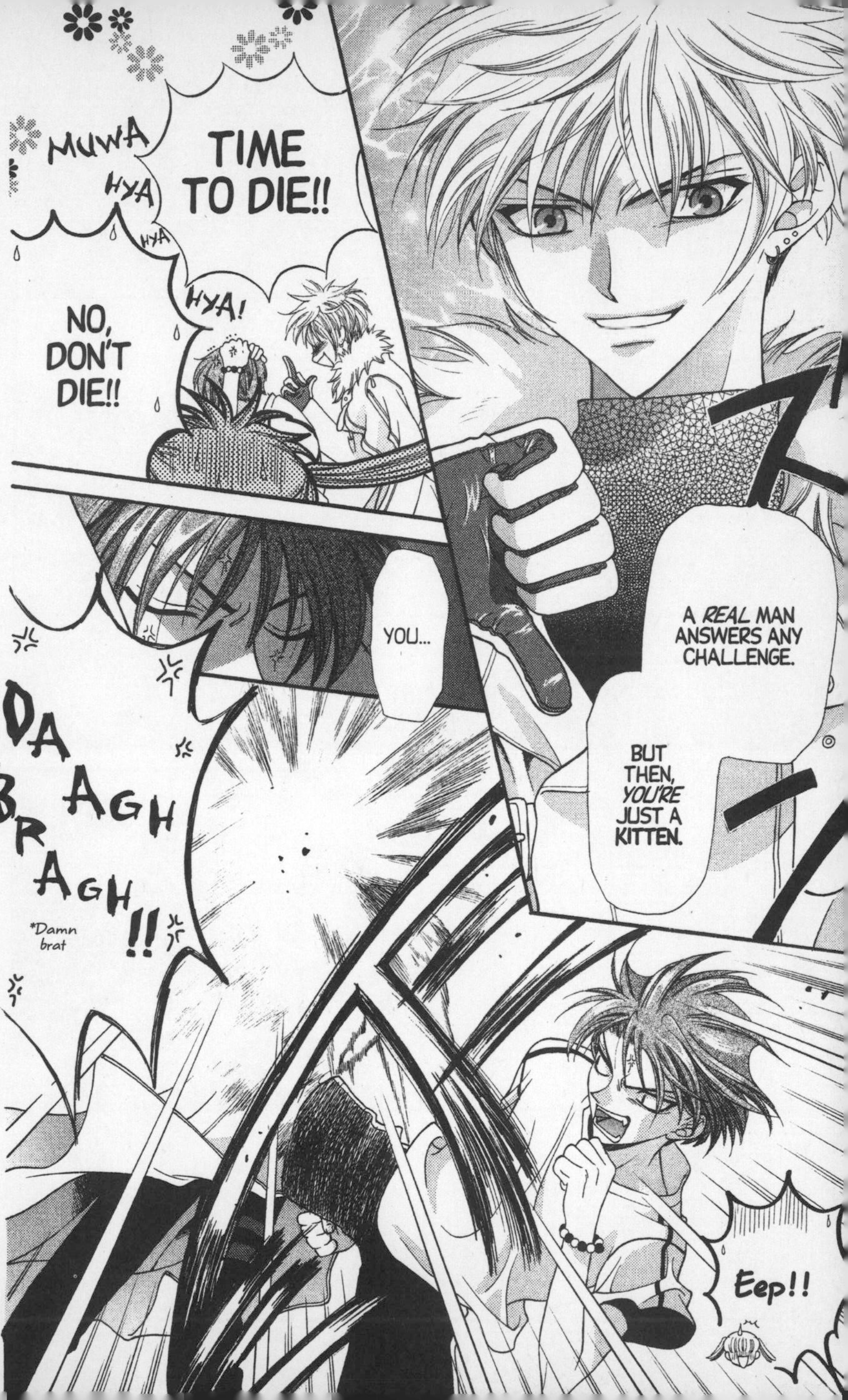
A *REAL* MAN ANSWERS ANY CHALLENGE.
BUT THEN, *YOU'RE* JUST A KITTEN.
TIME TO DIE!!
MUWA HYA HYA HYA!
NO, DON'T DIE!!
YOU...
DA AGH BRAGH!!
*Damn brat
Eep!!

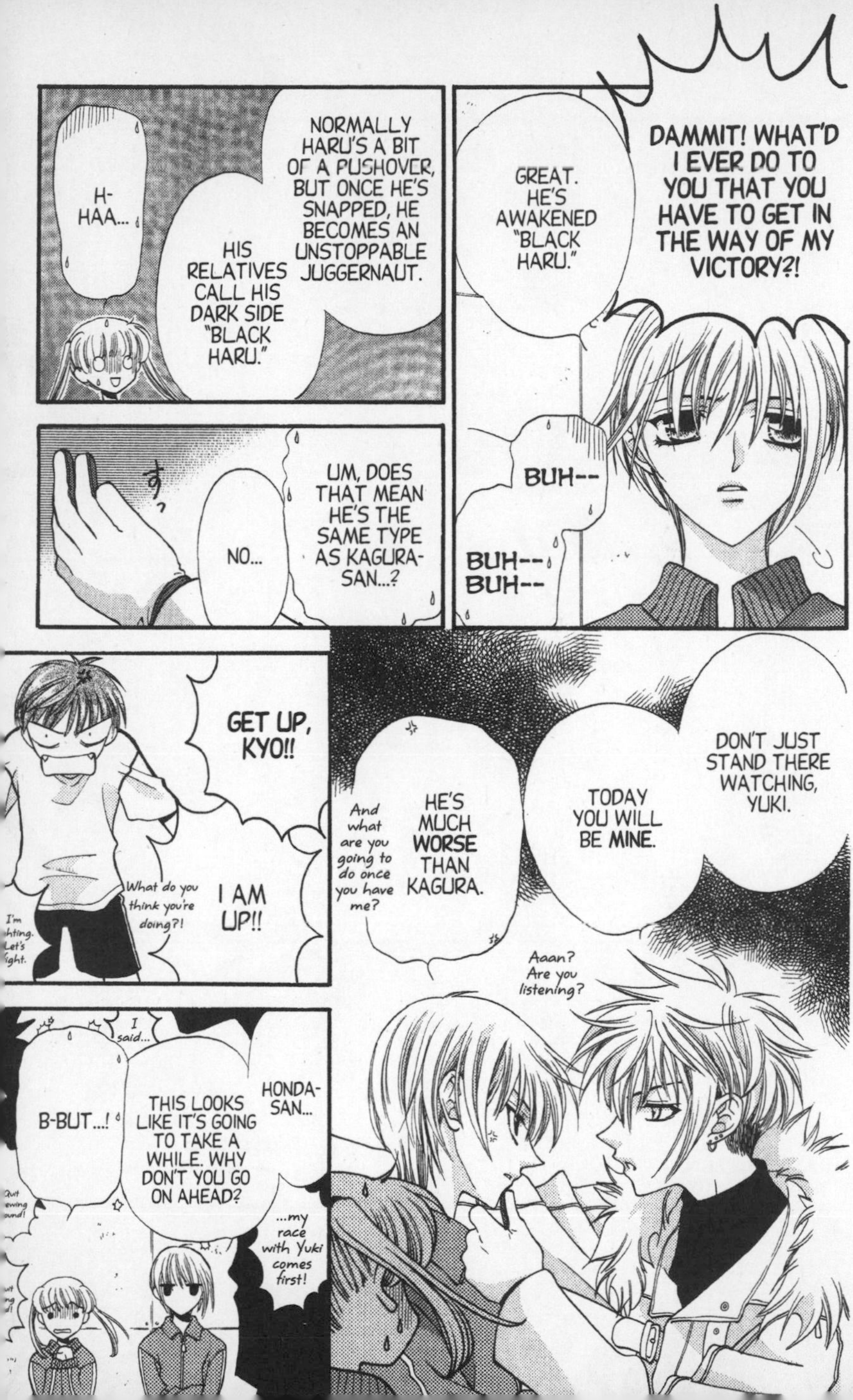
DAMMIT! WHAT'D I EVER DO TO YOU THAT YOU HAVE TO GET IN THE WAY OF MY VICTORY?!
GREAT. HE'S AWAKENED "BLACK HARU."
BUH--
BUH-- BUH--
NORMALLY HARU'S A BIT OF A PUSHOVER, BUT ONCE HE'S SNAPPED, HE BECOMES AN UNSTOPPABLE JUGGERNAUT.
HIS RELATIVES CALL HIS DARK SIDE "BLACK HARU."
H-HAA...
UM, DOES THAT MEAN HE'S THE SAME TYPE AS KAGURA-SAN...?
NO...
DON'T JUST STAND THERE WATCHING, YUKI.
TODAY YOU WILL BE MINE.
HE'S MUCH WORSE THAN KAGURA.
And what are you going to do once you have me?
Aaan? Are you listening?
GET UP, KYO!!
I AM UP!!
What do you think you're doing?!
HONDA-SAN...
THIS LOOKS LIKE IT'S GOING TO TAKE A WHILE. WHY DON'T YOU GO ON AHEAD?
I said...
B-BUT...!
...my race with Yuki comes first!

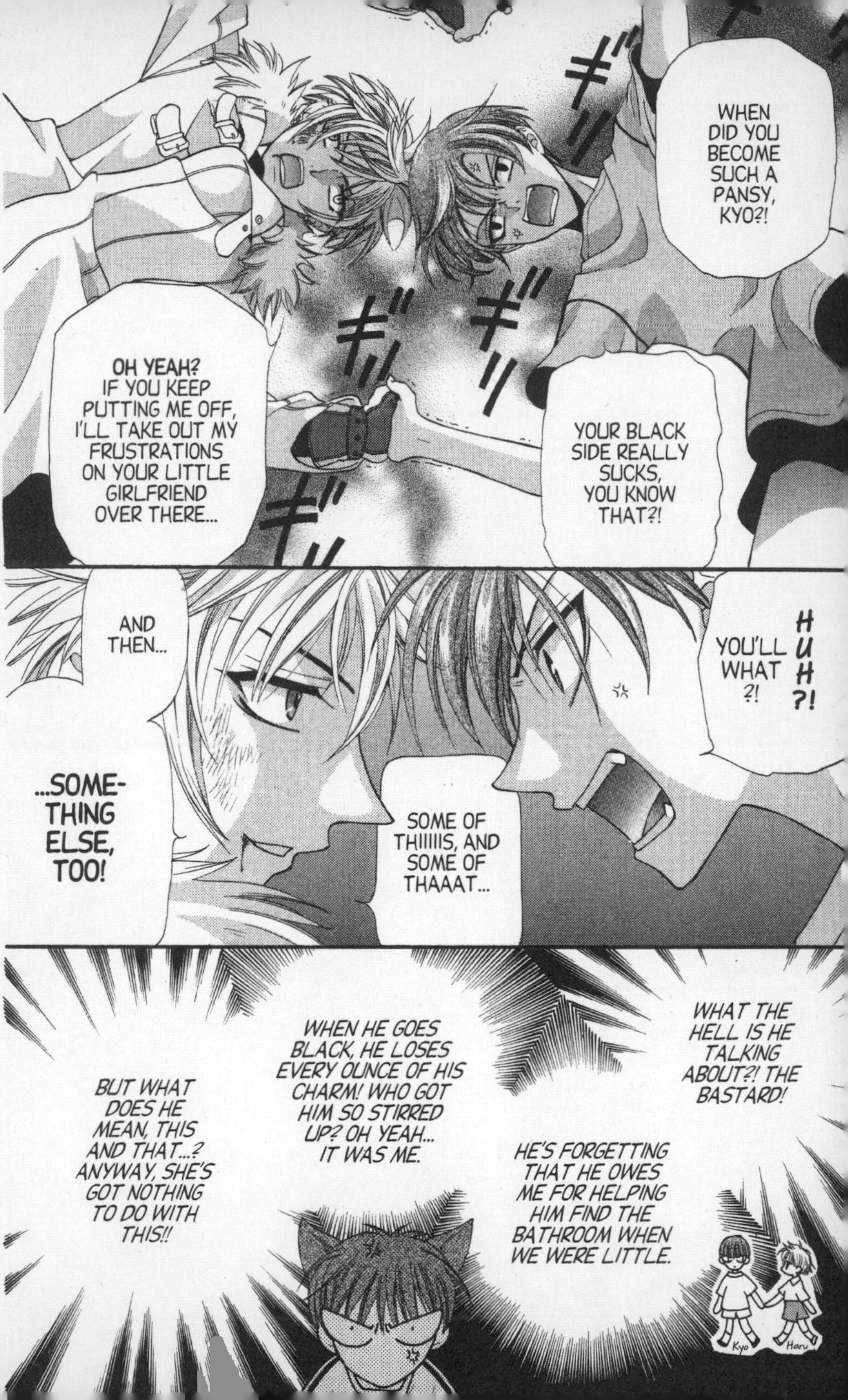
WHEN DID YOU BECOME SUCH A PANSY, KYO?!
YOUR BLACK SIDE REALLY SUCKS, YOU KNOW THAT?!
OH YEAH? IF YOU KEEP PUTTING ME OFF, I'LL TAKE OUT MY FRUSTRATIONS ON YOUR LITTLE GIRLFRIEND OVER THERE...
HUH?!
YOU'LL WHAT?!
AND THEN...
SOME OF THIIIIS, AND SOME OF THAAAT...
...SOME-THING ELSE, TOO!
WHAT THE HELL IS HE TALKING ABOUT?! THE BASTARD!
WHEN HE GOES BLACK, HE LOSES EVERY OUNCE OF HIS CHARM! WHO GOT HIM SO STIRRED UP? OH YEAH... IT WAS ME.
BUT WHAT DOES HE MEAN, THIS AND THAT...? ANYWAY, SHE'S GOT NOTHING TO DO WITH THIS!!
HE'S FORGETTING THAT HE OWES ME FOR HELPING HIM FIND THE BATHROOM WHEN WE WERE LITTLE.
Kyo
Haru

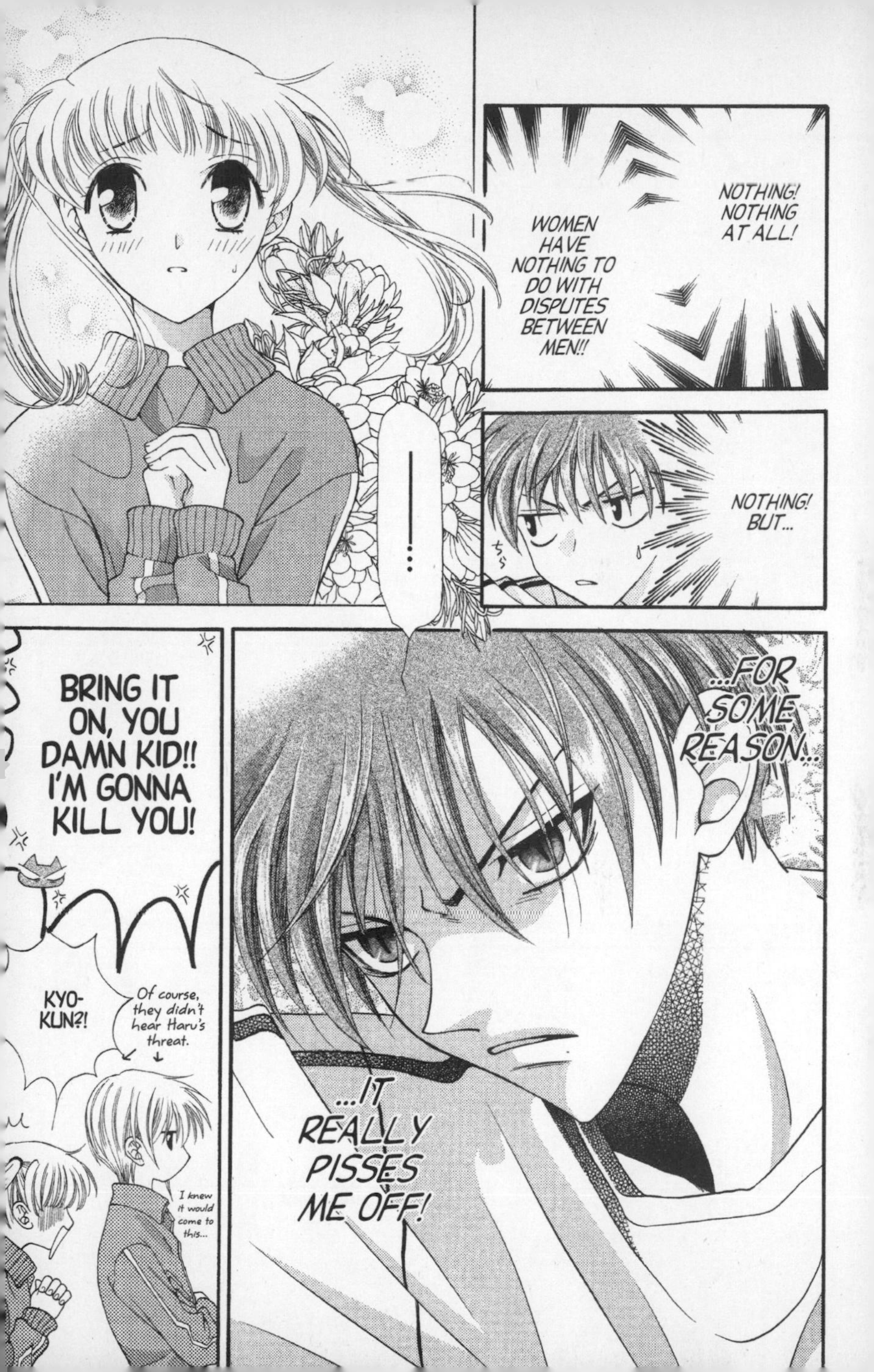
NOTHING! NOTHING AT ALL!
WOMEN HAVE NOTHING TO DO WITH DISPUTES BETWEEN MEN!!
NOTHING! BUT...
......
...FOR SOME REASON...
...IT REALLY PISSES ME OFF!
BRING IT ON, YOU DAMN KID!! I'M GONNA KILL YOU!
Of course, they didn't hear Haru's threat.
KYO-KUN?!
I knew it would come to this...

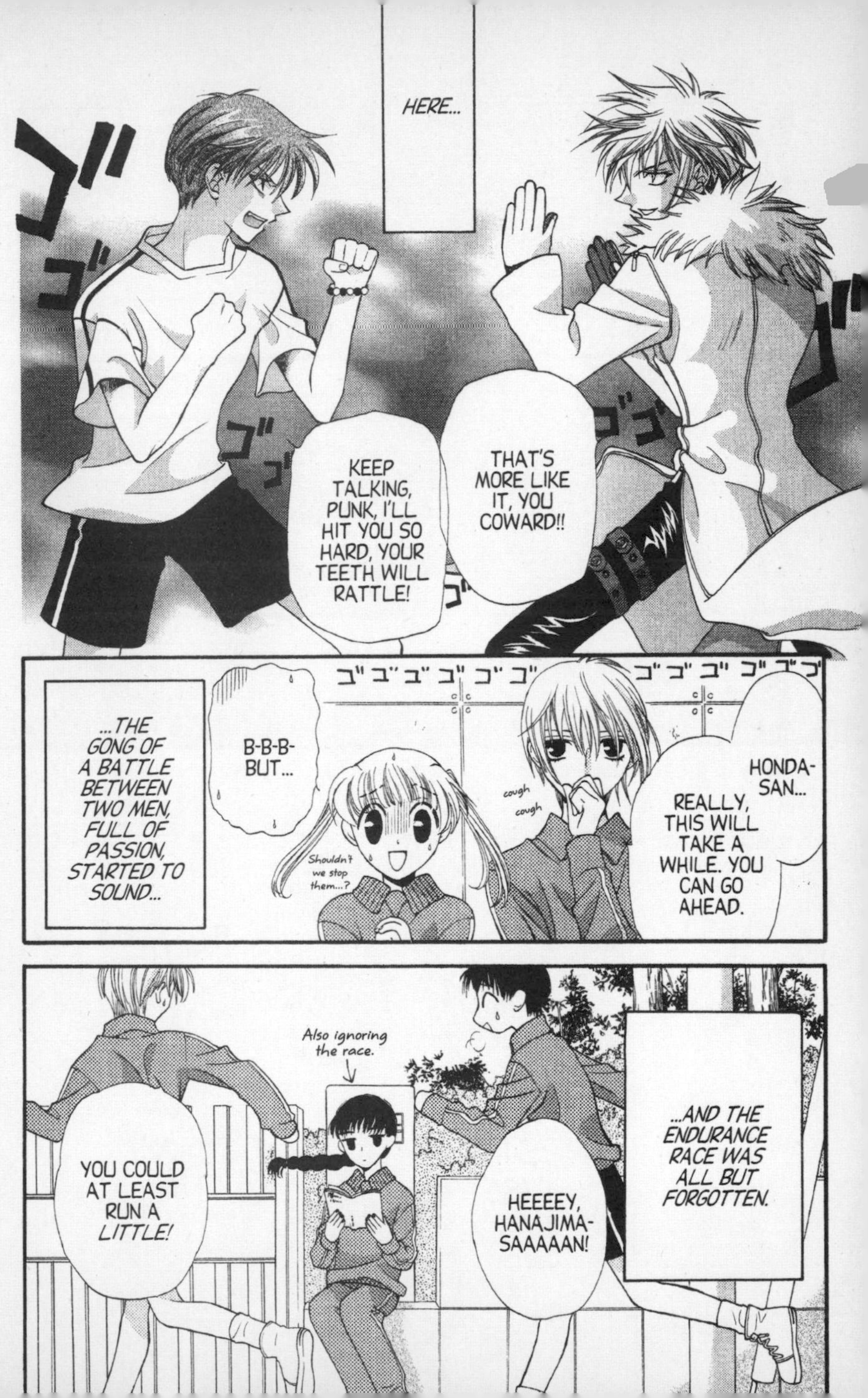
HERE...
THAT'S MORE LIKE IT, YOU COWARD!!
KEEP TALKING, PUNK, I'LL HIT YOU SO HARD, YOUR TEETH WILL RATTLE!
HONDA-SAN... REALLY, THIS WILL TAKE A WHILE. YOU CAN GO AHEAD.
cough cough
B-B-B-BUT...
Shouldn't we stop them...?
...THE GONG OF A BATTLE BETWEEN TWO MEN, FULL OF PASSION, STARTED TO SOUND...
...AND THE ENDURANCE RACE WAS ALL BUT FORGOTTEN.
HEEEEY, HANAJIMA-SAAAAAN!
Also ignoring the race.
YOU COULD AT LEAST RUN A LITTLE!

Chapter 14

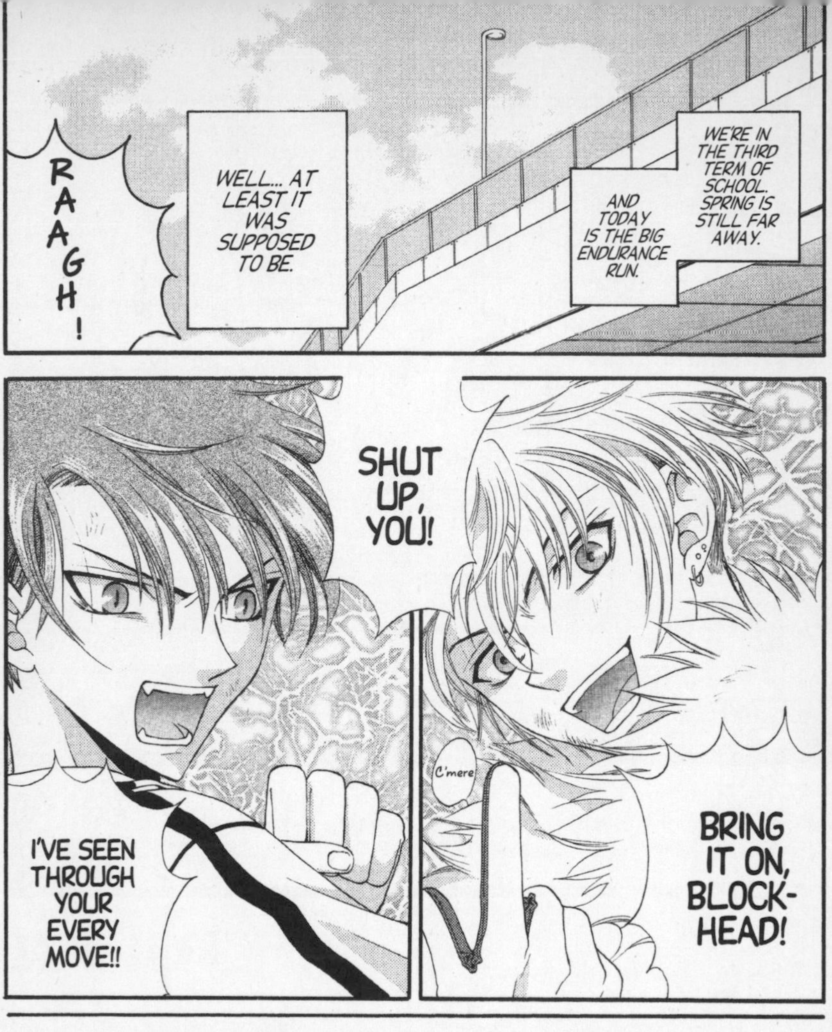
WE'RE IN THE THIRD TERM OF SCHOOL. SPRING IS STILL FAR AWAY.
AND TODAY IS THE BIG ENDURANCE RUN.
WELL... AT LEAST IT WAS SUPPOSED TO BE.
RAAGH!
SHUT UP, YOU!
C'mere
BRING IT ON, BLOCK-HEAD!
I'VE SEEN THROUGH YOUR EVERY MOVE!!

ULTRA SPECIAL BLAH BLAH BLAH 2

There were a lot of typos in this issue first time around...I got a lot of letters saying, "This line of dialogue is weird!" Of course it's weird--it's a typo! Oh well. We're human, we make mistakes. Let's be more tolerant. As it happens, I'm really bad at catching typos. (But I think I caught them all this time!)

*These words come from Takaya-sensei, but they apply to the editor as well!

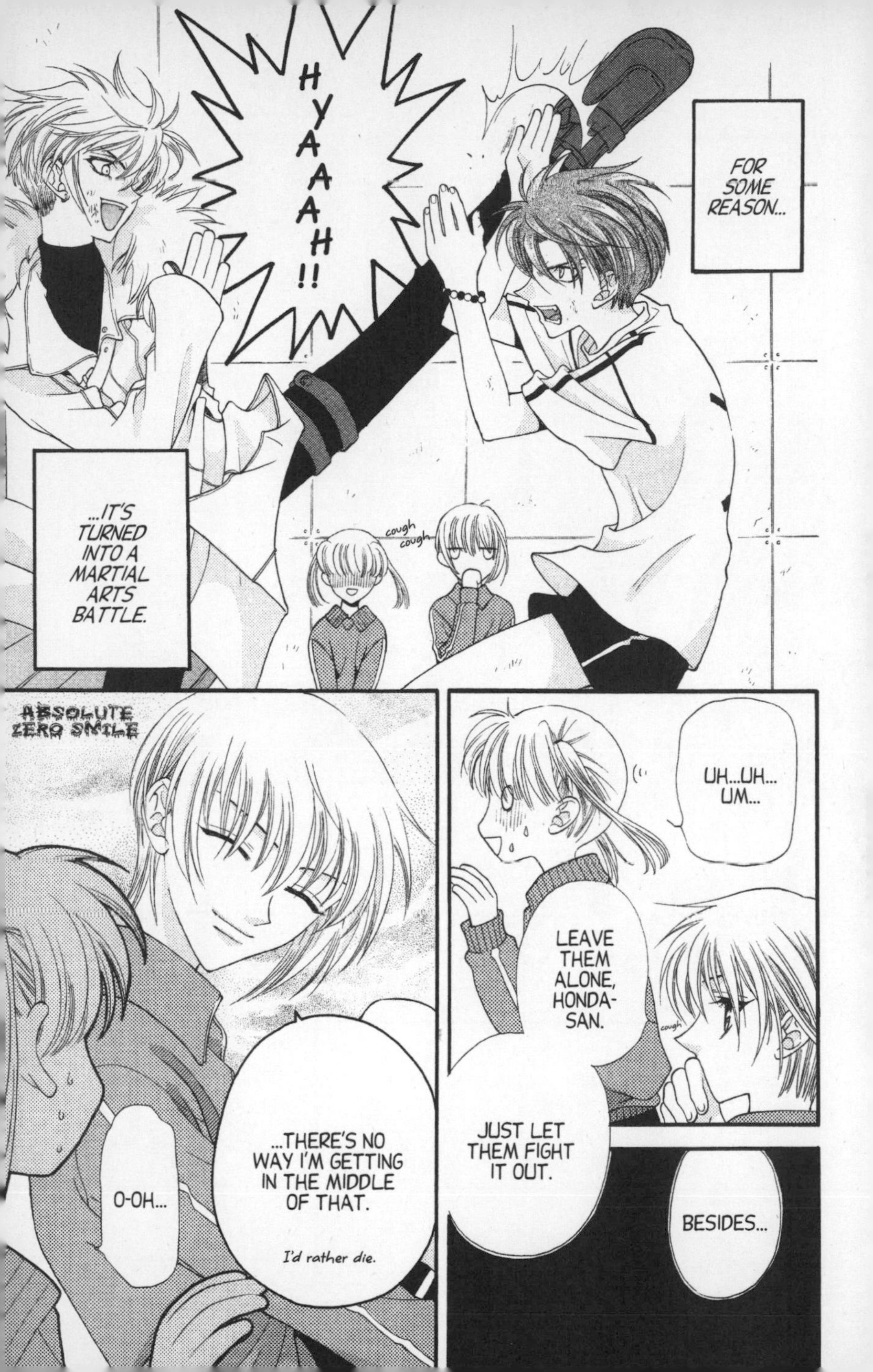

FOR SOME REASON...
HYAAAH!!
cough cough
...IT'S TURNED INTO A MARTIAL ARTS BATTLE.
UH...UH... UM...
LEAVE THEM ALONE, HONDA-SAN.
cough
JUST LET THEM FIGHT IT OUT.
BESIDES...
ABSOLUTE ZERO SMILE
...THERE'S NO WAY I'M GETTING IN THE MIDDLE OF THAT.
I'd rather die.
O-OH...

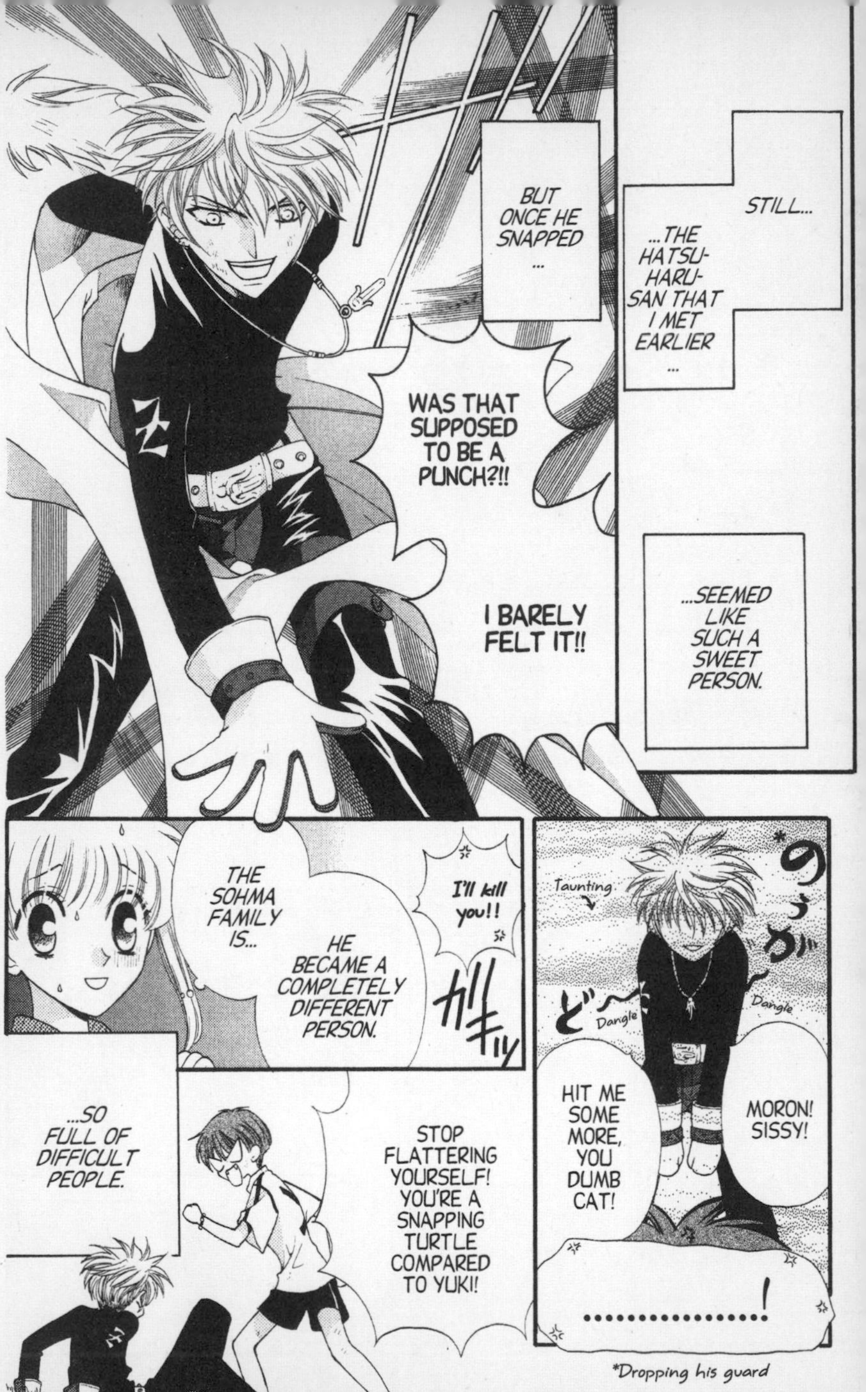
STILL...
...THE HATSUHARU-SAN THAT I MET EARLIER...
...SEEMED LIKE SUCH A SWEET PERSON.
BUT ONCE HE SNAPPED...
WAS THAT SUPPOSED TO BE A PUNCH?!!
I BARELY FELT IT!!
*のうが
Taunting
ど~
Dangle
Dangle
MORON! SISSY!
HIT ME SOME MORE, YOU DUMB CAT!
...............!
*Dropping his guard
I'll kill you!!
ガキッ
HE BECAME A COMPLETELY DIFFERENT PERSON.
THE SOHMA FAMILY IS...
STOP FLATTERING YOURSELF! YOU'RE A SNAPPING TURTLE COMPARED TO YUKI!!
...SO FULL OF DIFFICULT PEOPLE.

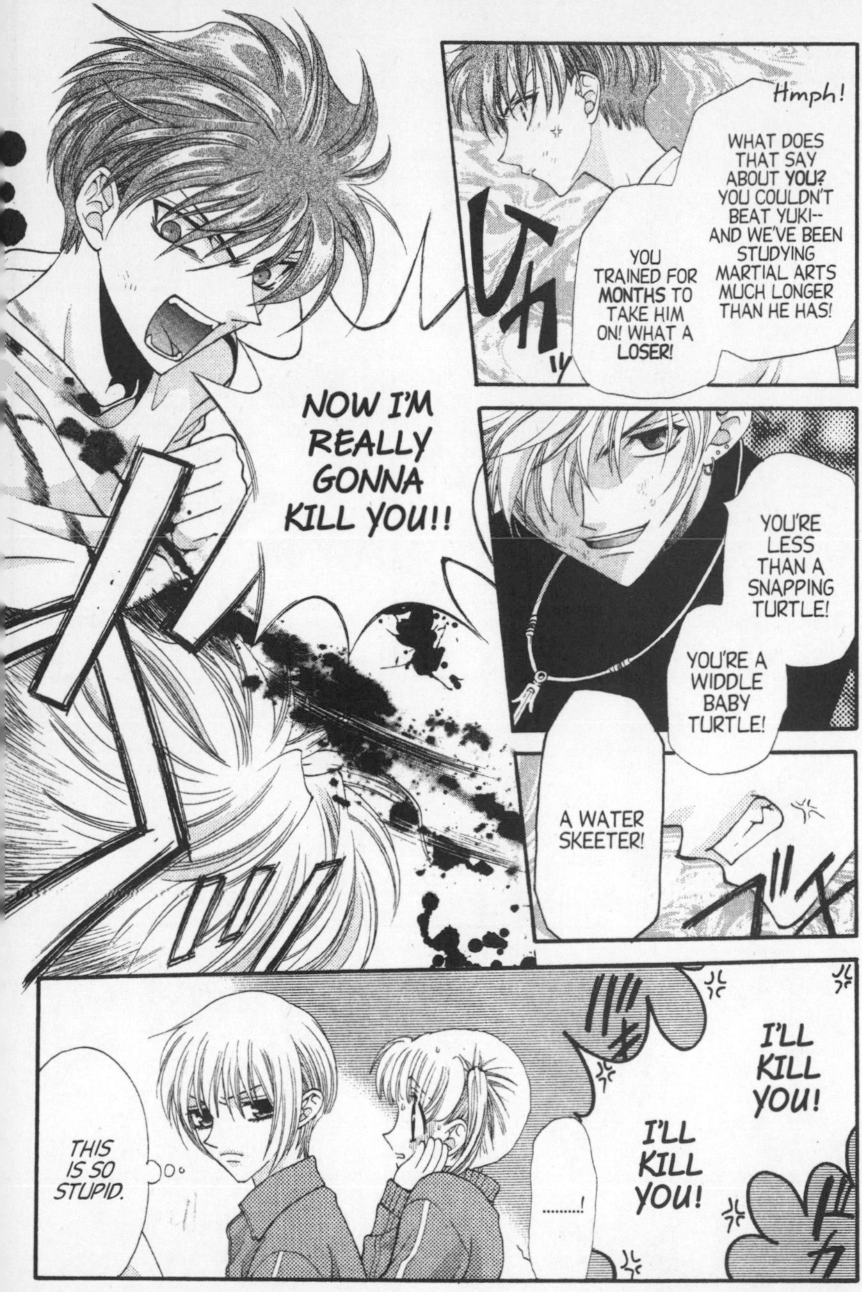
Himph!
WHAT DOES THAT SAY ABOUT YOU? YOU COULDN'T BEAT YUKI-- AND WE'VE BEEN STUDYING MARTIAL ARTS MUCH LONGER THAN HE HAS!
YOU TRAINED FOR MONTHS TO TAKE HIM ON! WHAT A LOSER!
YOU'RE LESS THAN A SNAPPING TURTLE!
YOU'RE A WIDDLE BABY TURTLE!
A WATER SKEETER!
NOW I'M REALLY GONNA KILL YOU!!
I'LL KILL YOU!
I'LL KILL YOU!
.........!
THIS IS SO STUPID.

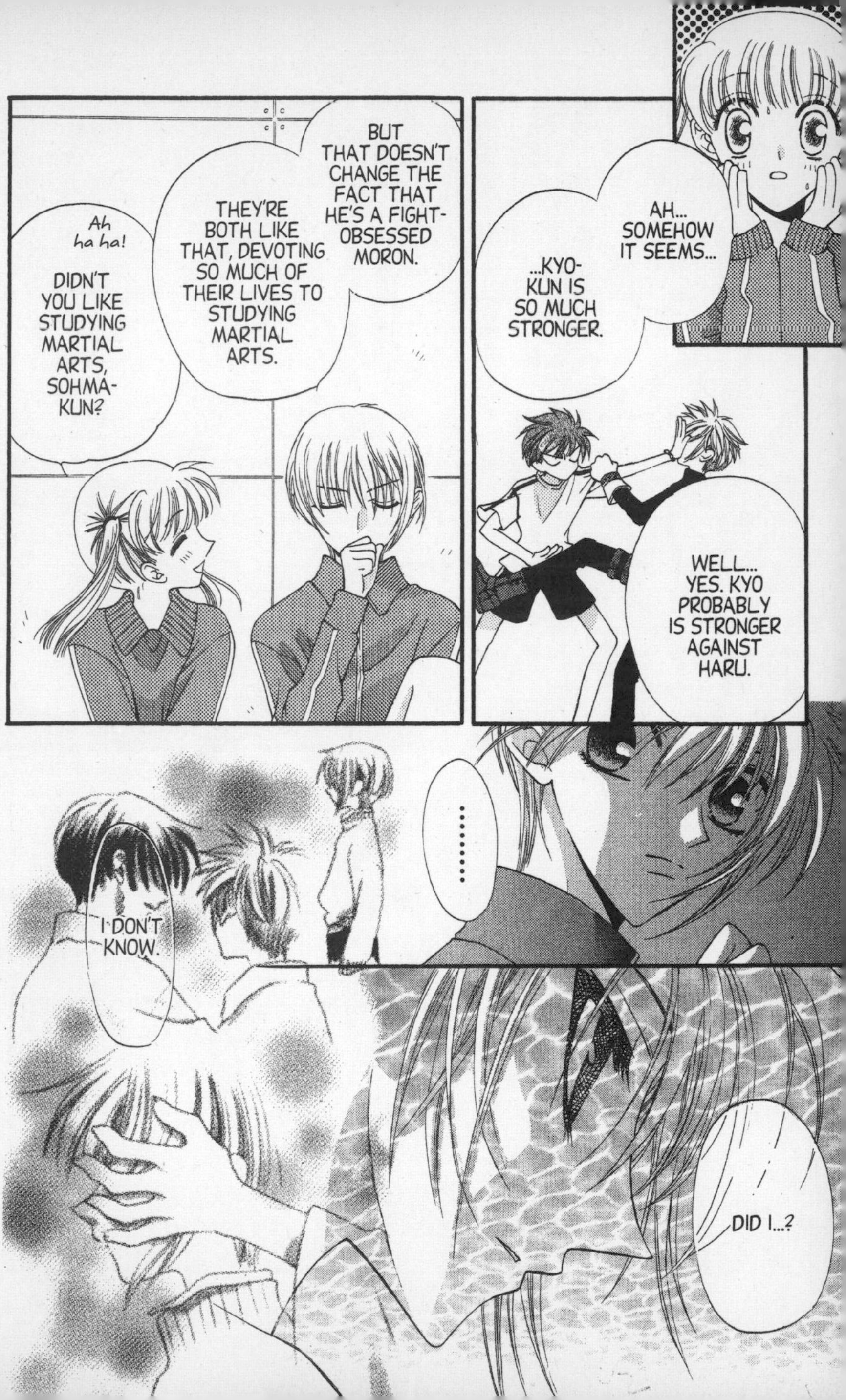
AH... SOMEHOW IT SEEMS...
...KYO-KUN IS SO MUCH STRONGER.
WELL... YES. KYO PROBABLY IS STRONGER AGAINST HARU.
BUT THAT DOESN'T CHANGE THE FACT THAT HE'S A FIGHT-OBSESSED MORON.
THEY'RE BOTH LIKE THAT, DEVOTING SO MUCH OF THEIR LIVES TO STUDYING MARTIAL ARTS.
Ah ha ha!
DIDN'T YOU LIKE STUDYING MARTIAL ARTS, SOHMA-KUN?
....
I DON'T KNOW.
DID I...?

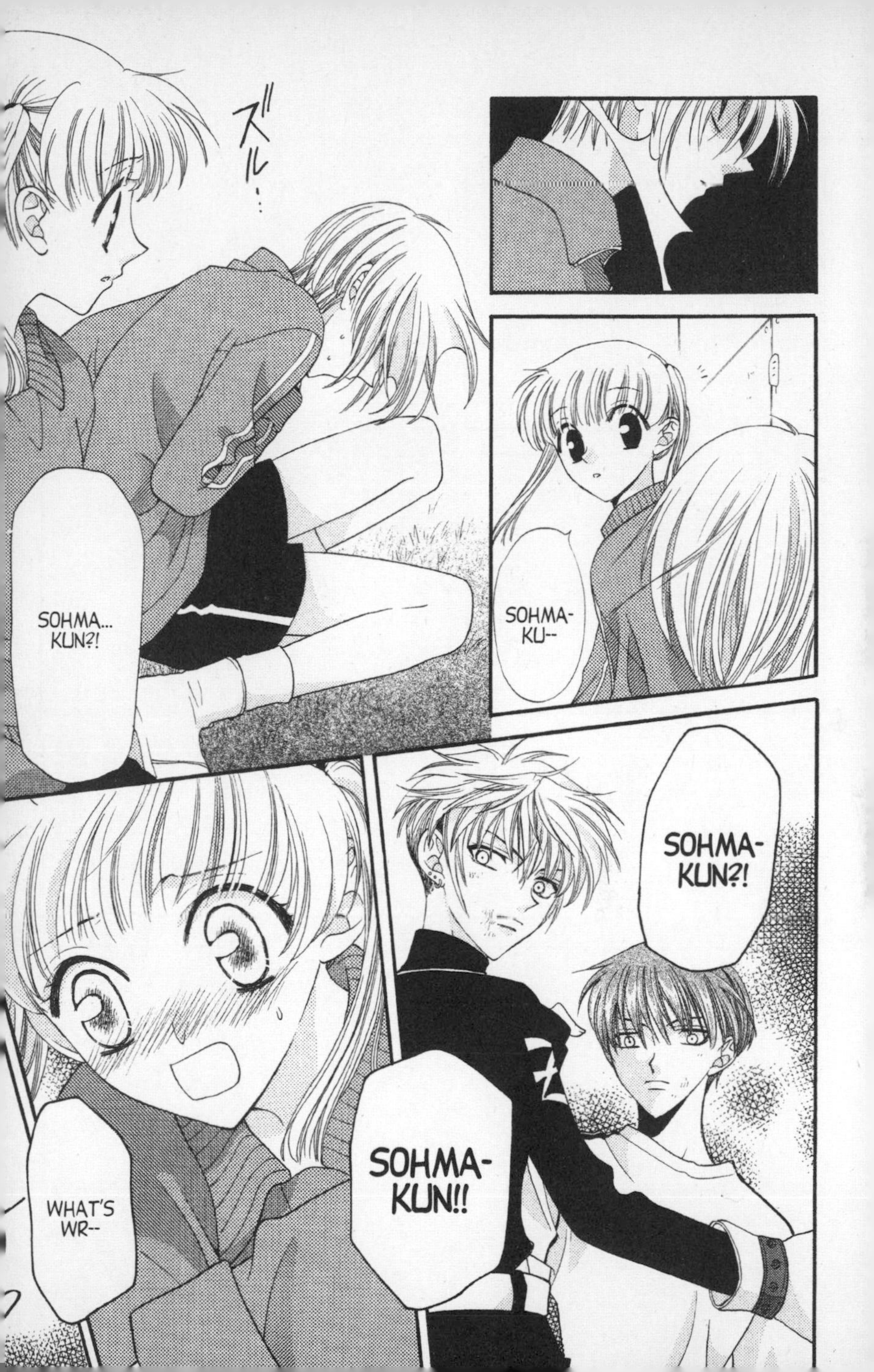
SOHMA-
KU--
ズル・・
SOHMA...
KUN?!
SOHMA-
KUN?!
SOHMA-
KUN!!
WHAT'S
WR--

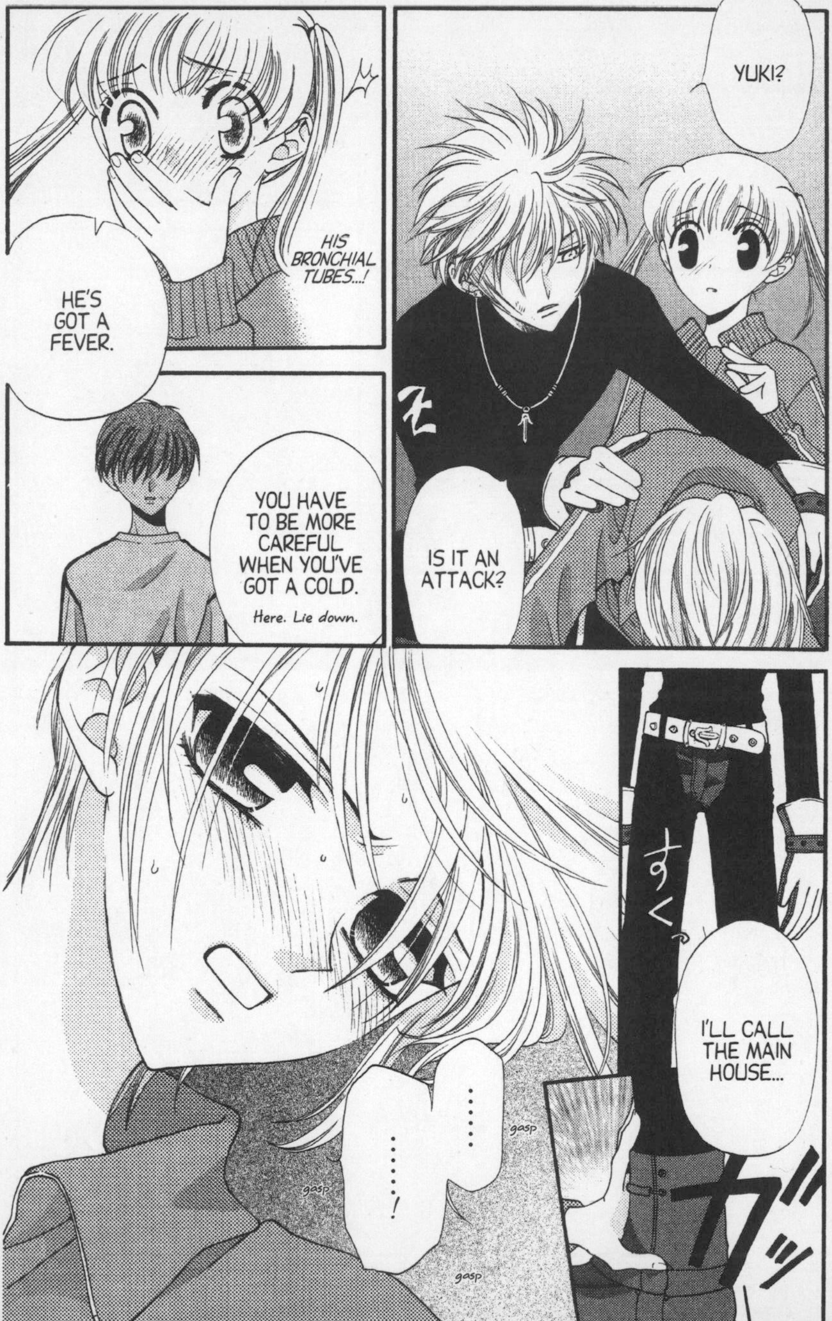
YUKI?
IS IT AN ATTACK?
HIS BRONCHIAL TUBES...!
HE'S GOT A FEVER.
YOU HAVE TO BE MORE CAREFUL WHEN YOU'VE GOT A COLD.
Here. Lie down.
すくっ
I'LL CALL THE MAIN HOUSE...
ガッ
gasp
......
......!
gasp
gasp

Fruits Basket 3 Part 2:

I got to meet my idol, Banri ♪ Hidaka-sensei! Isn't that great? Aren't you jealous?! Eh heh heeehh...♪ (Someday someone's gonna smack you.) There was a thing, and we were both invited, and I met her there. (I met other authors there, too, but I didn't get permission to write about them, so I can't tell you who they were.) Well, anyway-- I haven't met many other Hana-Yume authors, so it was very exciting! Maybe I haven't met them because I don't go anywhere...like New Year's parties... (This year I had the flu and thought it would be bad to go to a party and give it to everyone else.) Hidaka-sensei was very much like the manga she writes.

To be continued...

*Hidaka-sensei is the manga ka of SEKAI DE ICHIBAN DAIKIRAI.

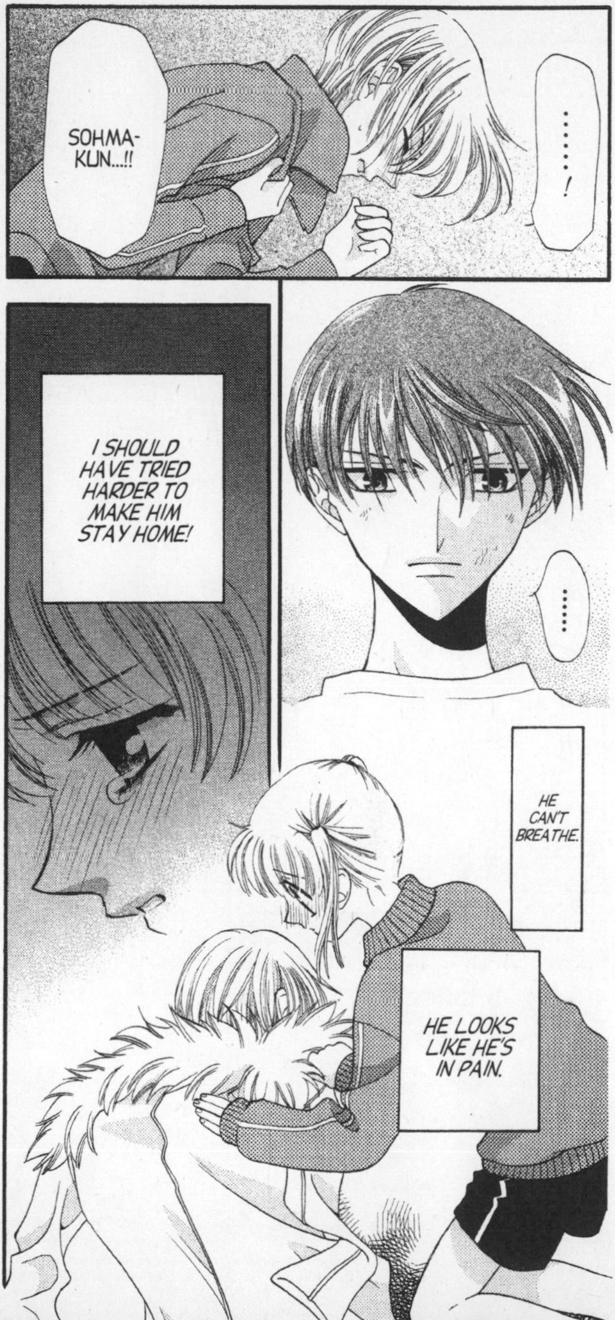
......!
SOHMA-KUN...!!
......
I SHOULD HAVE TRIED HARDER TO MAKE HIM STAY HOME!
HE CAN'T BREATHE.
HE LOOKS LIKE HE'S IN PAIN.

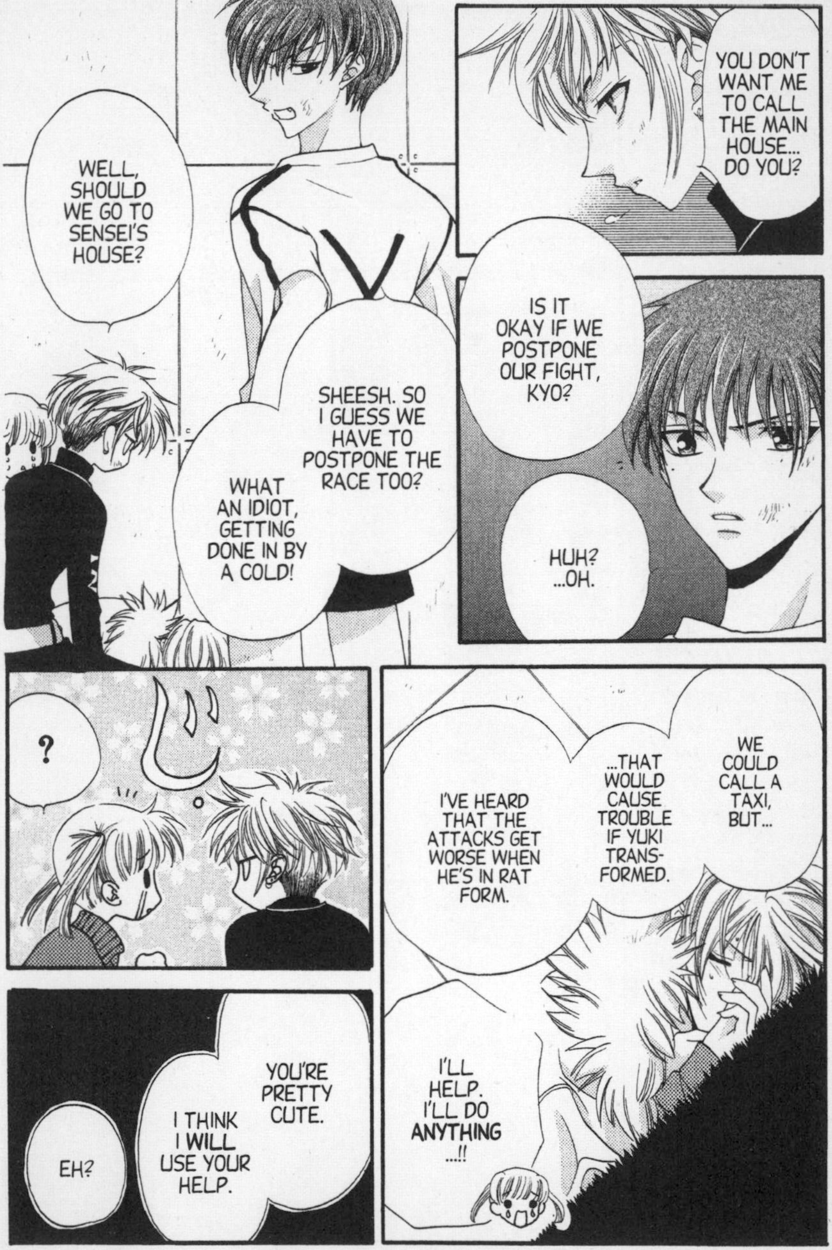
YOU DON'T WANT ME TO CALL THE MAIN HOUSE... DO YOU?
IS IT OKAY IF WE POSTPONE OUR FIGHT, KYO?
HUH? ...OH.
WELL, SHOULD WE GO TO SENSEI'S HOUSE?
SHEESH. SO I GUESS WE HAVE TO POSTPONE THE RACE TOO?
WHAT AN IDIOT, GETTING DONE IN BY A COLD!
WE COULD CALL A TAXI, BUT...
...THAT WOULD CAUSE TROUBLE IF YUKI TRANSFORMED.
I'VE HEARD THAT THE ATTACKS GET WORSE WHEN HE'S IN RAT FORM.
I'LL HELP. I'LL DO **ANYTHING** ...!!
?
YOU'RE PRETTY CUTE.
I THINK I **WILL** USE YOUR HELP.
EH?

* *Haru and some other Sohma members refer to Shigure as Sensei. Sensei can be applied to a master of a craft, like a novelist, or manga-ka, as well as an actual teacher.*

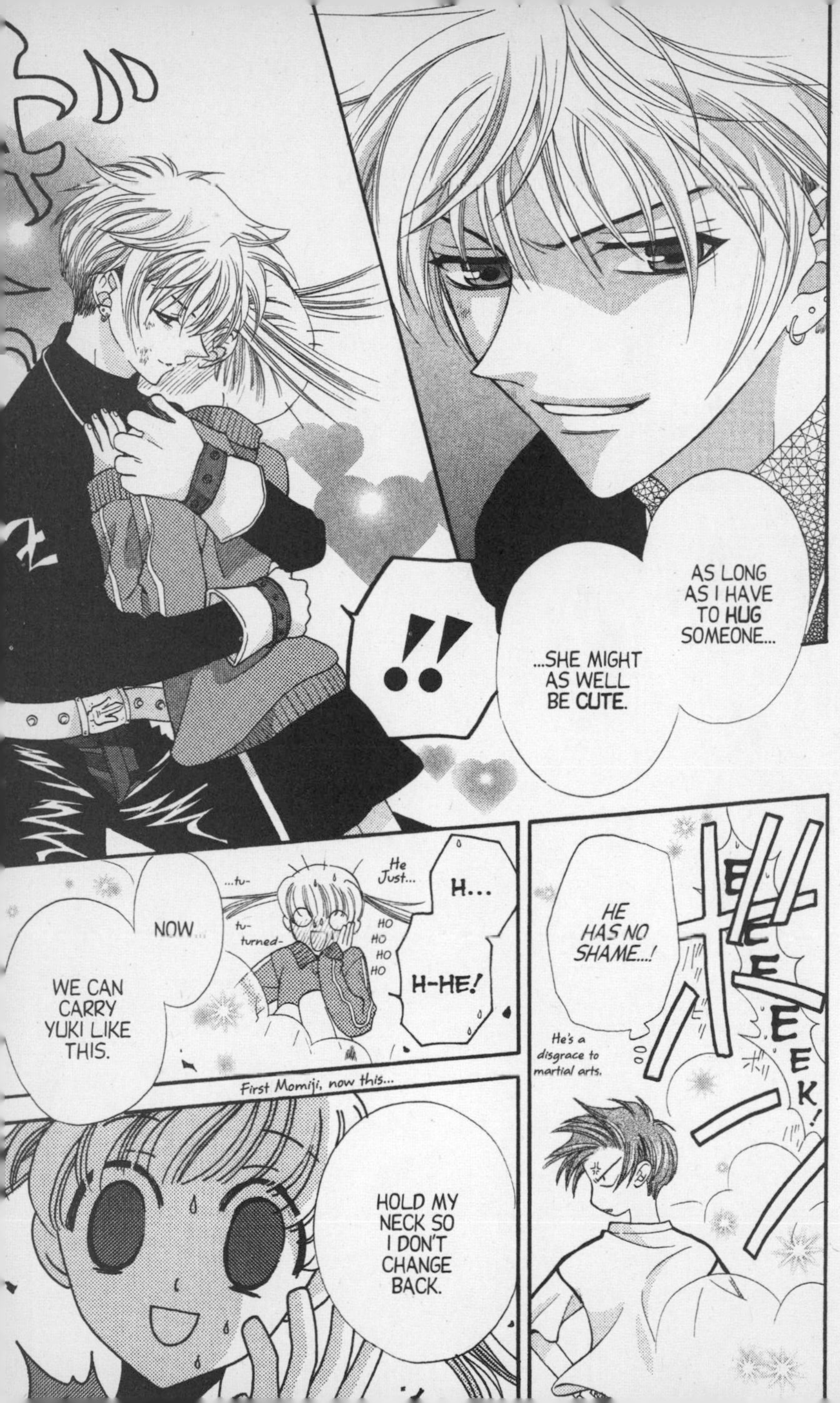
AS LONG AS I HAVE TO HUG SOMEONE...
...SHE MIGHT AS WELL BE CUTE.
!!
EEEEEK!
HE HAS NO SHAME...!
He's a disgrace to martial arts.
H...
H-HE!
He Just...
...tu-
tu-turned-
HO HO HO HO
NOW...
WE CAN CARRY YUKI LIKE THIS.
First Momiji, now this...
HOLD MY NECK SO I DON'T CHANGE BACK.

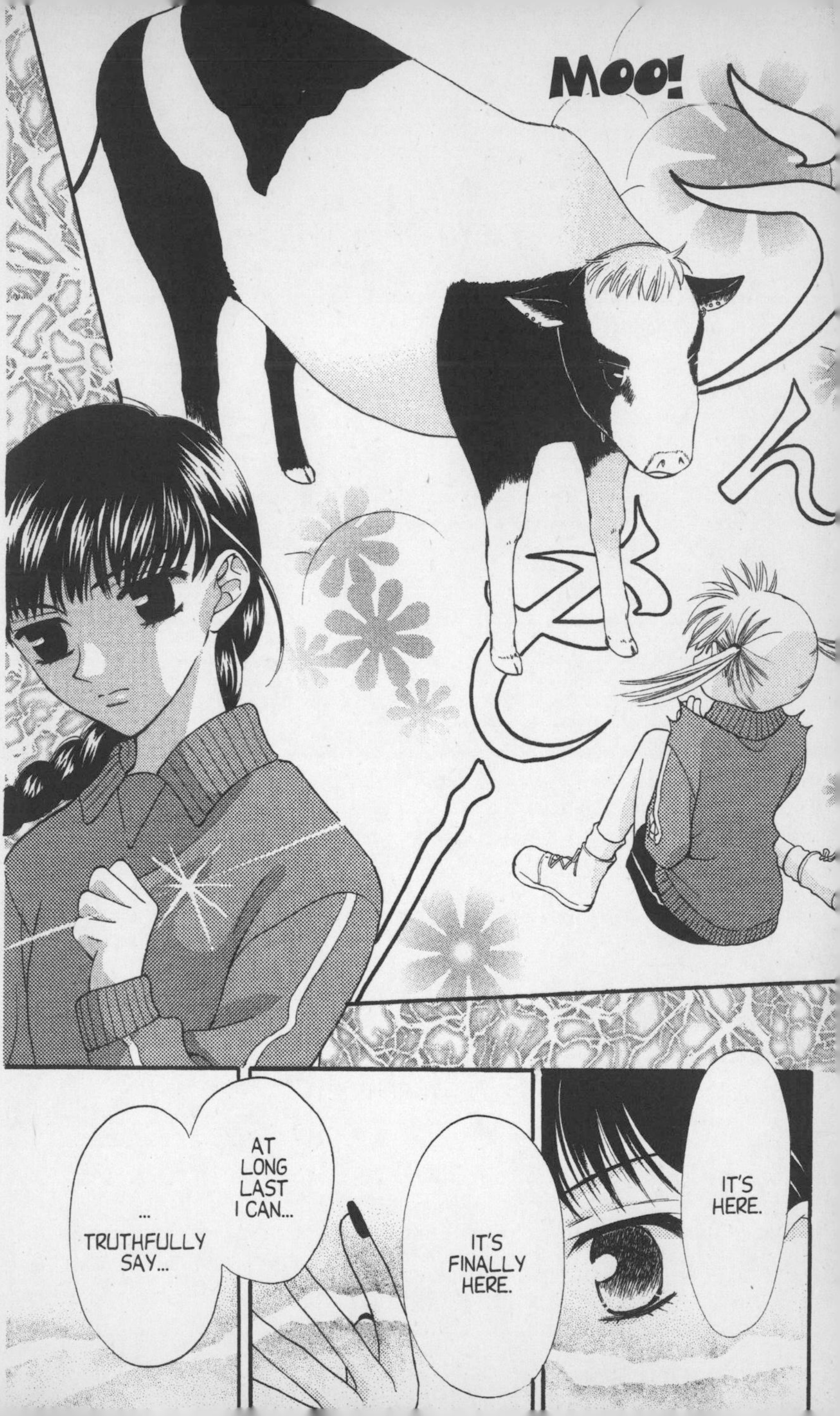
MOO!
IT'S HERE.
IT'S FINALLY HERE.
AT LONG LAST I CAN...
... TRUTHFULLY SAY...

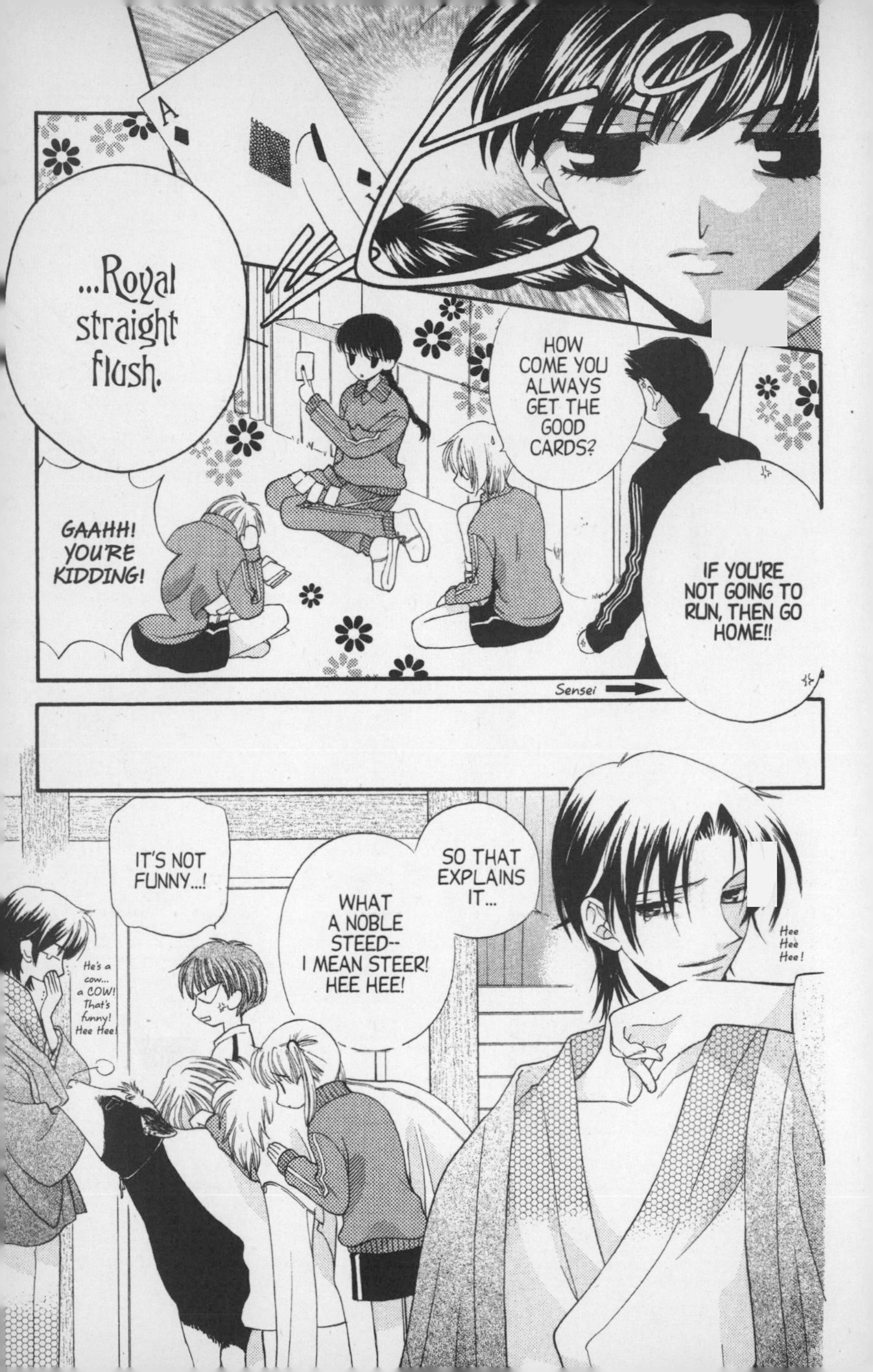
...Royal straight flush.
HOW COME YOU ALWAYS GET THE GOOD CARDS?
GAAHH! YOU'RE KIDDING!
IF YOU'RE NOT GOING TO RUN, THEN GO HOME!!
Sensei
Hee Hee Hee!
SO THAT EXPLAINS IT...
WHAT A NOBLE STEED-- I MEAN STEER! HEE HEE!
IT'S NOT FUNNY...!
He's a cow... a COW! That's funny! Hee Hee!

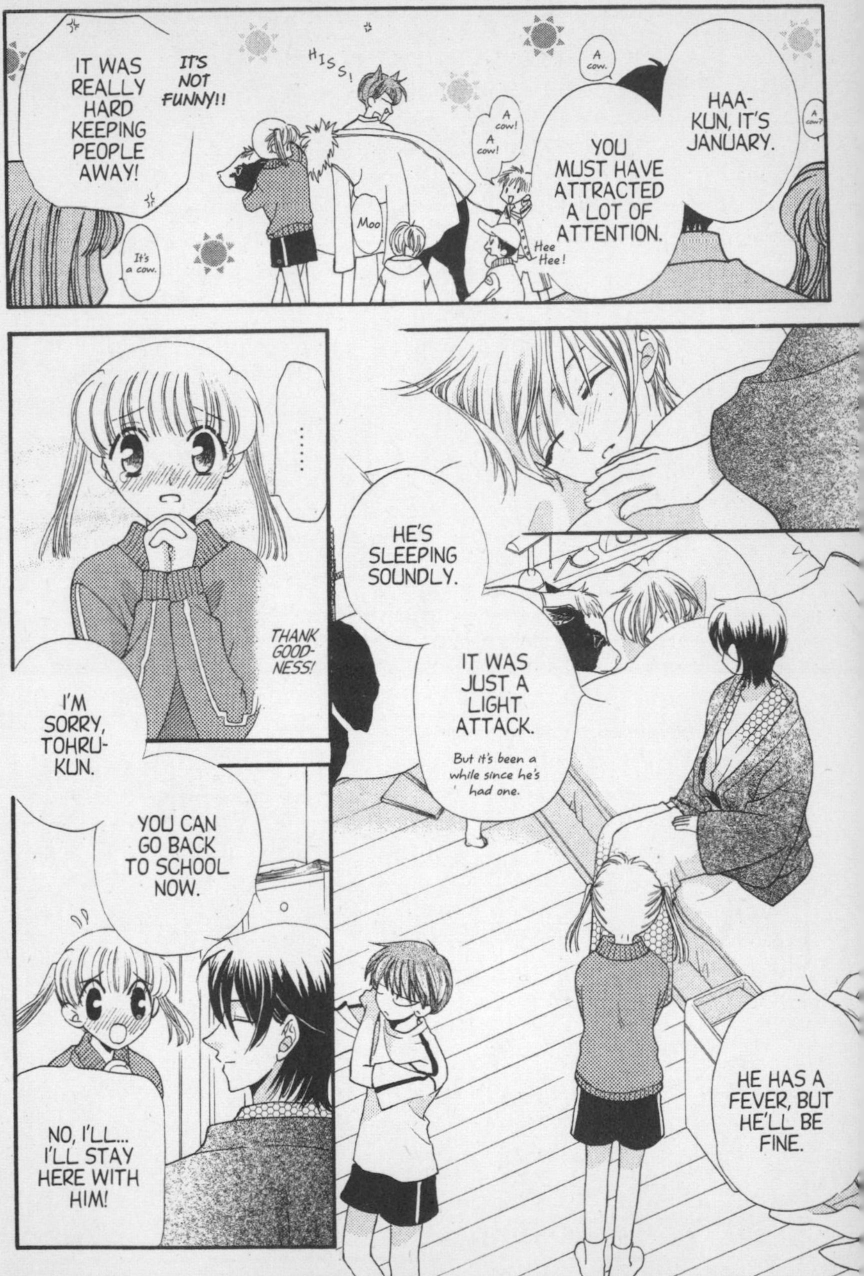
A cow?
HAA-KUN, IT'S JANUARY.
A cow.
YOU MUST HAVE ATTRACTED A LOT OF ATTENTION.
Hee Hee!
A cow!
A cow!
Moo
HISS!
IT'S NOT FUNNY!!
IT WAS REALLY HARD KEEPING PEOPLE AWAY!
It's a cow.
HE'S SLEEPING SOUNDLY.
HE HAS A FEVER, BUT HE'LL BE FINE.
IT WAS JUST A LIGHT ATTACK.
But it's been a while since he's had one.
......
THANK GOODNESS!
I'M SORRY, TOHRU-KUN.
YOU CAN GO BACK TO SCHOOL NOW.
NO, I'LL... I'LL STAY HERE WITH HIM!

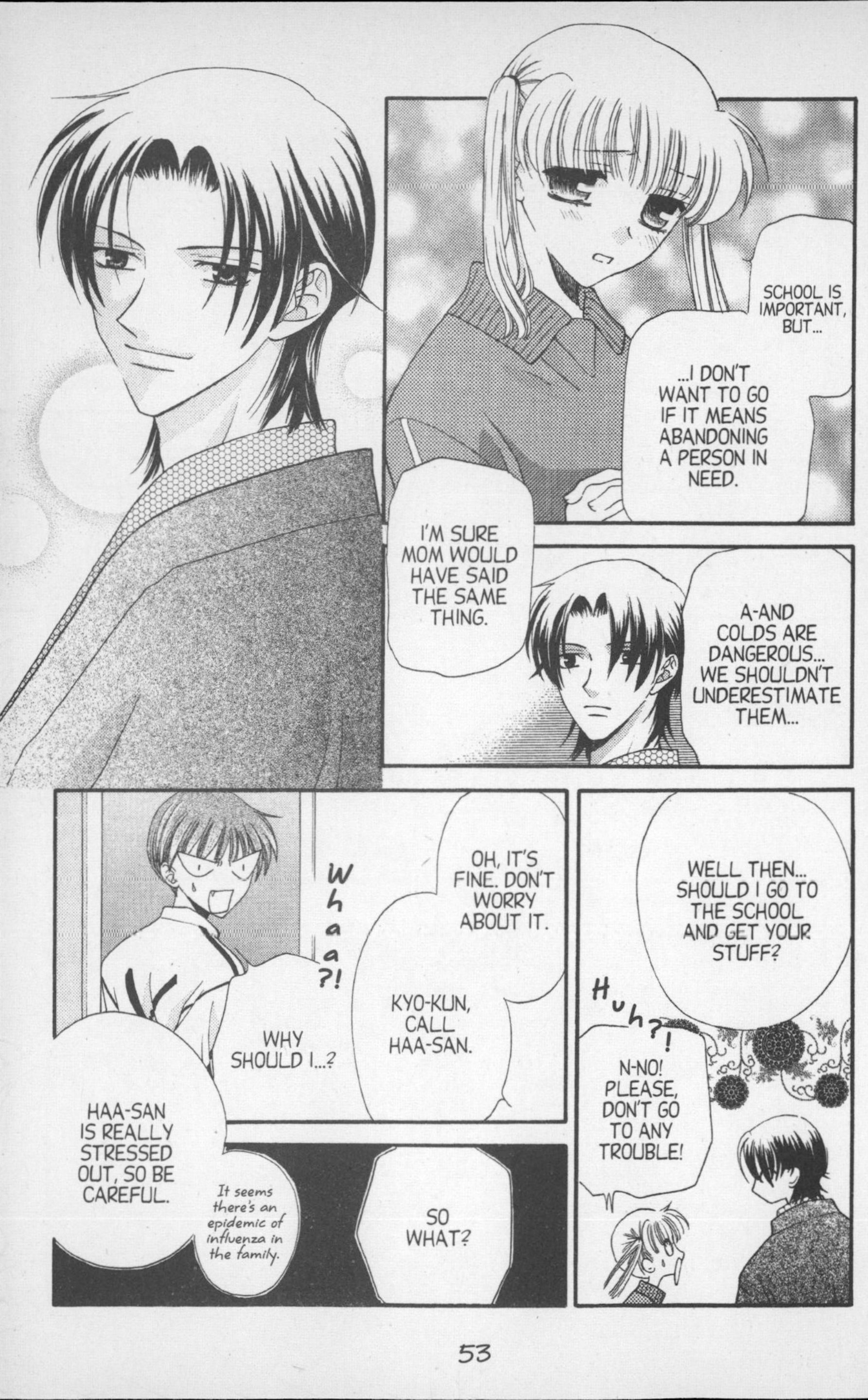
SCHOOL IS IMPORTANT, BUT...
...I DON'T WANT TO GO IF IT MEANS ABANDONING A PERSON IN NEED.
I'M SURE MOM WOULD HAVE SAID THE SAME THING.
A-AND COLDS ARE DANGEROUS... WE SHOULDN'T UNDERESTIMATE THEM...
WELL THEN... SHOULD I GO TO THE SCHOOL AND GET YOUR STUFF?
Huh?!
N-NO! PLEASE, DON'T GO TO ANY TROUBLE!
OH, IT'S FINE. DON'T WORRY ABOUT IT.
Whaaa?!
KYO-KUN, CALL HAA-SAN.
WHY SHOULD I...?
HAA-SAN IS REALLY STRESSED OUT, SO BE CAREFUL.
It seems there's an epidemic of influenza in the family.
SO WHAT?

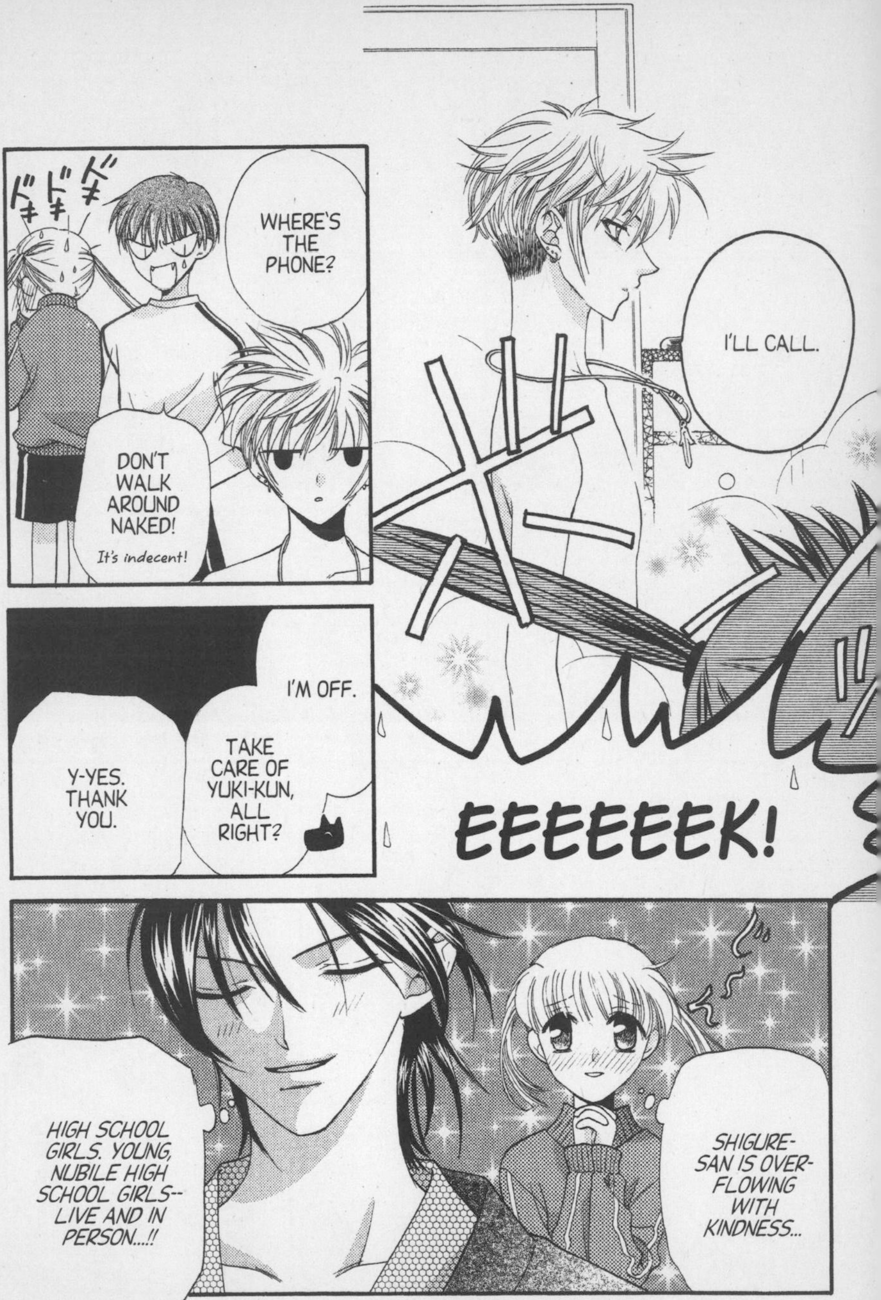
I'LL CALL.
EEEEEEEK!
WHERE'S THE PHONE?
ドキドキドキ
DON'T WALK AROUND NAKED!
It's indecent!
I'M OFF.
TAKE CARE OF YUKI-KUN, ALL RIGHT?
Y-YES. THANK YOU.
SHIGURE-SAN IS OVER-FLOWING WITH KINDNESS...
HIGH SCHOOL GIRLS. YOUNG, NUBILE HIGH SCHOOL GIRLS-- LIVE AND IN PERSON...!!

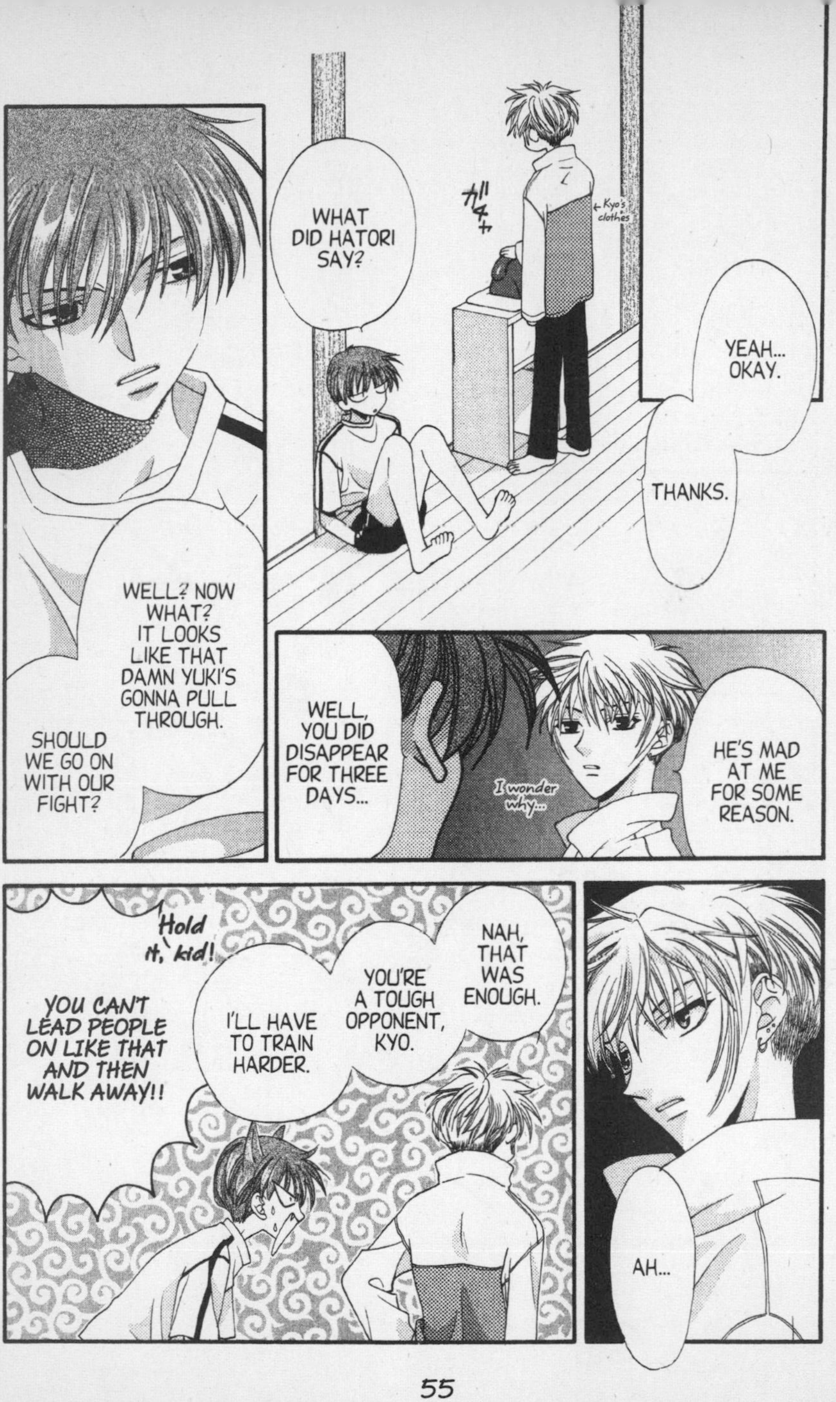

YEAH... OKAY.
THANKS.
Kyo's clothes
WHAT DID HATORI SAY?
HE'S MAD AT ME FOR SOME REASON.
I wonder why...
WELL, YOU DID DISAPPEAR FOR THREE DAYS...
WELL? NOW WHAT? IT LOOKS LIKE THAT DAMN YUKI'S GONNA PULL THROUGH.
SHOULD WE GO ON WITH OUR FIGHT?
AH...
NAH, THAT WAS ENOUGH.
YOU'RE A TOUGH OPPONENT, KYO.
I'LL HAVE TO TRAIN HARDER.
Hold it, kid!
YOU CAN'T LEAD PEOPLE ON LIKE THAT AND THEN WALK AWAY!!

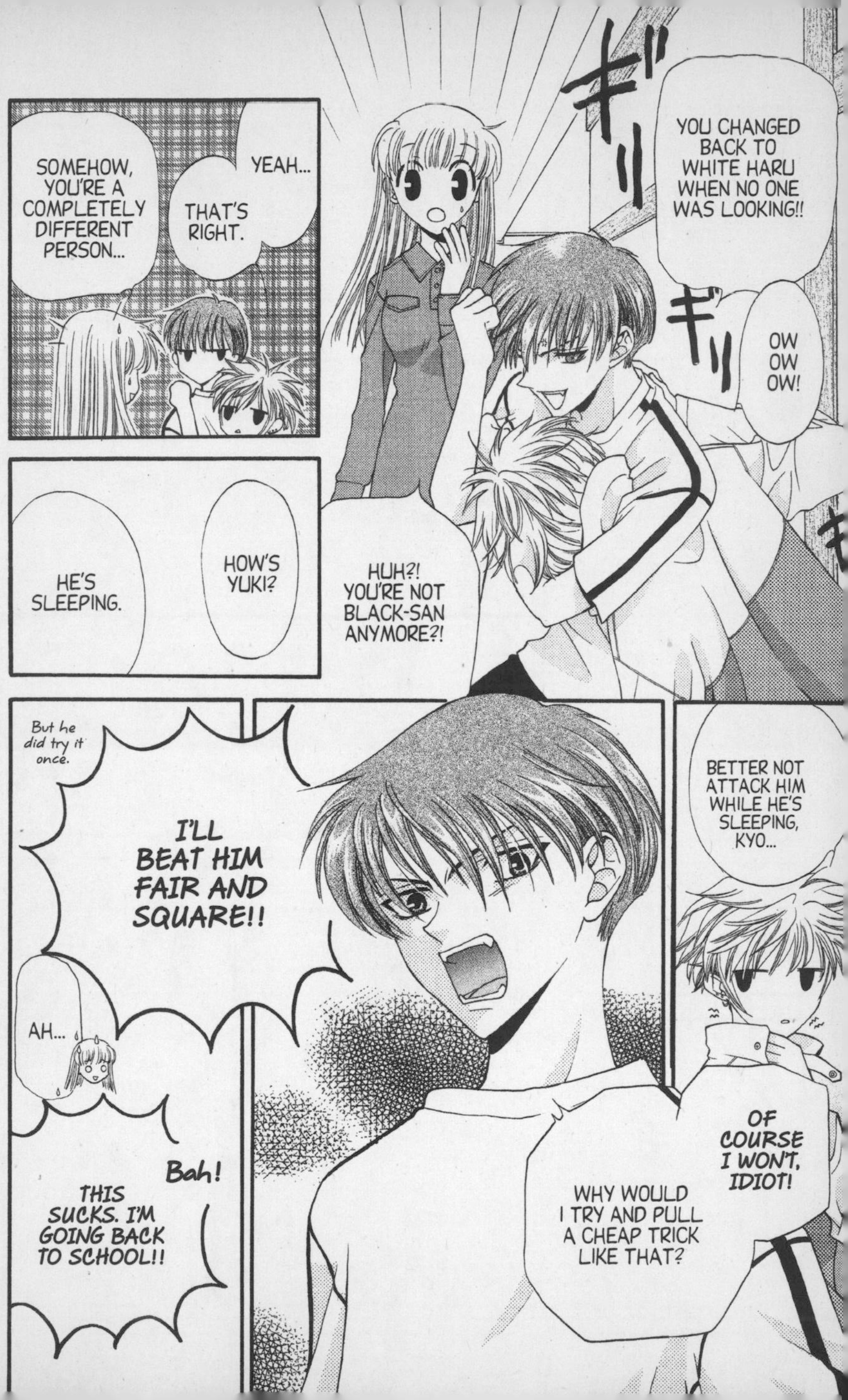

ギリ
YOU CHANGED BACK TO WHITE HARU WHEN NO ONE WAS LOOKING!!
ギリ
OW OW OW!
HUH?! YOU'RE NOT BLACK-SAN ANYMORE?!
YEAH... THAT'S RIGHT.
SOMEHOW, YOU'RE A COMPLETELY DIFFERENT PERSON...
HOW'S YUKI?
HE'S SLEEPING.
BETTER NOT ATTACK HIM WHILE HE'S SLEEPING, KYO...
OF COURSE I WON'T, IDIOT!
WHY WOULD I TRY AND PULL A CHEAP TRICK LIKE THAT?
I'LL BEAT HIM FAIR AND SQUARE!!
But he did try it once.
AH...
Bah!
THIS SUCKS. I'M GOING BACK TO SCHOOL!!

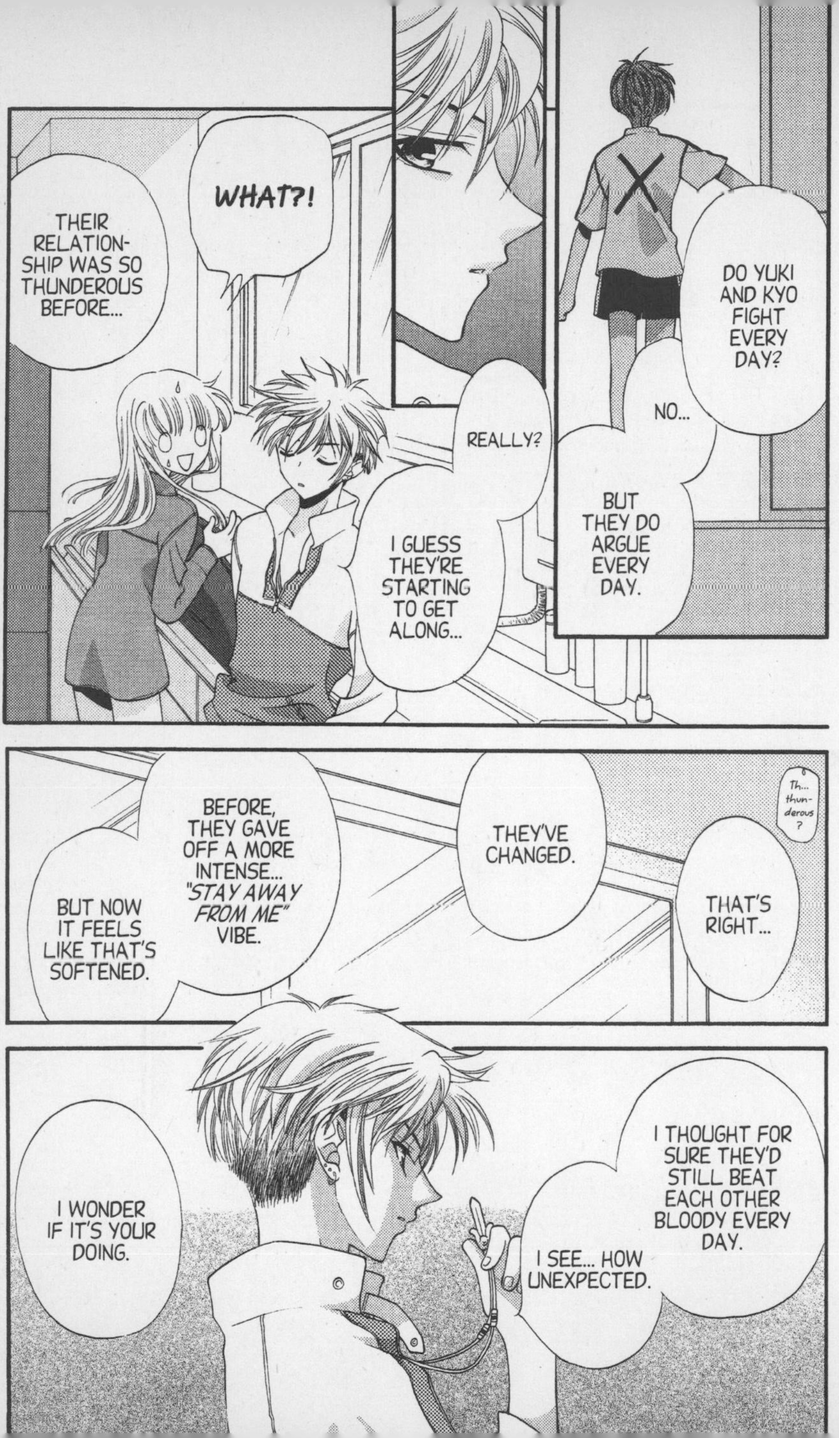
DO YUKI AND KYO FIGHT EVERY DAY?
NO...
BUT THEY DO ARGUE EVERY DAY.
REALLY?
I GUESS THEY'RE STARTING TO GET ALONG...
WHAT?!
THEIR RELATION-SHIP WAS SO THUNDEROUS BEFORE...
Th... thun-derous?
THAT'S RIGHT...
THEY'VE CHANGED.
BEFORE, THEY GAVE OFF A MORE INTENSE... "STAY AWAY FROM ME" VIBE.
BUT NOW IT FEELS LIKE THAT'S SOFTENED.
I THOUGHT FOR SURE THEY'D STILL BEAT EACH OTHER BLOODY EVERY DAY.
I SEE... HOW UNEXPECTED.
I WONDER IF IT'S YOUR DOING.

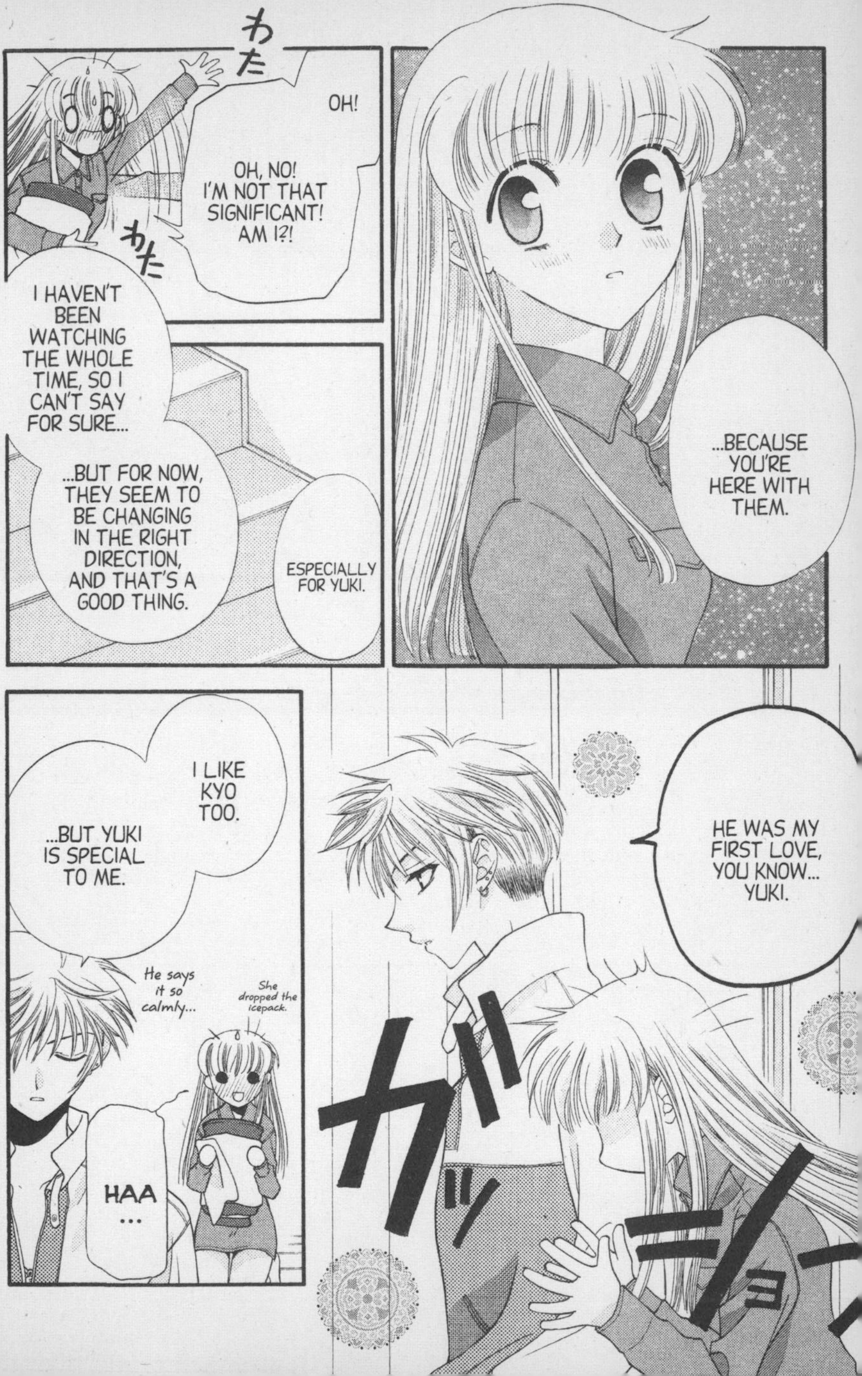
...BECAUSE YOU'RE HERE WITH THEM.
わた
OH!
OH, NO! I'M NOT THAT SIGNIFICANT! AM I?!
わた
I HAVEN'T BEEN WATCHING THE WHOLE TIME, SO I CAN'T SAY FOR SURE...
...BUT FOR NOW, THEY SEEM TO BE CHANGING IN THE RIGHT DIRECTION, AND THAT'S A GOOD THING.
ESPECIALLY FOR YUKI.
HE WAS MY FIRST LOVE, YOU KNOW... YUKI.
ガッ
I LIKE KYO TOO.
...BUT YUKI IS SPECIAL TO ME.
He says it so calmly...
She dropped the icepack.
HAA ...

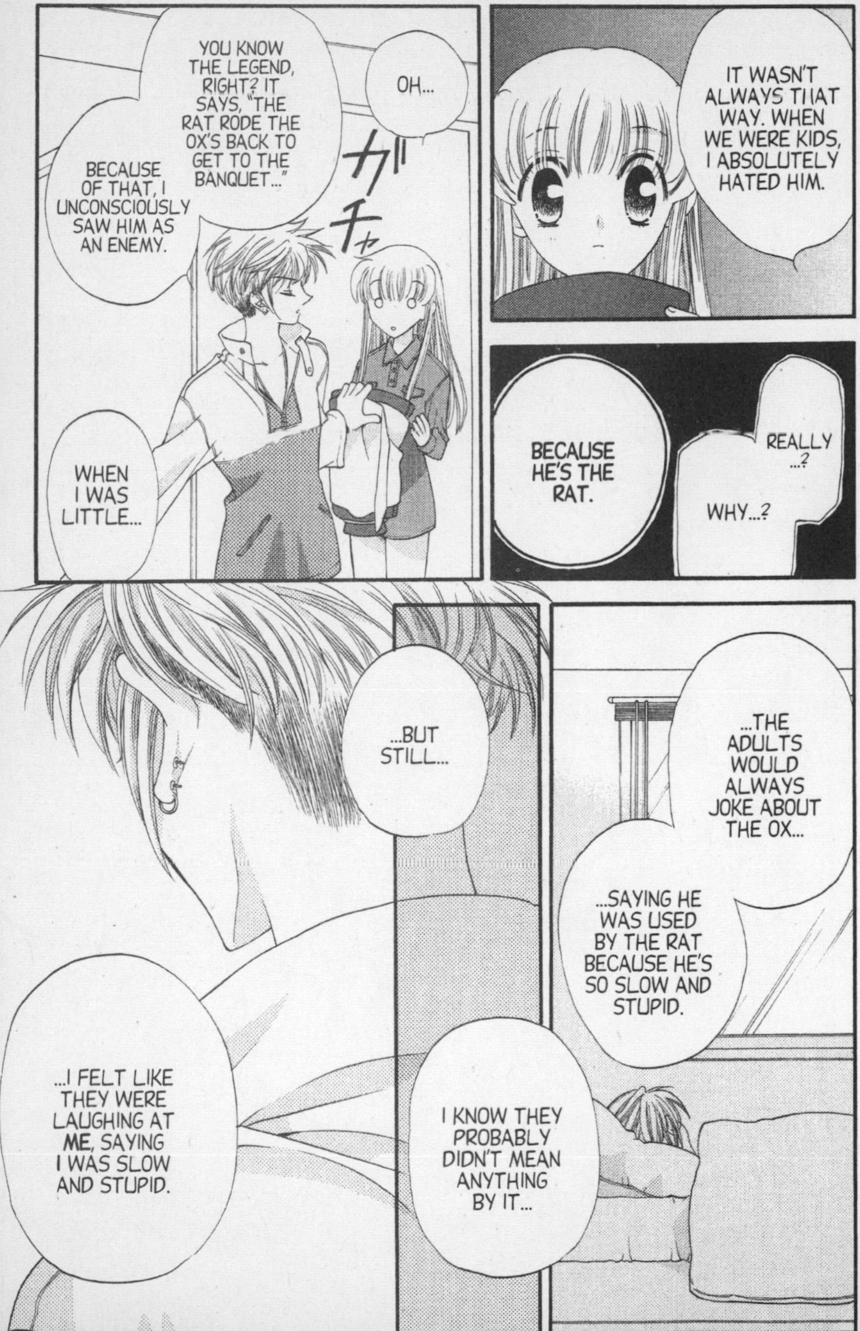
IT WASN'T ALWAYS THAT WAY. WHEN WE WERE KIDS, I ABSOLUTELY HATED HIM.
REALLY ...?
WHY...?
BECAUSE HE'S THE RAT.
OH...
ガチャ
YOU KNOW THE LEGEND, RIGHT? IT SAYS, "THE RAT RODE THE OX'S BACK TO GET TO THE BANQUET..."
BECAUSE OF THAT, I UNCONSCIOUSLY SAW HIM AS AN ENEMY.
WHEN I WAS LITTLE...
...THE ADULTS WOULD ALWAYS JOKE ABOUT THE OX...
...SAYING HE WAS USED BY THE RAT BECAUSE HE'S SO SLOW AND STUPID.
I KNOW THEY PROBABLY DIDN'T MEAN ANYTHING BY IT...
...BUT STILL...
...I FELT LIKE THEY WERE LAUGHING AT **ME**, SAYING I WAS SLOW AND STUPID.

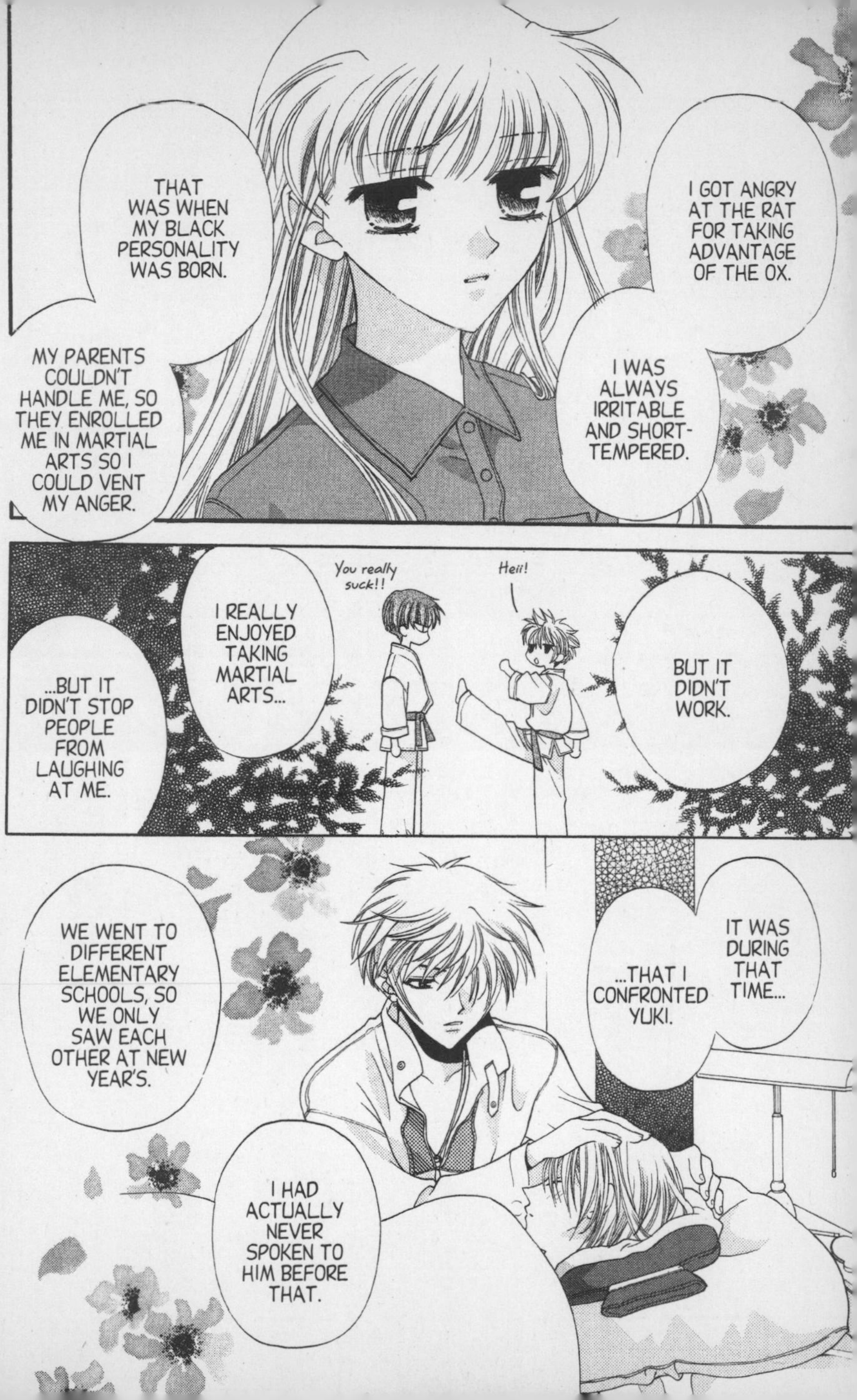
I GOT ANGRY AT THE RAT FOR TAKING ADVANTAGE OF THE OX.
I WAS ALWAYS IRRITABLE AND SHORT-TEMPERED.
THAT WAS WHEN MY BLACK PERSONALITY WAS BORN.
MY PARENTS COULDN'T HANDLE ME, SO THEY ENROLLED ME IN MARTIAL ARTS SO I COULD VENT MY ANGER.
BUT IT DIDN'T WORK.
Heii!
You really suck!!
I REALLY ENJOYED TAKING MARTIAL ARTS...
...BUT IT DIDN'T STOP PEOPLE FROM LAUGHING AT ME.
IT WAS DURING THAT TIME...
...THAT I CONFRONTED YUKI.
WE WENT TO DIFFERENT ELEMENTARY SCHOOLS, SO WE ONLY SAW EACH OTHER AT NEW YEAR'S.
I HAD ACTUALLY NEVER SPOKEN TO HIM BEFORE THAT.

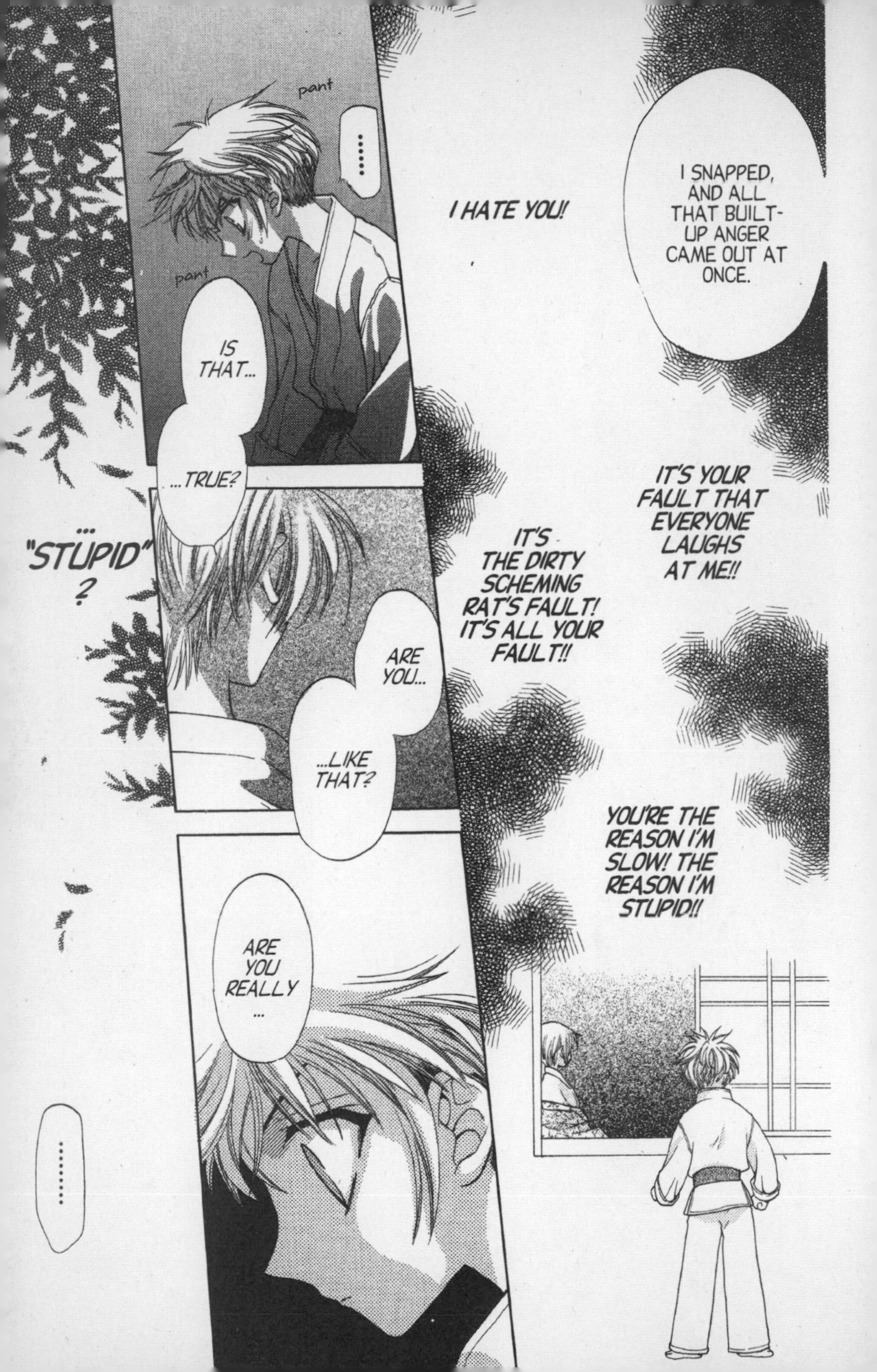
I SNAPPED, AND ALL THAT BUILT-UP ANGER CAME OUT AT ONCE.
I HATE YOU!
IT'S YOUR FAULT THAT EVERYONE LAUGHS AT ME!!
IT'S THE DIRTY SCHEMING RAT'S FAULT! IT'S ALL YOUR FAULT!!
YOU'RE THE REASON I'M SLOW! THE REASON I'M STUPID!!
pant
......
pant
IS THAT...
...TRUE?
... "STUPID" ?
ARE YOU...
...LIKE THAT?
ARE YOU REALLY ...
......

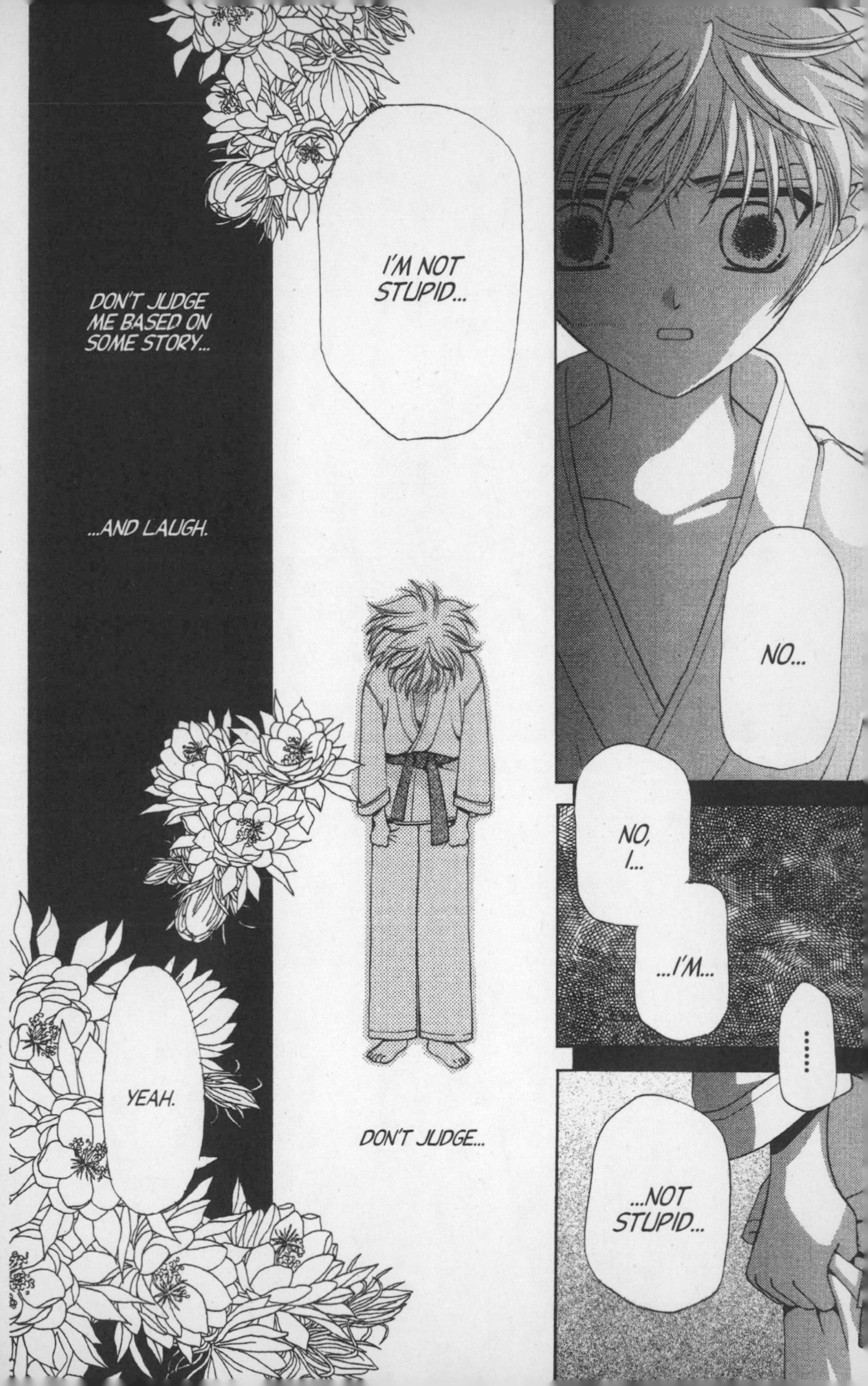
NO...
NO, I...
...I'M...
......
...NOT STUPID...
I'M NOT STUPID...
DON'T JUDGE ME BASED ON SOME STORY...
...AND LAUGH.
DON'T JUDGE...
YEAH.

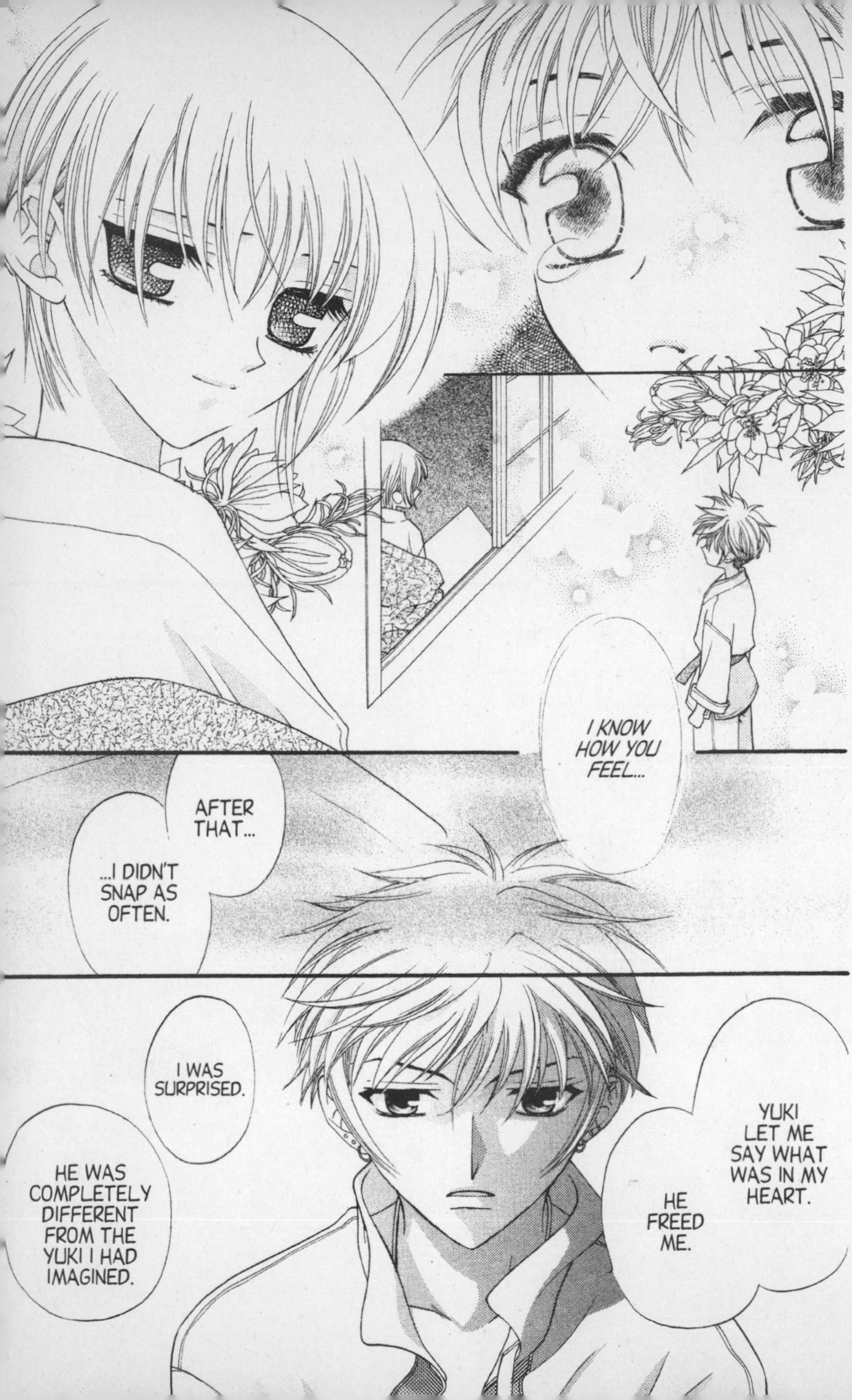
I KNOW HOW YOU FEEL...
AFTER THAT...
...I DIDN'T SNAP AS OFTEN.
YUKI LET ME SAY WHAT WAS IN MY HEART.
HE FREED ME.
I WAS SURPRISED.
HE WAS COMPLETELY DIFFERENT FROM THE YUKI I HAD IMAGINED.

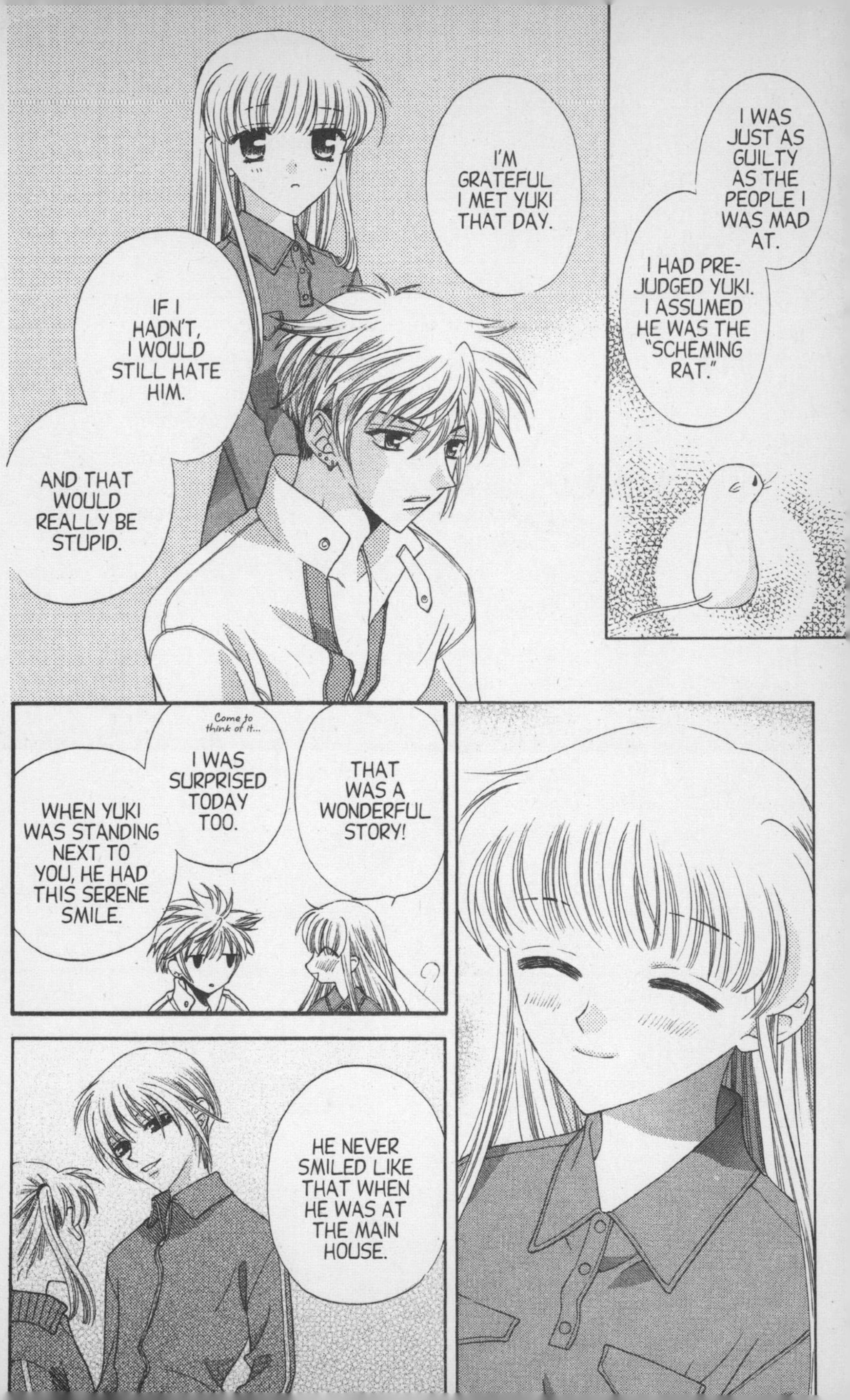
I WAS JUST AS GUILTY AS THE PEOPLE I WAS MAD AT.
I HAD PRE-JUDGED YUKI. I ASSUMED HE WAS THE "SCHEMING RAT."
I'M GRATEFUL I MET YUKI THAT DAY.
IF I HADN'T, I WOULD STILL HATE HIM.
AND THAT WOULD REALLY BE STUPID.
THAT WAS A WONDERFUL STORY!
Come to think of it...
I WAS SURPRISED TODAY TOO.
WHEN YUKI WAS STANDING NEXT TO YOU, HE HAD THIS SERENE SMILE.
HE NEVER SMILED LIKE THAT WHEN HE WAS AT THE MAIN HOUSE.

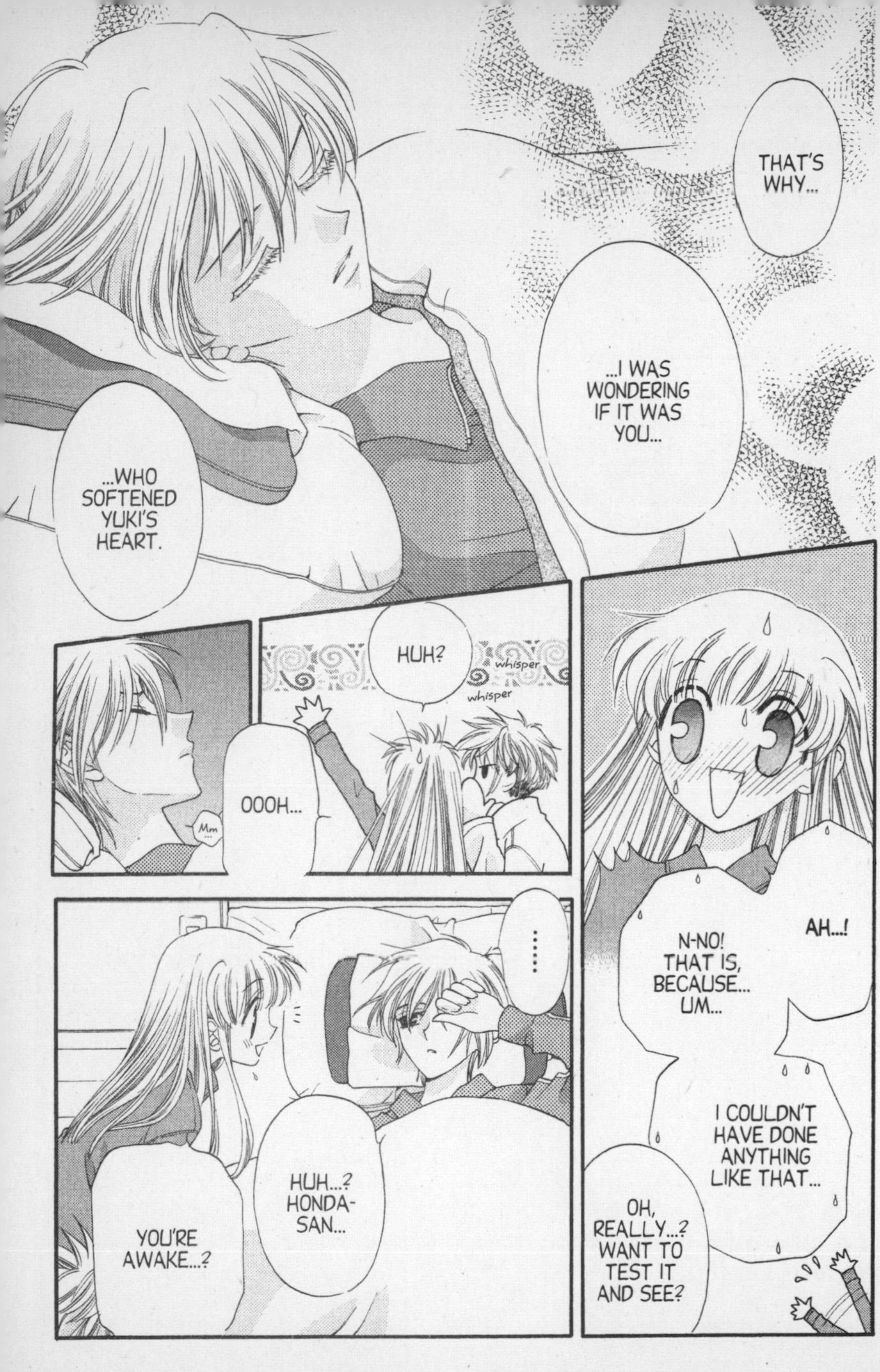
THAT'S WHY...
...I WAS WONDERING IF IT WAS YOU...
...WHO SOFTENED YUKI'S HEART.
AH...!
N-NO! THAT IS, BECAUSE... UM...
I COULDN'T HAVE DONE ANYTHING LIKE THAT...
OH, REALLY...? WANT TO TEST IT AND SEE?
HUH?
whisper
whisper
OOOH...
Mm...
......
HUH...? HONDA-SAN...
YOU'RE AWAKE...?

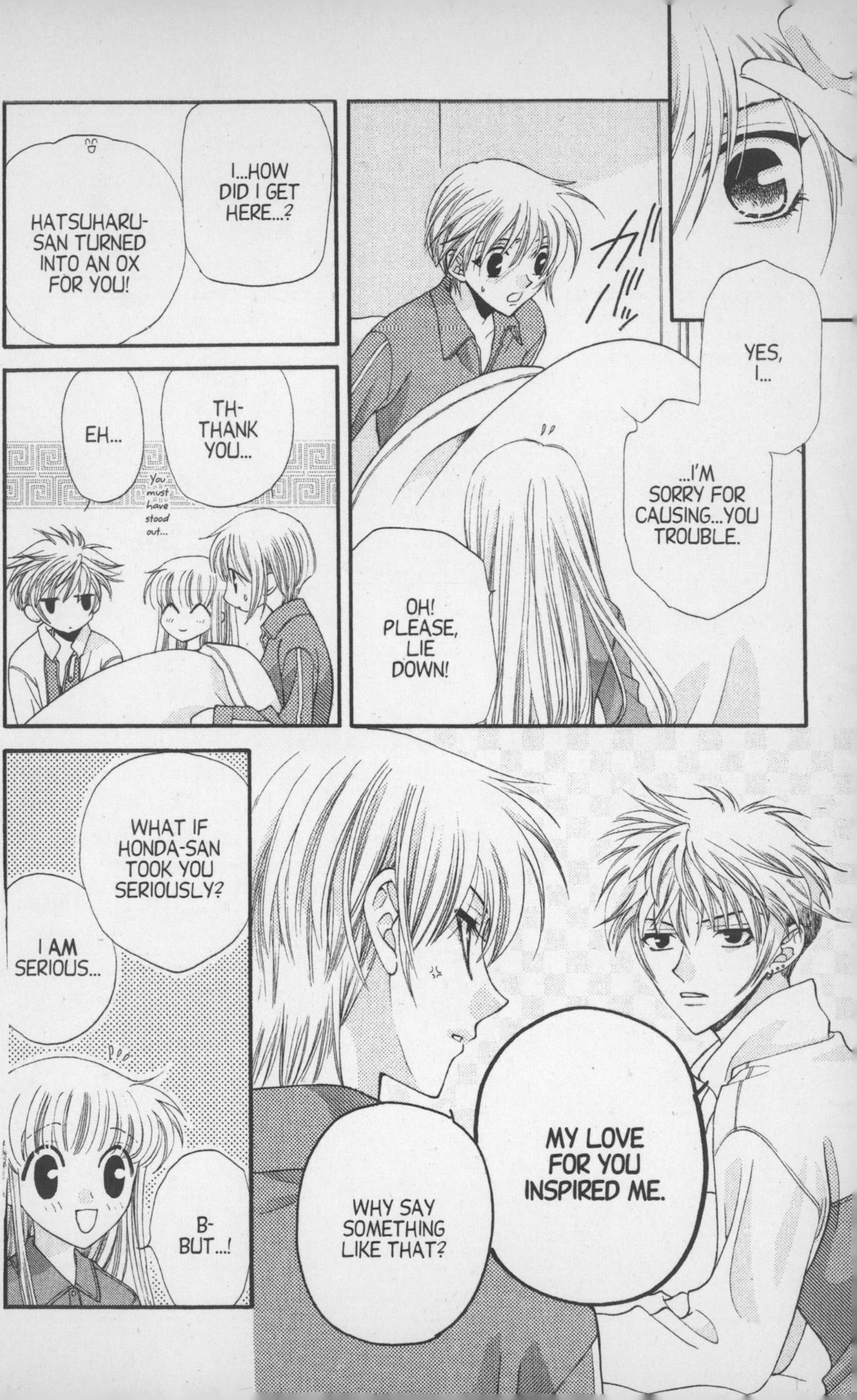
ガバッ
YES, I...
...I'M SORRY FOR CAUSING...YOU TROUBLE.
OH! PLEASE, LIE DOWN!
I...HOW DID I GET HERE...?
HATSUHARU-SAN TURNED INTO AN OX FOR YOU!
TH-THANK YOU...
EH...
You must have stood out...
MY LOVE FOR YOU INSPIRED ME.
WHY SAY SOMETHING LIKE THAT?
WHAT IF HONDA-SAN TOOK YOU SERIOUSLY?
I AM SERIOUS...
B-BUT...!

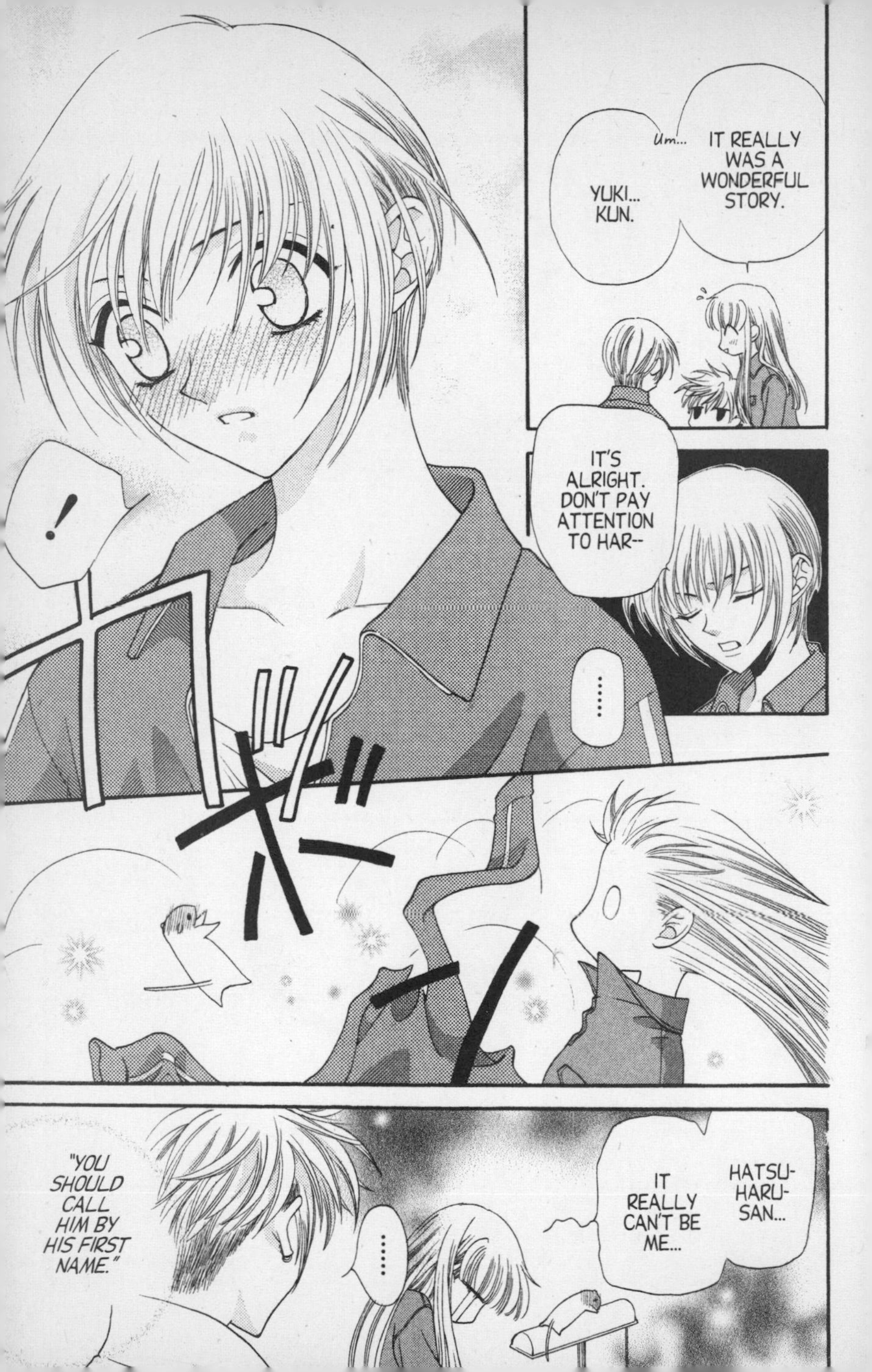
IT REALLY WAS A WONDERFUL STORY.
Um...
YUKI... KUN.
IT'S ALRIGHT. DON'T PAY ATTENTION TO HAR--
!
......
HATSU-HARU-SAN...
IT REALLY CAN'T BE ME...
......
"YOU SHOULD CALL HIM BY HIS FIRST NAME."

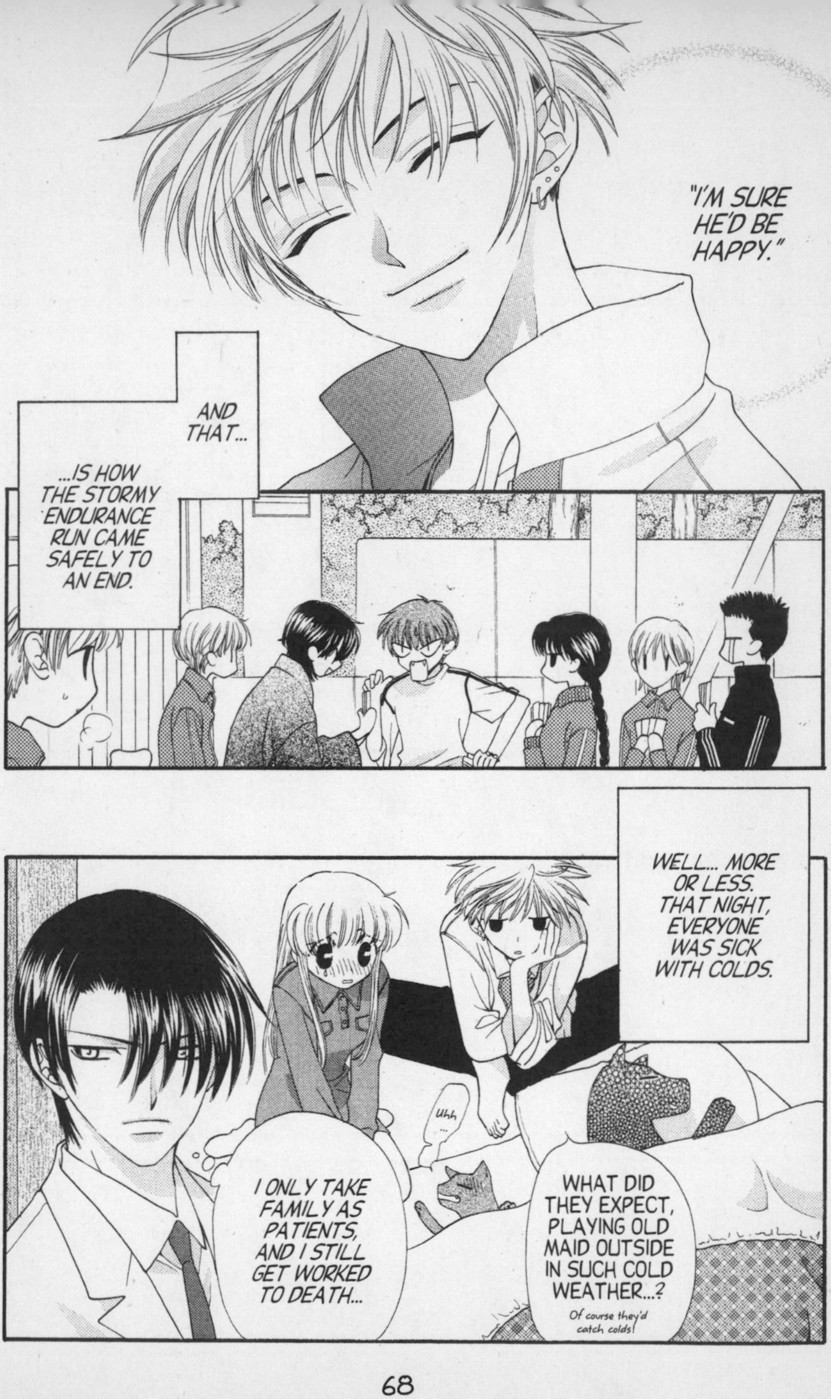
"I'M SURE HE'D BE HAPPY."
AND THAT...
...IS HOW THE STORMY ENDURANCE RUN CAME SAFELY TO AN END.
WELL... MORE OR LESS. THAT NIGHT, EVERYONE WAS SICK WITH COLDS.
WHAT DID THEY EXPECT, PLAYING OLD MAID OUTSIDE IN SUCH COLD WEATHER...?
Of course they'd catch colds!
Uhh...
I ONLY TAKE FAMILY AS PATIENTS, AND I STILL GET WORKED TO DEATH...

Chapter 15

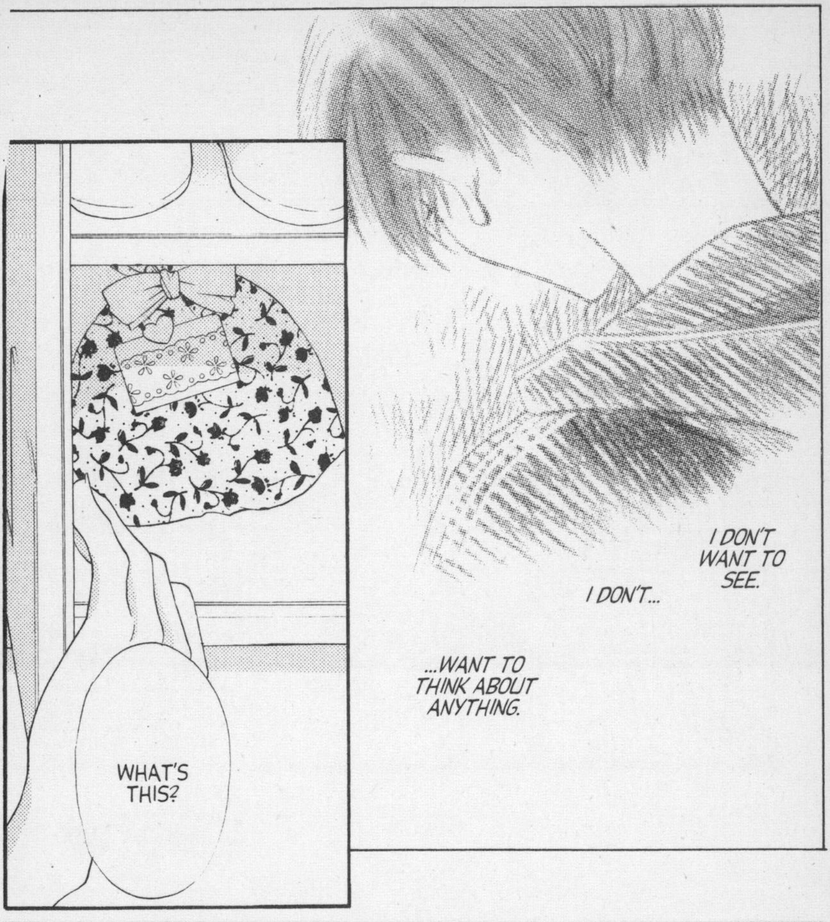
I DON'T WANT TO SEE.
I DON'T...
...WANT TO THINK ABOUT ANYTHING.
WHAT'S THIS?

ULTRA SPECIAL BLAH BLAH BLAH 3

This is a little off topic, but it's about Hatsuharu. His personality is split into Black and White. The White side represents his true self, but he retains all of his memories when he's Black too. (Of course, he probably doesn't think much besides, "Aahh... I've gone Black again!")

Fruits Basket 3 Part 3

The mood of manga--I know that's a very sensuous way of phrasing it--but every author has his or her own style that evokes a certain mood. Definitely. Well, what is mine like...? (Ha ha!) Anyway, a while back, Hana-Yume magazine allowed me to interview Hidaka-sensei, and I remember that she said, "I'm told I look like Sachiko-chan." * I thought, "Oohh, come to think of it, she kinda does!" (Of course I didn't say anything out loud--I just thought it.) Oh, but it was such an honor to meet her! Please accept my insane faxes (Hee hee!), Hidaka-san! And please treat Natsuki Takaya kindly...

* Sachiko is the protagonist of Hidaka Banri's SEKAI DE ICHIBAN DAIKIRAI.

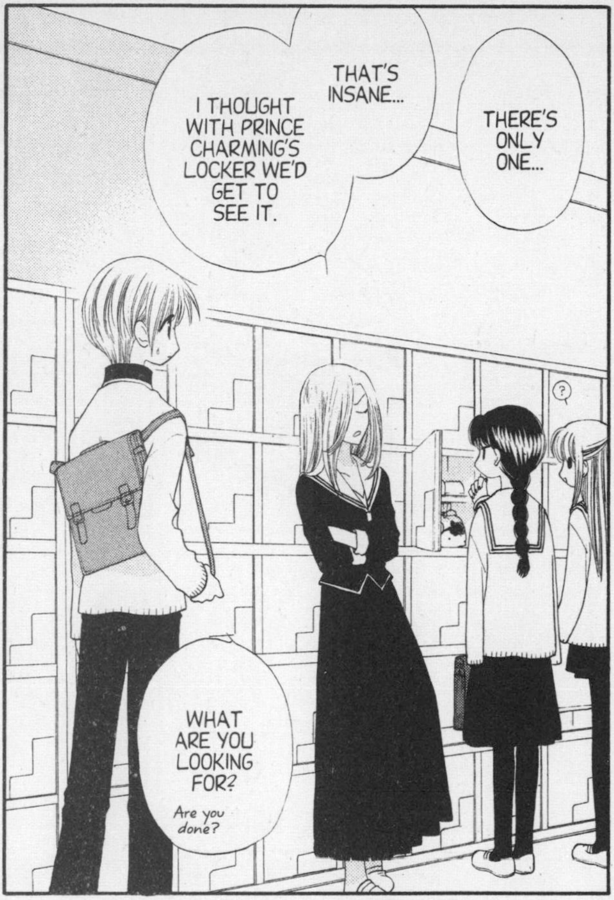
THERE'S ONLY ONE...
THAT'S INSANE...
I THOUGHT WITH PRINCE CHARMING'S LOCKER WE'D GET TO SEE IT.
?
WHAT ARE YOU LOOKING FOR?
Are you done?

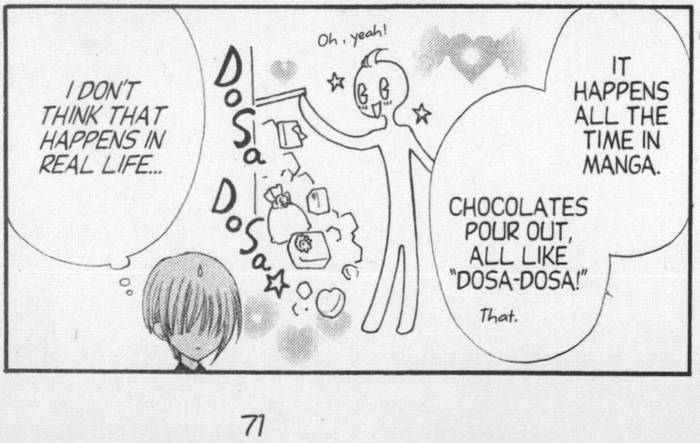
IT HAPPENS ALL THE TIME IN MANGA.
CHOCOLATES POUR OUT, ALL LIKE "DOSA-DOSA!"
That.
Oh, yeah!
DoSa DoSa
I DON'T THINK THAT HAPPENS IN REAL LIFE...

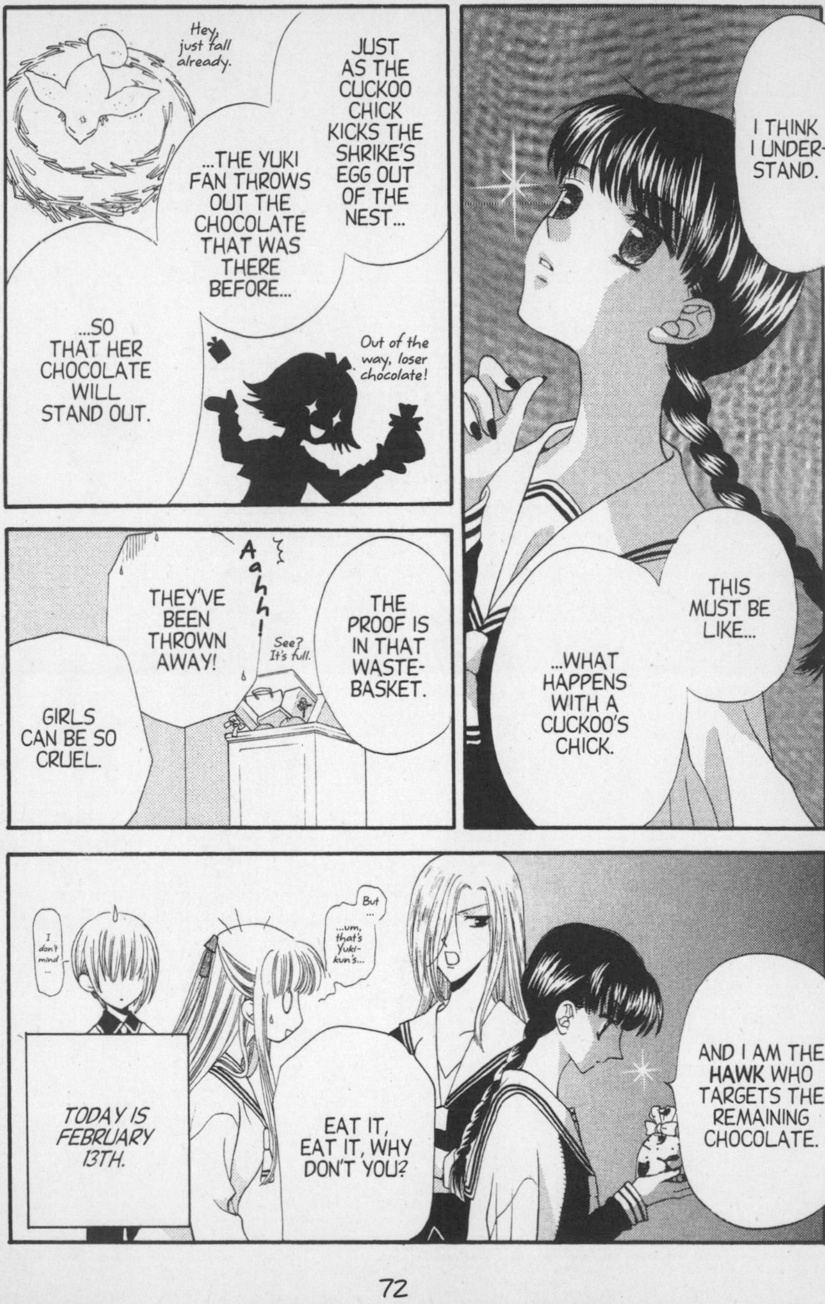
I THINK I UNDER-STAND.
THIS MUST BE LIKE...
...WHAT HAPPENS WITH A CUCKOO'S CHICK.
JUST AS THE CUCKOO CHICK KICKS THE SHRIKE'S EGG OUT OF THE NEST...
Hey, just fall already.
...THE YUKI FAN THROWS OUT THE CHOCOLATE THAT WAS THERE BEFORE...
Out of the way, loser chocolate!
...SO THAT HER CHOCOLATE WILL STAND OUT.
THE PROOF IS IN THAT WASTE-BASKET.
See? It's full.
Aahh!
THEY'VE BEEN THROWN AWAY!
GIRLS CAN BE SO CRUEL.
AND I AM THE HAWK WHO TARGETS THE REMAINING CHOCOLATE.
But ...
...um, that's Yuki-kun's...
EAT IT, EAT IT, WHY DON'T YOU?
I don't mind ...
TODAY IS FEBRUARY 13TH.

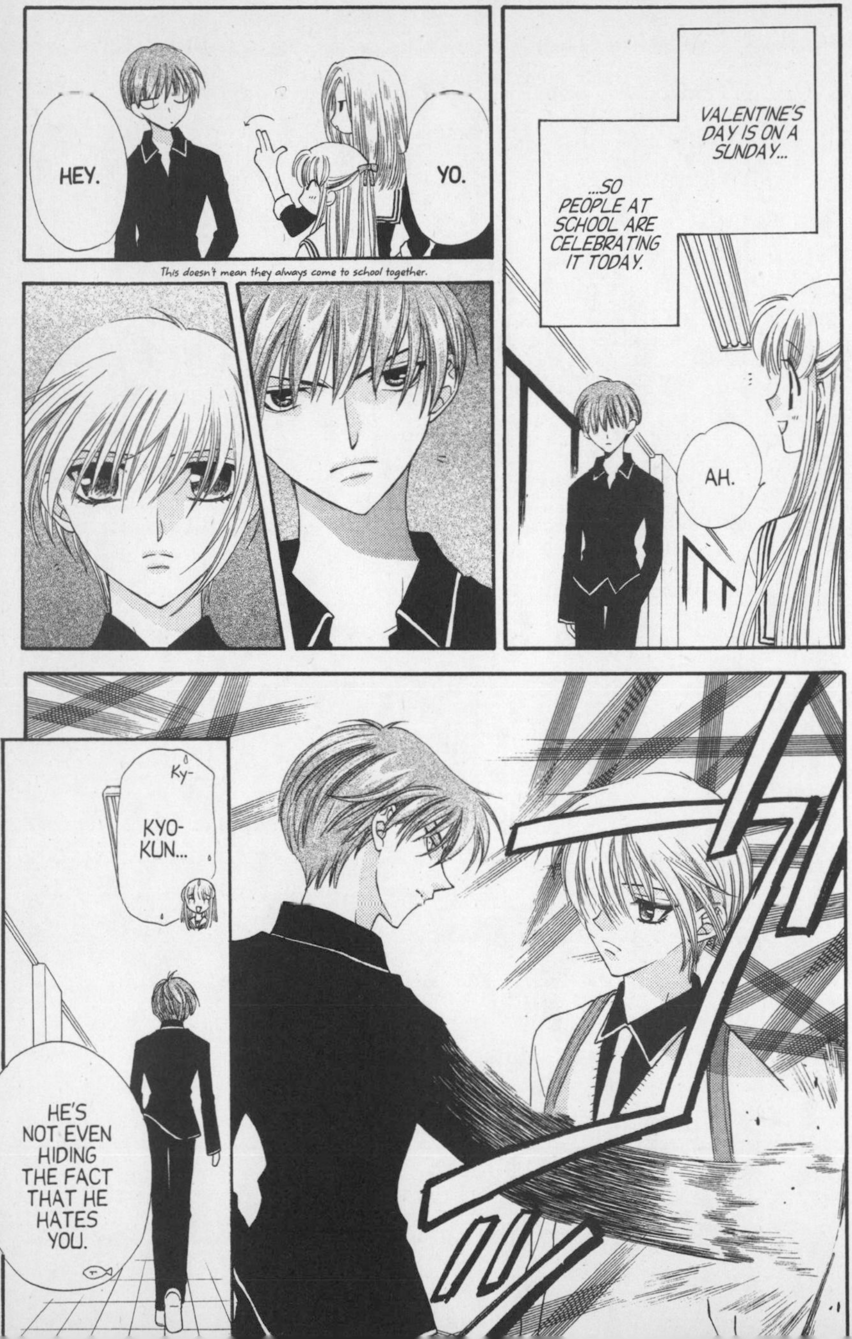
VALENTINE'S DAY IS ON A SUNDAY...
...SO PEOPLE AT SCHOOL ARE CELEBRATING IT TODAY.
AH.
YO.
HEY.
This doesn't mean they always come to school together.
Ky-
KYO-KUN...
HE'S NOT EVEN HIDING THE FACT THAT HE HATES YOU.

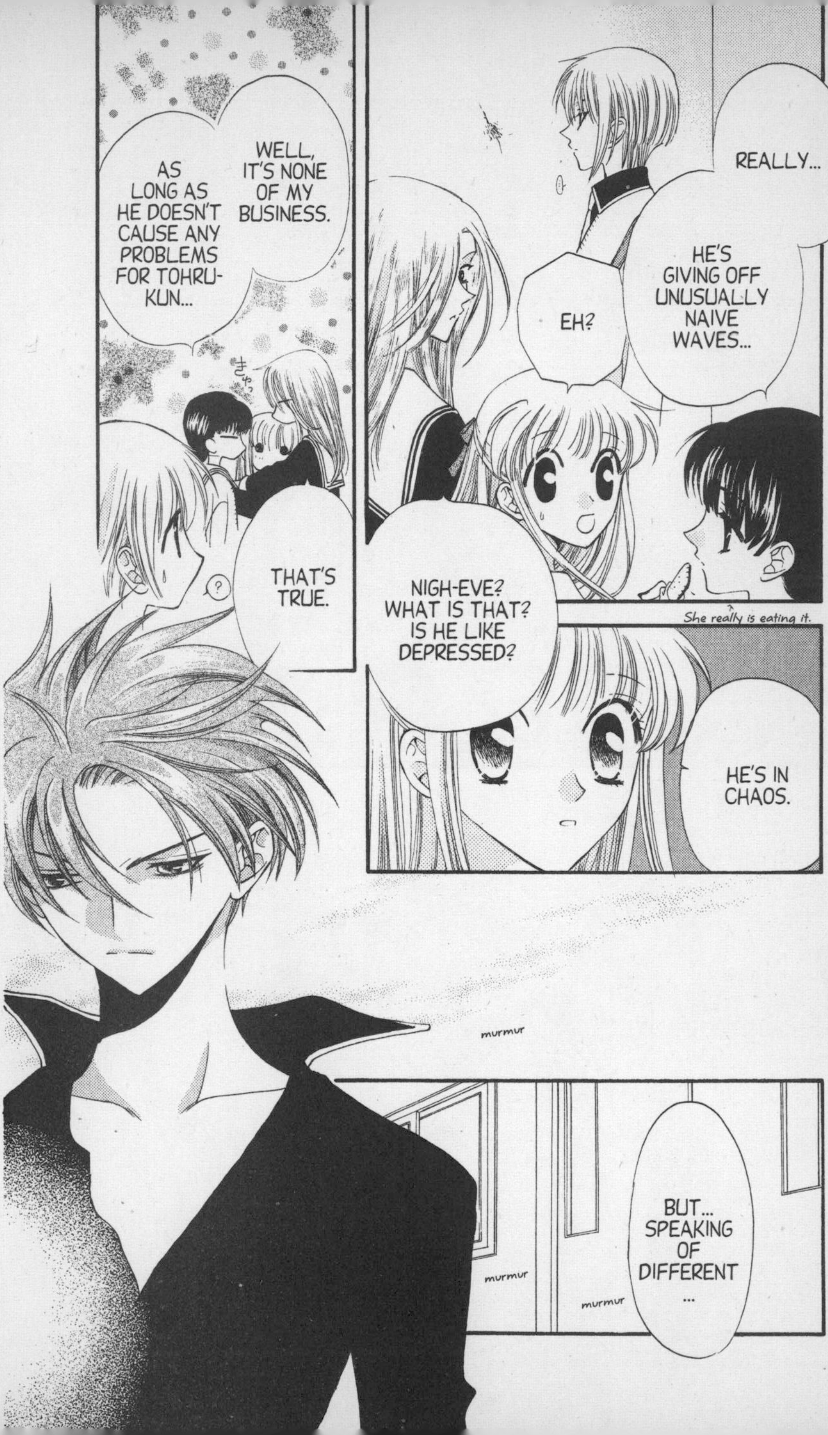
REALLY...
HE'S GIVING OFF UNUSUALLY NAIVE WAVES...
EH?
She really is eating it.
NIGH-EVE? WHAT IS THAT? IS HE LIKE DEPRESSED?
HE'S IN CHAOS.
WELL, IT'S NONE OF MY BUSINESS.
AS LONG AS HE DOESN'T CAUSE ANY PROBLEMS FOR TOHRU-KUN...
THAT'S TRUE.
murmur
BUT... SPEAKING OF DIFFERENT...
murmur
murmur

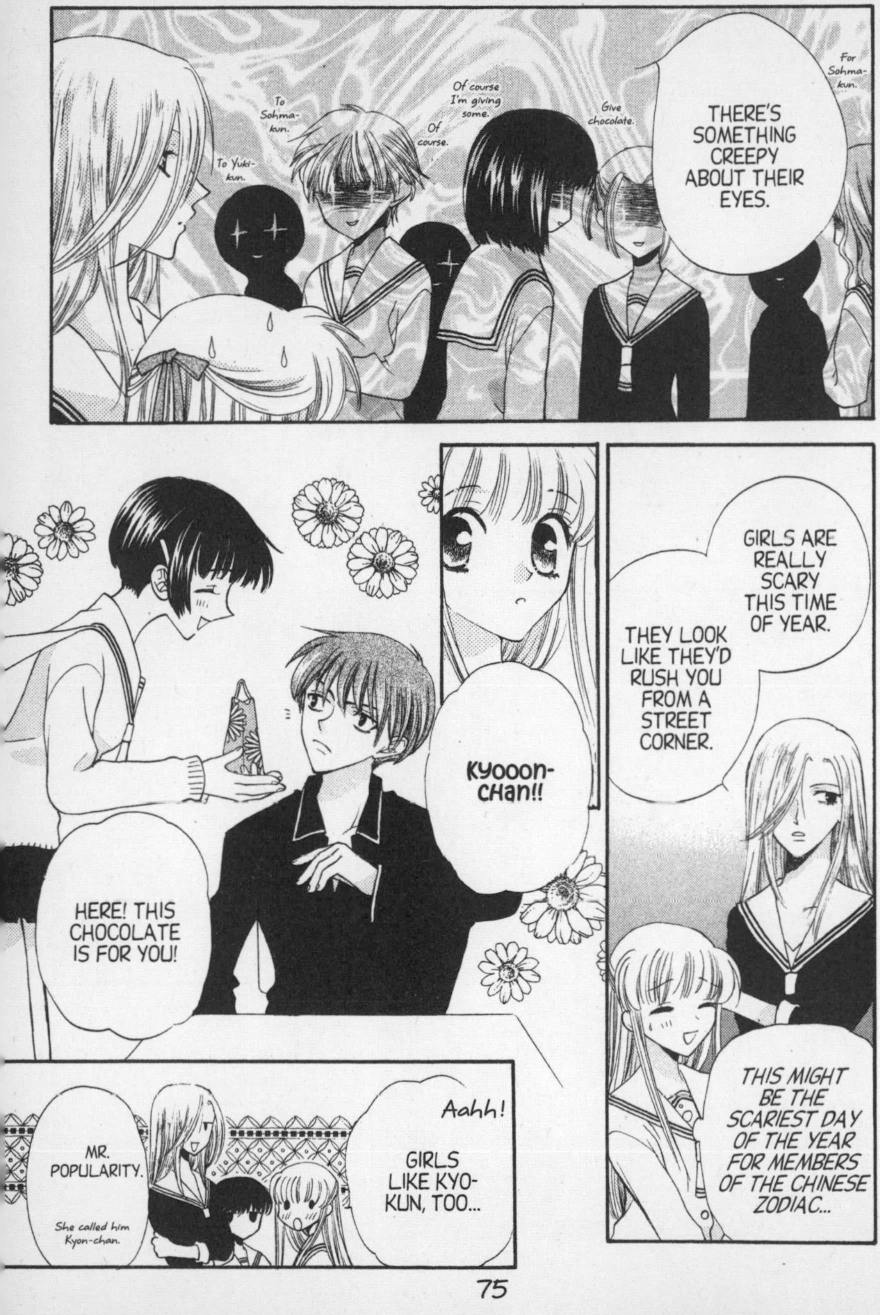
For Sohma-kun.
THERE'S SOMETHING CREEPY ABOUT THEIR EYES.
Give chocolate.
Of course I'm giving some.
Of course.
To Sohma-kun.
To Yuki-kun.
GIRLS ARE REALLY SCARY THIS TIME OF YEAR.
THEY LOOK LIKE THEY'D RUSH YOU FROM A STREET CORNER.
THIS MIGHT BE THE SCARIEST DAY OF THE YEAR FOR MEMBERS OF THE CHINESE ZODIAC...
KYOOON-CHAN!!
HERE! THIS CHOCOLATE IS FOR YOU!
Aahh!
GIRLS LIKE KYO-KUN, TOO...
MR. POPULARITY.
She called him Kyon-chan.

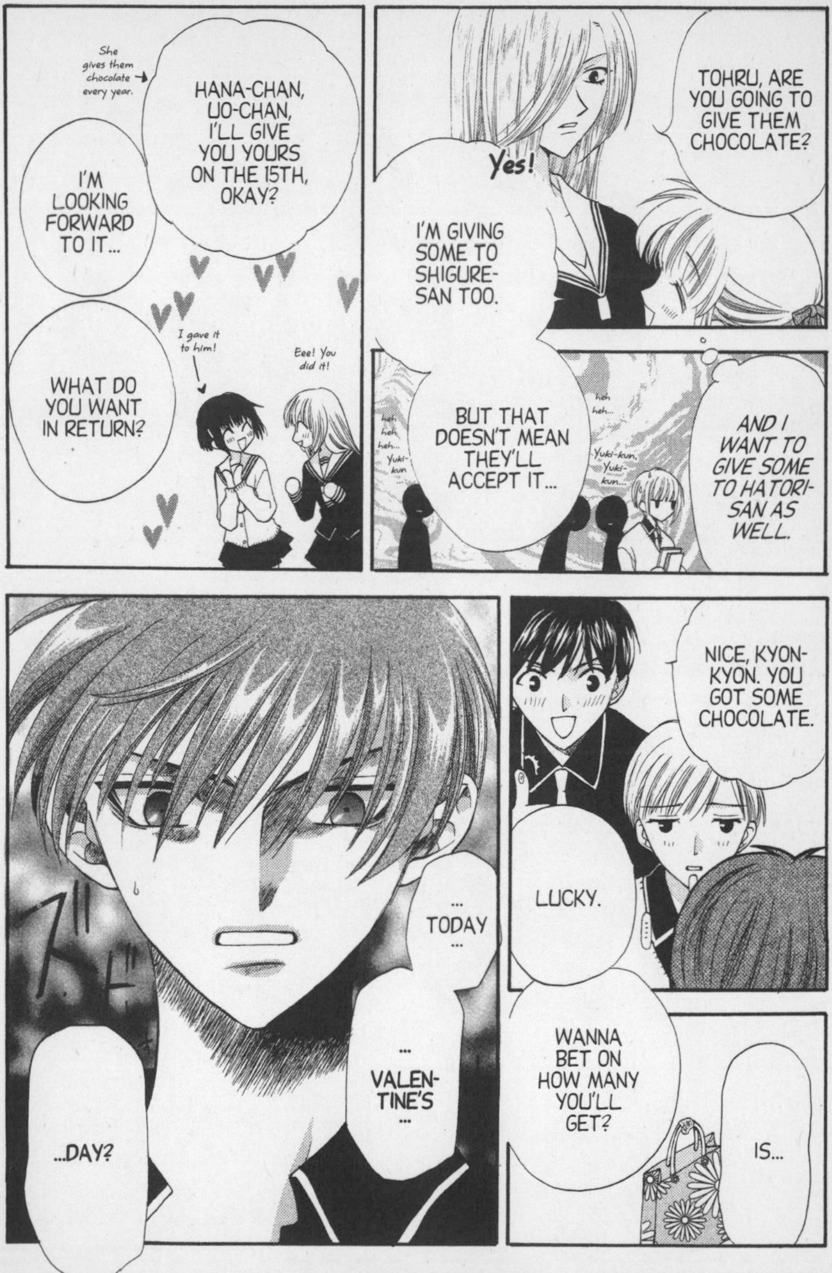
TOHRU, ARE YOU GOING TO GIVE THEM CHOCOLATE?
Yes!
I'M GIVING SOME TO SHIGURE-SAN TOO.
AND I WANT TO GIVE SOME TO HATORI-SAN AS WELL.
heh heh... Yuki-kun, Yuki-kun...
BUT THAT DOESN'T MEAN THEY'LL ACCEPT IT...
heh heh heh... Yuki-kun...
HANA-CHAN, UO-CHAN, I'LL GIVE YOU YOURS ON THE 15TH, OKAY?
She gives them chocolate every year.
I'M LOOKING FORWARD TO IT...
Eee! You did it!
I gave it to him!
WHAT DO YOU WANT IN RETURN?
NICE, KYON-KYON. YOU GOT SOME CHOCOLATE.
LUCKY.
WANNA BET ON HOW MANY YOU'LL GET?
IS...
...TODAY...
...VALENTINE'S...
...DAY?

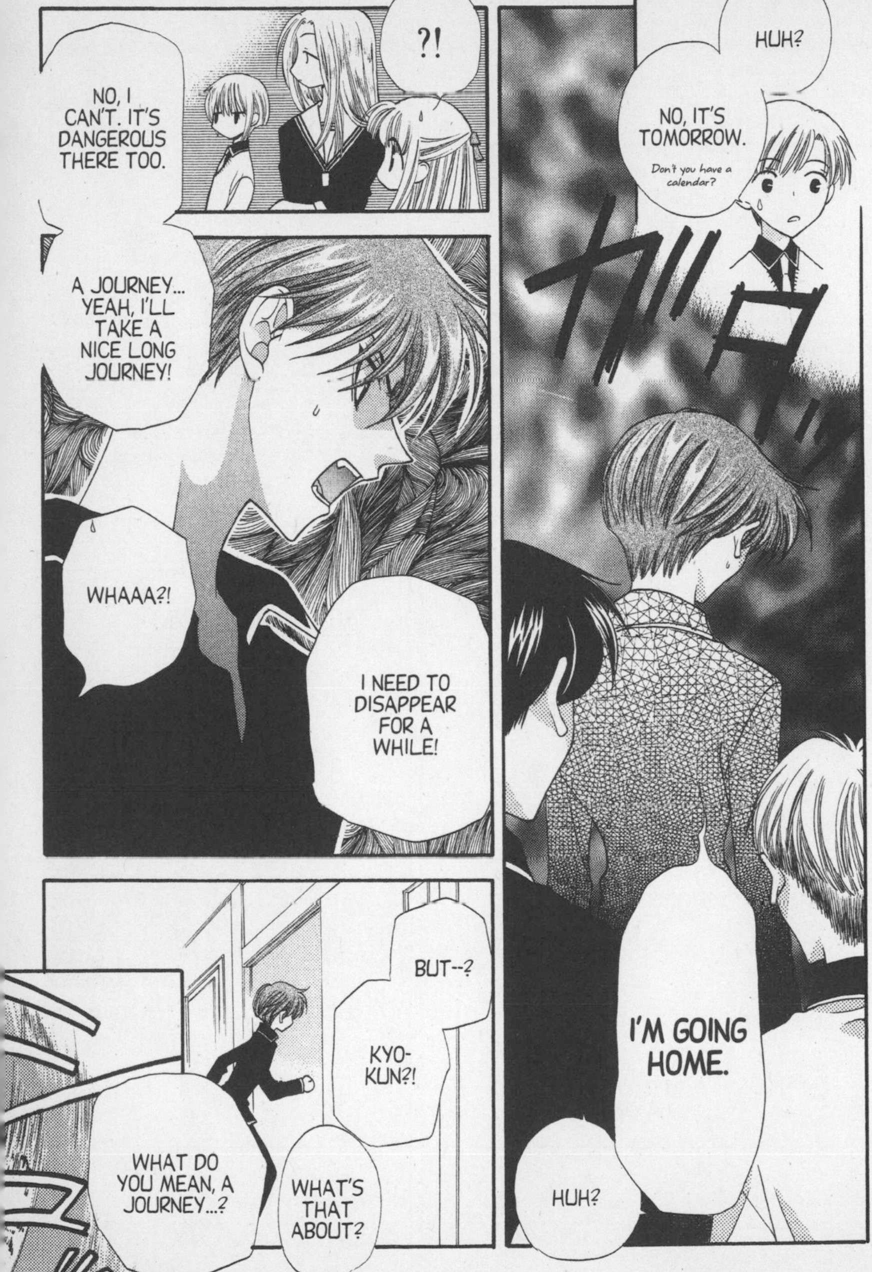
HUH?
NO, IT'S TOMORROW.
Don't you have a calendar?
I'M GOING HOME.
HUH?
?!
NO, I CAN'T. IT'S DANGEROUS THERE TOO.
A JOURNEY... YEAH, I'LL TAKE A NICE LONG JOURNEY!
WHAAA?!
I NEED TO DISAPPEAR FOR A WHILE!
BUT--?
KYO-KUN?!
WHAT DO YOU MEAN, A JOURNEY...?
WHAT'S THAT ABOUT?

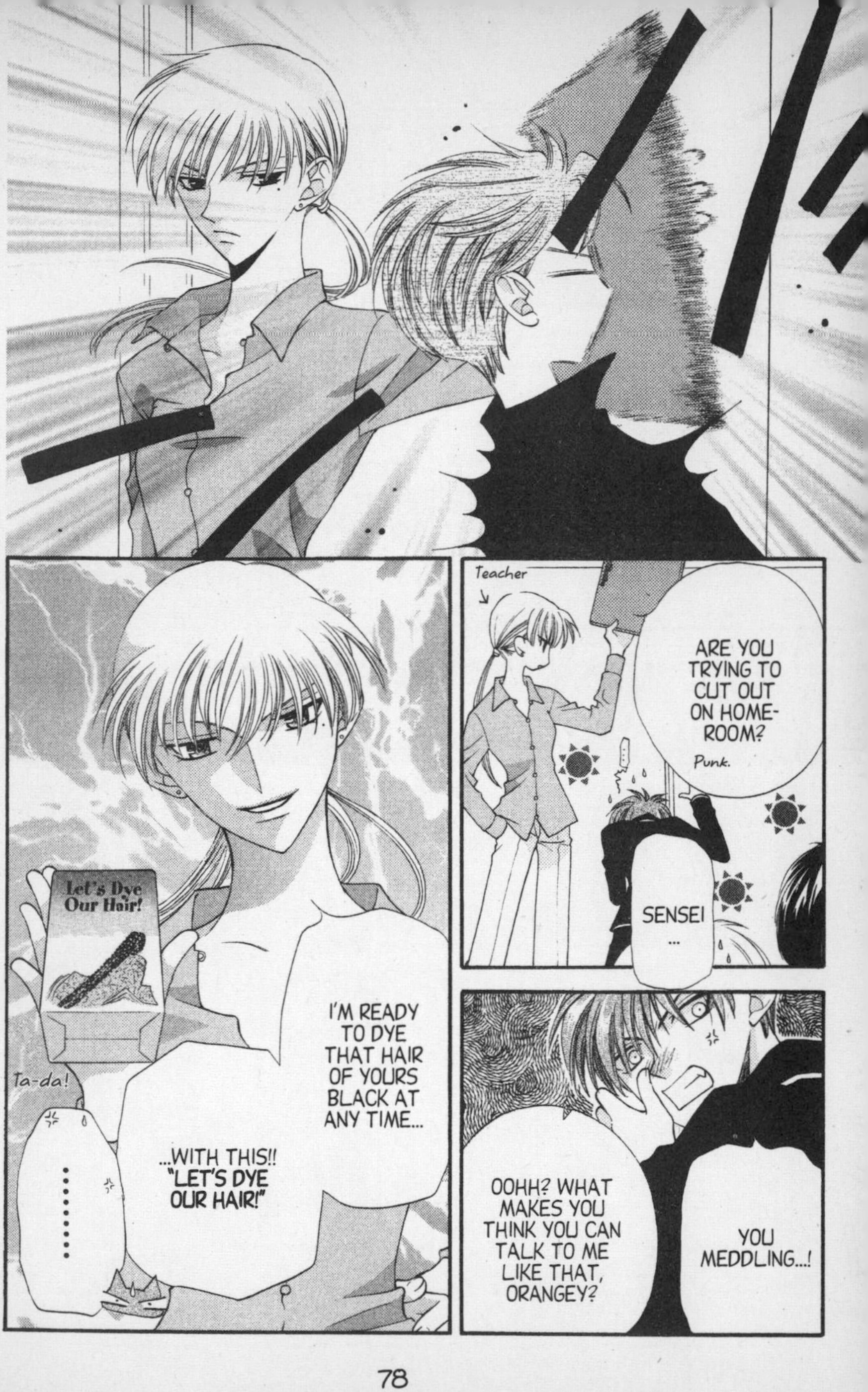
Teacher
ARE YOU TRYING TO CUT OUT ON HOME-ROOM?
Punk.
SENSEI ...
YOU MEDDLING...!
OOHH? WHAT MAKES YOU THINK YOU CAN TALK TO ME LIKE THAT, ORANGEY?
Let's Dye Our Hair!
I'M READY TO DYE THAT HAIR OF YOURS BLACK AT ANY TIME...
...WITH THIS!! "LET'S DYE OUR HAIR!"
Ta-da!
....

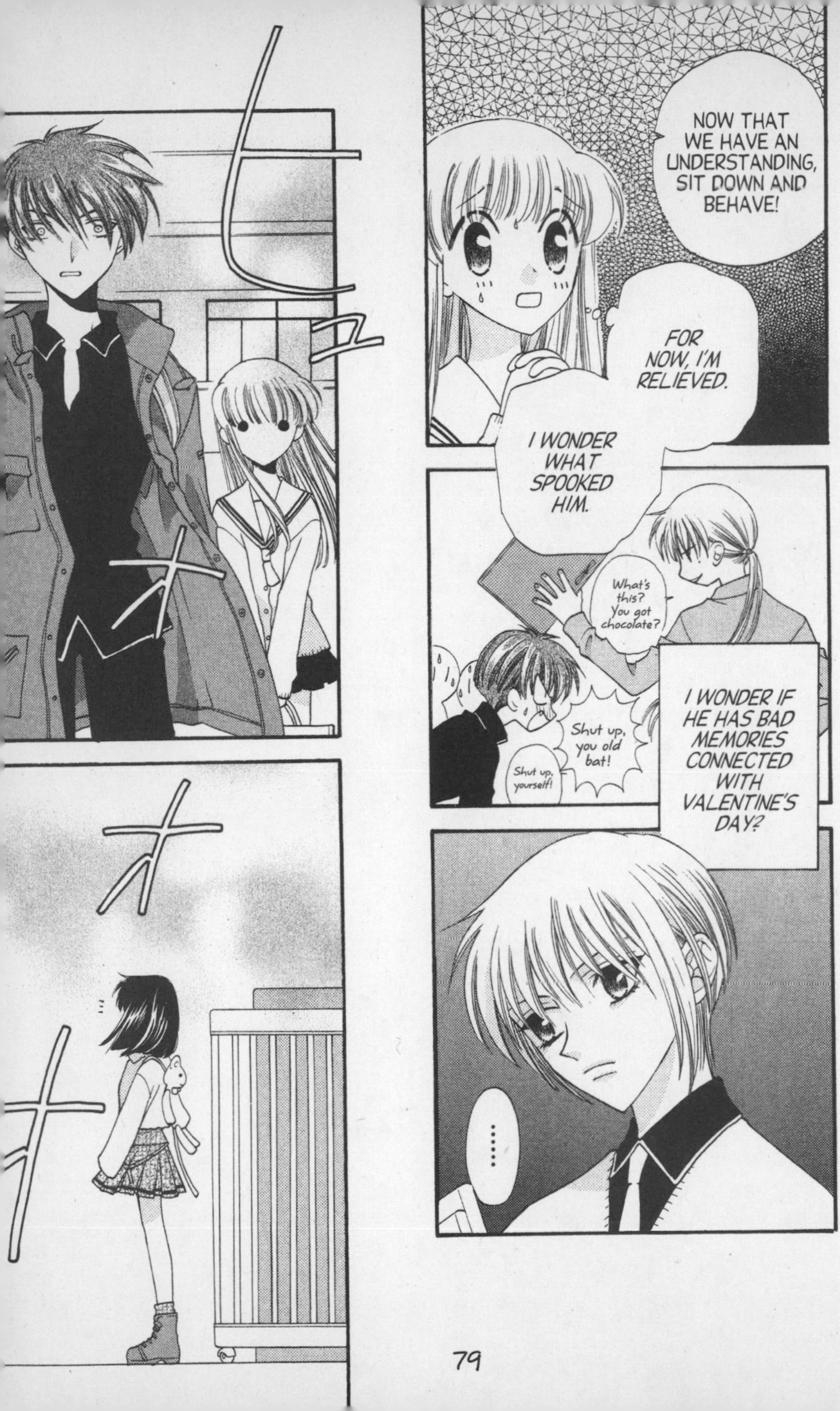
NOW THAT WE HAVE AN UNDERSTANDING, SIT DOWN AND BEHAVE!
FOR NOW, I'M RELIEVED.
I WONDER WHAT SPOOKED HIM.
What's this? You got chocolate?
Shut up, you old bat!
Shut up, yourself!
I WONDER IF HE HAS BAD MEMORIES CONNECTED WITH VALENTINE'S DAY?
......

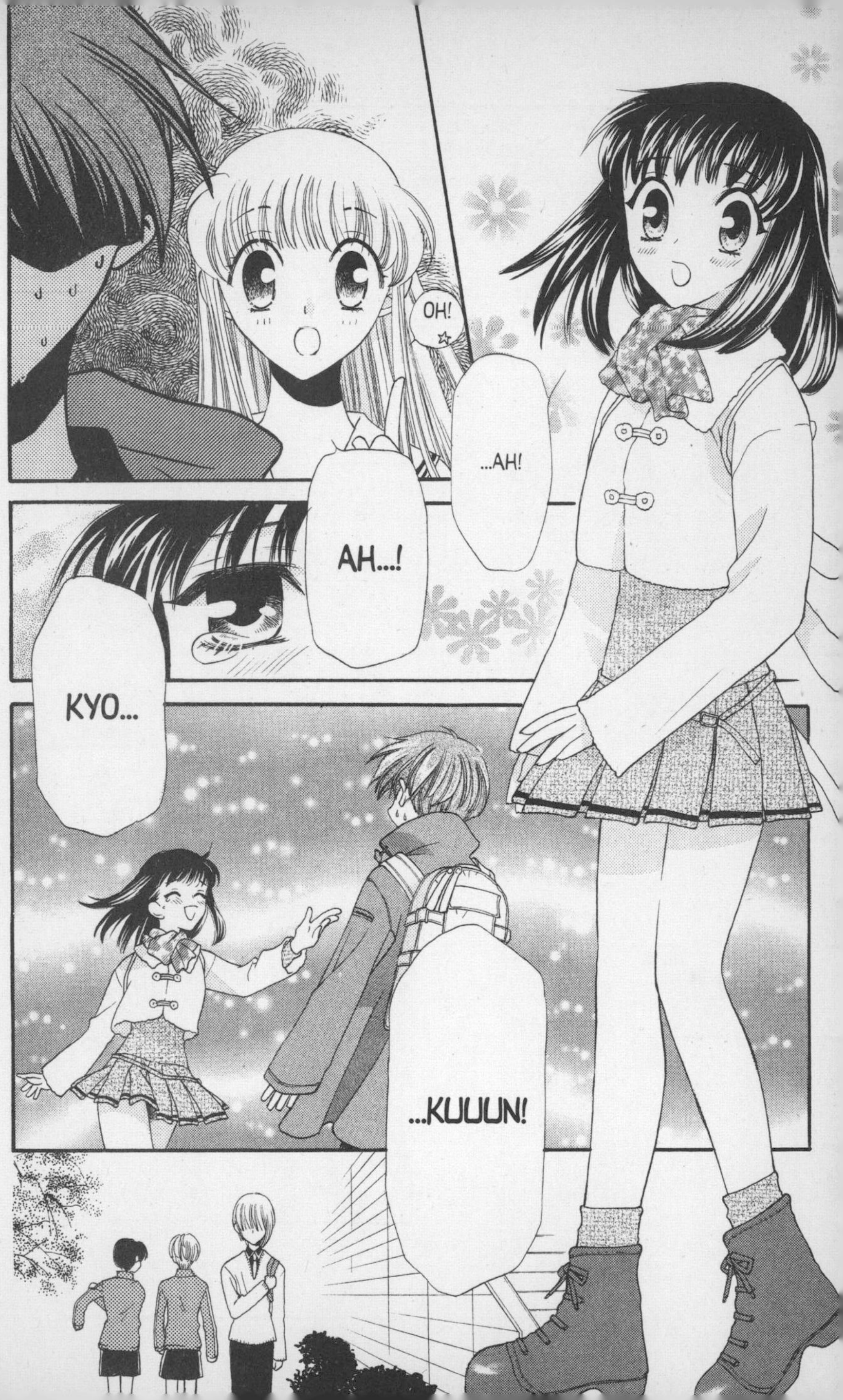
...AH!
OH!
AH...!
KYO...
...KUUUN!

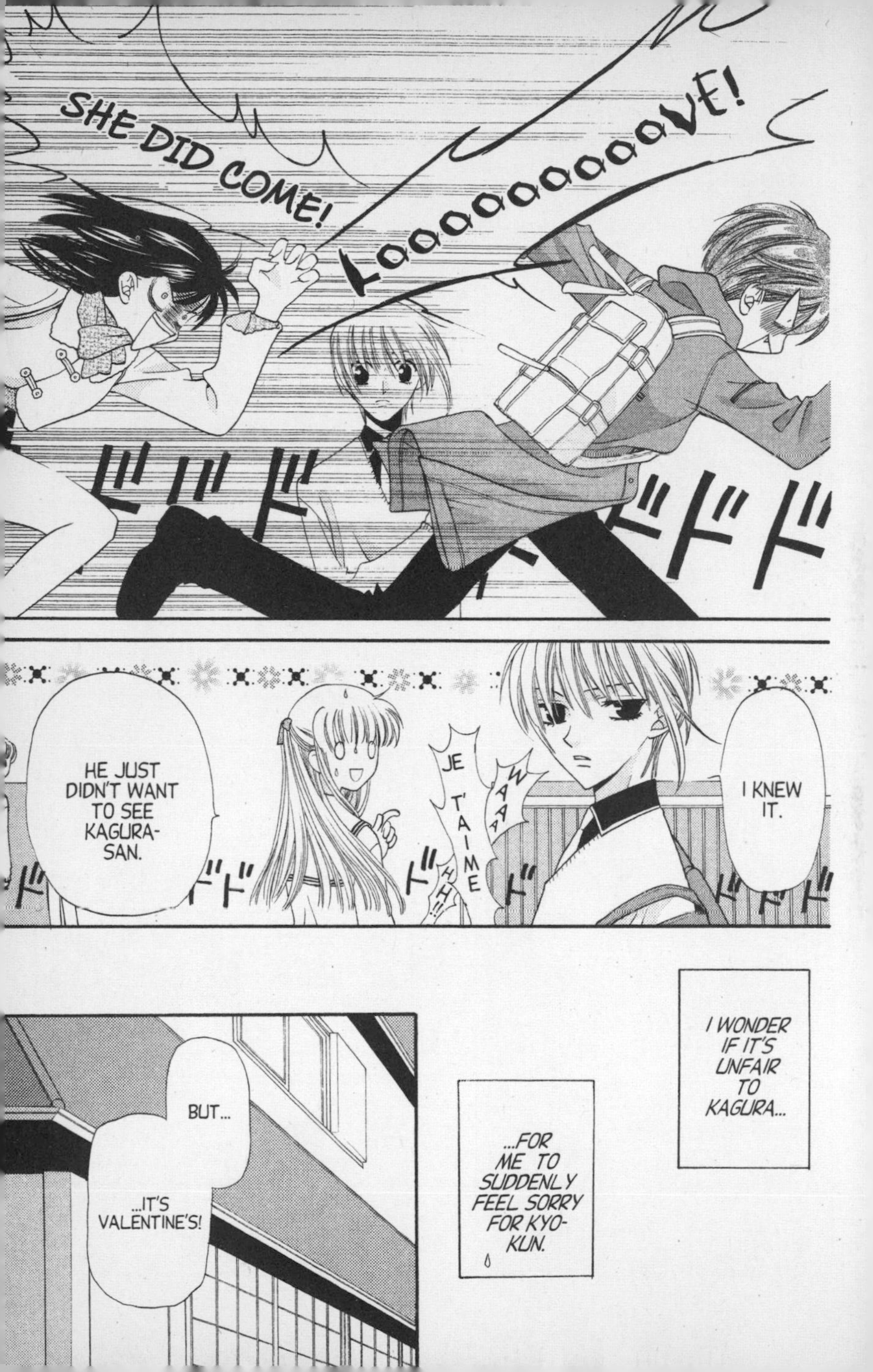
LOOOOOOOOOVE!
SHE DID COME!
ドドド
ドドド
I KNEW IT.
JE T'AIME
WAAAHH!!
HE JUST DIDN'T WANT TO SEE KAGURA-SAN.
ドドド
I WONDER IF IT'S UNFAIR TO KAGURA...
...FOR ME TO SUDDENLY FEEL SORRY FOR KYO-KUN.
BUT...
...IT'S VALENTINE'S!

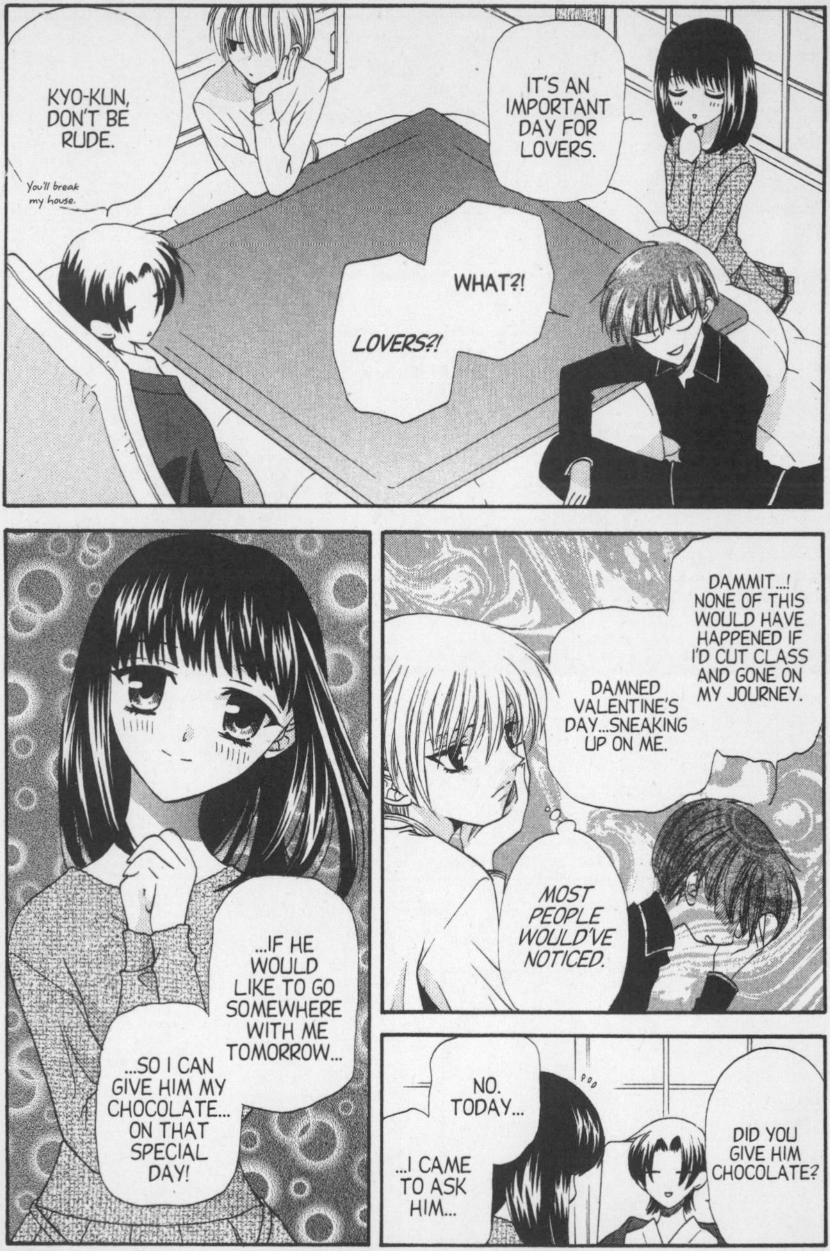
IT'S AN IMPORTANT DAY FOR LOVERS.
WHAT?!
LOVERS?!
KYO-KUN, DON'T BE RUDE.
You'll break my house.
DAMMIT...! NONE OF THIS WOULD HAVE HAPPENED IF I'D CUT CLASS AND GONE ON MY JOURNEY.
DAMNED VALENTINE'S DAY...SNEAKING UP ON ME.
MOST PEOPLE WOULD'VE NOTICED.
DID YOU GIVE HIM CHOCOLATE?
NO. TODAY...
...I CAME TO ASK HIM...
...IF HE WOULD LIKE TO GO SOMEWHERE WITH ME TOMORROW...
...SO I CAN GIVE HIM MY CHOCOLATE... ON THAT SPECIAL DAY!

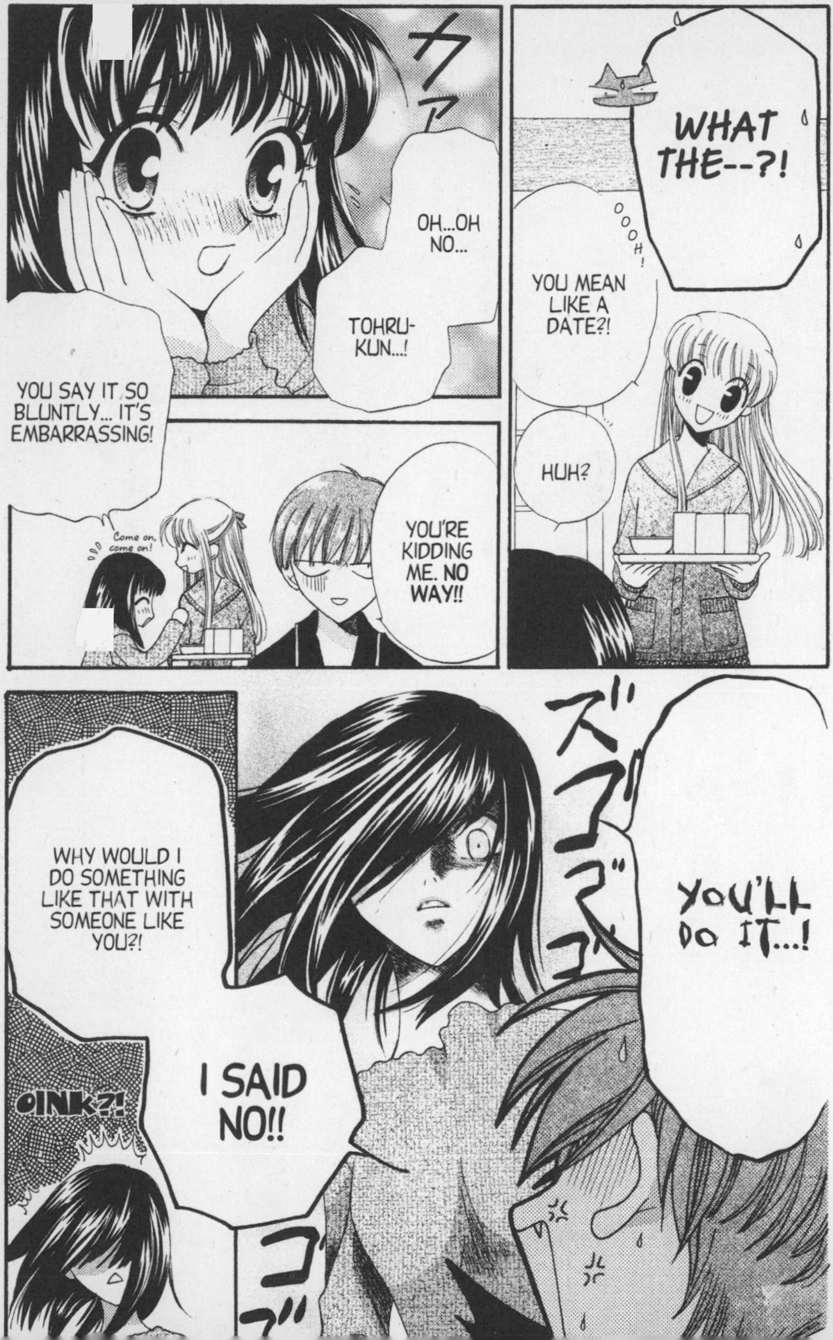
WHAT THE--?!
OOOH!
YOU MEAN LIKE A DATE?!
HUH?
カァ
OH...OH NO...
TOHRU-KUN...!
YOU SAY IT SO BLUNTLY... IT'S EMBARRASSING!
YOU'RE KIDDING ME. NO WAY!!
Come on, come on!
YOU'LL DO IT...!
WHY WOULD I DO SOMETHING LIKE THAT WITH SOMEONE LIKE YOU?!
I SAID NO!!
OINK?!

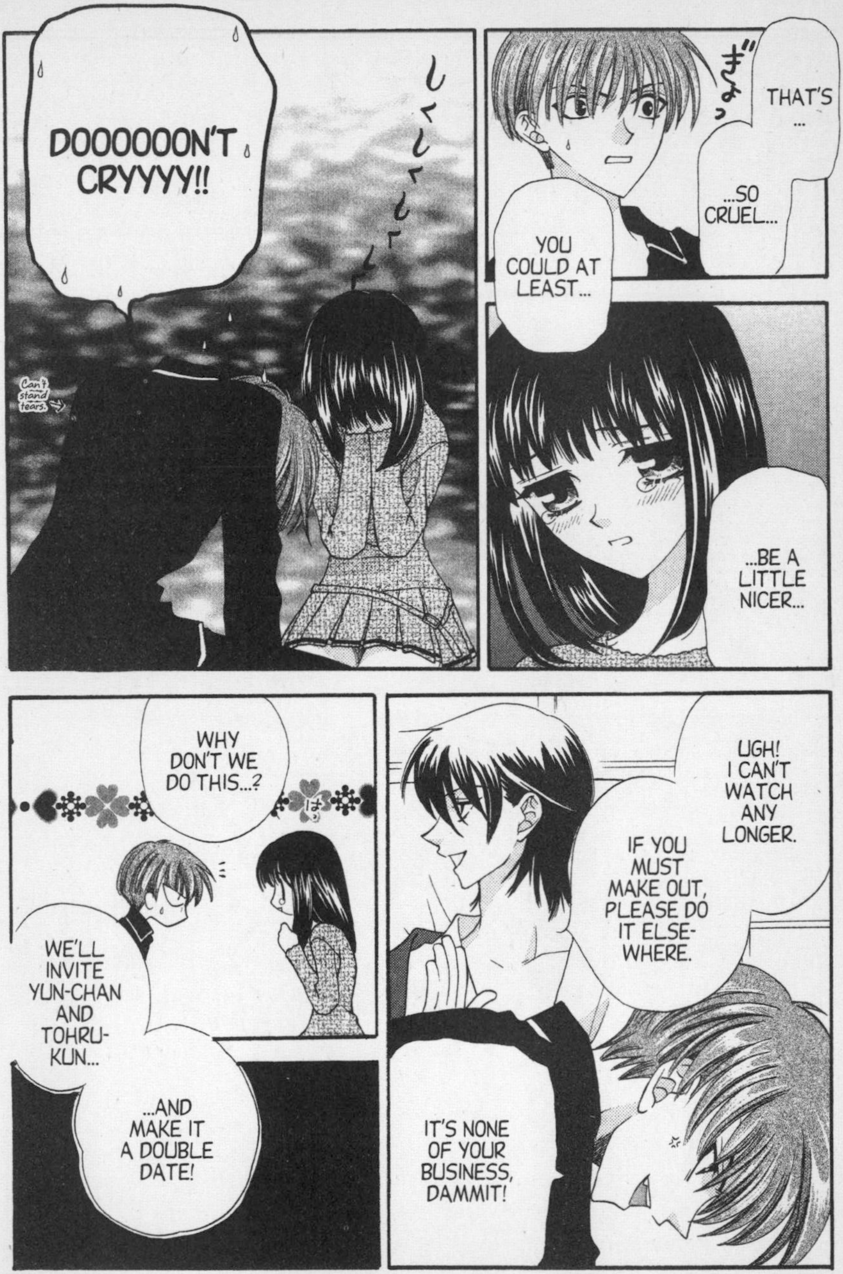
ぎょっ
THAT'S ...
...SO CRUEL...
YOU COULD AT LEAST...
...BE A LITTLE NICER...
しくしくしくしく
DOOOOOON'T CRYYYY!!
Can't stand tears.
UGH! I CAN'T WATCH ANY LONGER.
IF YOU MUST MAKE OUT, PLEASE DO IT ELSE-WHERE.
IT'S NONE OF YOUR BUSINESS, DAMMIT!
WHY DON'T WE DO THIS...?
は
WE'LL INVITE YUN-CHAN AND TOHRU-KUN...
...AND MAKE IT A DOUBLE DATE!

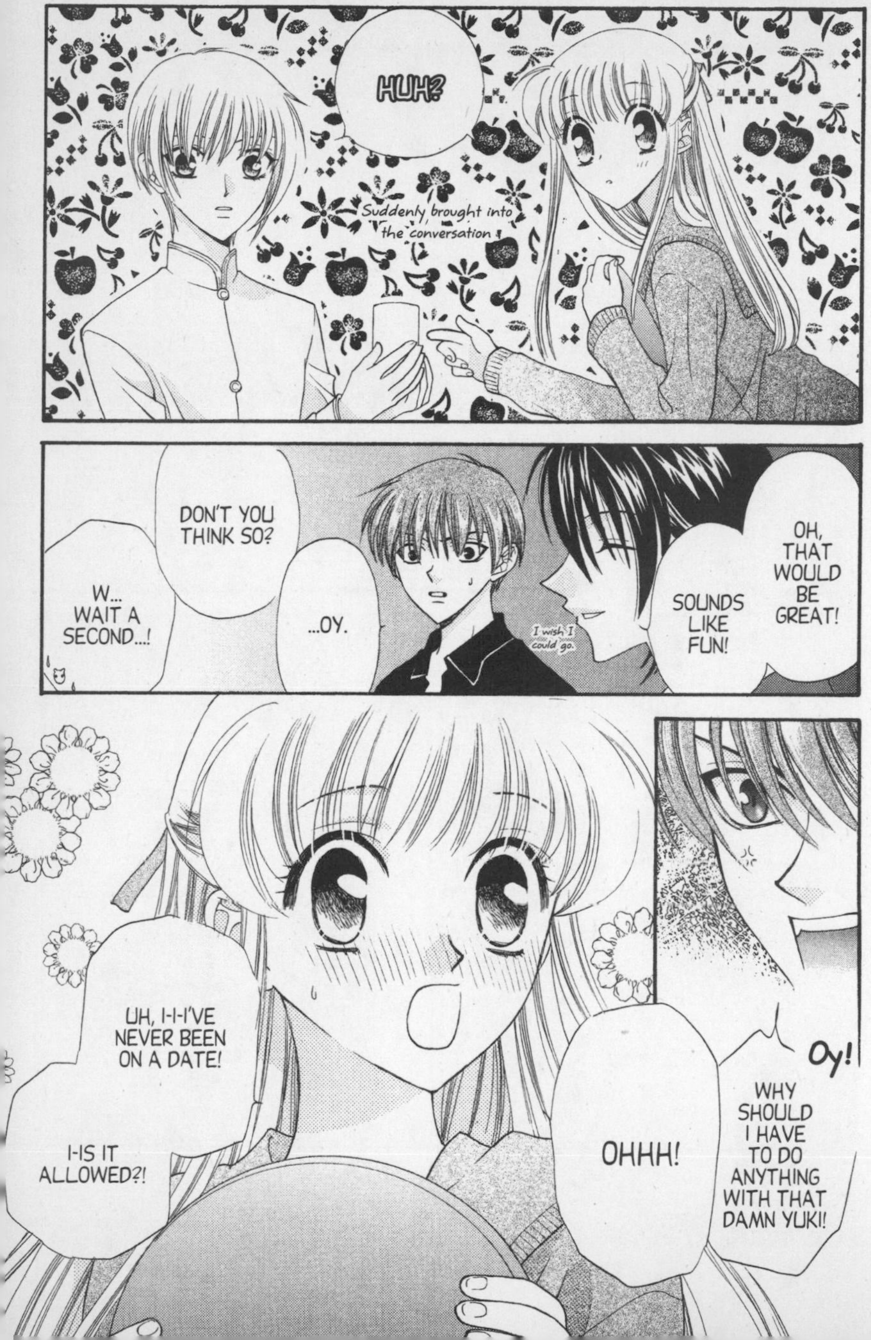
HUH?
Suddenly brought into the conversation
OH, THAT WOULD BE GREAT!
SOUNDS LIKE FUN!
I wish I could go.
...OY.
DON'T YOU THINK SO?
W... WAIT A SECOND...!
Oy!
WHY SHOULD I HAVE TO DO ANYTHING WITH THAT DAMN YUKI!
OHHH!
UH, I-I-I'VE NEVER BEEN ON A DATE!
I-IS IT ALLOWED?!

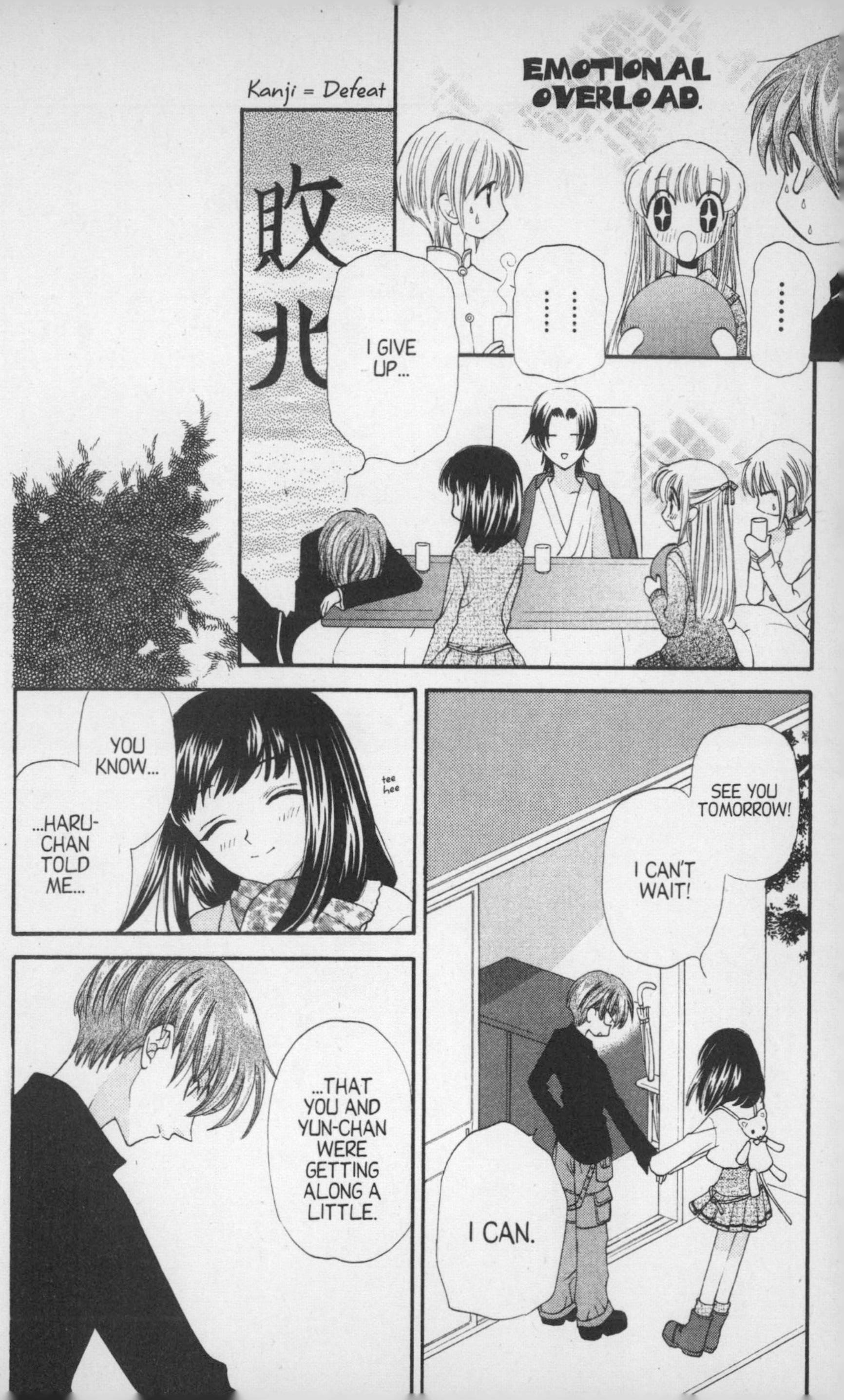
EMOTIONAL OVERLOAD.
......
......
I GIVE UP...
Kanji = Defeat
敗北
SEE YOU TOMORROW!
I CAN'T WAIT!
I CAN.
YOU KNOW...
...HARU-CHAN TOLD ME...
tee hee
...THAT YOU AND YUN-CHAN WERE GETTING ALONG A LITTLE.

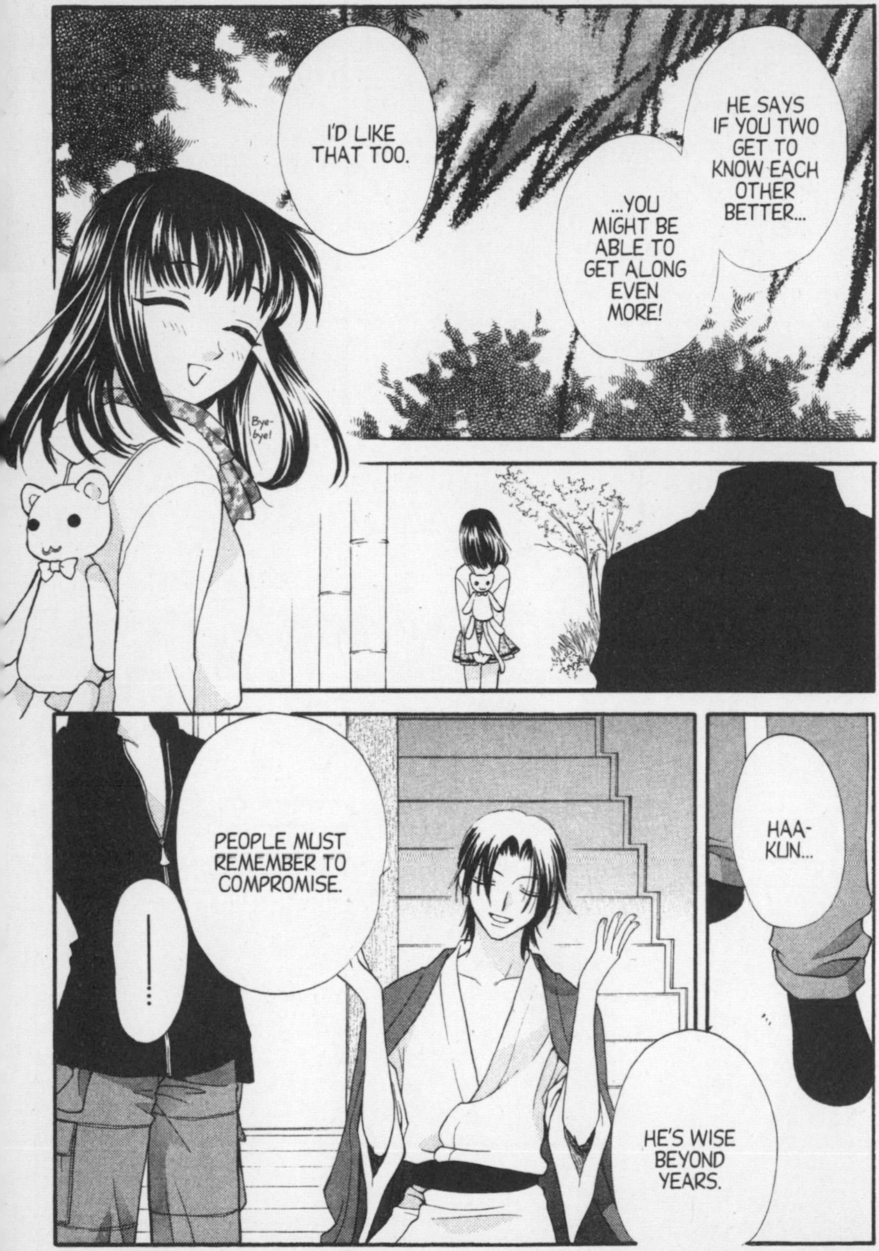
HE SAYS IF YOU TWO GET TO KNOW EACH OTHER BETTER...
...YOU MIGHT BE ABLE TO GET ALONG EVEN MORE!
I'D LIKE THAT TOO.
Bye-bye!
HAA-KUN...
PEOPLE MUST REMEMBER TO COMPROMISE.
...!
HE'S WISE BEYOND YEARS.

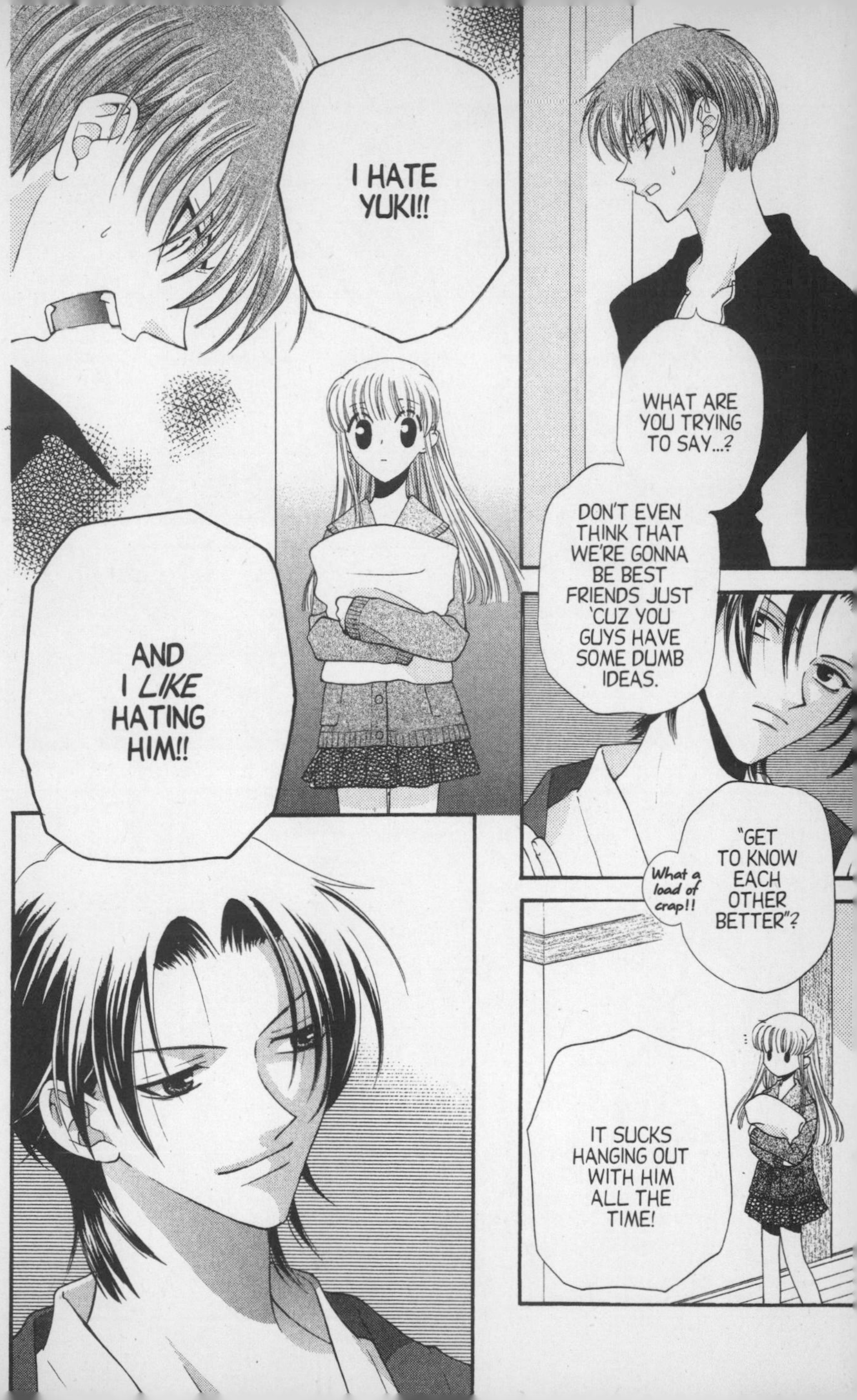
WHAT ARE YOU TRYING TO SAY...?
DON'T EVEN THINK THAT WE'RE GONNA BE BEST FRIENDS JUST 'CUZ YOU GUYS HAVE SOME DUMB IDEAS.
"GET TO KNOW EACH OTHER BETTER"?
What a load of crap!!
IT SUCKS HANGING OUT WITH HIM ALL THE TIME!
I HATE YUKI!!
AND I *LIKE* HATING HIM!!

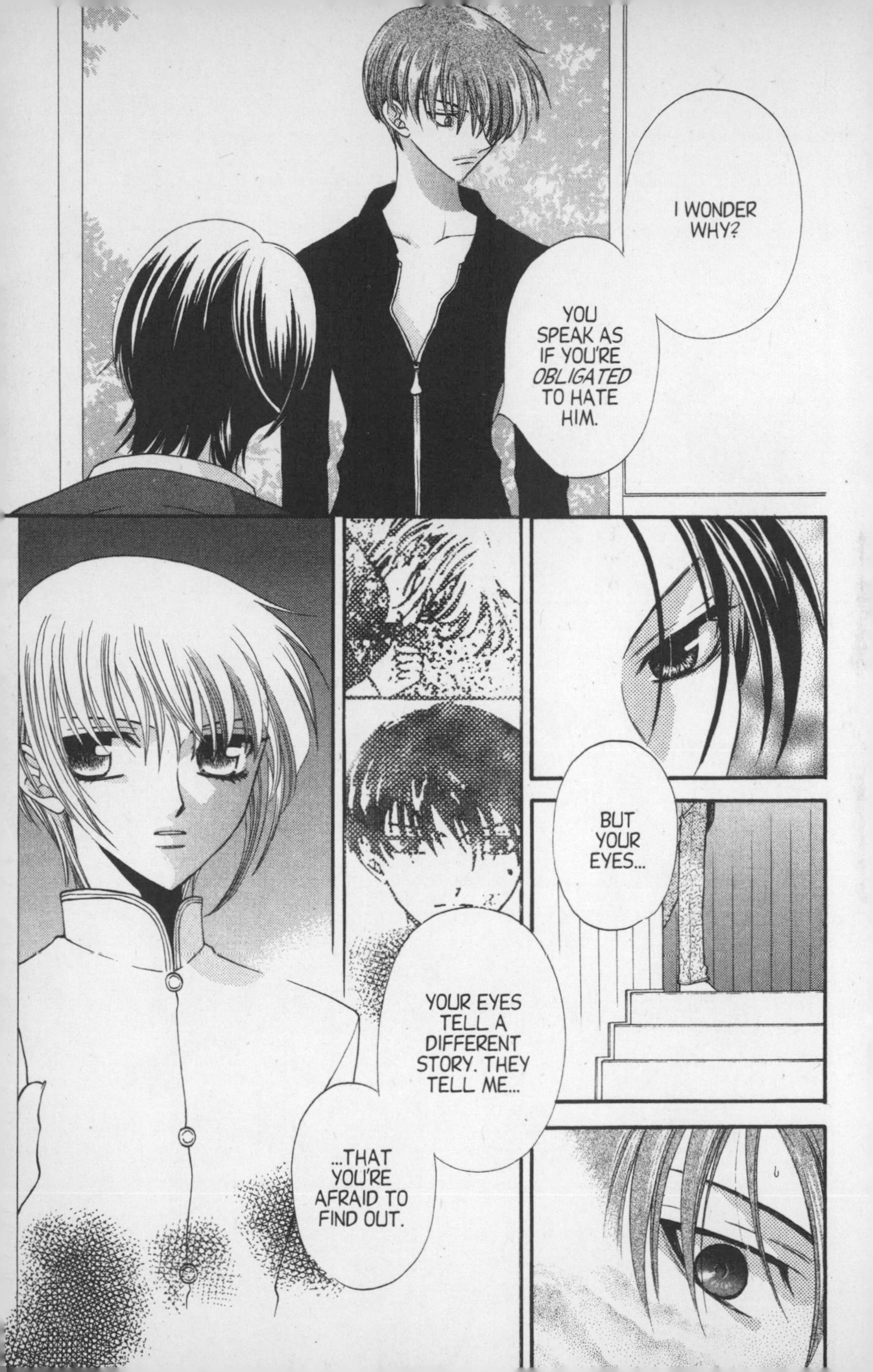
I WONDER WHY?
YOU SPEAK AS IF YOU'RE *OBLIGATED* TO HATE HIM.
BUT YOUR EYES...
YOUR EYES TELL A DIFFERENT STORY. THEY TELL ME...
...THAT YOU'RE AFRAID TO FIND OUT.

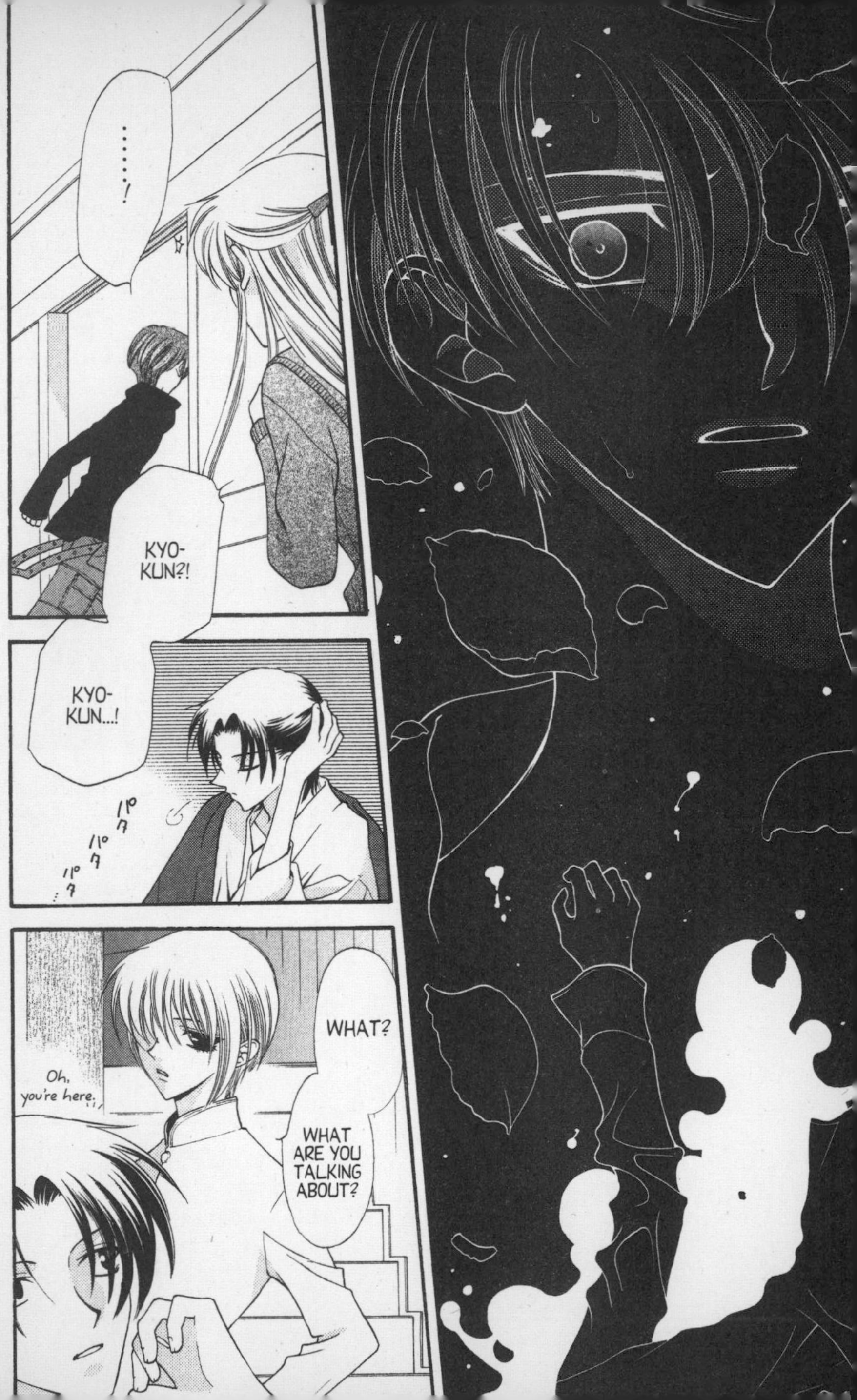
......!
KYO-KUN?!
KYO-KUN...!
パタ
パタ
パタ...
WHAT?
WHAT ARE YOU TALKING ABOUT?
Oh, you're here.

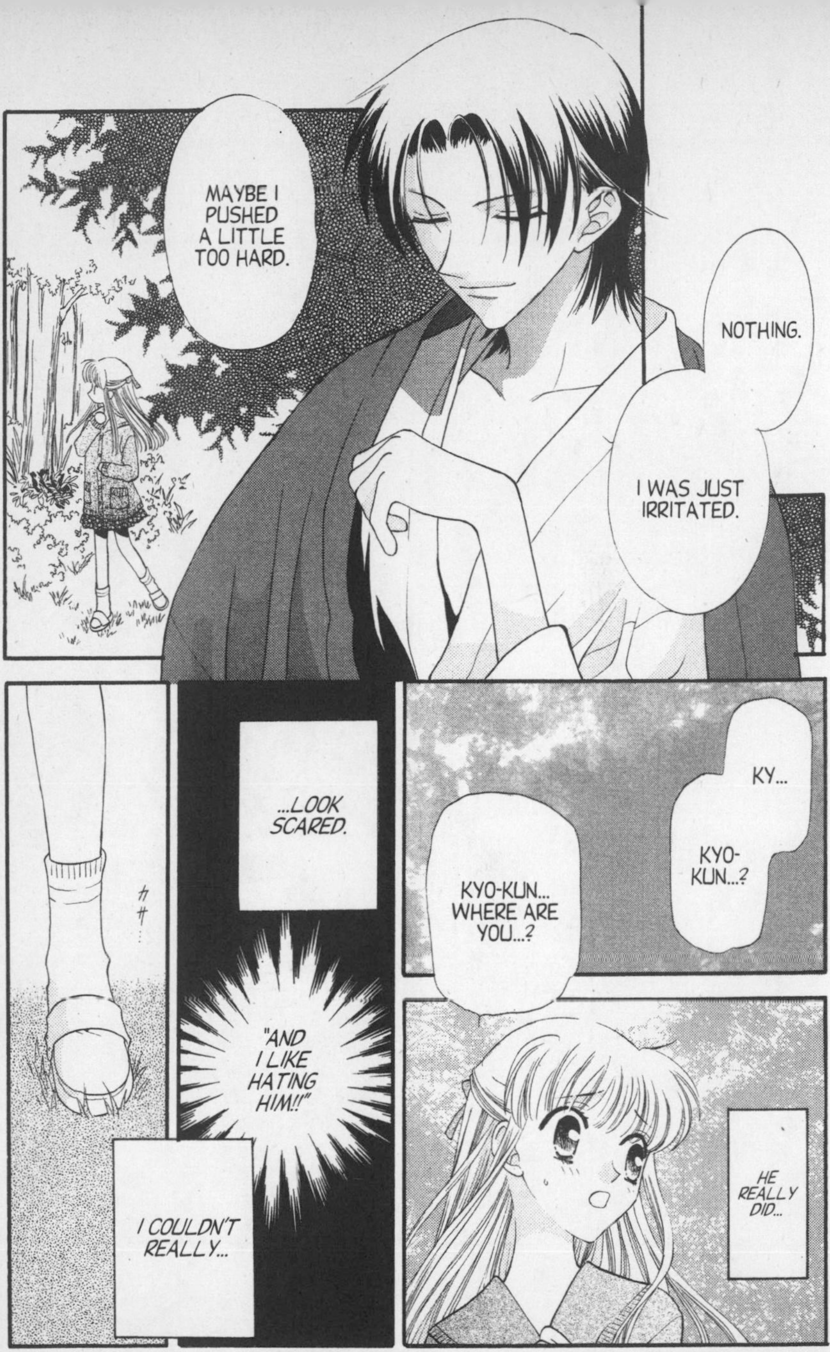
NOTHING.
I WAS JUST IRRITATED.
MAYBE I PUSHED A LITTLE TOO HARD.
KY... KYO-KUN...?
KYO-KUN... WHERE ARE YOU...?
HE REALLY DID...
...LOOK SCARED.
"AND I LIKE HATING HIM!!"
カサ...
I COULDN'T REALLY...

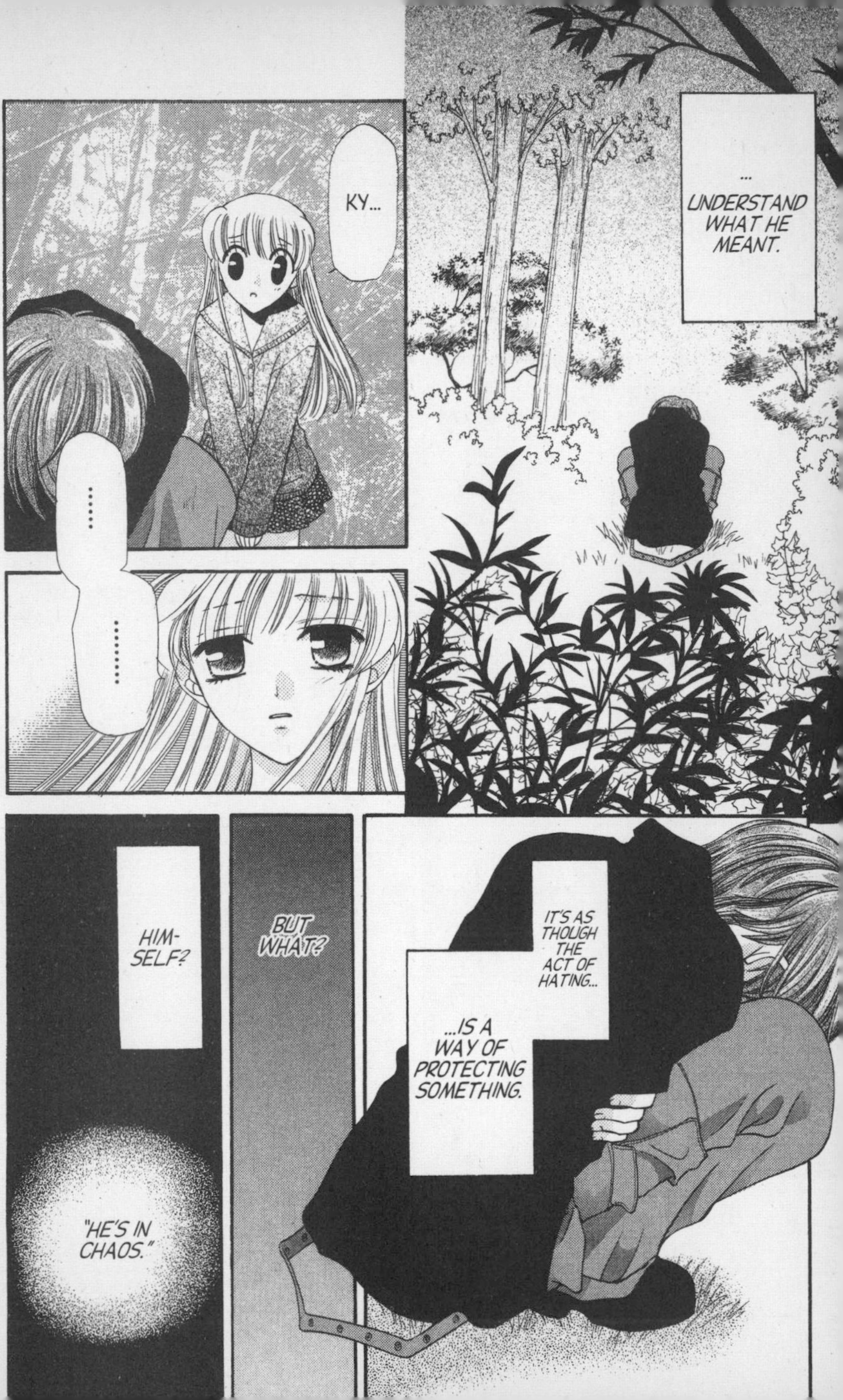
...
UNDERSTAND WHAT HE MEANT.
KY...
......
......
IT'S AS THOUGH THE ACT OF HATING...
...IS A WAY OF PROTECTING SOMETHING.
BUT WHAT?
HIM-SELF?
"HE'S IN CHAOS."

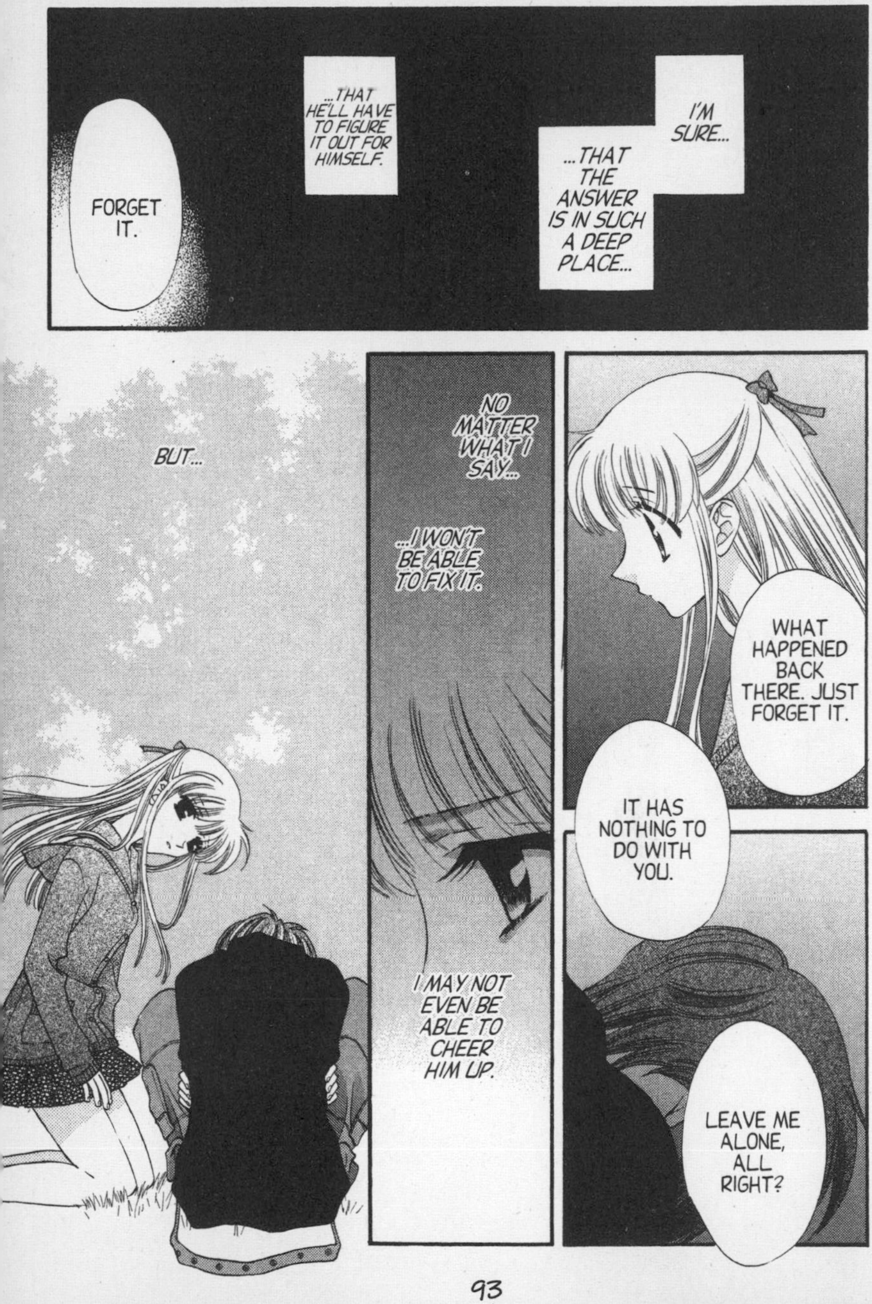
I'M SURE...
...THAT THE ANSWER IS IN SUCH A DEEP PLACE...
...THAT HE'LL HAVE TO FIGURE IT OUT FOR HIMSELF.
FORGET IT.
WHAT HAPPENED BACK THERE. JUST FORGET IT.
IT HAS NOTHING TO DO WITH YOU.
LEAVE ME ALONE, ALL RIGHT?
NO MATTER WHAT I SAY...
...I WON'T BE ABLE TO FIX IT.
I MAY NOT EVEN BE ABLE TO CHEER HIM UP.
BUT...

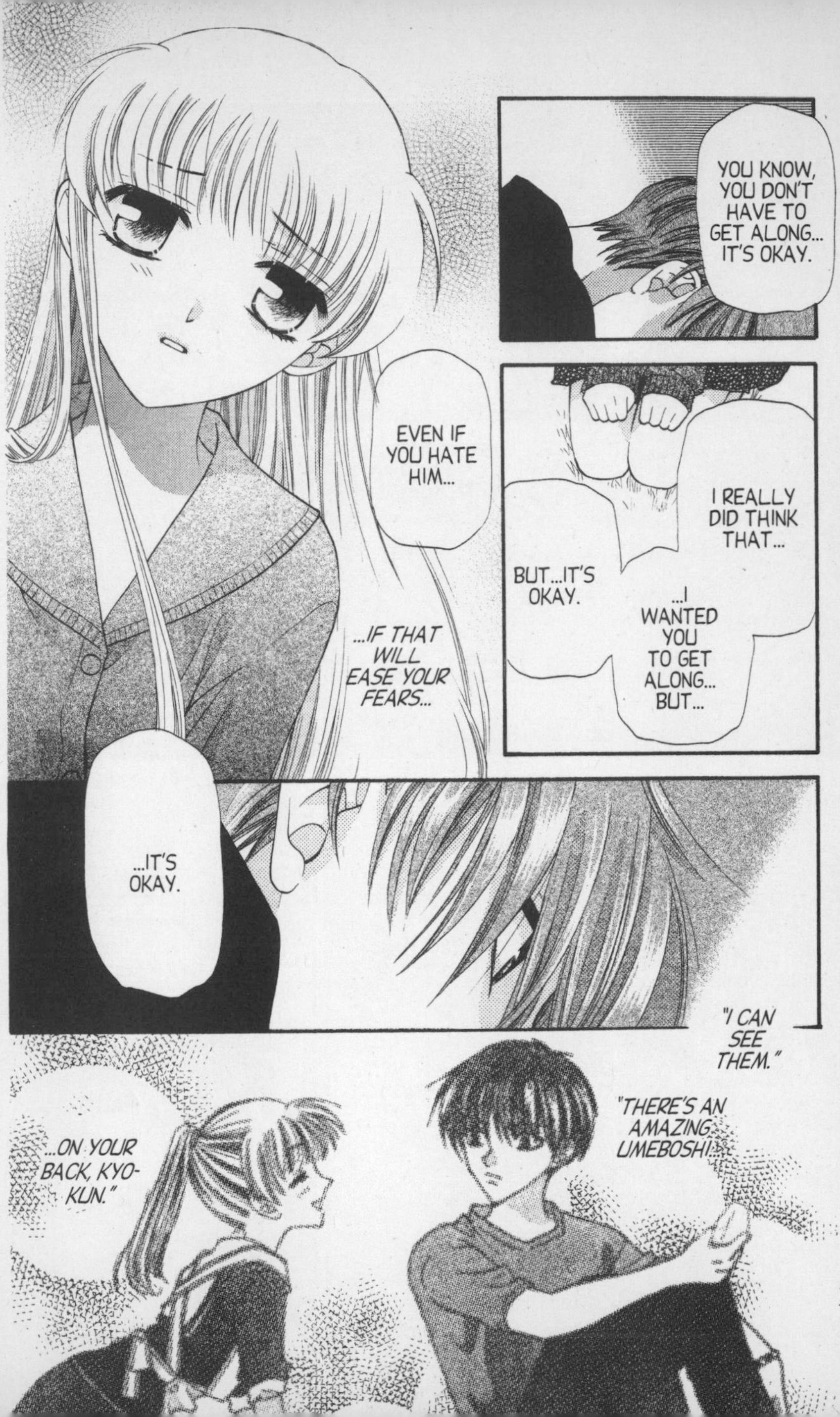
YOU KNOW, YOU DON'T HAVE TO GET ALONG... IT'S OKAY.
I REALLY DID THINK THAT...
...I WANTED YOU TO GET ALONG... BUT...
BUT...IT'S OKAY.
EVEN IF YOU HATE HIM...
...IF THAT WILL EASE YOUR FEARS...
...IT'S OKAY.
"I CAN SEE THEM."
"THERE'S AN AMAZING UMEBOSHI...
...ON YOUR BACK, KYO-KUN."

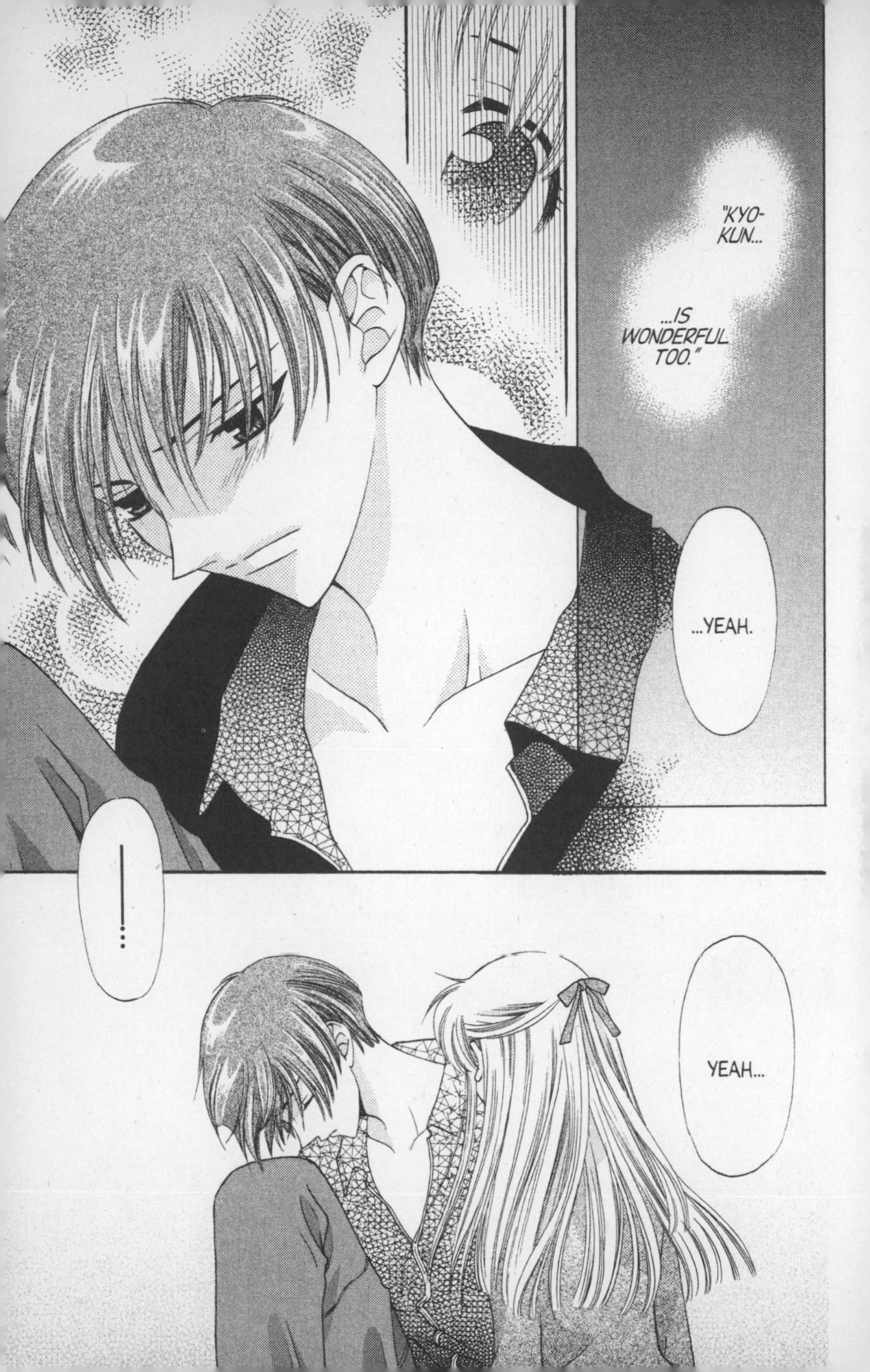
"KYO-KUN...
...IS WONDERFUL TOO."
...YEAH.
—....
YEAH...

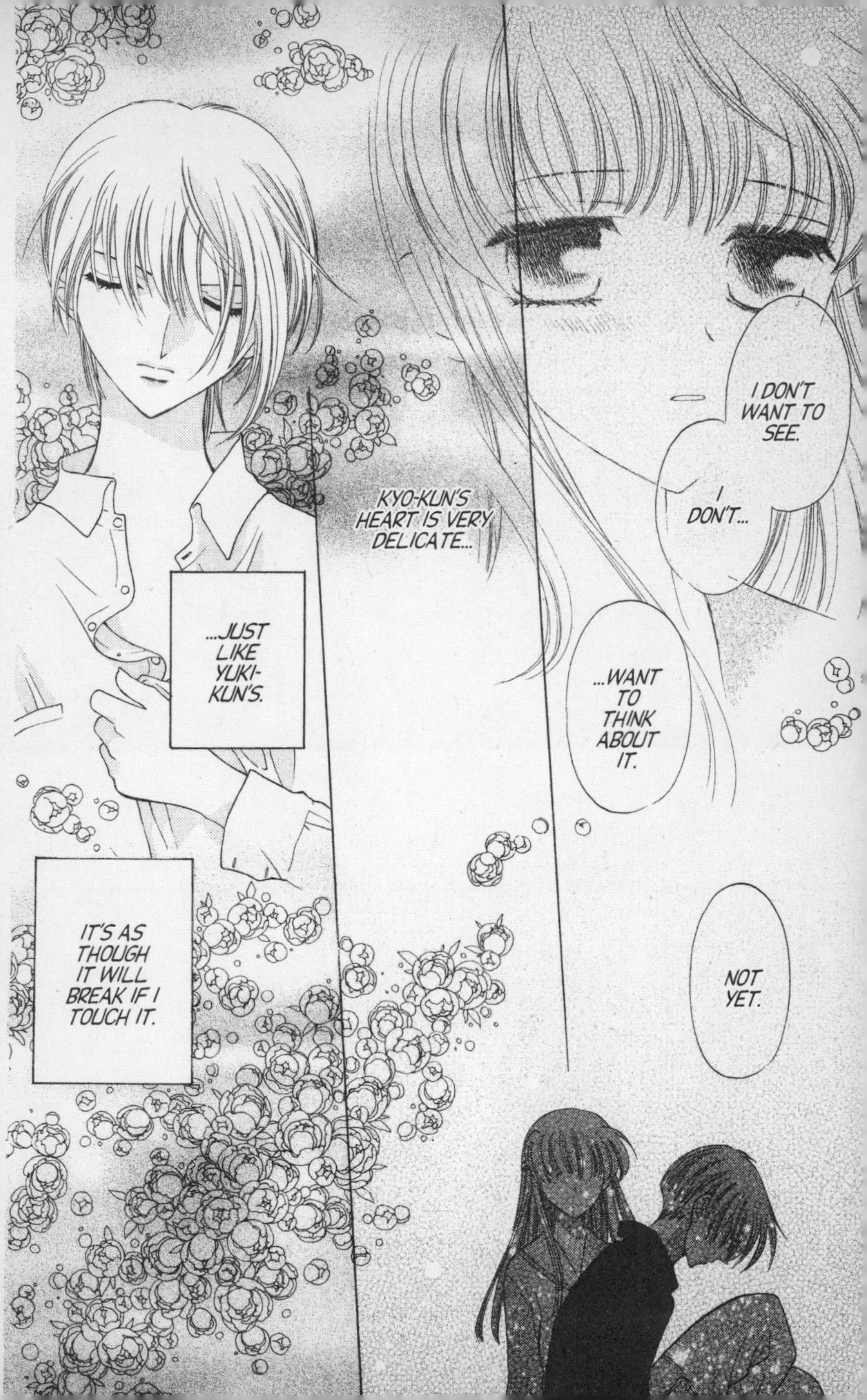
I DON'T WANT TO SEE.
I DON'T...
...WANT TO THINK ABOUT IT.
NOT YET.
KYO-KUN'S HEART IS VERY DELICATE...
...JUST LIKE YUKI-KUN'S.
IT'S AS THOUGH IT WILL BREAK IF I TOUCH IT.

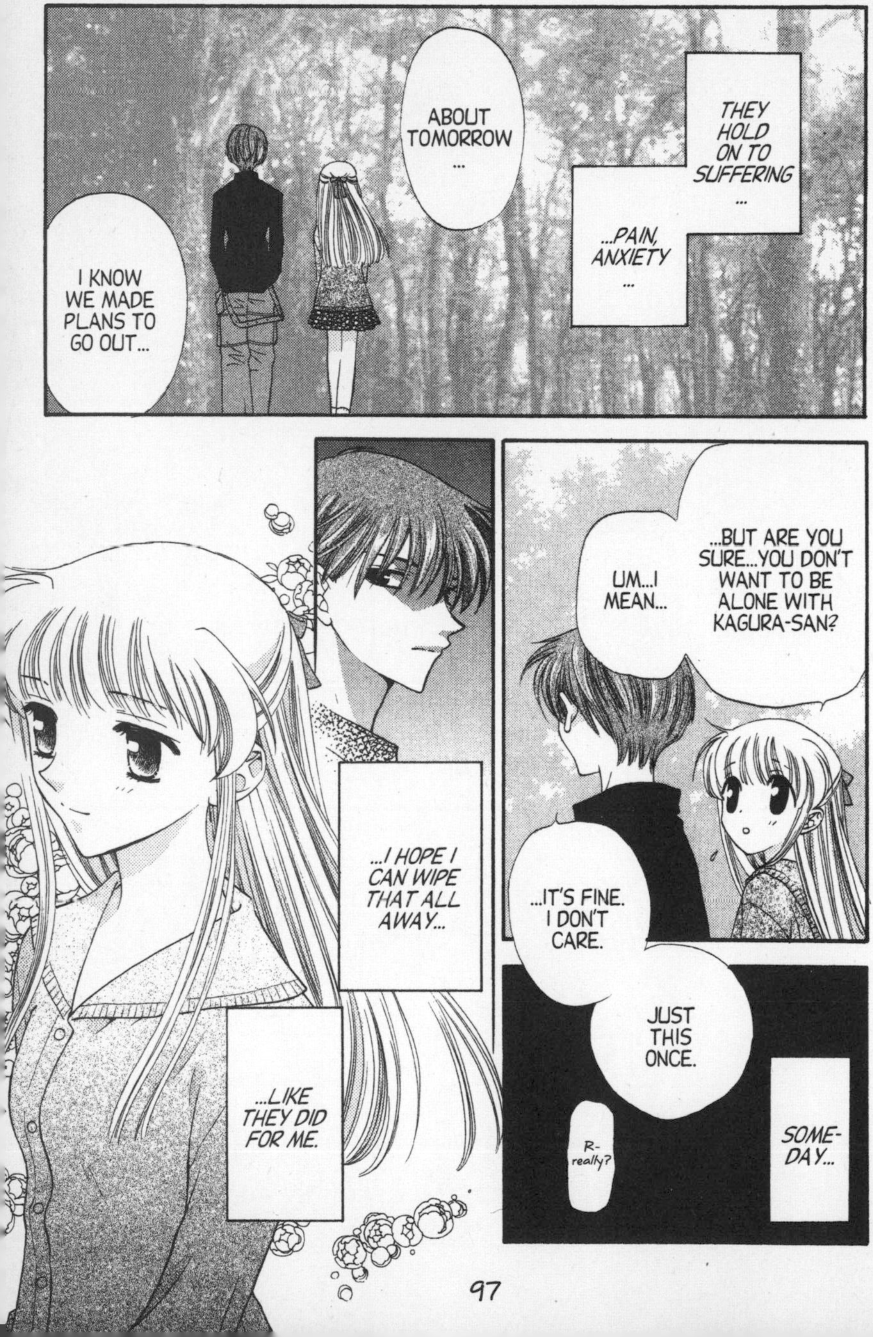
THEY HOLD ON TO SUFFERING ...
...PAIN, ANXIETY ...
ABOUT TOMORROW ...
I KNOW WE MADE PLANS TO GO OUT...
UM...I MEAN...
...BUT ARE YOU SURE...YOU DON'T WANT TO BE ALONE WITH KAGURA-SAN?
...IT'S FINE. I DON'T CARE.
JUST THIS ONCE.
SOME-DAY...
R-really?
...I HOPE I CAN WIPE THAT ALL AWAY...
...LIKE THEY DID FOR ME.

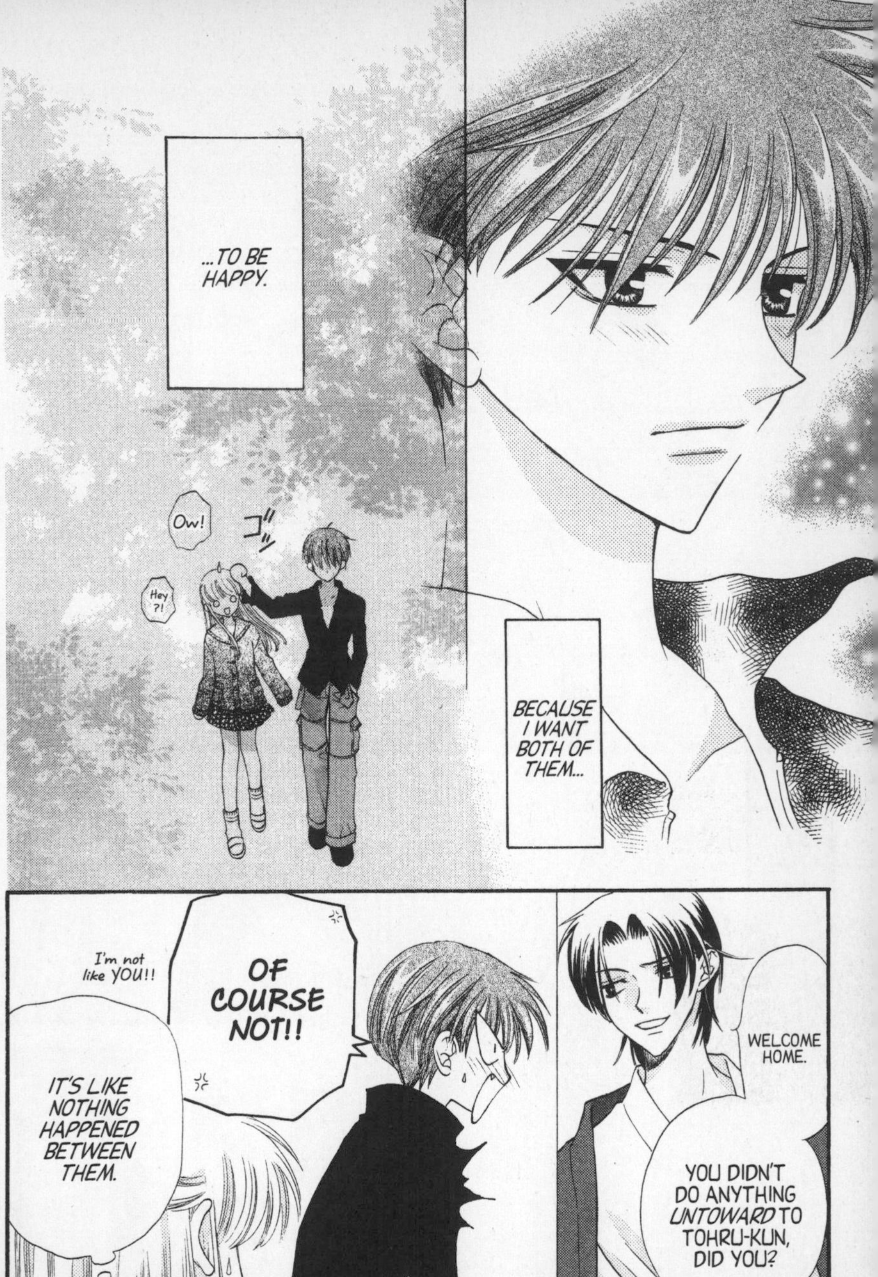
BECAUSE I WANT BOTH OF THEM...
...TO BE HAPPY.
Ow!
ゴッ
Hey ?!
WELCOME HOME.
YOU DIDN'T DO ANYTHING UNTOWARD TO TOHRU-KUN, DID YOU?
OF COURSE NOT!!
I'm not like YOU!!
IT'S LIKE NOTHING HAPPENED BETWEEN THEM.

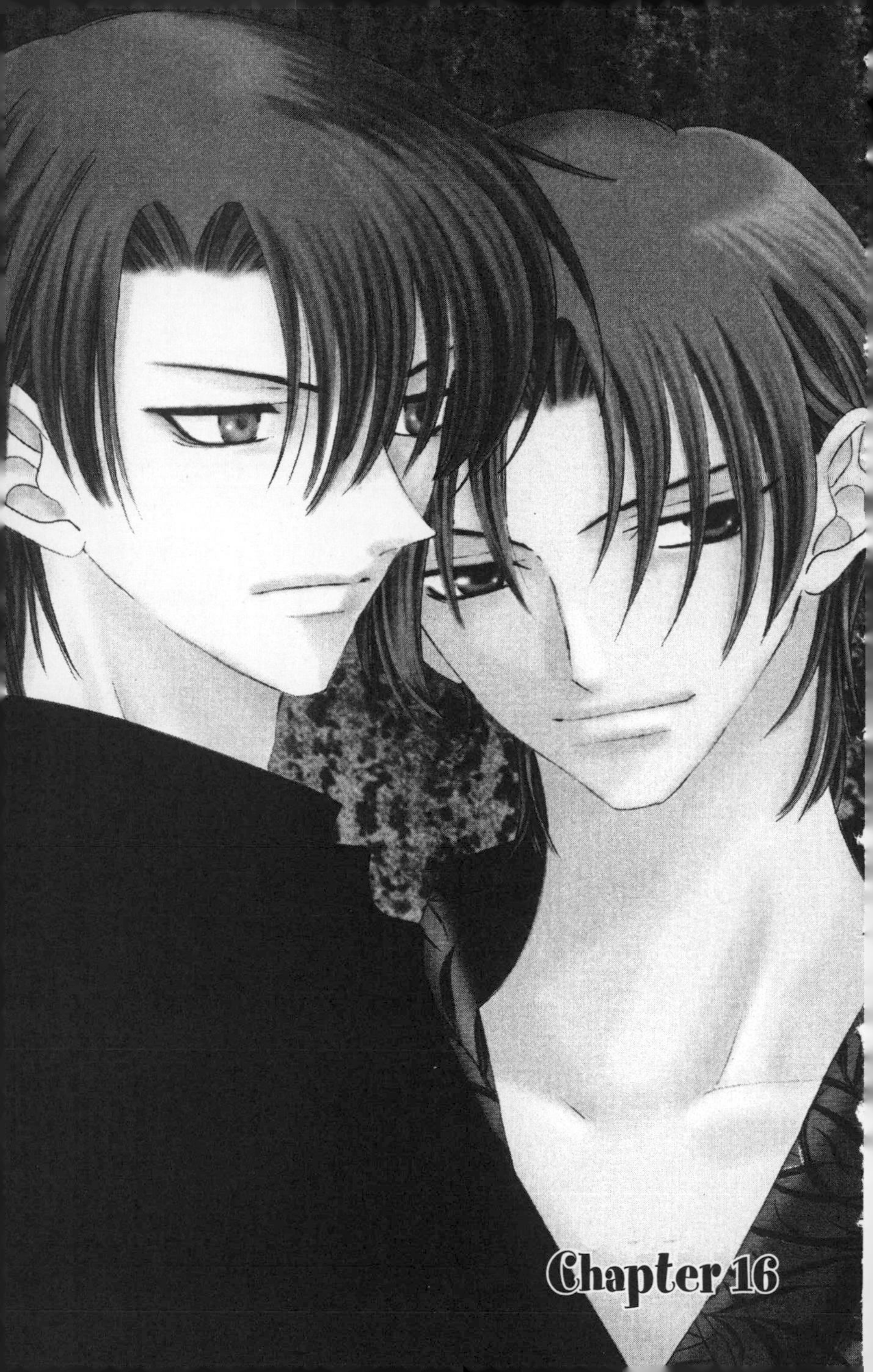
Chapter 16

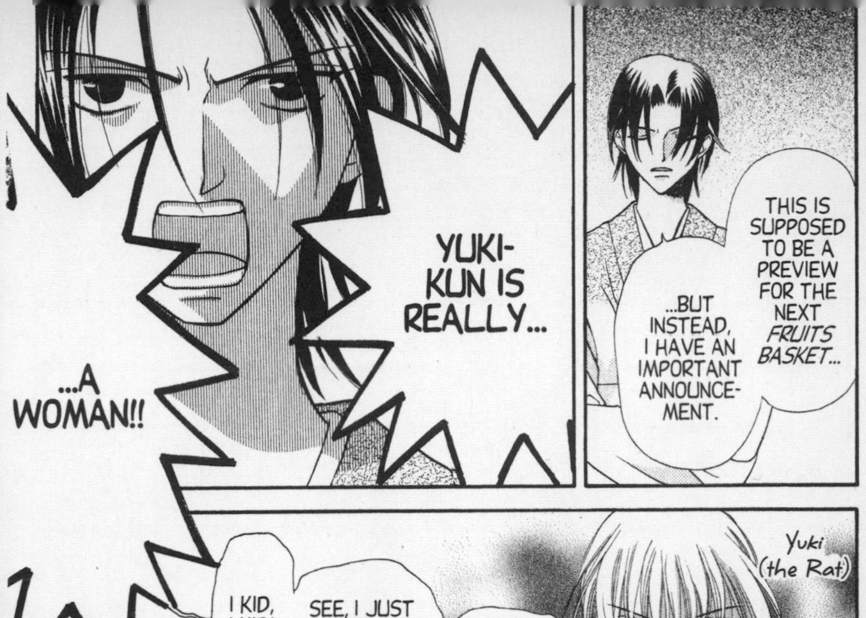
THIS IS SUPPOSED TO BE A PREVIEW FOR THE NEXT *FRUITS BASKET*...
...BUT INSTEAD, I HAVE AN IMPORTANT ANNOUNCE-MENT.
YUKI-KUN IS REALLY...
...A WOMAN!!
Yuki (the Rat)
Shigure (the Dog)
I KID, I KID!
SEE, I JUST THOUGHT IT WOULD MAKE MORE OF AN IMPACT...
...IF I SAID SOMETHING DRAMATIC. YOU'RE 100% MALE, YUKI-KUN. WELL...AT LEAST 80%
Tohru (the Heroine)
Kyo (the Cat)
IT'S STARTING! ♡

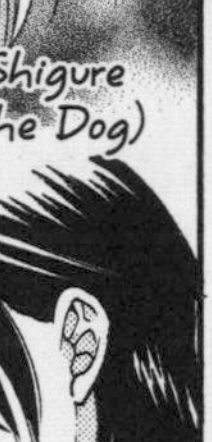

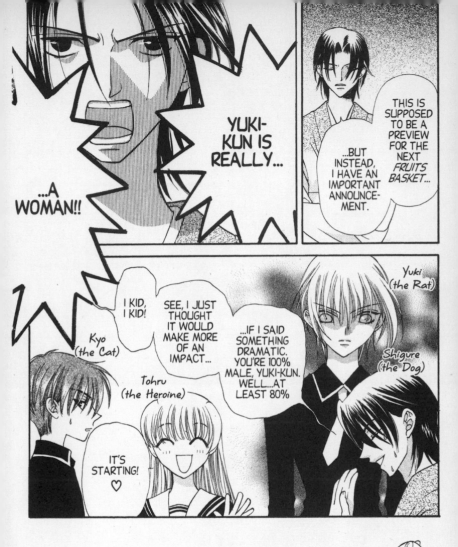

Omake Theater, Part 2

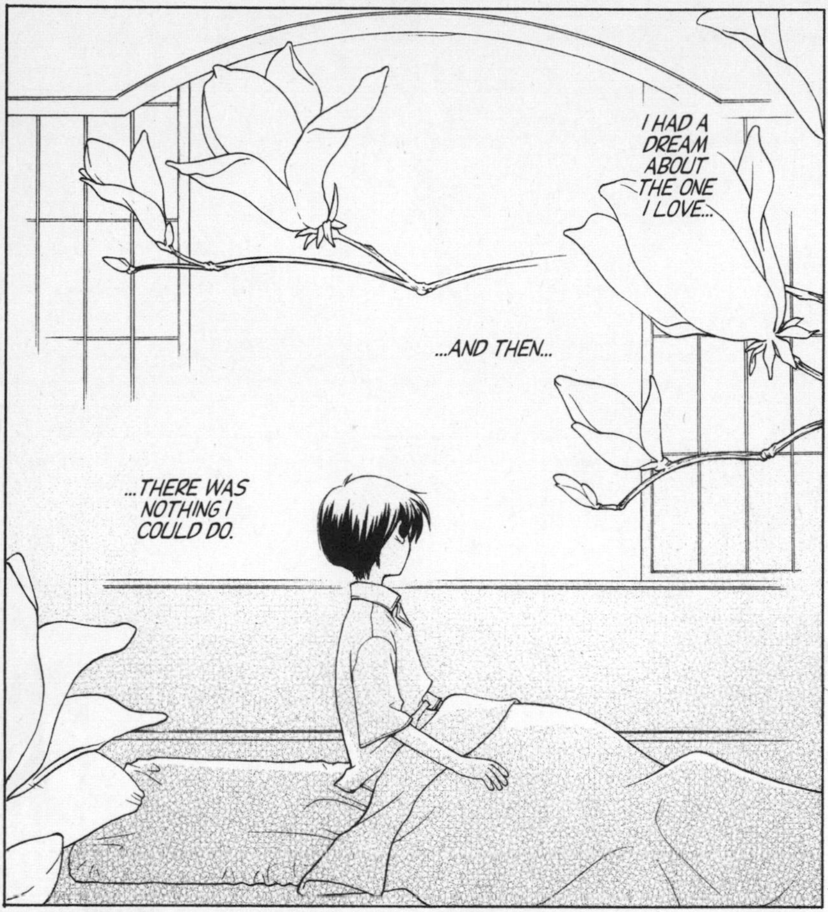
I HAD A DREAM ABOUT THE ONE I LOVE...
...AND THEN...
...THERE WAS NOTHING I COULD DO.

ULTRA SPECIAL BLAH BLAH BLAH 4

The main character of this episode is a fellow by the name of Mogeta! Okay, not really, but the name does come up. So does Aaya. I will explain the Mabudachi Trio in Volume 4! Anyway, don't you think it's cute when adults call their friends by pet names?

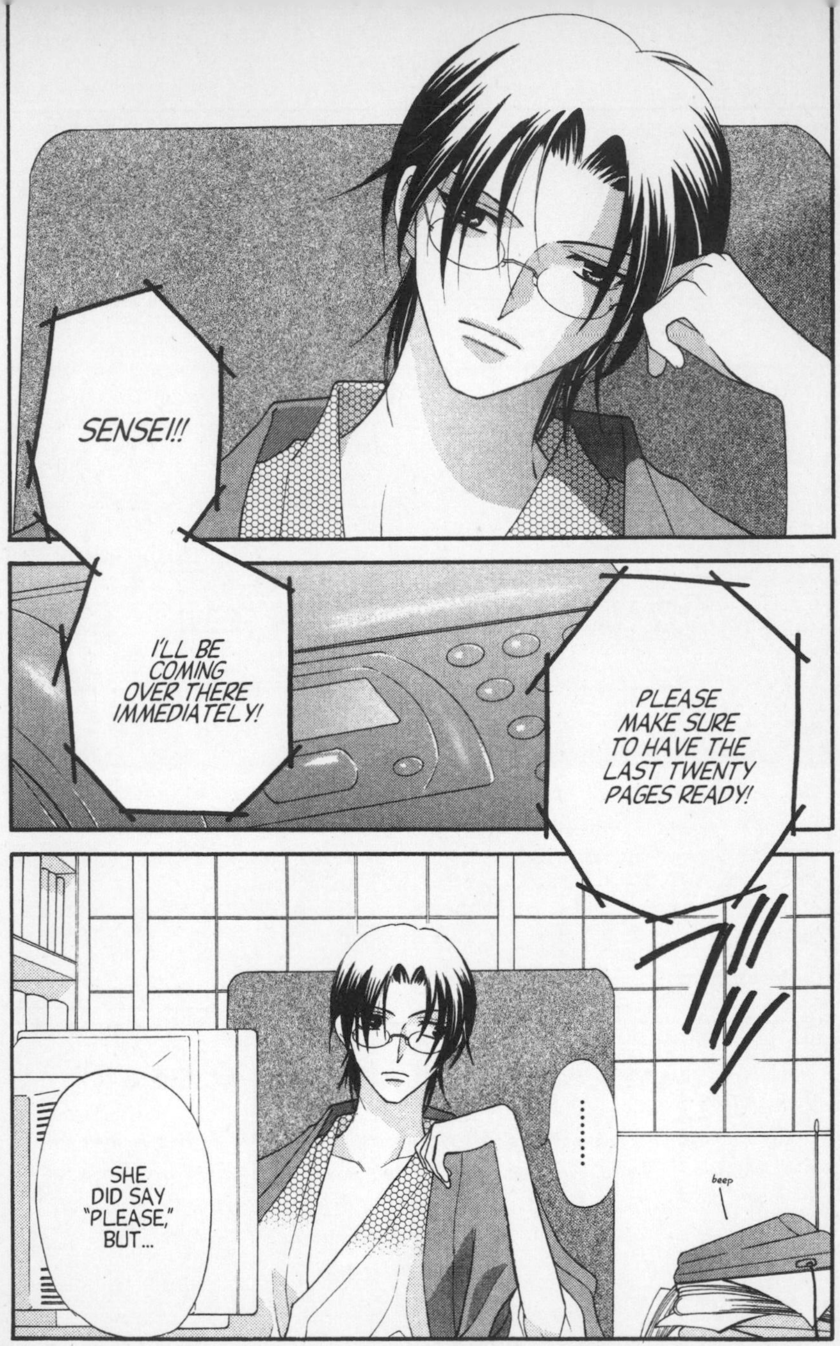
SENSEI!!
I'LL BE COMING OVER THERE IMMEDIATELY!
PLEASE MAKE SURE TO HAVE THE LAST TWENTY PAGES READY!
beep
......
SHE DID SAY "PLEASE," BUT...

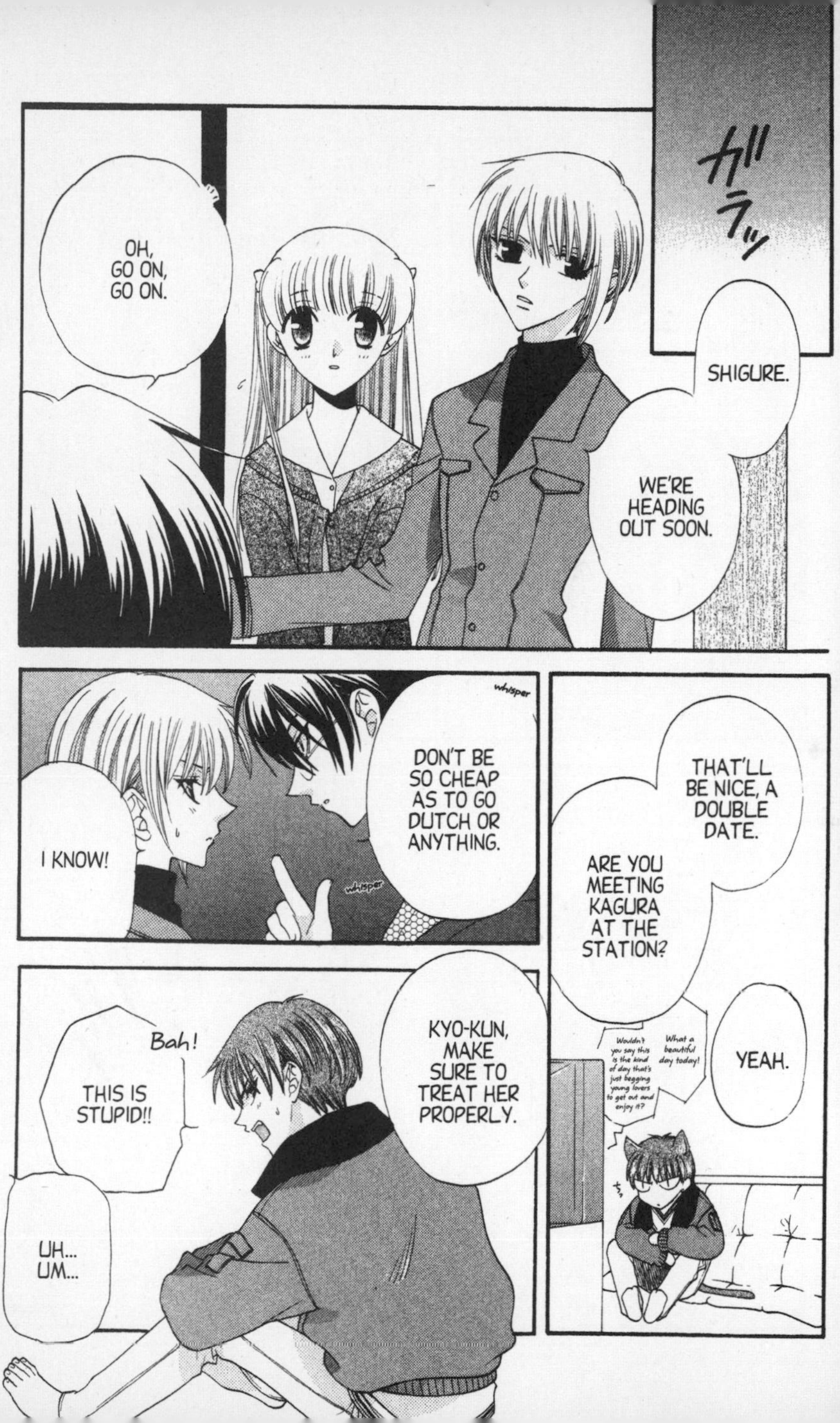
ガラッ
SHIGURE.
WE'RE HEADING OUT SOON.
OH, GO ON, GO ON.
THAT'LL BE NICE, A DOUBLE DATE.
ARE YOU MEETING KAGURA AT THE STATION?
YEAH.
What a beautiful day today!
Wouldn't you say this is the kind of day that's just begging young lovers to get out and enjoy it?
whisper
DON'T BE SO CHEAP AS TO GO DUTCH OR ANYTHING.
whisper
I KNOW!
KYO-KUN, MAKE SURE TO TREAT HER PROPERLY.
Bah!
THIS IS STUPID!!
UH... UM...

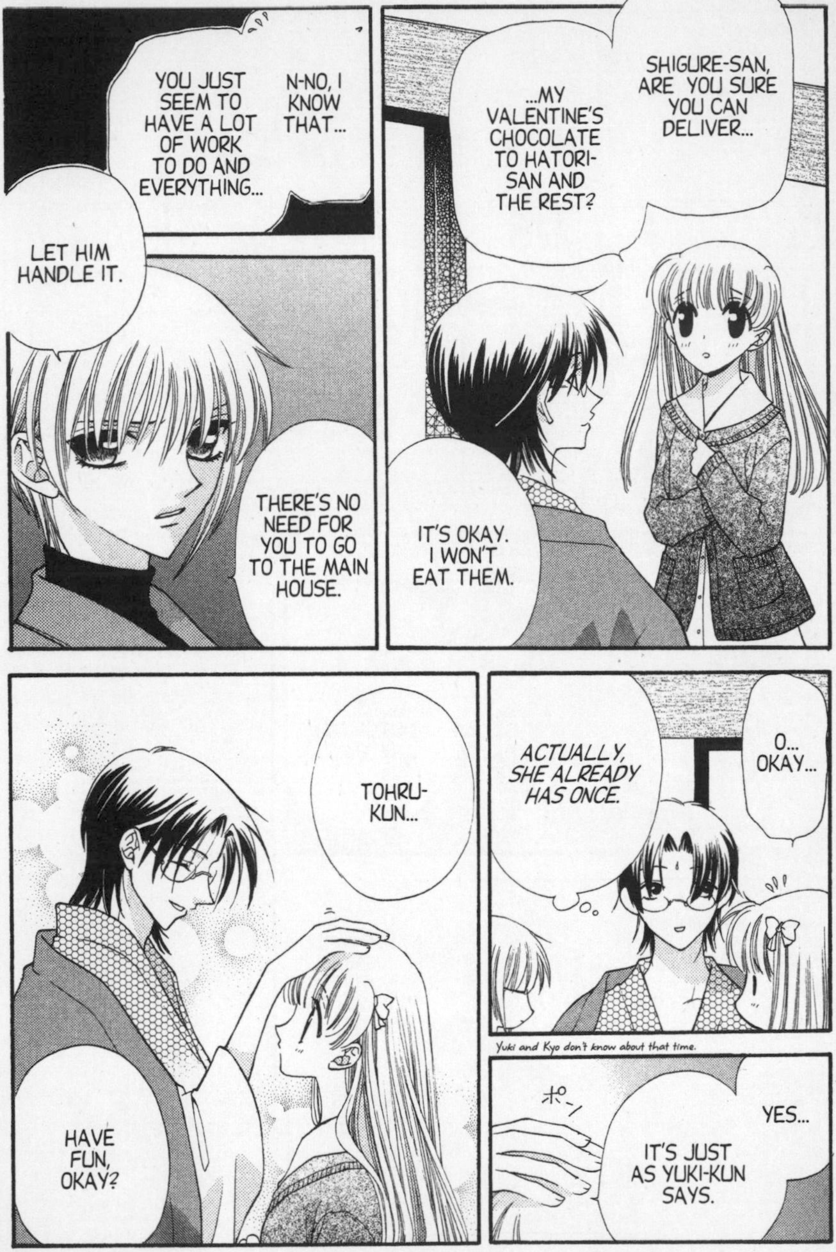
SHIGURE-SAN, ARE YOU SURE YOU CAN DELIVER...
...MY VALENTINE'S CHOCOLATE TO HATORI-SAN AND THE REST?
IT'S OKAY. I WON'T EAT THEM.
N-NO, I KNOW THAT...
YOU JUST SEEM TO HAVE A LOT OF WORK TO DO AND EVERYTHING...
LET HIM HANDLE IT.
THERE'S NO NEED FOR YOU TO GO TO THE MAIN HOUSE.
O... OKAY...
ACTUALLY, SHE ALREADY HAS ONCE.
Yuki and Kyo don't know about that time.
YES...
ポーッ
IT'S JUST AS YUKI-KUN SAYS.
TOHRU-KUN...
HAVE FUN, OKAY?

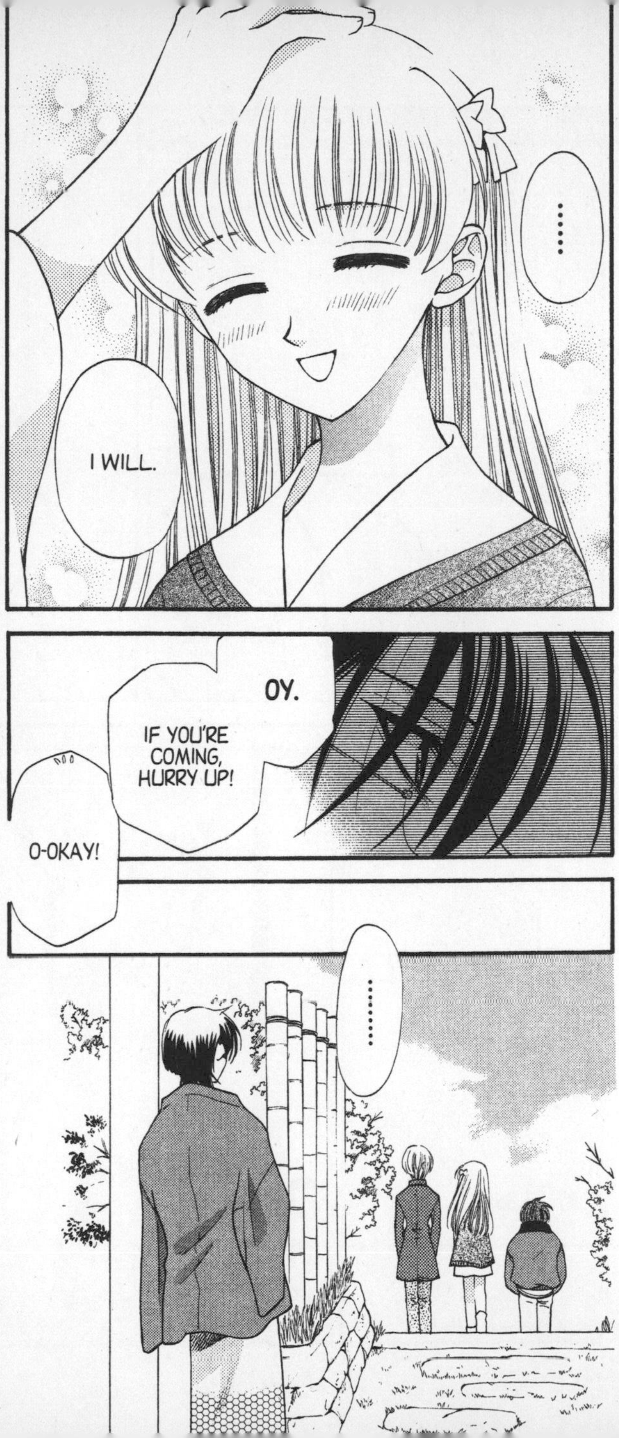
......
I WILL.
OY.
IF YOU'RE COMING, HURRY UP!
O-OKAY!
......

Fruits Basket Part 4

I think people who read the magazine already know this, but I built my own home page. It was called "Chotto Ippuku." It took forever. First, I don't understand html tags. It's like learning alien language! I gave that up pretty quickly. I got some software that helps you build a home page without knowing tags, and little by little, I learned how to do it. There was no one around I could ask about it, so it was really hard. I'm updating regularly, but...I wonder how long I can keep this up...?

Editor's note: (Chotto Ippuku went offline in September 2002)

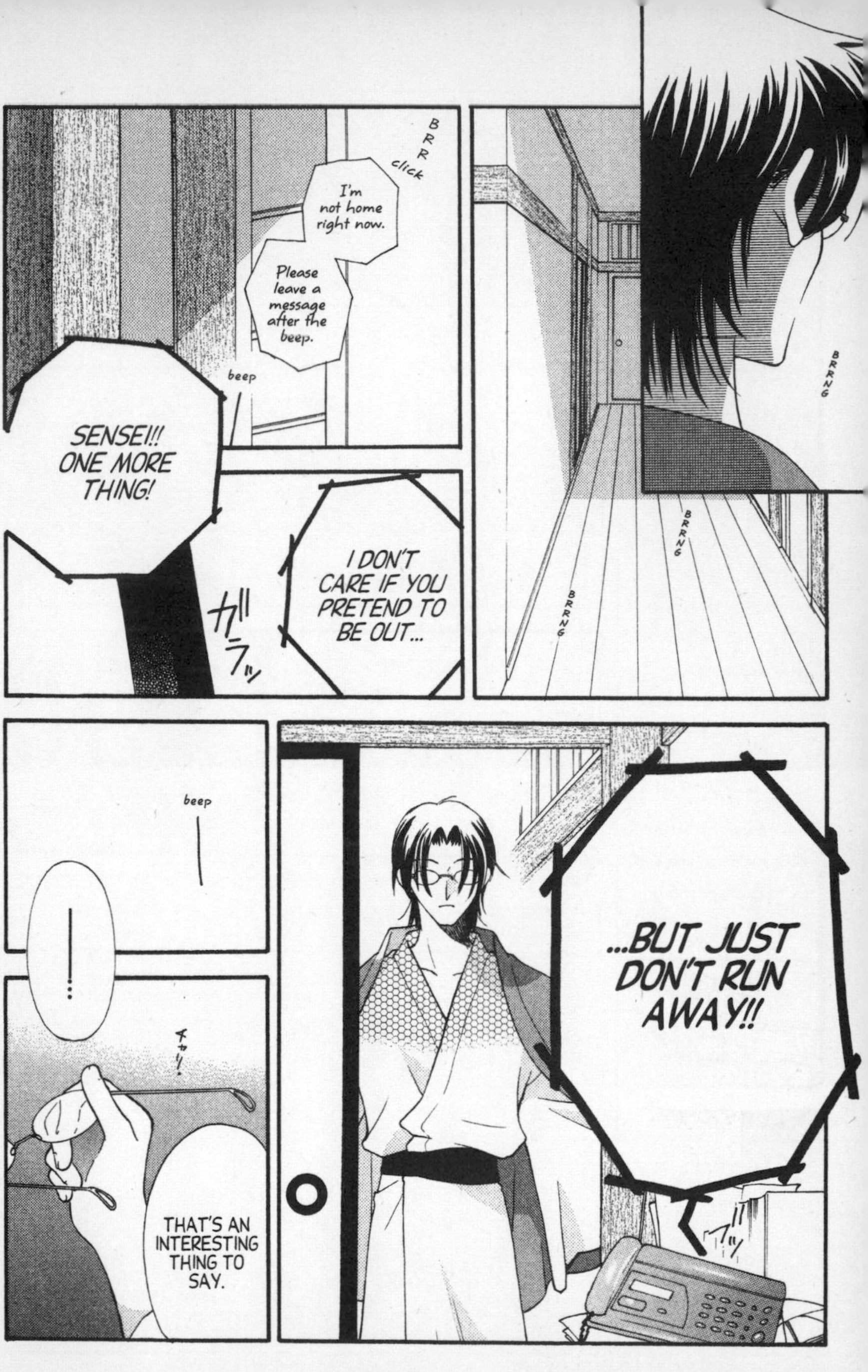
BRRNG
BRRNG
BRRNG
BRR click
I'm not home right now.
Please leave a message after the beep.
beep
SENSEI!! ONE MORE THING!
I DON'T CARE IF YOU PRETEND TO BE OUT...
ガラッ
...BUT JUST DON'T RUN AWAY!!
beep
—
...!
THAT'S AN INTERESTING THING TO SAY.

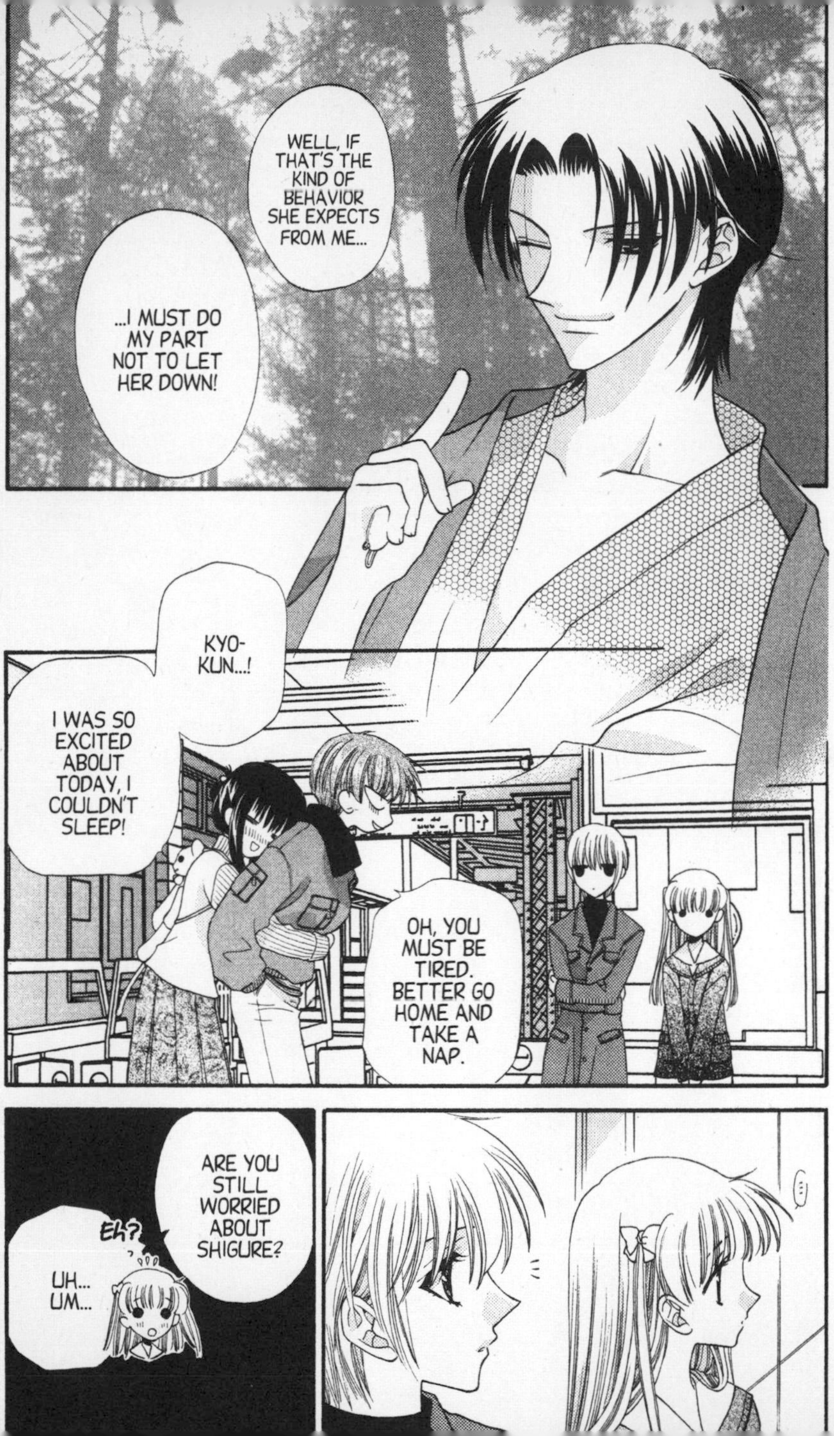
WELL, IF THAT'S THE KIND OF BEHAVIOR SHE EXPECTS FROM ME...
...I MUST DO MY PART NOT TO LET HER DOWN!
KYO-KUN...!
I WAS SO EXCITED ABOUT TODAY, I COULDN'T SLEEP!
OH, YOU MUST BE TIRED. BETTER GO HOME AND TAKE A NAP.
ARE YOU STILL WORRIED ABOUT SHIGURE?
EH?
UH... UM...

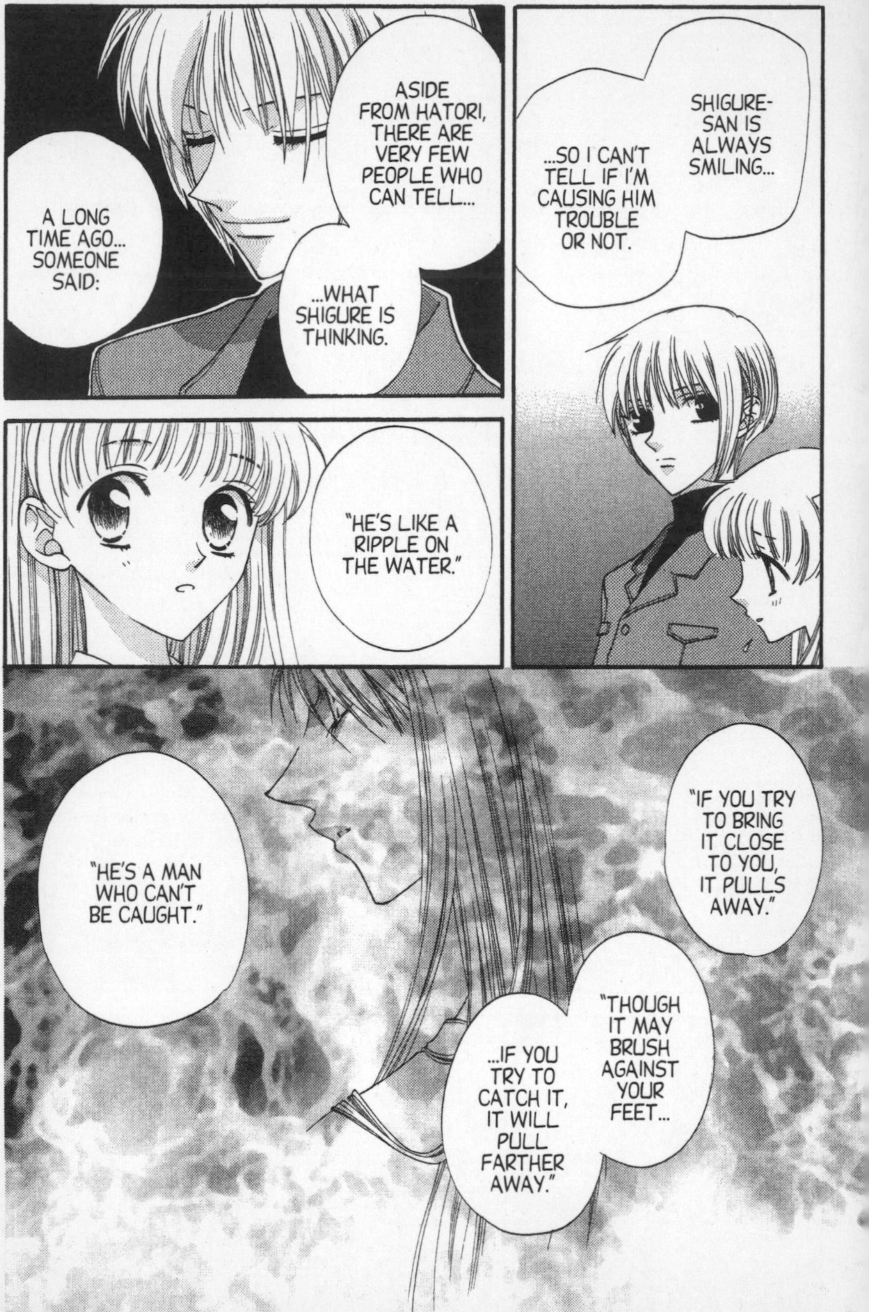
SHIGURE-SAN IS ALWAYS SMILING...
...SO I CAN'T TELL IF I'M CAUSING HIM TROUBLE OR NOT.
ASIDE FROM HATORI, THERE ARE VERY FEW PEOPLE WHO CAN TELL...
...WHAT SHIGURE IS THINKING.
A LONG TIME AGO... SOMEONE SAID:
"HE'S LIKE A RIPPLE ON THE WATER."
"IF YOU TRY TO BRING IT CLOSE TO YOU, IT PULLS AWAY."
"THOUGH IT MAY BRUSH AGAINST YOUR FEET...
...IF YOU TRY TO CATCH IT, IT WILL PULL FARTHER AWAY."
"HE'S A MAN WHO CAN'T BE CAUGHT."

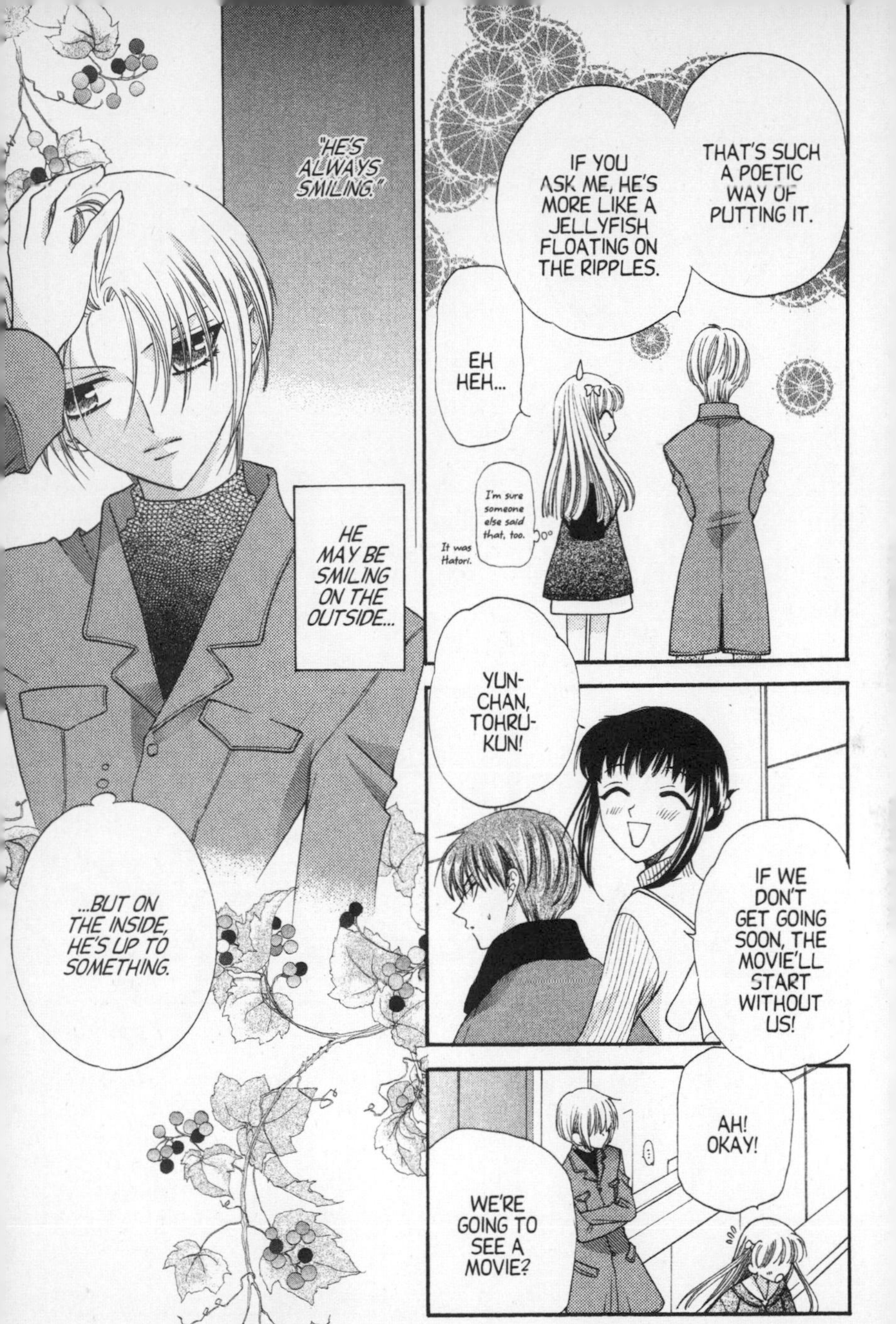
THAT'S SUCH A POETIC WAY OF PUTTING IT.
IF YOU ASK ME, HE'S MORE LIKE A JELLYFISH FLOATING ON THE RIPPLES.
EH HEH...
I'm sure someone else said that, too.
It was Hatori.
YUN-CHAN, TOHRU-KUN!
IF WE DON'T GET GOING SOON, THE MOVIE'LL START WITHOUT US!
AH! OKAY!
WE'RE GOING TO SEE A MOVIE?
"HE'S ALWAYS SMILING."
HE MAY BE SMILING ON THE OUTSIDE...
...BUT ON THE INSIDE, HE'S UP TO SOMETHING.

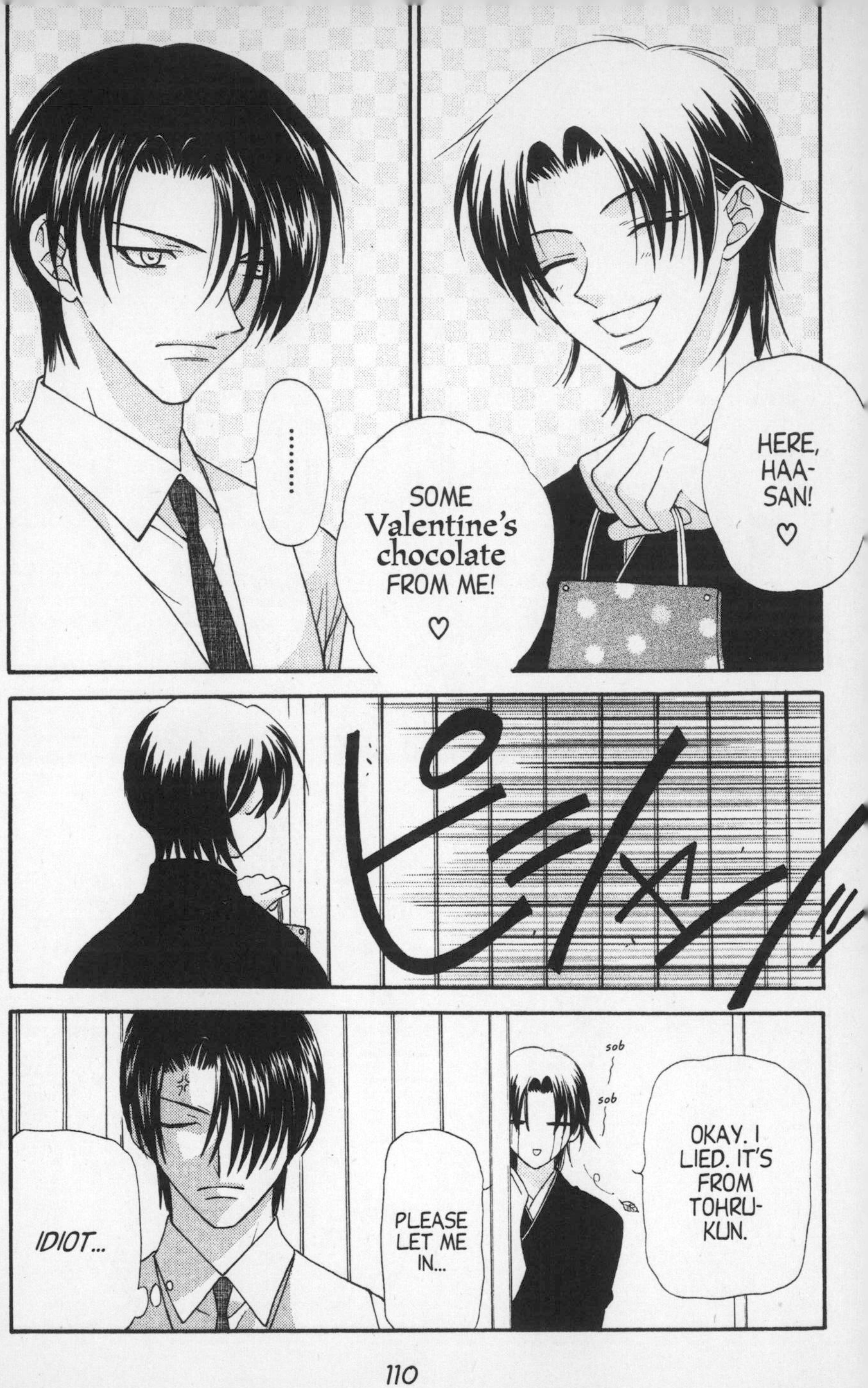
HERE, HAA-SAN! ♡
SOME Valentine's chocolate FROM ME! ♡
....
sob
sob
OKAY. I LIED. IT'S FROM TOHRU-KUN.
PLEASE LET ME IN...
IDIOT...

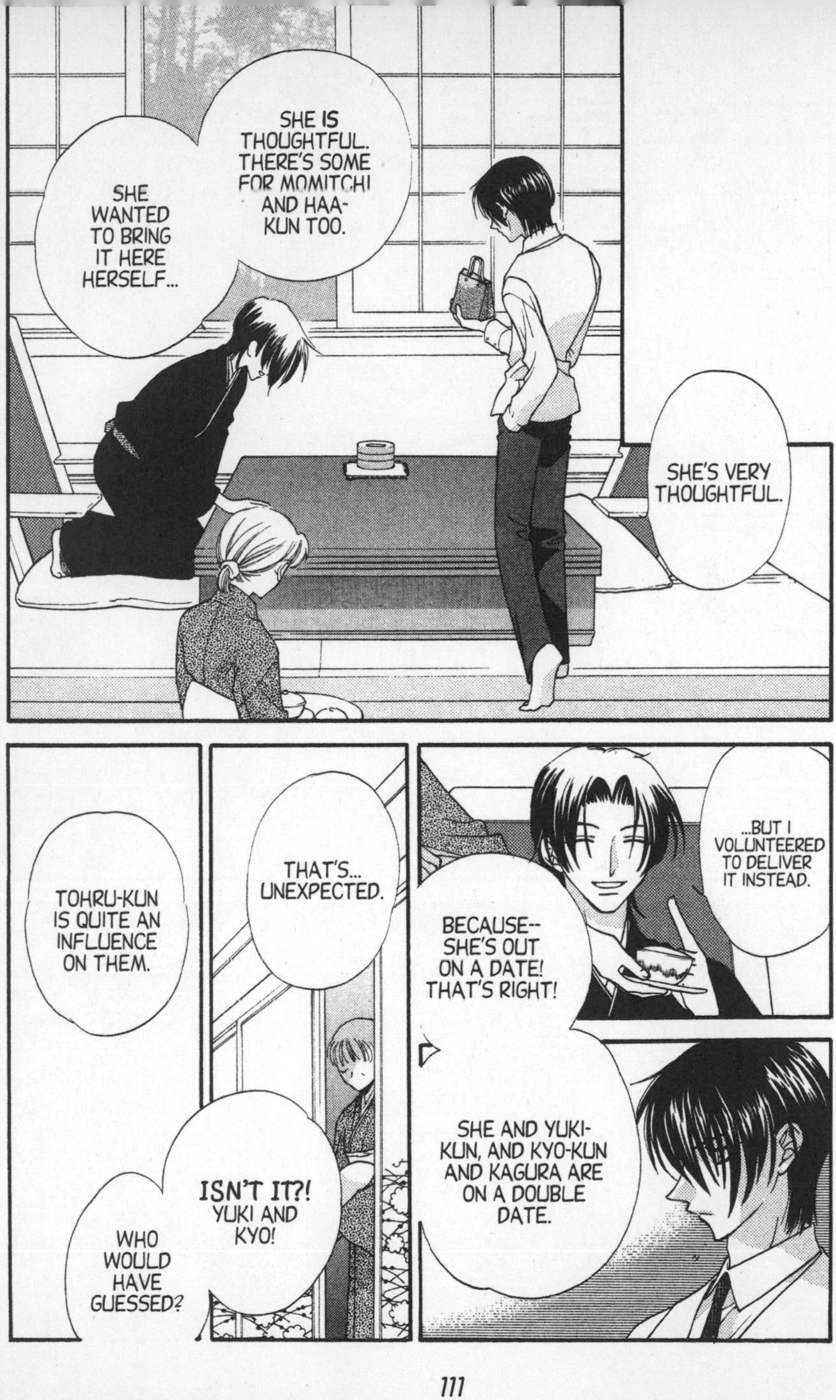
SHE IS THOUGHTFUL. THERE'S SOME FOR MOMITCHI AND HAA-KUN TOO.
SHE'S VERY THOUGHTFUL.
SHE WANTED TO BRING IT HERE HERSELF...
...BUT I VOLUNTEERED TO DELIVER IT INSTEAD.
BECAUSE-- SHE'S OUT ON A DATE! THAT'S RIGHT!
SHE AND YUKI-KUN, AND KYO-KUN AND KAGURA ARE ON A DOUBLE DATE.
THAT'S... UNEXPECTED.
ISN'T IT?! YUKI AND KYO!
WHO WOULD HAVE GUESSED?
TOHRU-KUN IS QUITE AN INFLUENCE ON THEM.

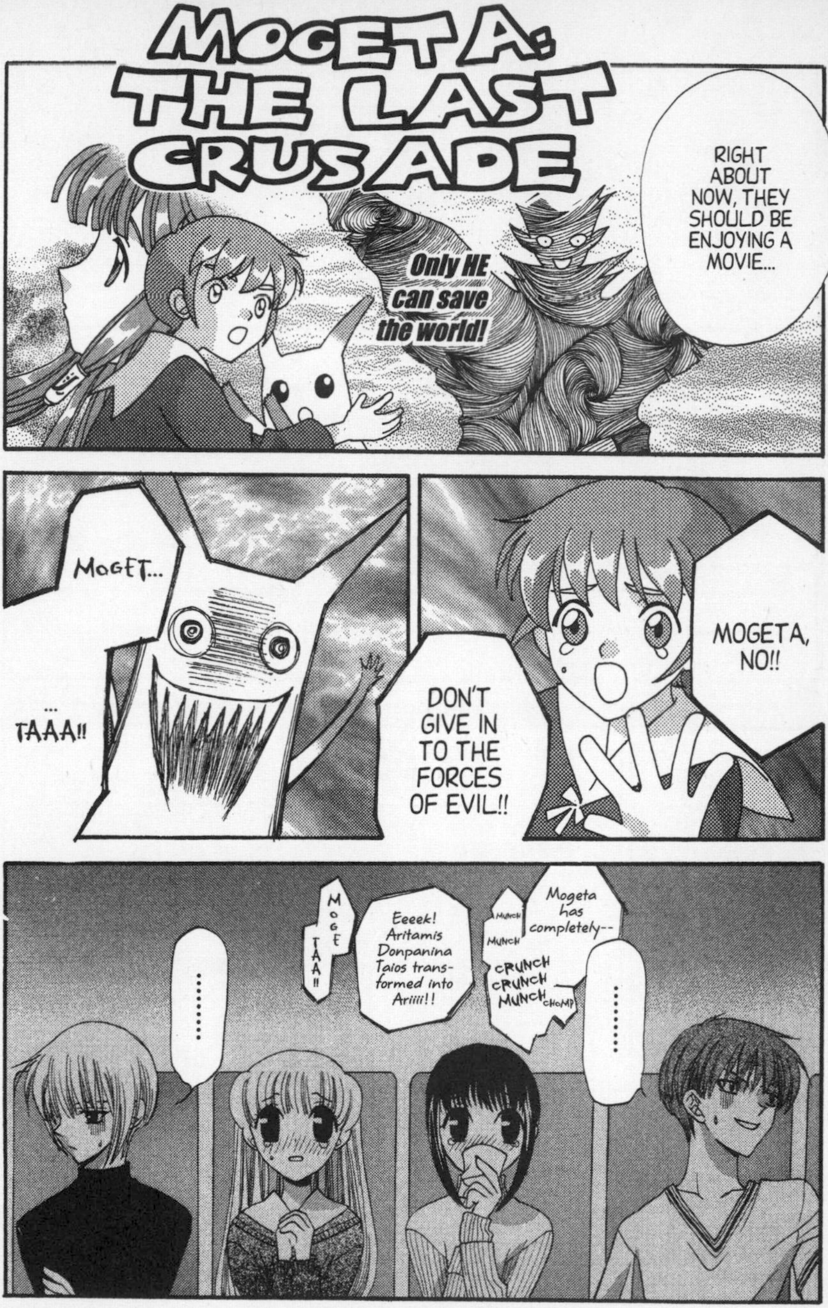
MOGETA: THE LAST CRUSADE
RIGHT ABOUT NOW, THEY SHOULD BE ENJOYING A MOVIE...
Only HE can save the world!
MOGETA, NO!!
DON'T GIVE IN TO THE FORCES OF EVIL!!
MOGET...
...TAAA!!
......
Mogeta has completely--
MUNCH MUNCH CRUNCH CRUNCH MUNCH CHOMP
Eeeek! Aritamis Donpanina Taios transformed into Ariiii!!
MOGE TAA!!
......

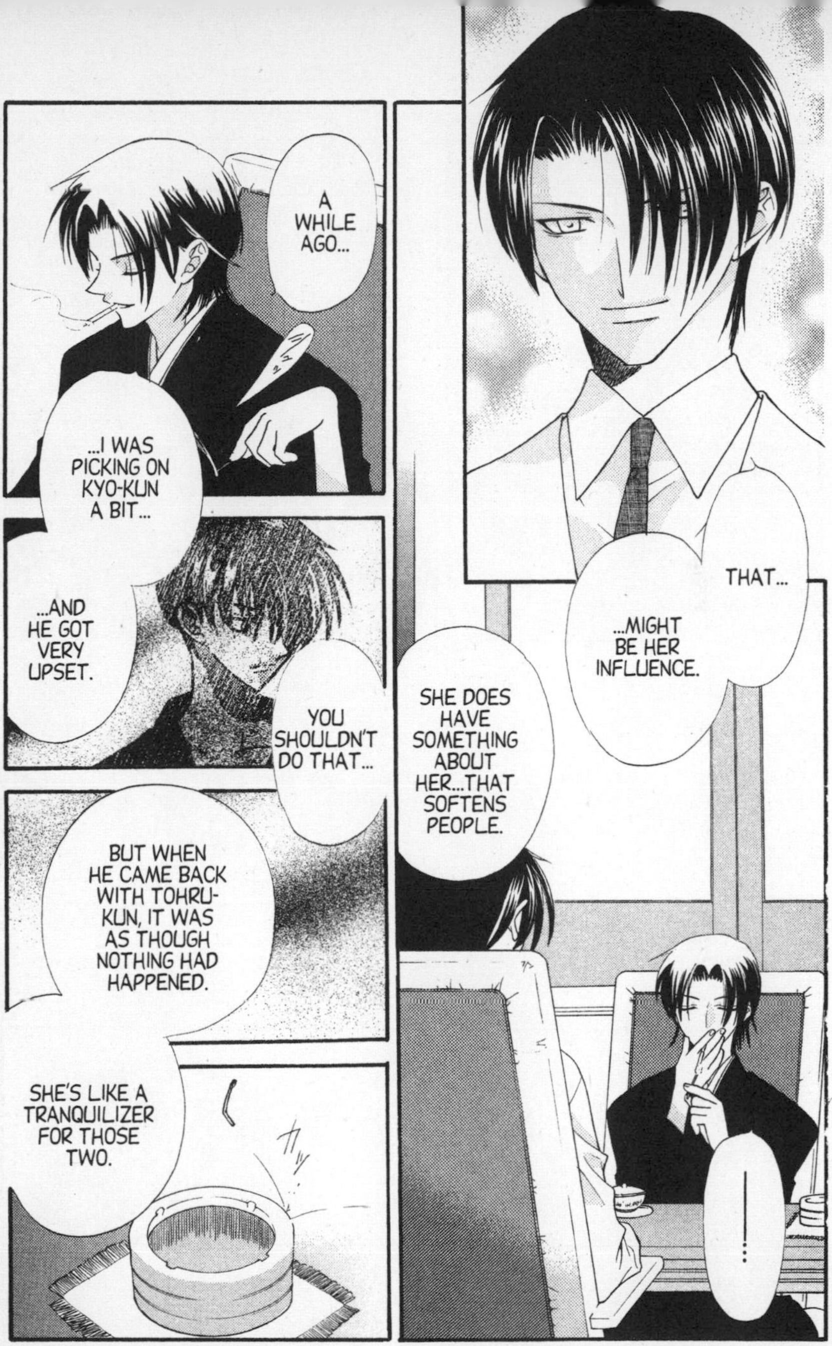
A WHILE AGO...
...I WAS PICKING ON KYO-KUN A BIT...
...AND HE GOT VERY UPSET.
YOU SHOULDN'T DO THAT...
BUT WHEN HE CAME BACK WITH TOHRU-KUN, IT WAS AS THOUGH NOTHING HAD HAPPENED.
SHE'S LIKE A TRANQUILIZER FOR THOSE TWO.
THAT...
...MIGHT BE HER INFLUENCE.
SHE DOES HAVE SOMETHING ABOUT HER...THAT SOFTENS PEOPLE.
......!

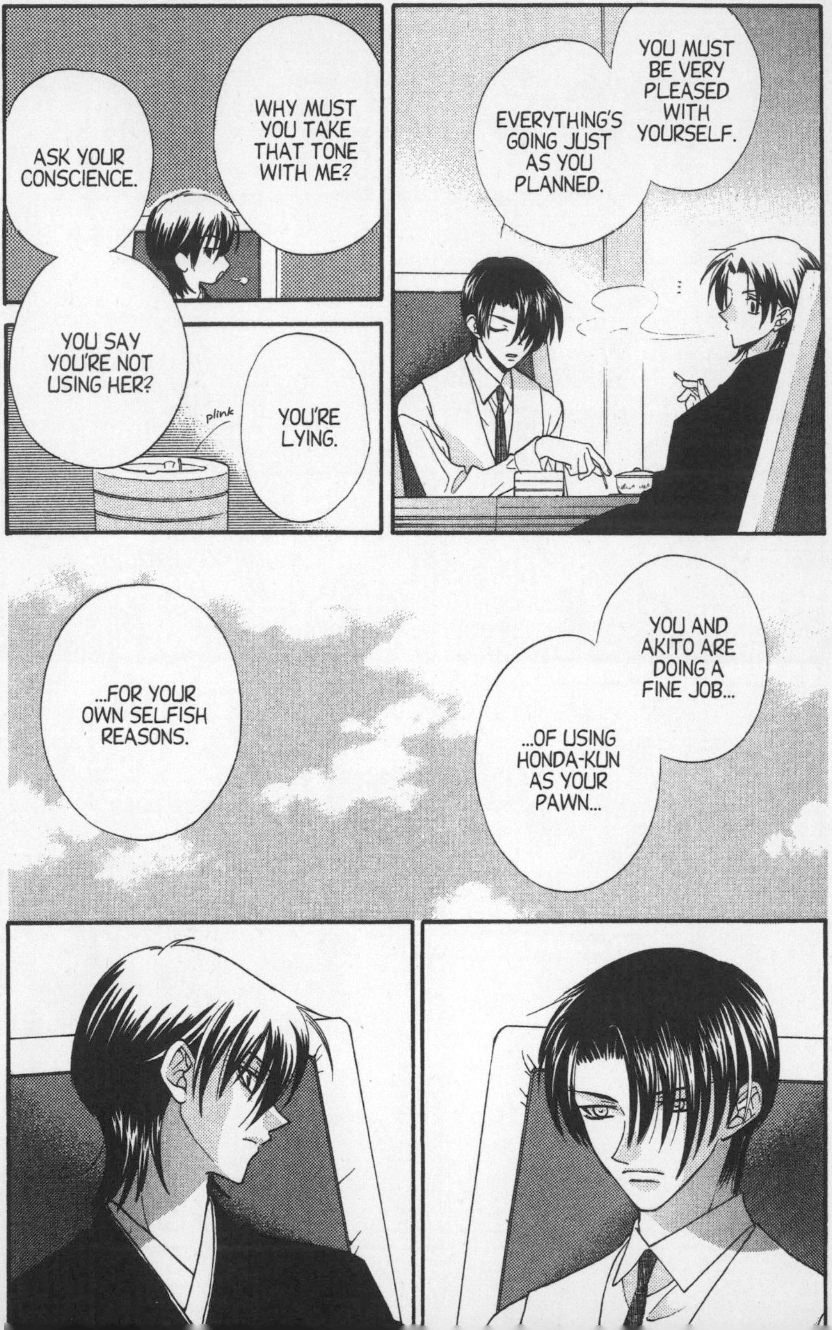
YOU MUST BE VERY PLEASED WITH YOURSELF.
EVERYTHING'S GOING JUST AS YOU PLANNED.
WHY MUST YOU TAKE THAT TONE WITH ME?
ASK YOUR CONSCIENCE.
YOU SAY YOU'RE NOT USING HER?
YOU'RE LYING.
plink
YOU AND AKITO ARE DOING A FINE JOB...
...OF USING HONDA-KUN AS YOUR PAWN...
...FOR YOUR OWN SELFISH REASONS.

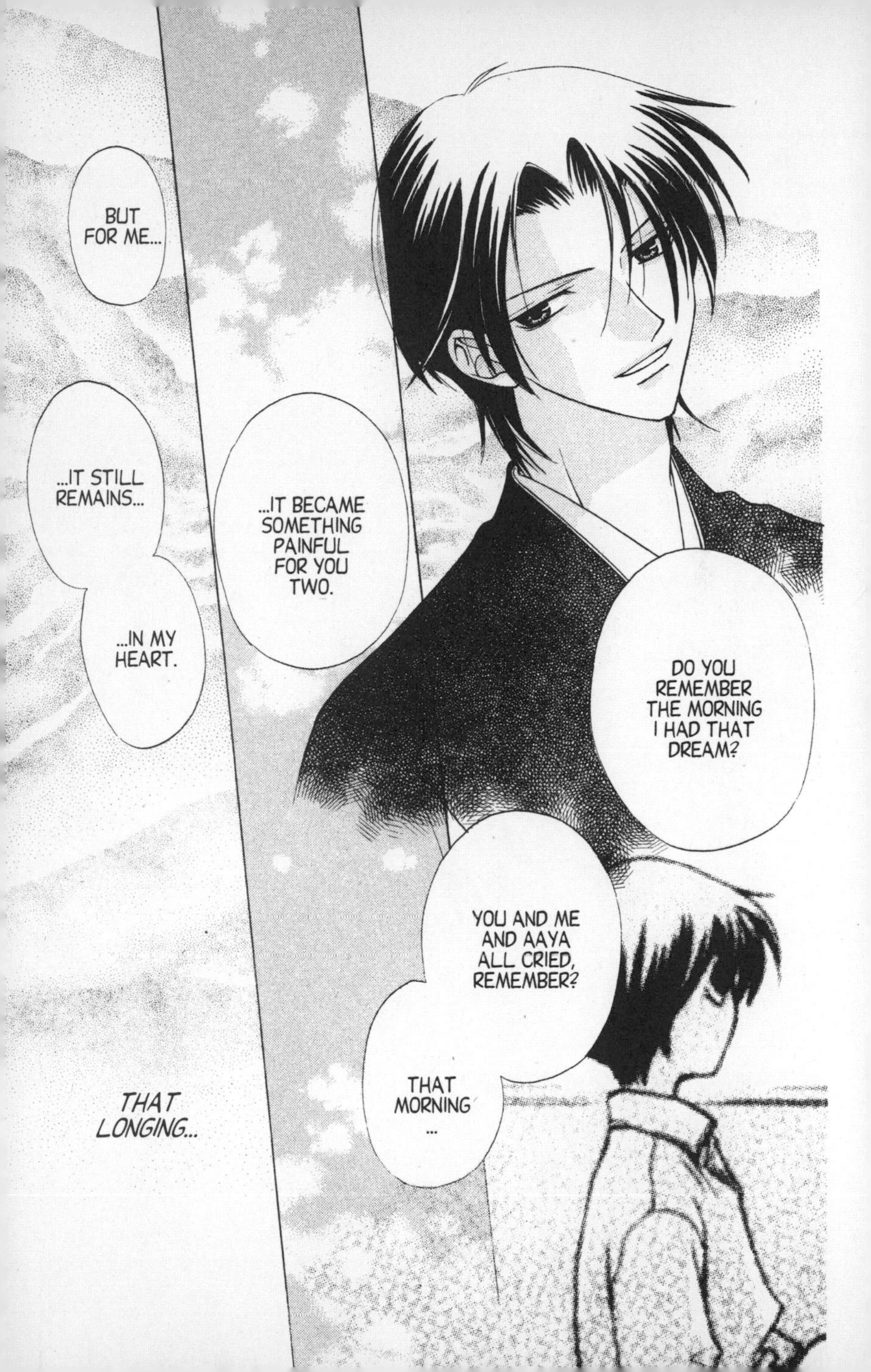
DO YOU REMEMBER THE MORNING I HAD THAT DREAM?
YOU AND ME AND AAYA ALL CRIED, REMEMBER?
THAT MORNING ...
...IT BECAME SOMETHING PAINFUL FOR YOU TWO.
BUT FOR ME...
...IT STILL REMAINS...
...IN MY HEART.
THAT LONGING...

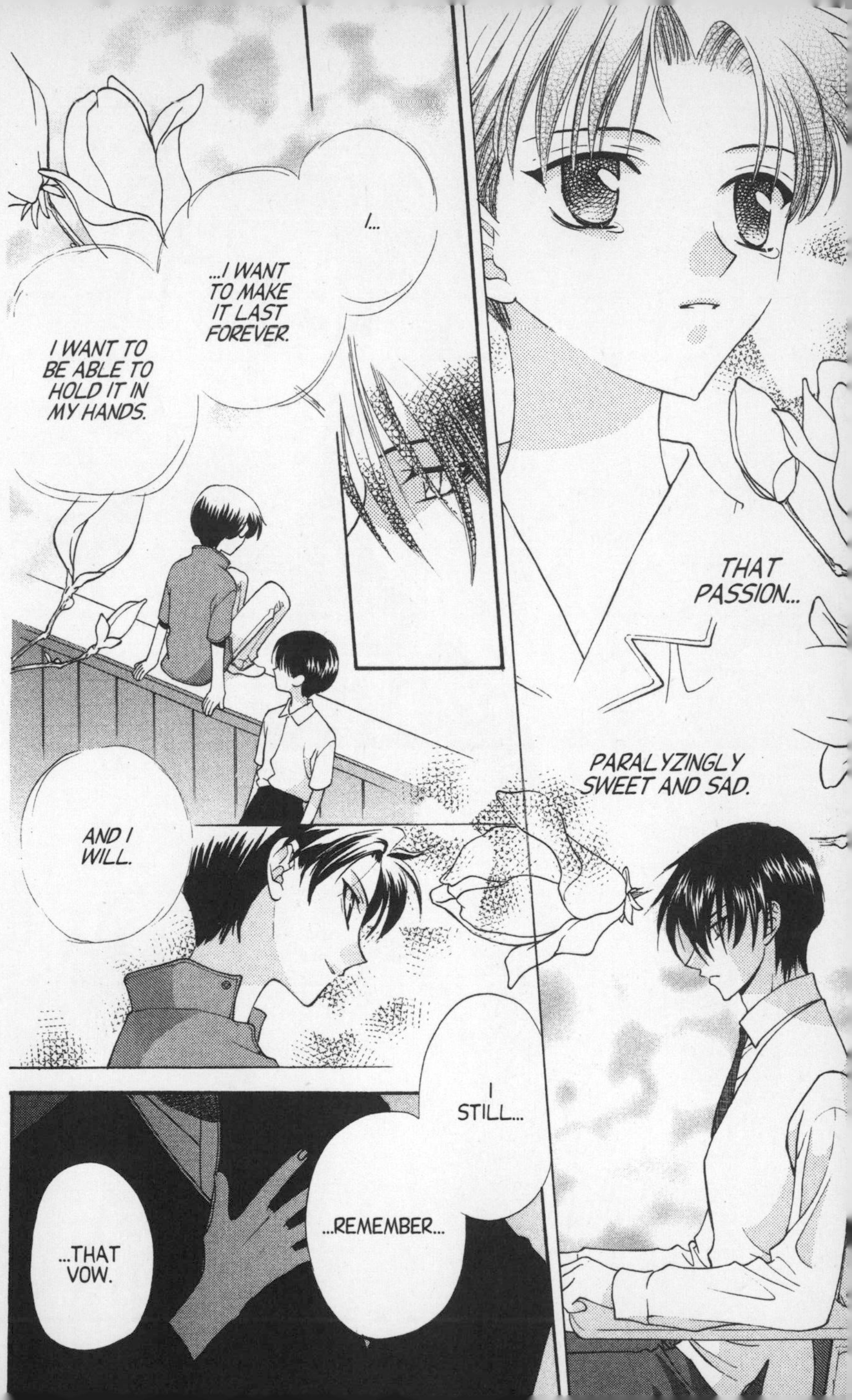
THAT PASSION...
PARALYZINGLY SWEET AND SAD.
I...
...I WANT TO MAKE IT LAST FOREVER.
I WANT TO BE ABLE TO HOLD IT IN MY HANDS.
AND I WILL.
I STILL...
...REMEMBER...
...THAT VOW.

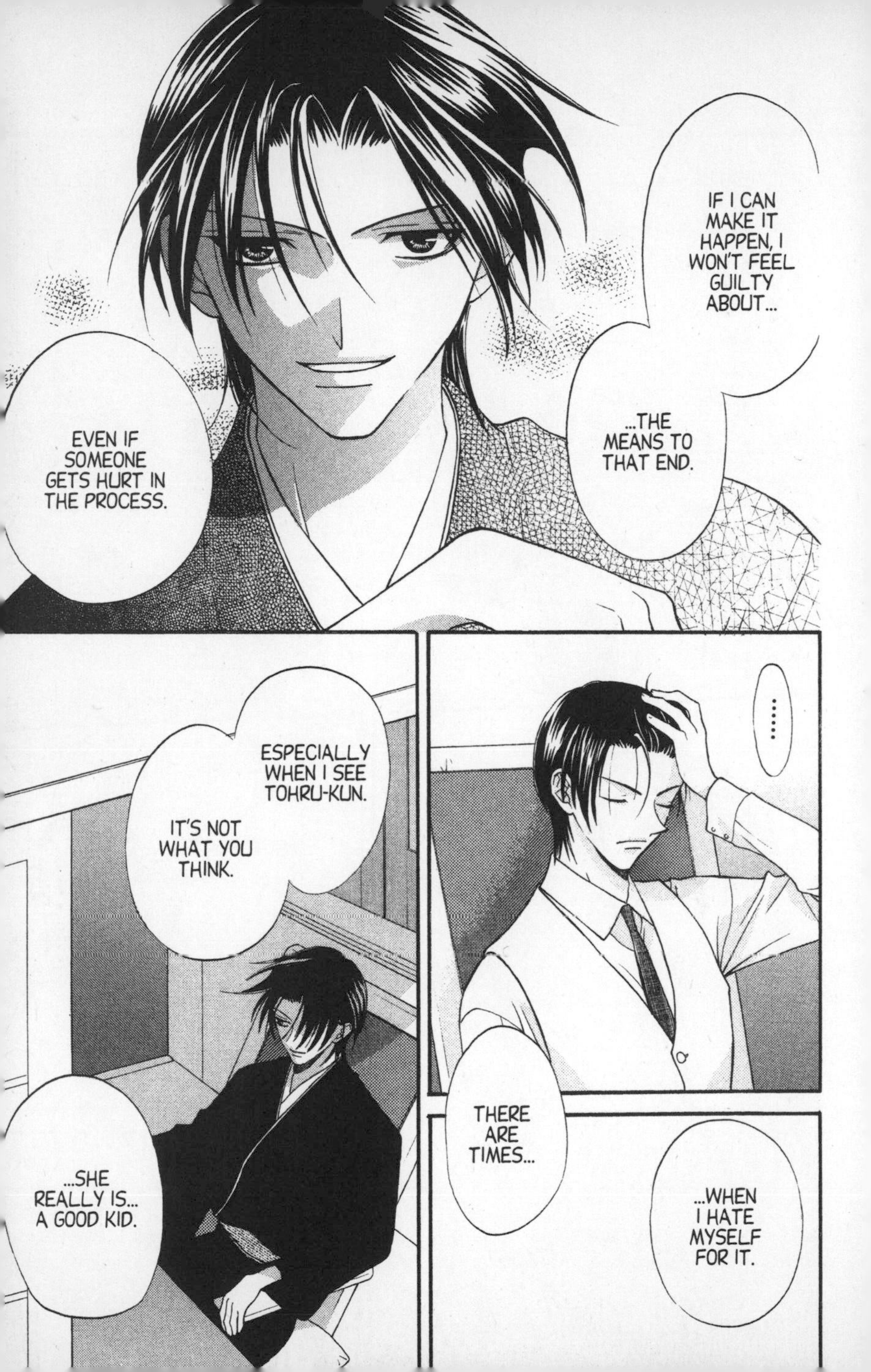
IF I CAN MAKE IT HAPPEN, I WON'T FEEL GUILTY ABOUT...
...THE MEANS TO THAT END.
EVEN IF SOMEONE GETS HURT IN THE PROCESS.
......
THERE ARE TIMES...
...WHEN I HATE MYSELF FOR IT.
ESPECIALLY WHEN I SEE TOHRU-KUN.
IT'S NOT WHAT YOU THINK.
...SHE REALLY IS... A GOOD KID.

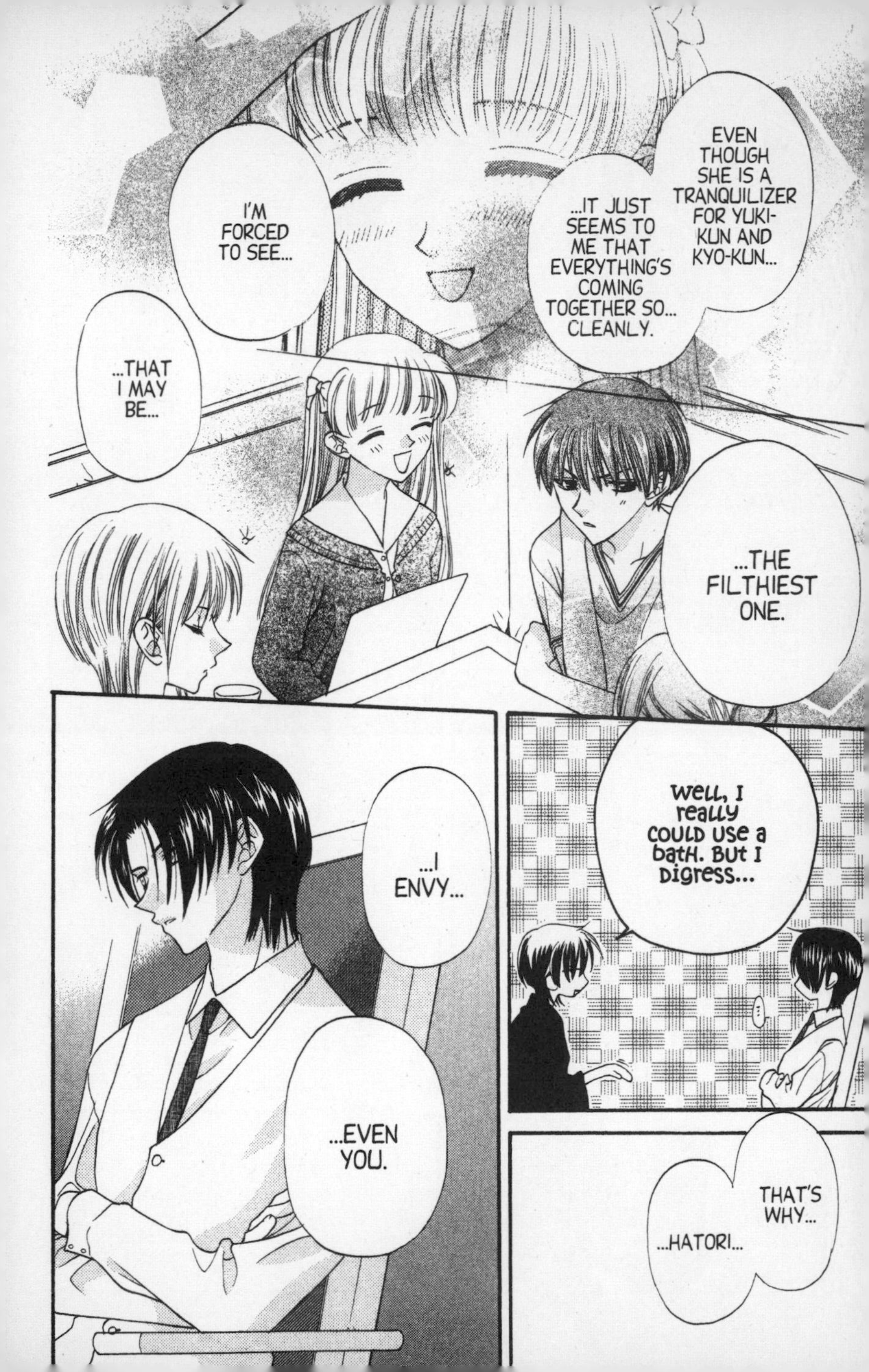
EVEN THOUGH SHE IS A TRANQUILIZER FOR YUKI-KUN AND KYO-KUN...
...IT JUST SEEMS TO ME THAT EVERYTHING'S COMING TOGETHER SO... CLEANLY.
I'M FORCED TO SEE...
...THAT I MAY BE...
...THE FILTHIEST ONE.
Well, I really could use a bath. But I digress...
THAT'S WHY...
...HATORI...
...I ENVY...
...EVEN YOU.

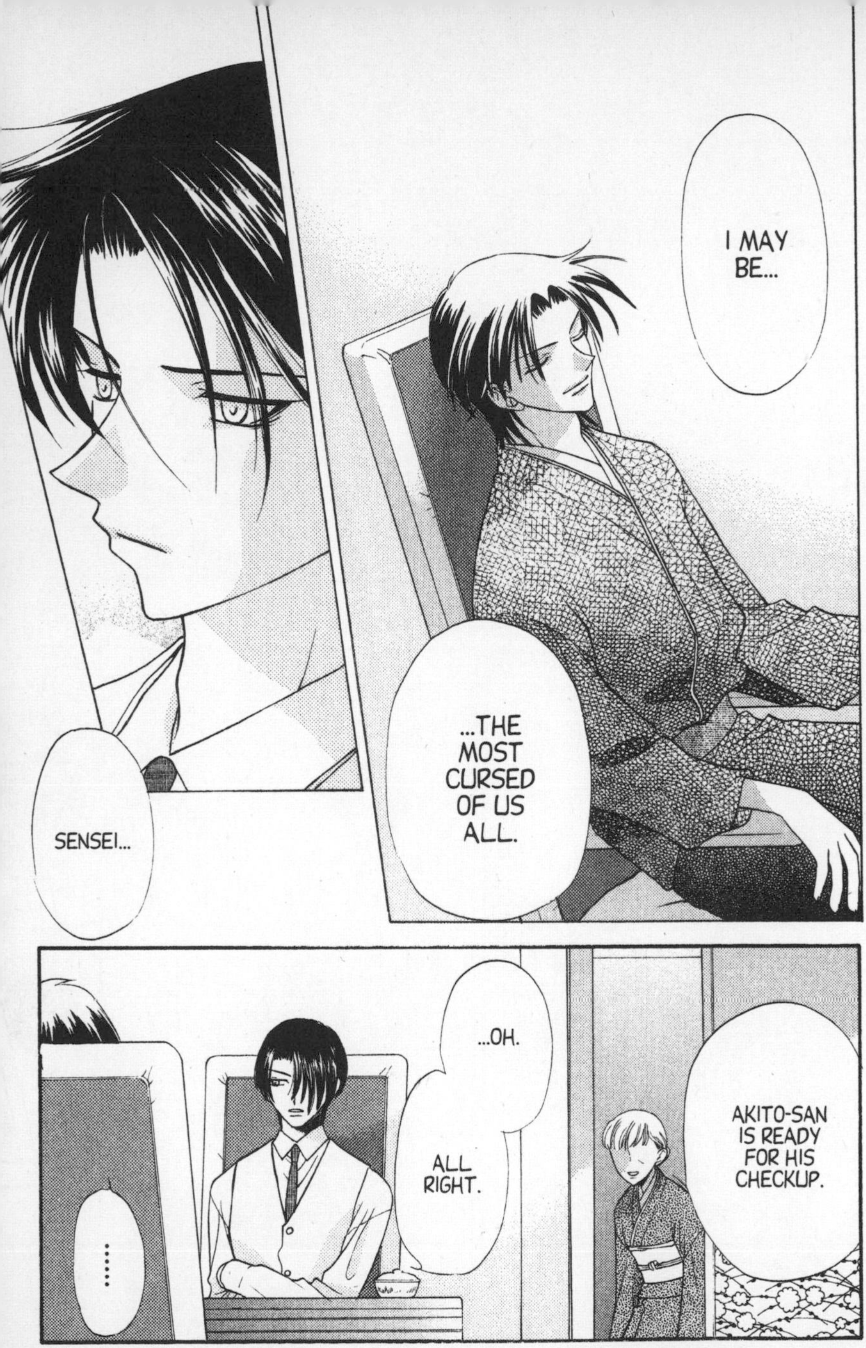
I MAY BE...
...THE MOST CURSED OF US ALL.
SENSEI...
AKITO-SAN IS READY FOR HIS CHECKUP.
...OH.
ALL RIGHT.
......

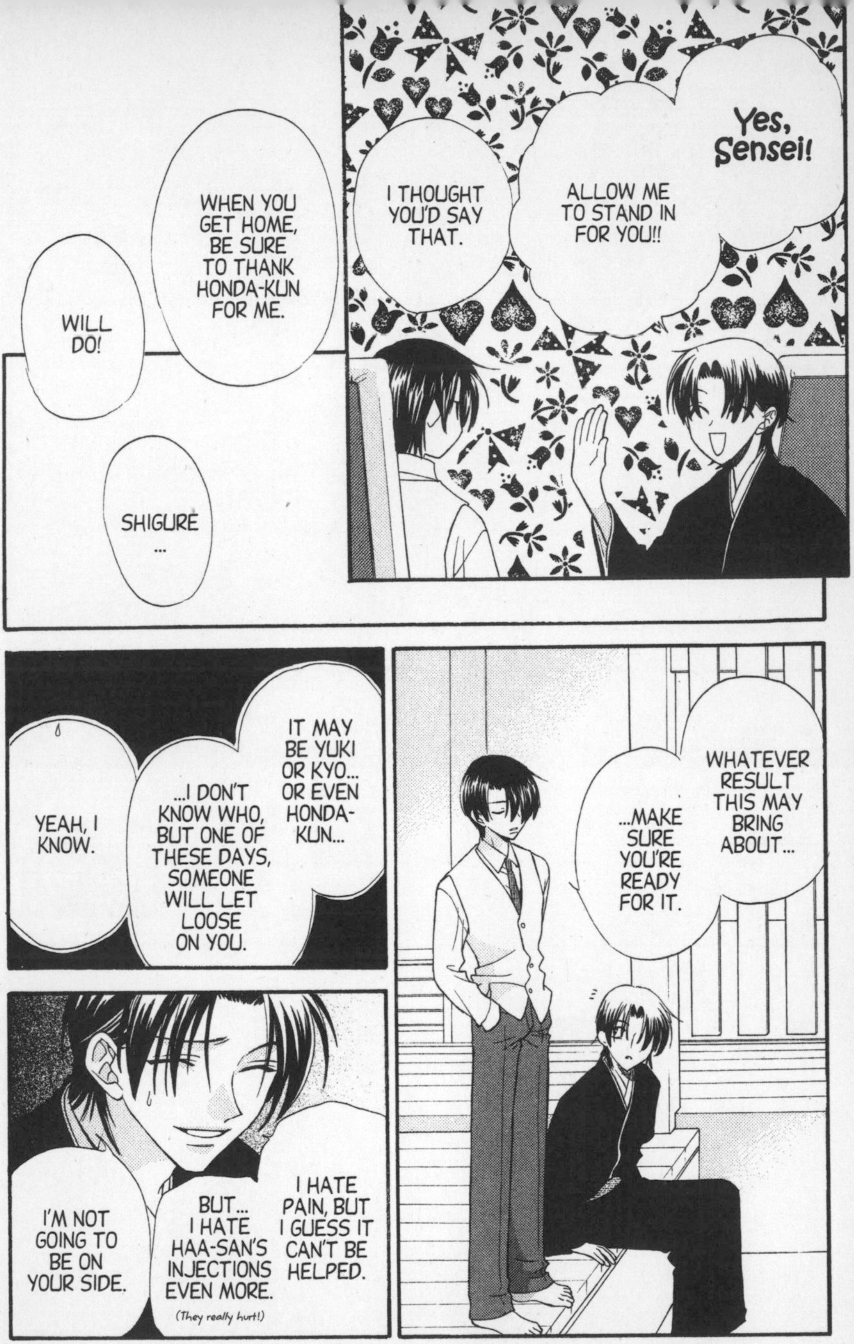
Yes, Sensei!
ALLOW ME TO STAND IN FOR YOU!!
I THOUGHT YOU'D SAY THAT.
WHEN YOU GET HOME, BE SURE TO THANK HONDA-KUN FOR ME.
WILL DO!
SHIGURE ...
WHATEVER RESULT THIS MAY BRING ABOUT...
...MAKE SURE YOU'RE READY FOR IT.
IT MAY BE YUKI OR KYO... OR EVEN HONDA-KUN...
...I DON'T KNOW WHO, BUT ONE OF THESE DAYS, SOMEONE WILL LET LOOSE ON YOU.
YEAH, I KNOW.
I HATE PAIN, BUT I GUESS IT CAN'T BE HELPED.
BUT... I HATE HAA-SAN'S INJECTIONS EVEN MORE.
(They really hurt!)
I'M NOT GOING TO BE ON YOUR SIDE.

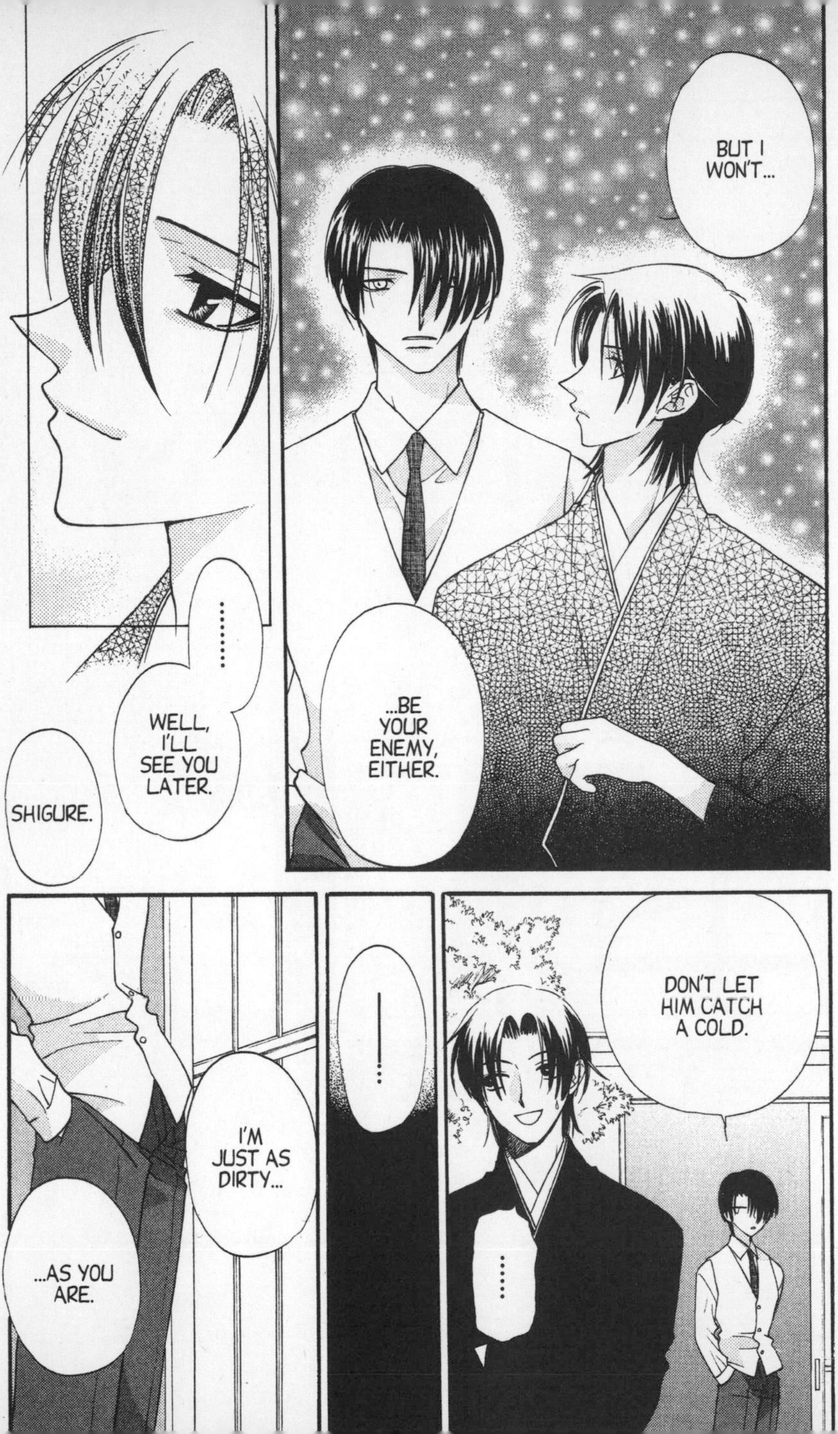
BUT I WON'T...
...BE YOUR ENEMY, EITHER.
......
WELL, I'LL SEE YOU LATER.
SHIGURE.
DON'T LET HIM CATCH A COLD.
......
......!
I'M JUST AS DIRTY...
...AS YOU ARE.

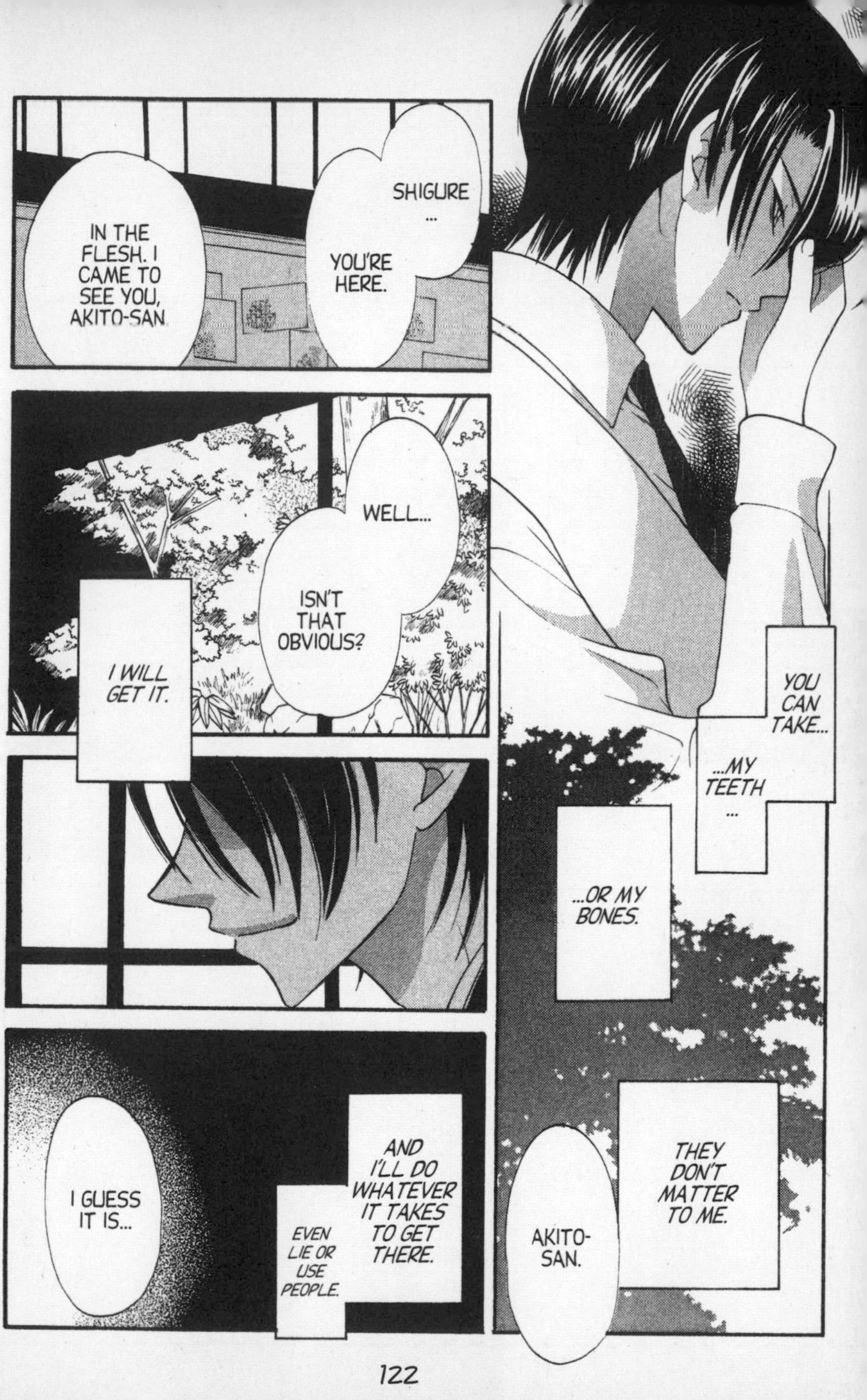
SHIGURE ...
YOU'RE HERE.
IN THE FLESH. I CAME TO SEE YOU, AKITO-SAN.
WELL...
ISN'T THAT OBVIOUS?
I WILL GET IT.
I GUESS IT IS...
AND I'LL DO WHATEVER IT TAKES TO GET THERE.
EVEN LIE OR USE PEOPLE.
YOU CAN TAKE...
...MY TEETH ...
...OR MY BONES.
THEY DON'T MATTER TO ME.
AKITO-SAN.

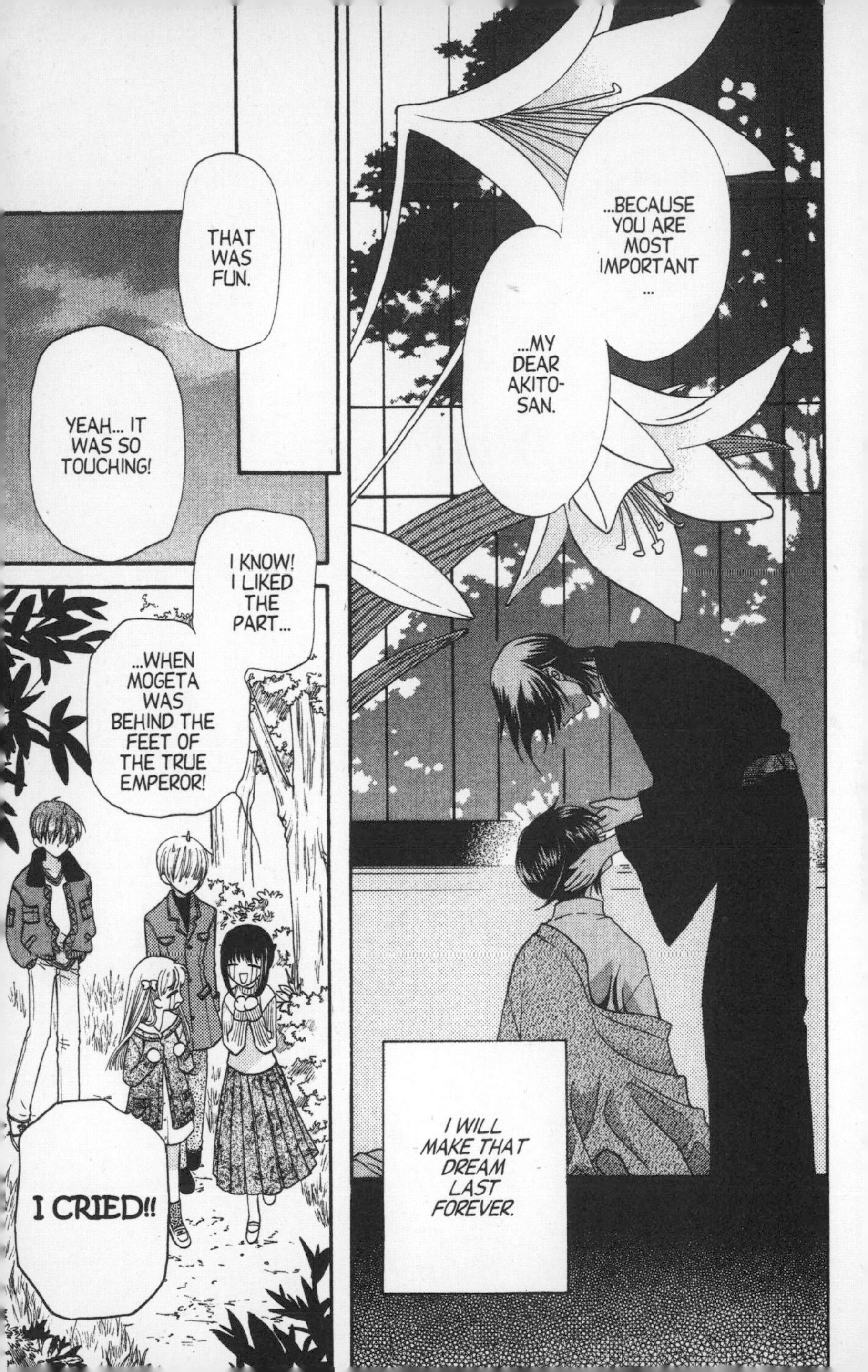
...BECAUSE YOU ARE MOST IMPORTANT ...
...MY DEAR AKITO-SAN.
I WILL MAKE THAT DREAM LAST FOREVER.
THAT WAS FUN.
YEAH... IT WAS SO TOUCHING!
I KNOW! I LIKED THE PART...
...WHEN MOGETA WAS BEHIND THE FEET OF THE TRUE EMPEROR!
I CRIED!!

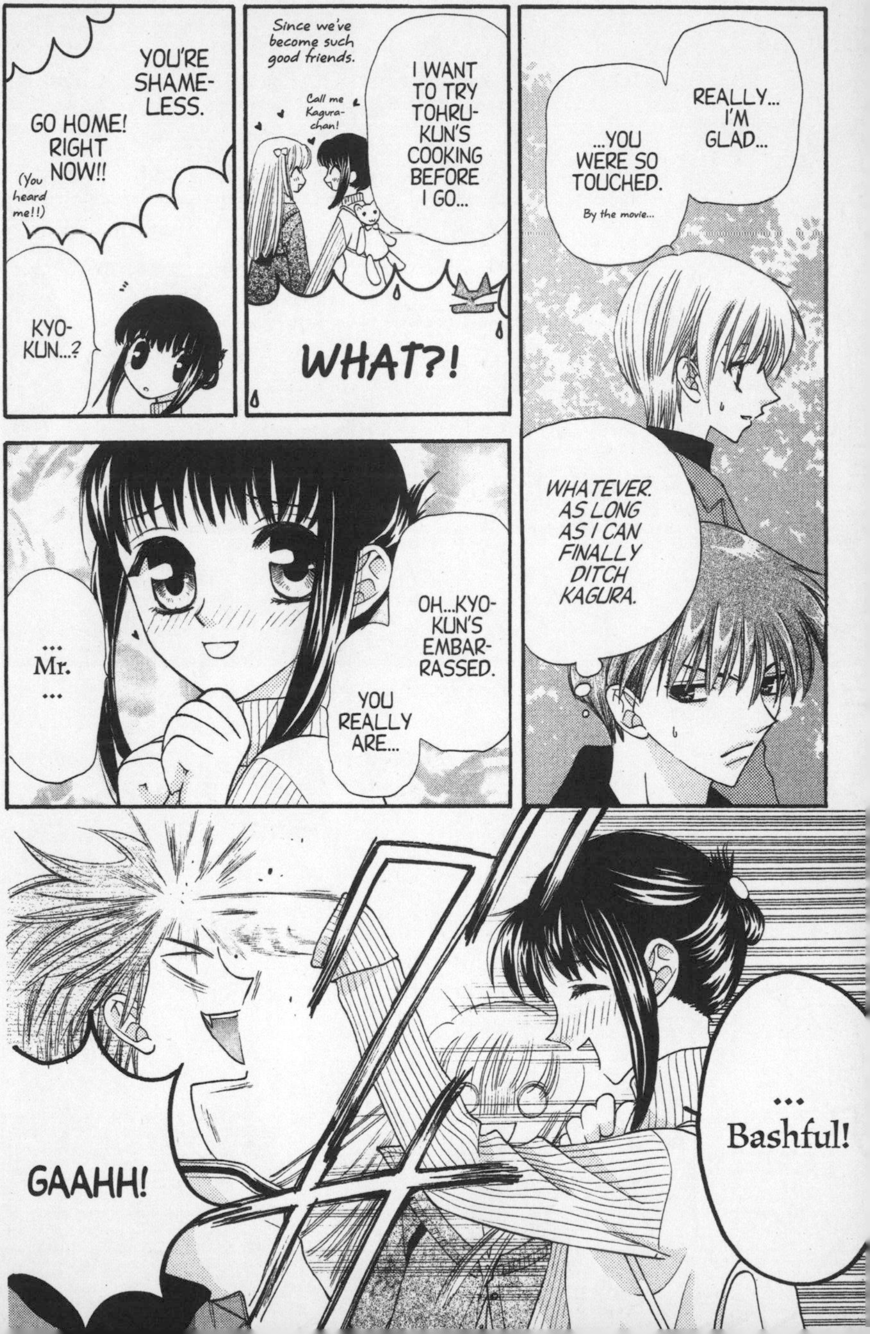

REALLY... I'M GLAD...
...YOU WERE SO TOUCHED.
By the movie...
WHATEVER. AS LONG AS I CAN FINALLY DITCH KAGURA.
I WANT TO TRY TOHRU-KUN'S COOKING BEFORE I GO...
Since we've become such good friends.
Call me Kagura-chan!
WHAT?!
YOU'RE SHAMELESS.
GO HOME! RIGHT NOW!!
(You heard me!!)
KYO-KUN...?
OH...KYO-KUN'S EMBARRASSED.
YOU REALLY ARE...
...Mr. ...
...Bashful!
GAAHH!

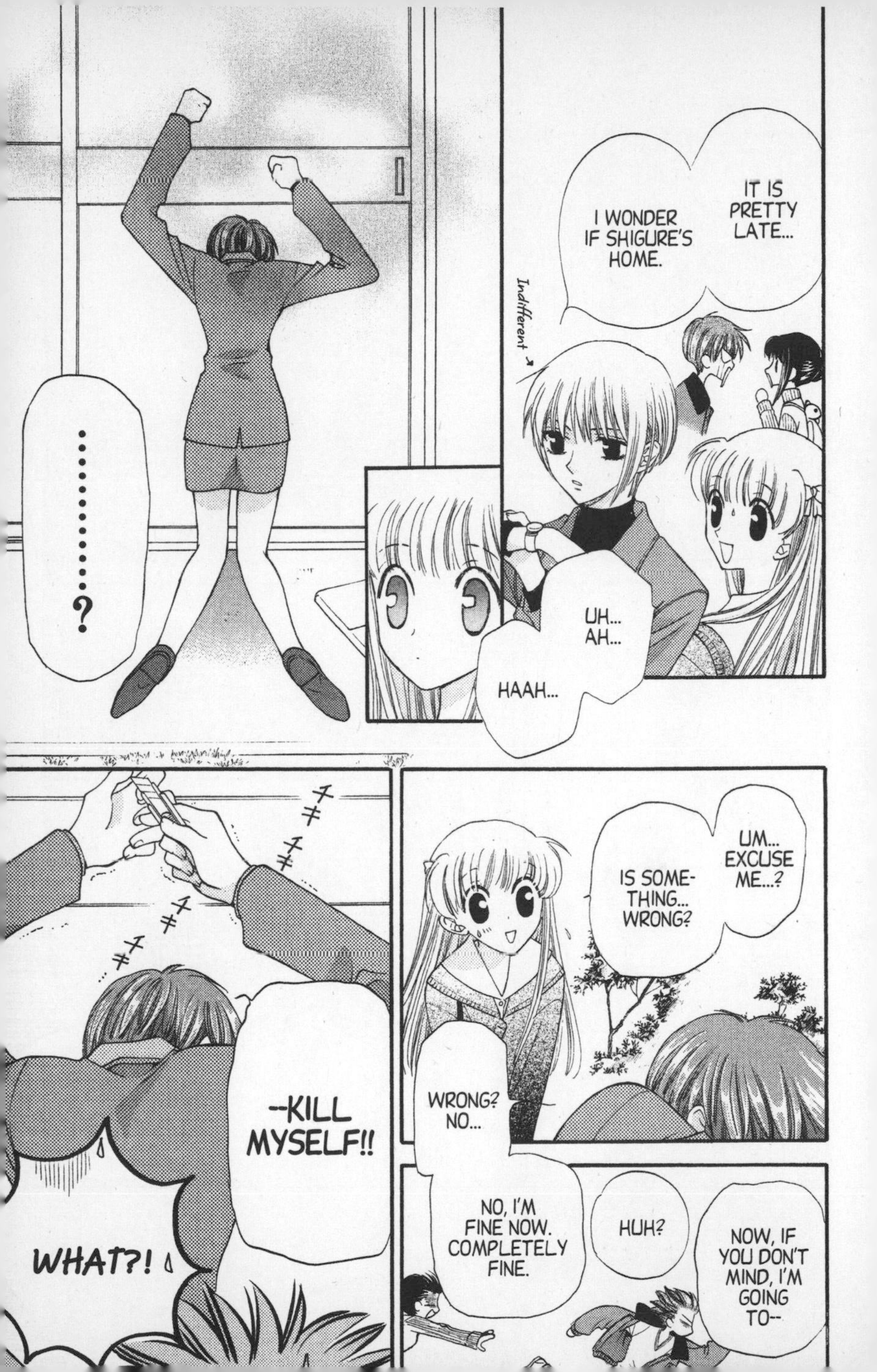
IT IS PRETTY LATE...
I WONDER IF SHIGURE'S HOME.
Indifferent
UH... AH...
HAAH...
..........?
UM... EXCUSE ME...?
IS SOME-THING... WRONG?
WRONG? NO...
NOW, IF YOU DON'T MIND, I'M GOING TO--
HUH?
NO, I'M FINE NOW. COMPLETELY FINE.
チキ チキ チキ チキ
--KILL MYSELF!!
WHAT?!

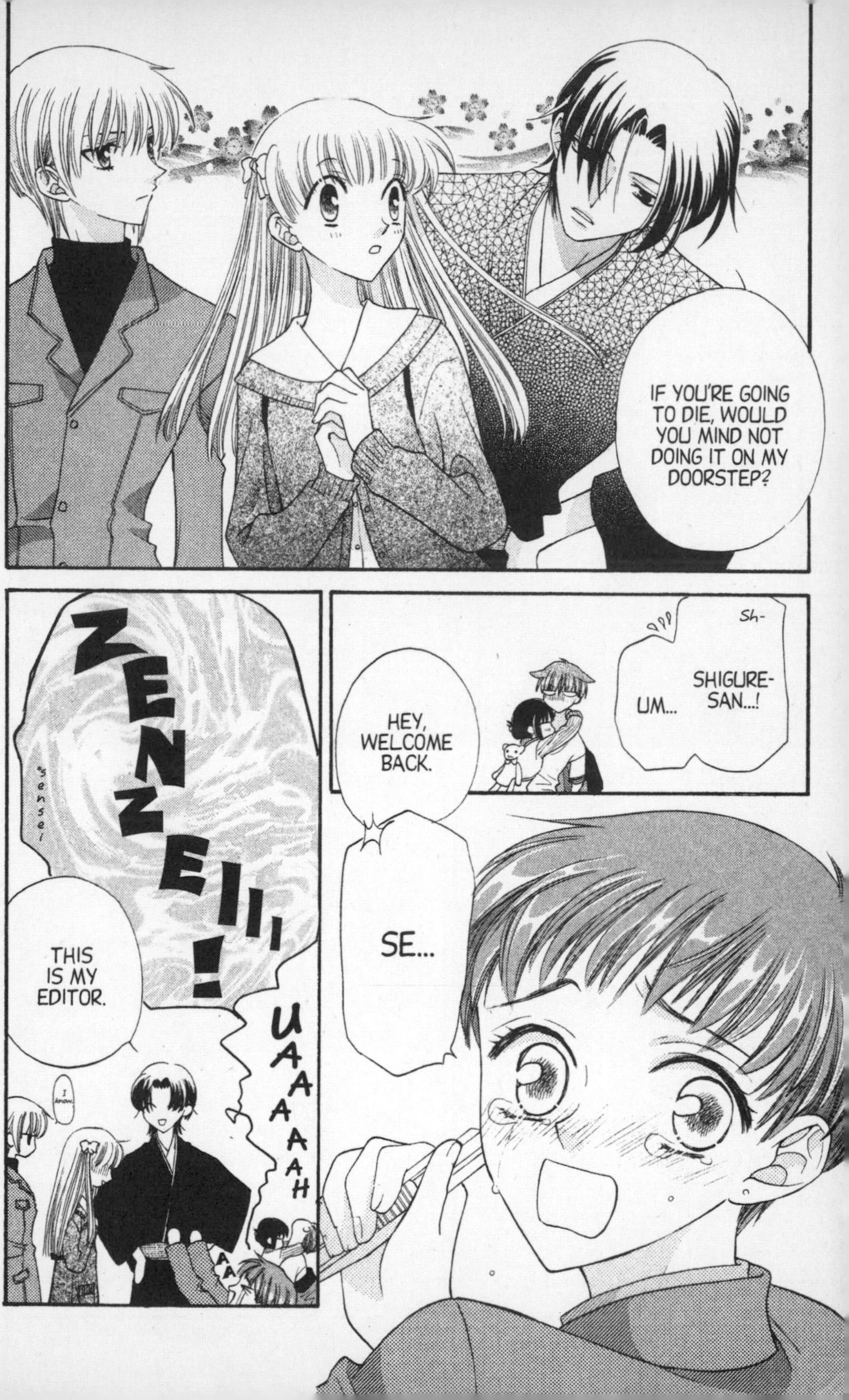
IF YOU'RE GOING TO DIE, WOULD YOU MIND NOT DOING IT ON MY DOORSTEP?
Sh-
SHIGURE-SAN...!
UM...
HEY, WELCOME BACK.
SE...
ZENZEI!!!
*sensei
UAAAAAAAH
THIS IS MY EDITOR.
I know.

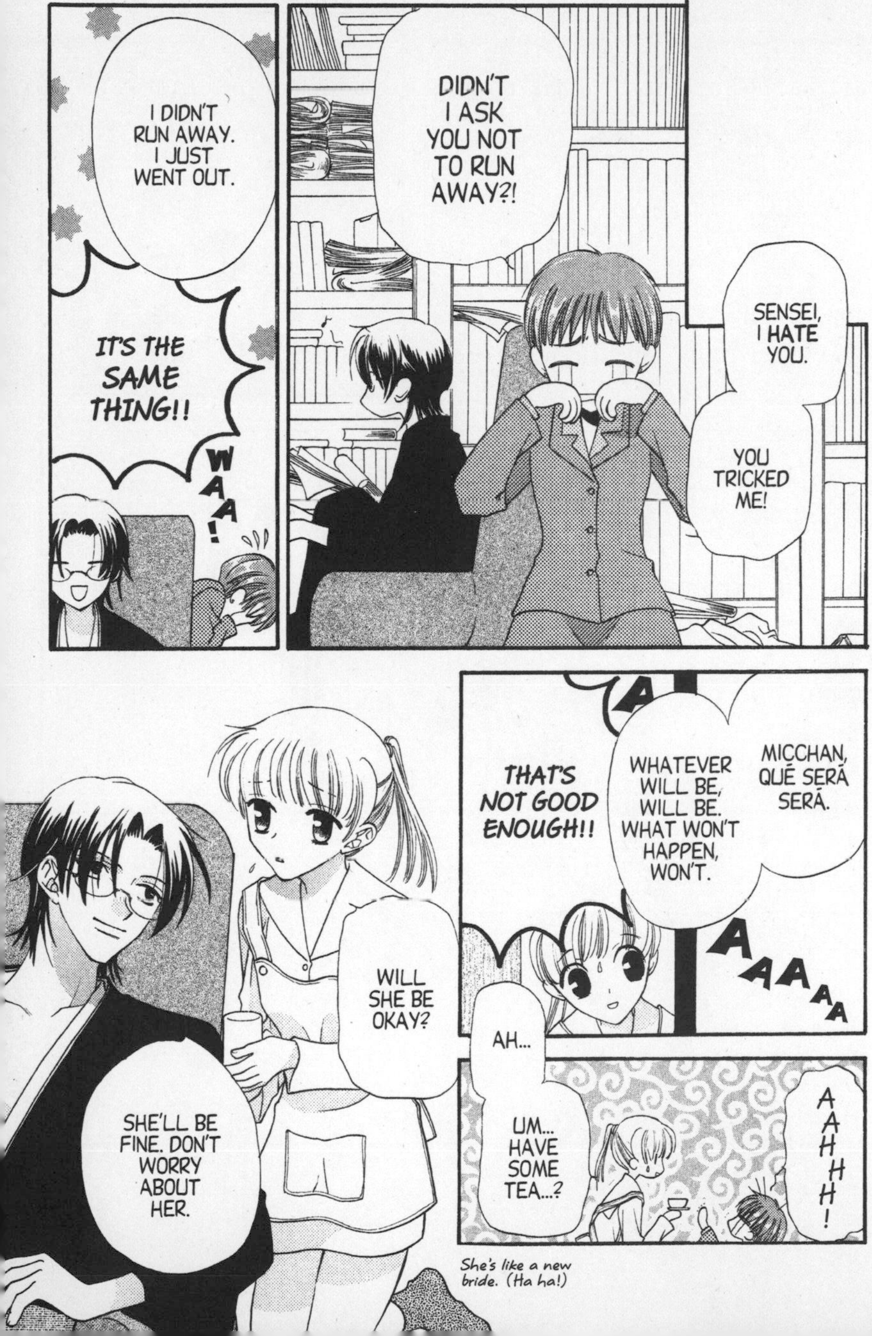
SENSEI, I HATE YOU.
YOU TRICKED ME!
DIDN'T I ASK YOU NOT TO RUN AWAY?!
I DIDN'T RUN AWAY. I JUST WENT OUT.
IT'S THE SAME THING!!
WAAA!
MICCHAN, QUÉ SERÁ SERÁ.
WHATEVER WILL BE, WILL BE. WHAT WON'T HAPPEN, WON'T.
THAT'S NOT GOOD ENOUGH!!
AAAAAA
AAHHH!
UM... HAVE SOME TEA...?
AH...
WILL SHE BE OKAY?
SHE'LL BE FINE. DON'T WORRY ABOUT HER.
She's like a new bride. (Ha ha!)

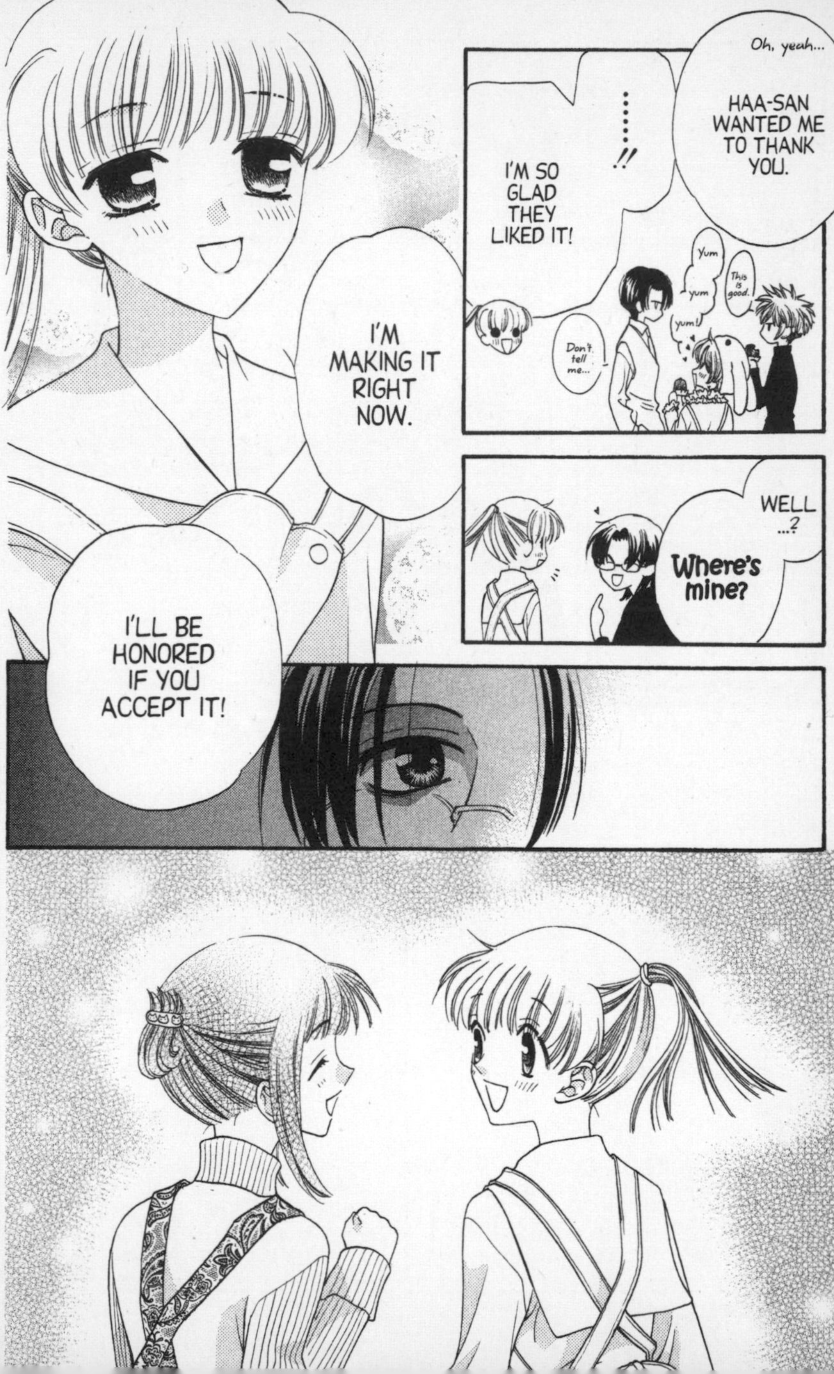
Oh, yeah...
HAA-SAN WANTED ME TO THANK YOU.
......!!
I'M SO GLAD THEY LIKED IT!
This is good.
Yum
yum
yum!
Don't tell me...
WELL ...?
Where's mine?
I'M MAKING IT RIGHT NOW.
I'LL BE HONORED IF YOU ACCEPT IT!

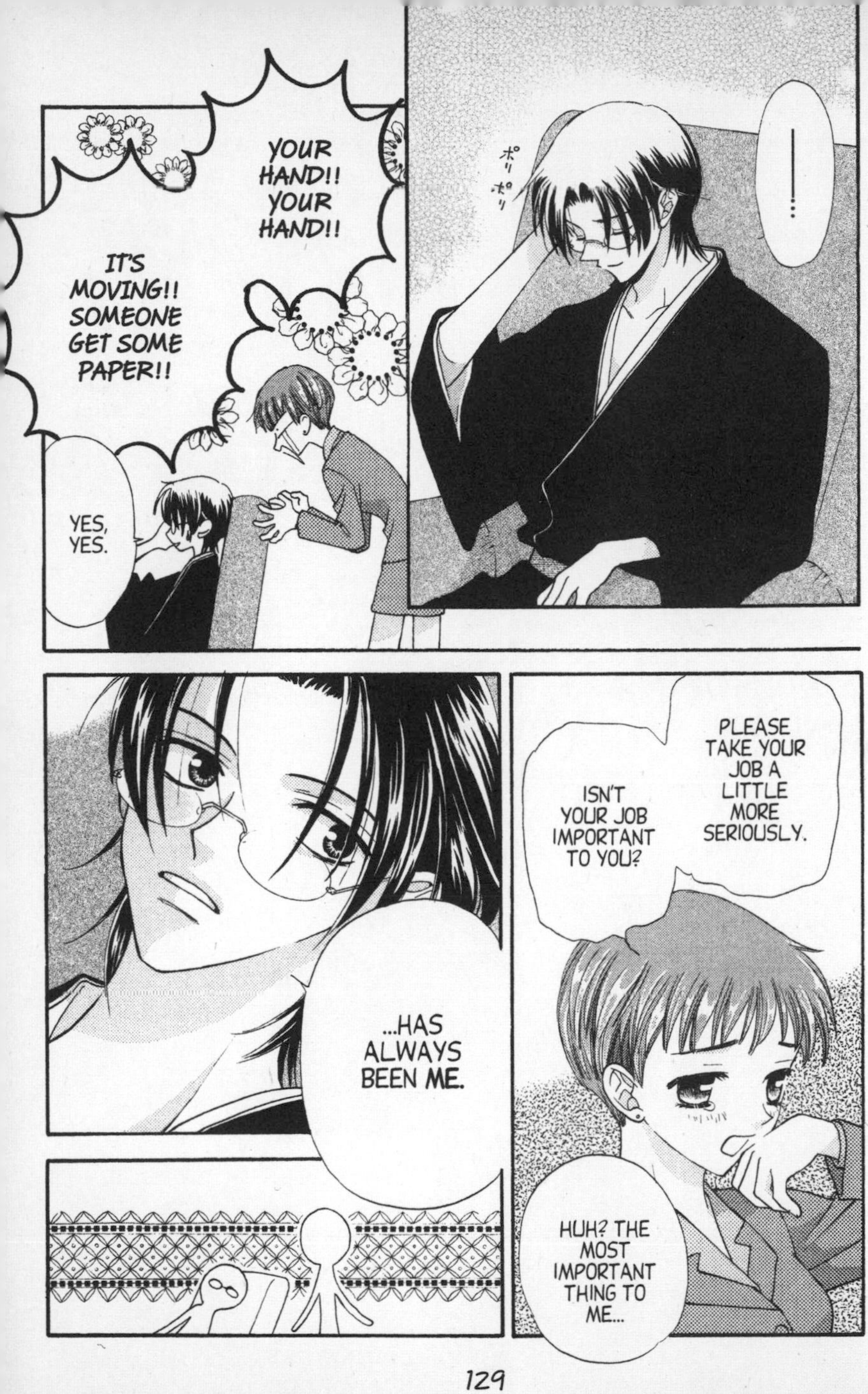
...!
ポリポリ
YOUR HAND!! YOUR HAND!!
IT'S MOVING!! SOMEONE GET SOME PAPER!!
YES, YES.
PLEASE TAKE YOUR JOB A LITTLE MORE SERIOUSLY.
ISN'T YOUR JOB IMPORTANT TO YOU?
HUH? THE MOST IMPORTANT THING TO ME...
...HAS ALWAYS BEEN ME.

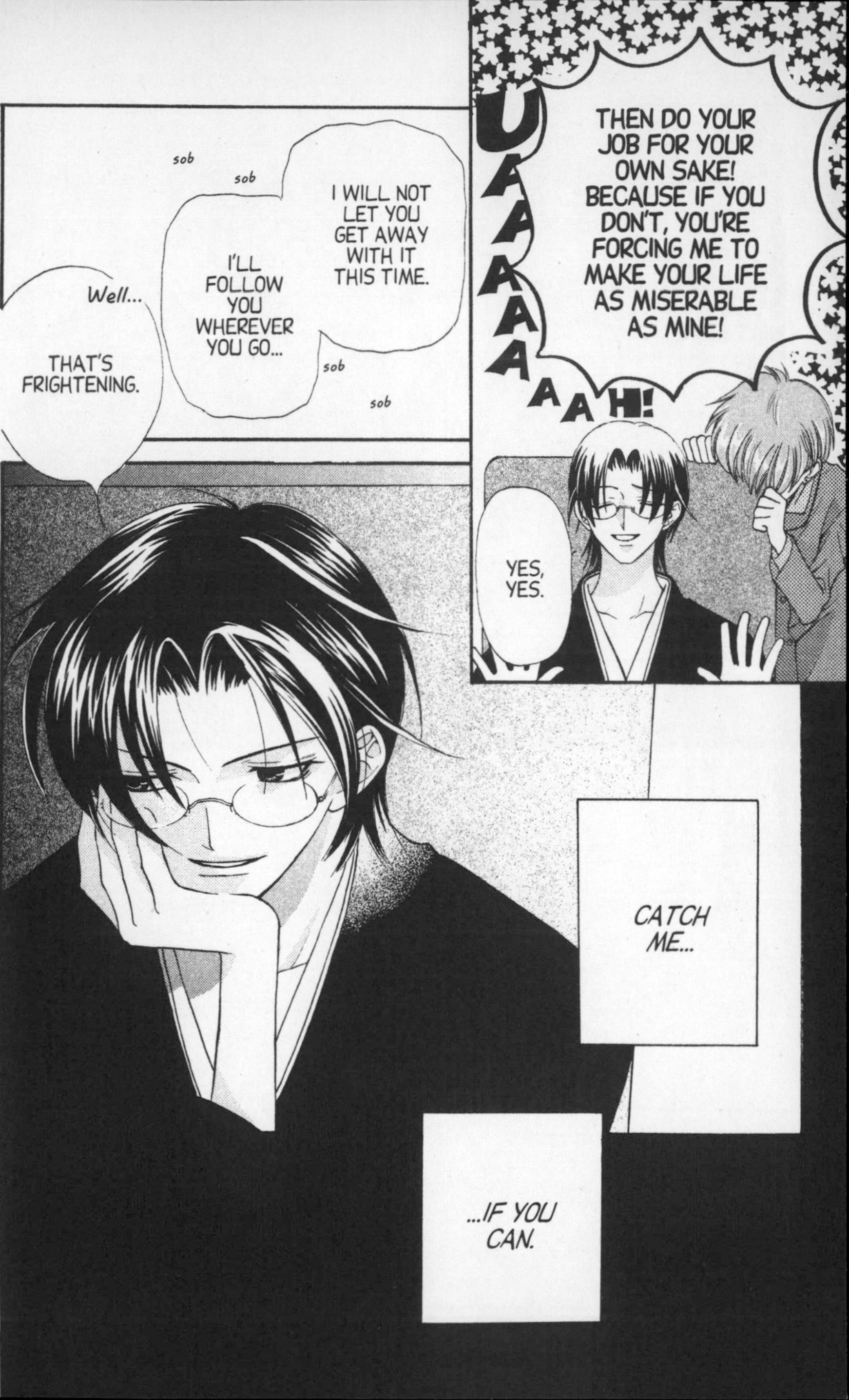
THEN DO YOUR JOB FOR YOUR OWN SAKE! BECAUSE IF YOU DON'T, YOU'RE FORCING ME TO MAKE YOUR LIFE AS MISERABLE AS MINE!
UAAAAAAAAH!
YES, YES.
I WILL NOT LET YOU GET AWAY WITH IT THIS TIME.
I'LL FOLLOW YOU WHEREVER YOU GO...
sob
sob
sob
sob
Well...
THAT'S FRIGHTENING.
CATCH ME...
...IF YOU CAN.

Chapter 17

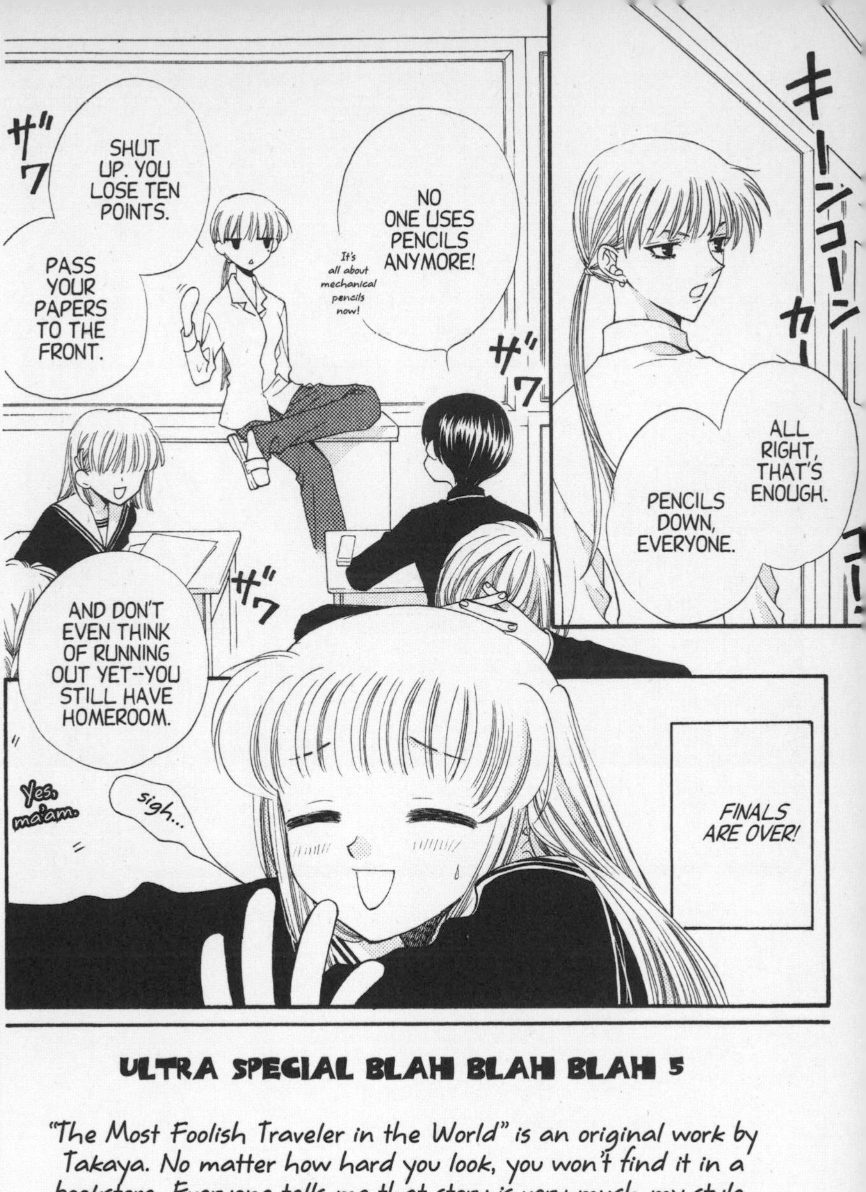
ALL RIGHT, THAT'S ENOUGH.
PENCILS DOWN, EVERYONE.
NO ONE USES PENCILS ANYMORE!
It's all about mechanical pencils now!
ザワ
SHUT UP. YOU LOSE TEN POINTS.
PASS YOUR PAPERS TO THE FRONT.
ザワ
AND DON'T EVEN THINK OF RUNNING OUT YET--YOU STILL HAVE HOMEROOM.
ザワ
FINALS ARE OVER!
sigh...
Yes, ma'am.

ULTRA SPECIAL BLAH BLAH BLAH 5

"The Most Foolish Traveler in the World" is an original work by Takaya. No matter how hard you look, you won't find it in a bookstore. Everyone tells me that story is very much my style. Rather than try to elicit a cheap cry, I really wanted to make readers face their own emotions.

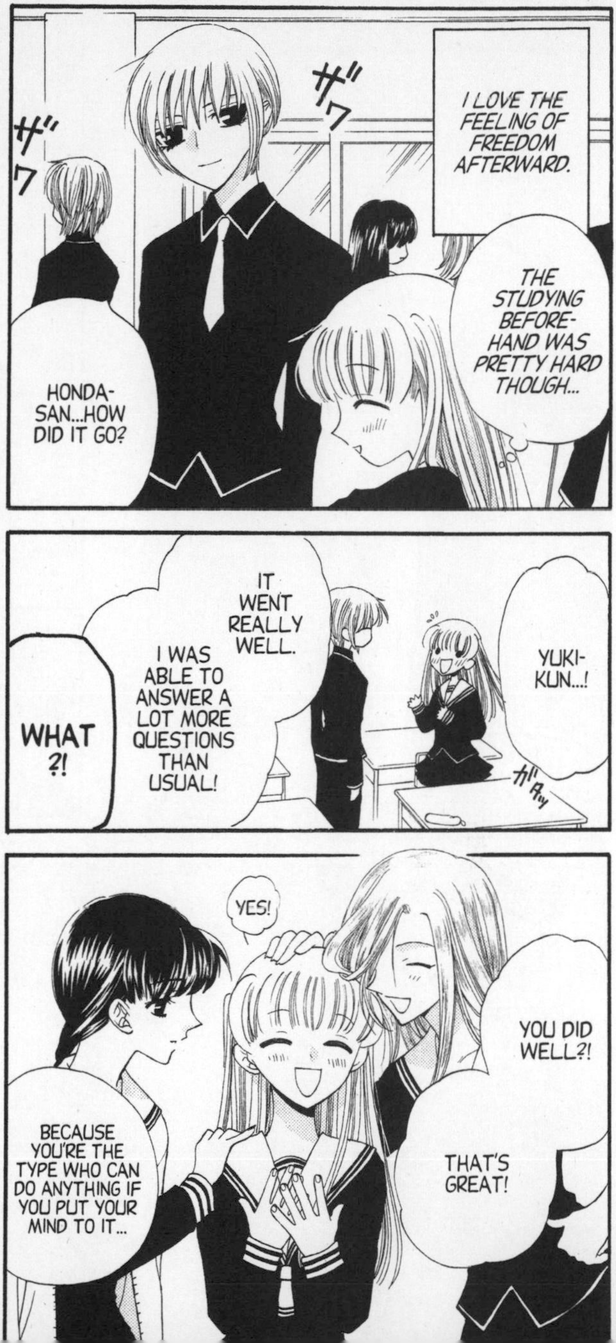
I LOVE THE FEELING OF FREEDOM AFTERWARD.
ザワ
ザワ
THE STUDYING BEFORE-HAND WAS PRETTY HARD THOUGH...
HONDA-SAN...HOW DID IT GO?
YUKI-KUN...!
IT WENT REALLY WELL.
I WAS ABLE TO ANSWER A LOT MORE QUESTIONS THAN USUAL!
WHAT?!
YOU DID WELL?!
THAT'S GREAT!
YES!
BECAUSE YOU'RE THE TYPE WHO CAN DO ANYTHING IF YOU PUT YOUR MIND TO IT...

Fruits Basket 3 Part 5

In Vol. 2 I said there weren't any plans for it, but a Furuba CD drama is coming out after all! It's a special offer, so it's not being sold to the public. These things happen suddenly, so it might be a good idea to check the magazine. Currently, the script isn't even done, but I hope it turns out to be fun! It's an oasis in the desert of my heart!! King of MidoriXXXX-san (it probably won't mean anything to censor his name at this point...) is... not in it. Sometimes I hate myself because I get serious at strange times. I really like all the voice actors who have agreed to be in Furuba, so I'm still very happy! I'm looking forward to it!

To be continued...

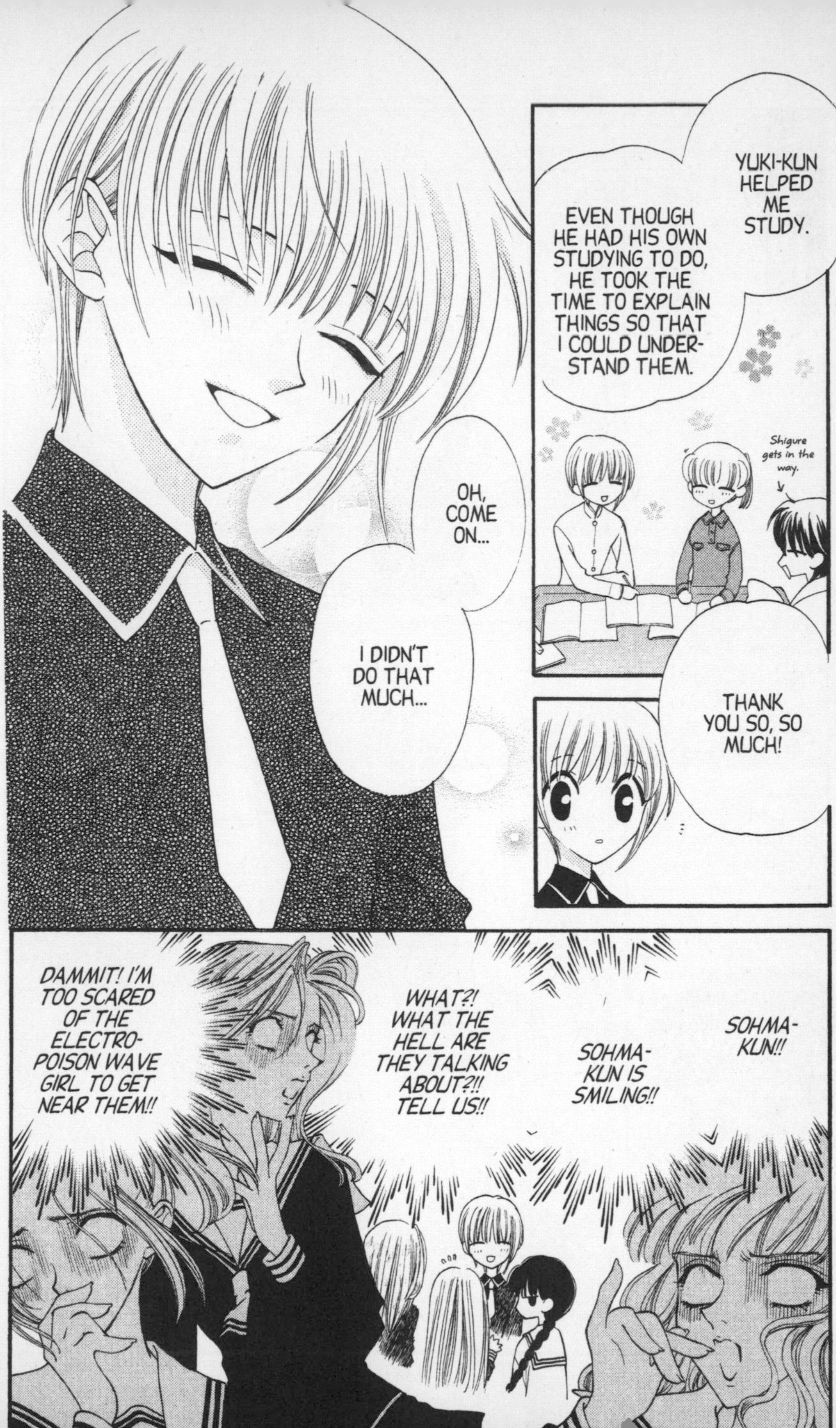
YUKI-KUN HELPED ME STUDY.
EVEN THOUGH HE HAD HIS OWN STUDYING TO DO, HE TOOK THE TIME TO EXPLAIN THINGS SO THAT I COULD UNDER-STAND THEM.
Shigure gets in the way.
THANK YOU SO, SO MUCH!
OH, COME ON...
I DIDN'T DO THAT MUCH...
SOHMA-KUN!!
SOHMA-KUN IS SMILING!!
WHAT?! WHAT THE HELL ARE THEY TALKING ABOUT?!! TELL US!!
DAMMIT! I'M TOO SCARED OF THE ELECTRO-POISON WAVE GIRL TO GET NEAR THEM!!

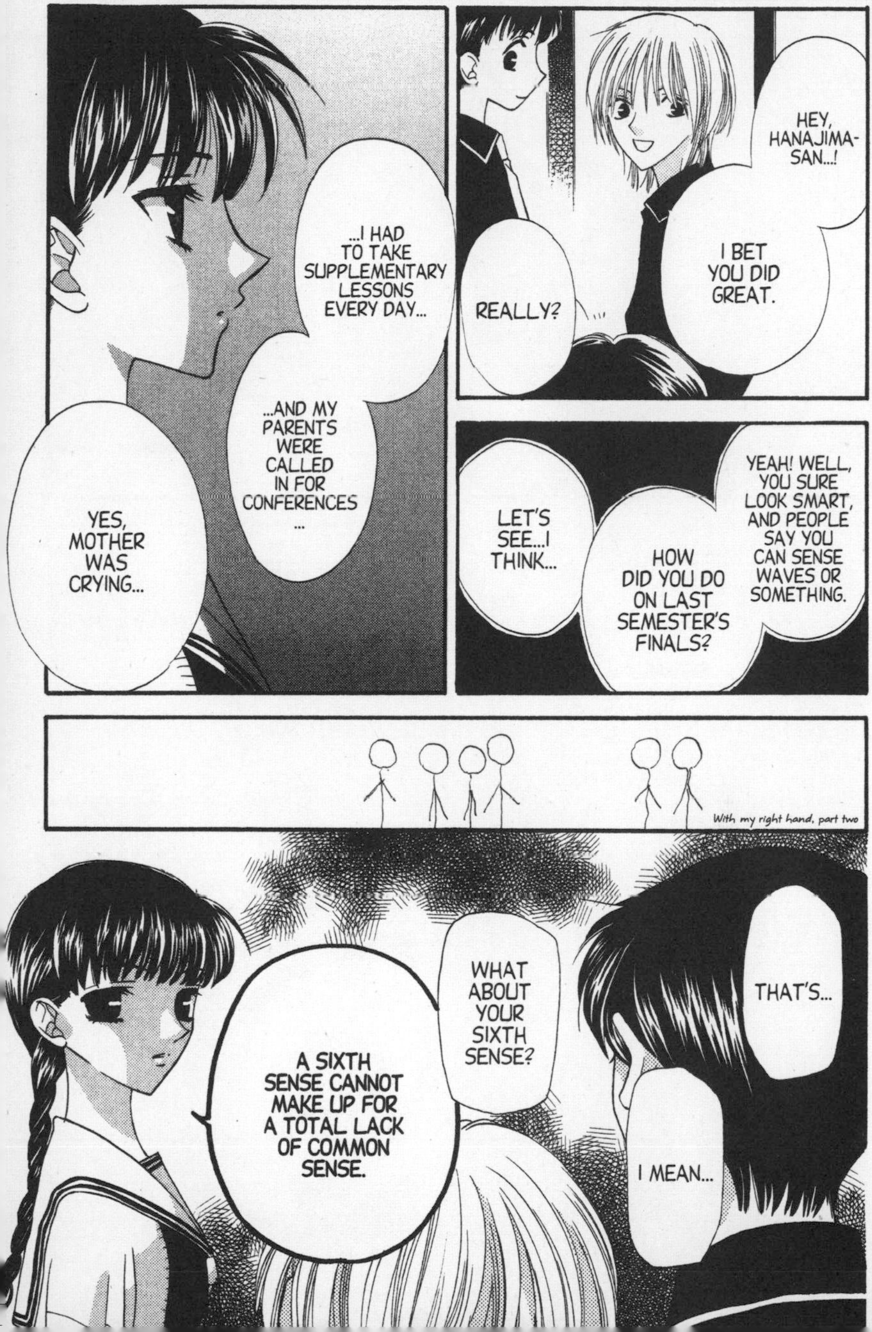
HEY, HANAJIMA-SAN...!
I BET YOU DID GREAT.
REALLY?
YEAH! WELL, YOU SURE LOOK SMART, AND PEOPLE SAY YOU CAN SENSE WAVES OR SOMETHING.
HOW DID YOU DO ON LAST SEMESTER'S FINALS?
LET'S SEE...I THINK...
...I HAD TO TAKE SUPPLEMENTARY LESSONS EVERY DAY...
...AND MY PARENTS WERE CALLED IN FOR CONFERENCES ...
YES, MOTHER WAS CRYING...
With my right hand, part two
THAT'S...
I MEAN...
WHAT ABOUT YOUR SIXTH SENSE?
A SIXTH SENSE CANNOT MAKE UP FOR A TOTAL LACK OF COMMON SENSE.

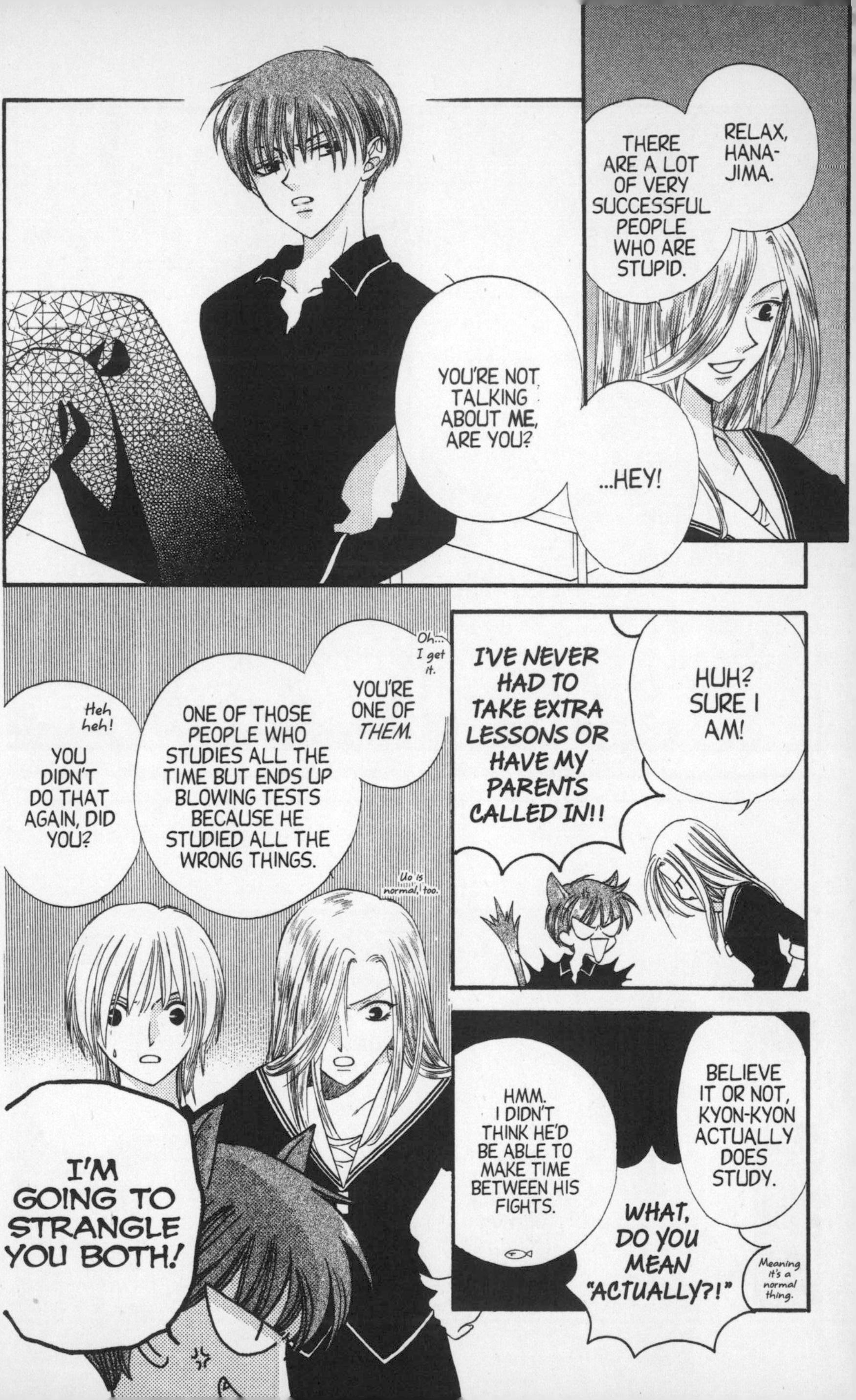
RELAX, HANA-JIMA.
THERE ARE A LOT OF VERY SUCCESSFUL PEOPLE WHO ARE STUPID.
YOU'RE NOT TALKING ABOUT ME, ARE YOU?
...HEY!
HUH? SURE I AM!
I'VE NEVER HAD TO TAKE EXTRA LESSONS OR HAVE MY PARENTS CALLED IN!!
BELIEVE IT OR NOT, KYON-KYON ACTUALLY DOES STUDY.
HMM. I DIDN'T THINK HE'D BE ABLE TO MAKE TIME BETWEEN HIS FIGHTS.
WHAT, DO YOU MEAN "ACTUALLY?!"
Meaning it's a normal thing.
Oh... I get it.
YOU'RE ONE OF *THEM*.
ONE OF THOSE PEOPLE WHO STUDIES ALL THE TIME BUT ENDS UP BLOWING TESTS BECAUSE HE STUDIED ALL THE WRONG THINGS.
Heh heh!
YOU DIDN'T DO THAT AGAIN, DID YOU?
Uo is normal, too.
I'M GOING TO STRANGLE YOU BOTH!

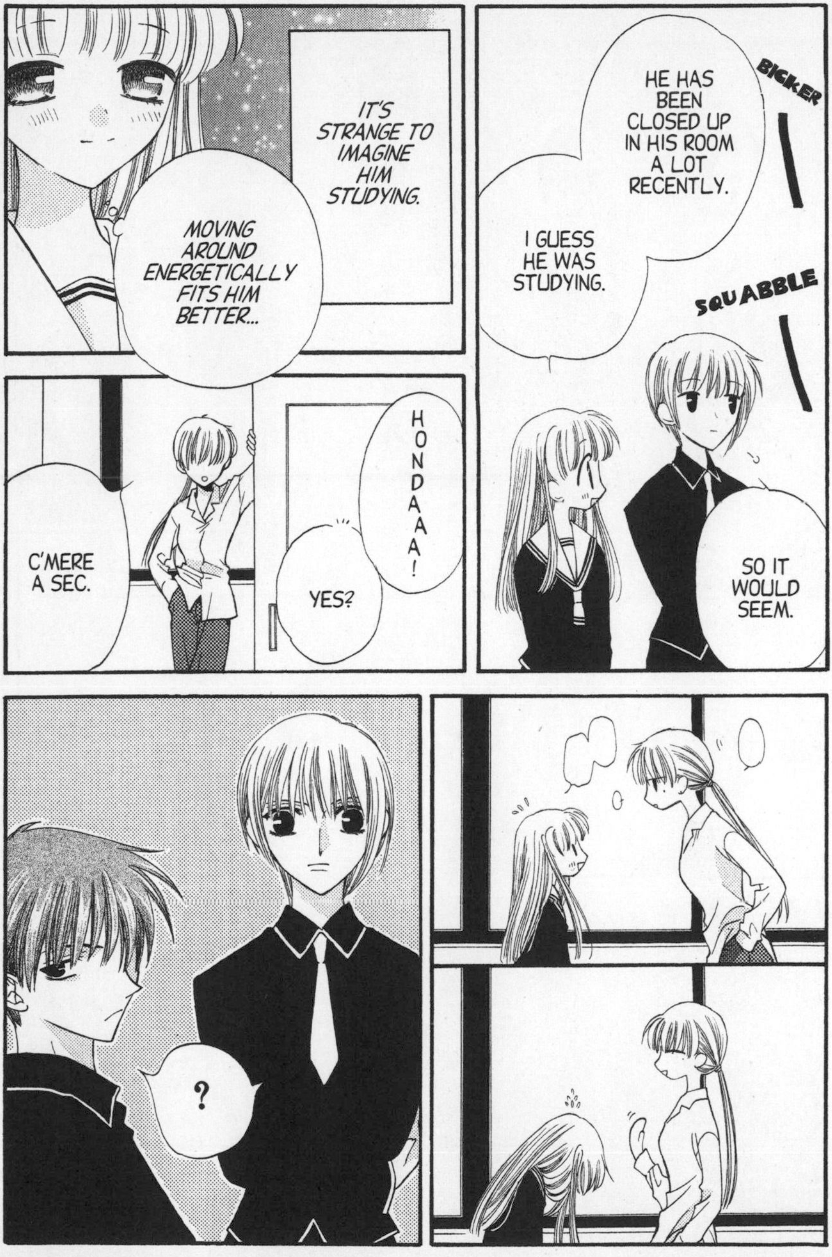
BICKER
HE HAS BEEN CLOSED UP IN HIS ROOM A LOT RECENTLY.
I GUESS HE WAS STUDYING.
SQUABBLE
SO IT WOULD SEEM.
IT'S STRANGE TO IMAGINE HIM STUDYING.
MOVING AROUND ENERGETICALLY FITS HIM BETTER...
HONDAAAA!
YES?
C'MERE A SEC.
?

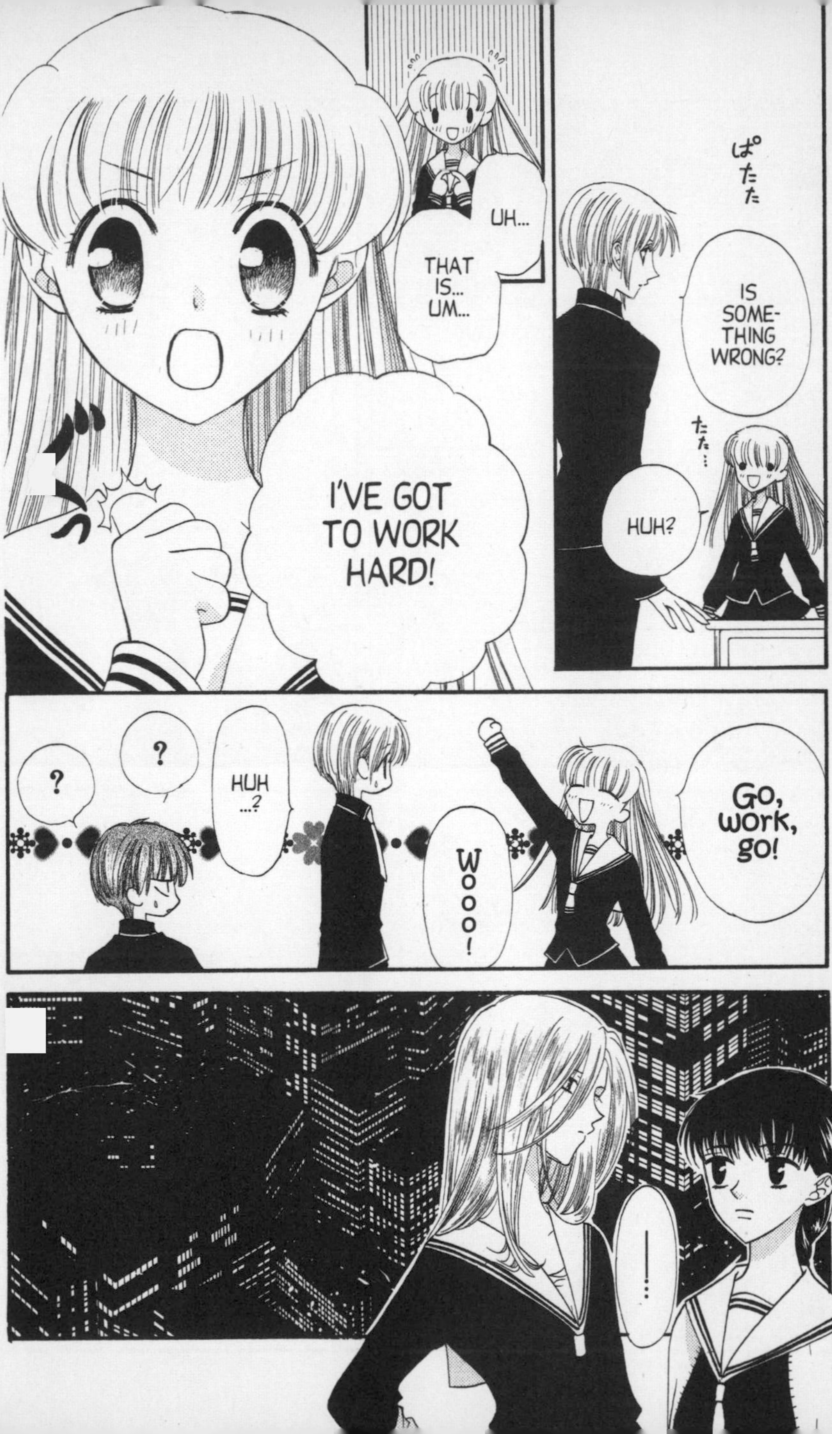
ぱたた
IS SOMETHING WRONG?
たた…
HUH?
UH...
THAT IS... UM...
I'VE GOT TO WORK HARD!
Go, work, go!
Wooo!
HUH ...?
?
?
!...

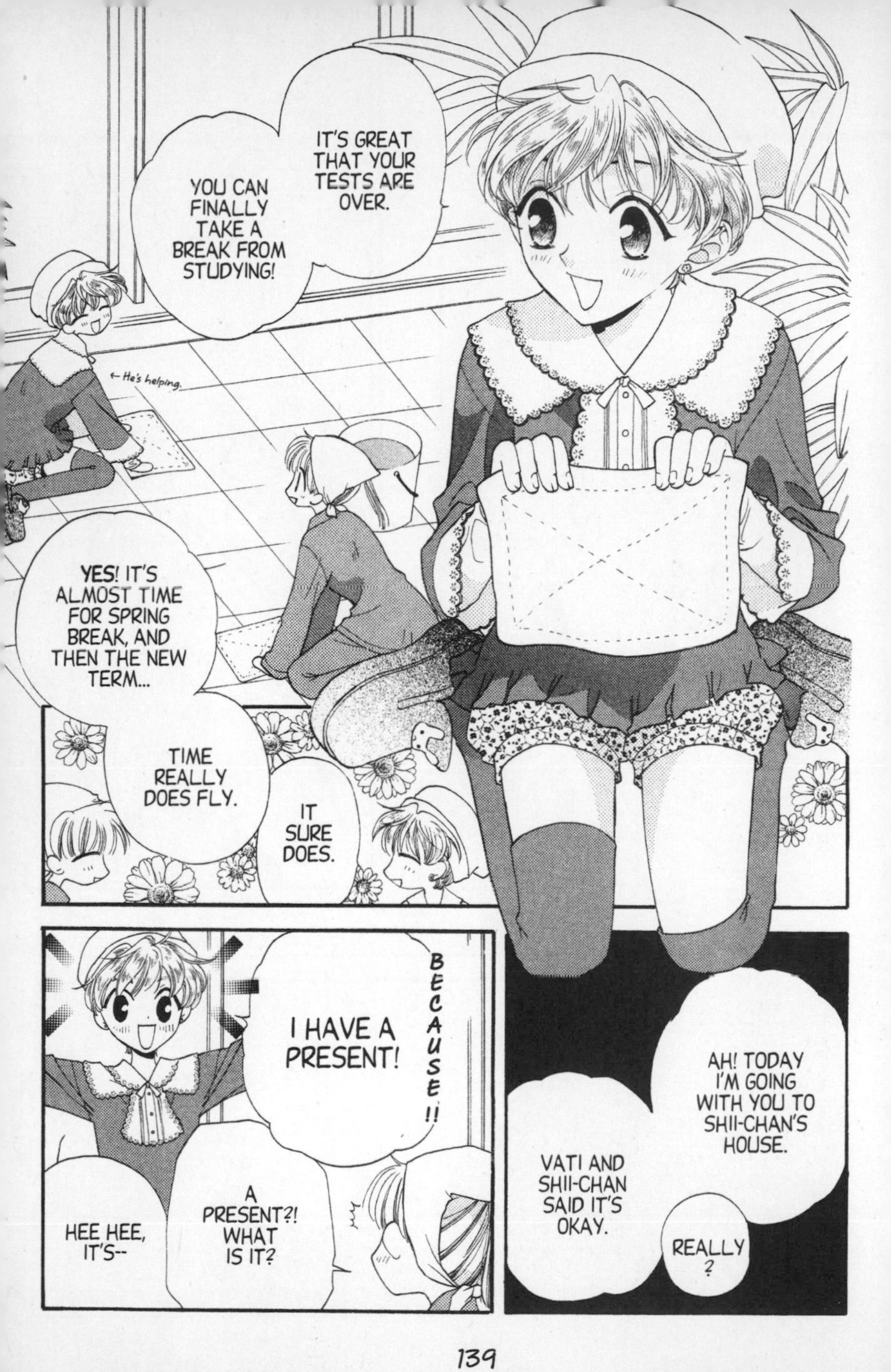
IT'S GREAT THAT YOUR TESTS ARE OVER.
YOU CAN FINALLY TAKE A BREAK FROM STUDYING!
← He's helping.
YES! IT'S ALMOST TIME FOR SPRING BREAK, AND THEN THE NEW TERM...
TIME REALLY DOES FLY.
IT SURE DOES.
AH! TODAY I'M GOING WITH YOU TO SHII-CHAN'S HOUSE.
VATI AND SHII-CHAN SAID IT'S OKAY.
REALLY?
BECAUSE!!
I HAVE A PRESENT!
A PRESENT?! WHAT IS IT?
HEE HEE, IT'S--

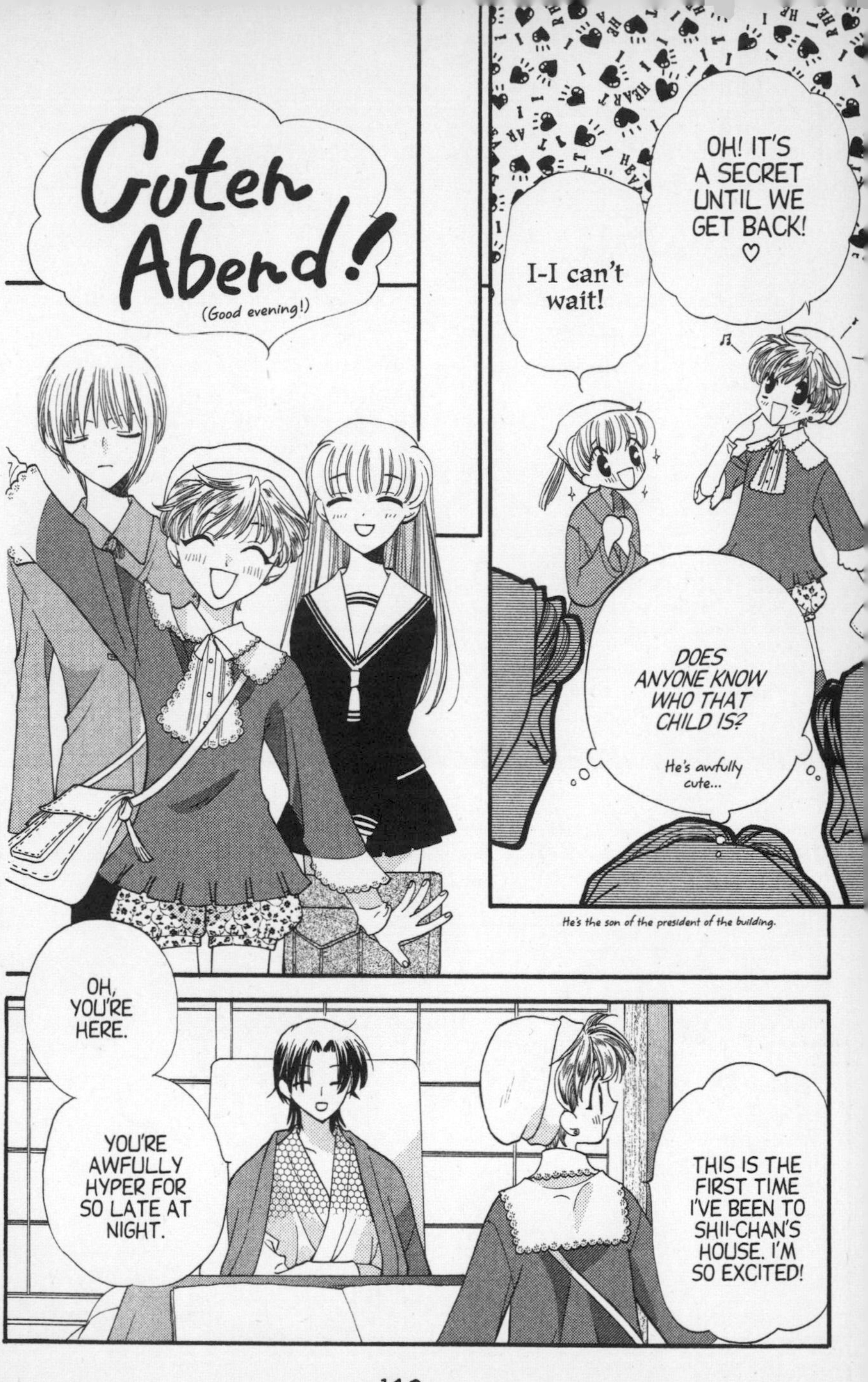
OH! IT'S A SECRET UNTIL WE GET BACK! ♡
I-I can't wait!
DOES ANYONE KNOW WHO THAT CHILD IS?
He's awfully cute...
He's the son of the president of the building.
Guten Abend!
(Good evening!)
THIS IS THE FIRST TIME I'VE BEEN TO SHII-CHAN'S HOUSE. I'M SO EXCITED!
OH, YOU'RE HERE.
YOU'RE AWFULLY HYPER FOR SO LATE AT NIGHT.

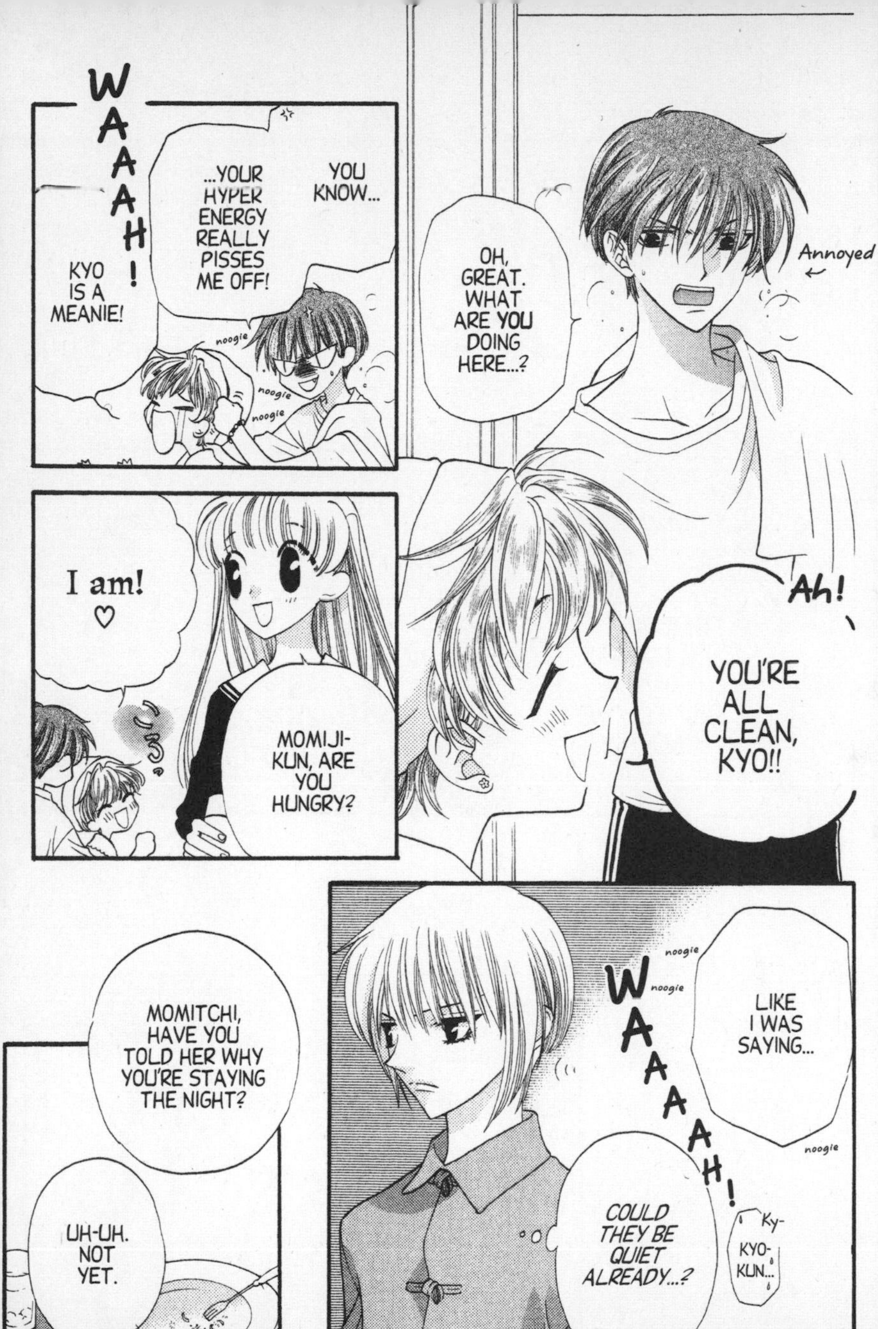
OH, GREAT. WHAT ARE YOU DOING HERE...?
Annoyed
Ah!
YOU'RE ALL CLEAN, KYO!!
YOU KNOW...
...YOUR HYPER ENERGY REALLY PISSES ME OFF!
WAAAAH!
KYO IS A MEANIE!
noogie
noogie
noogie
MOMIJI-KUN, ARE YOU HUNGRY?
I am! ♡
LIKE I WAS SAYING...
noogie
noogie
WAAAAAH!
noogie
Ky- KYO-KUN...
COULD THEY BE QUIET ALREADY...?
MOMITCHI, HAVE YOU TOLD HER WHY YOU'RE STAYING THE NIGHT?
UH-UH. NOT YET.

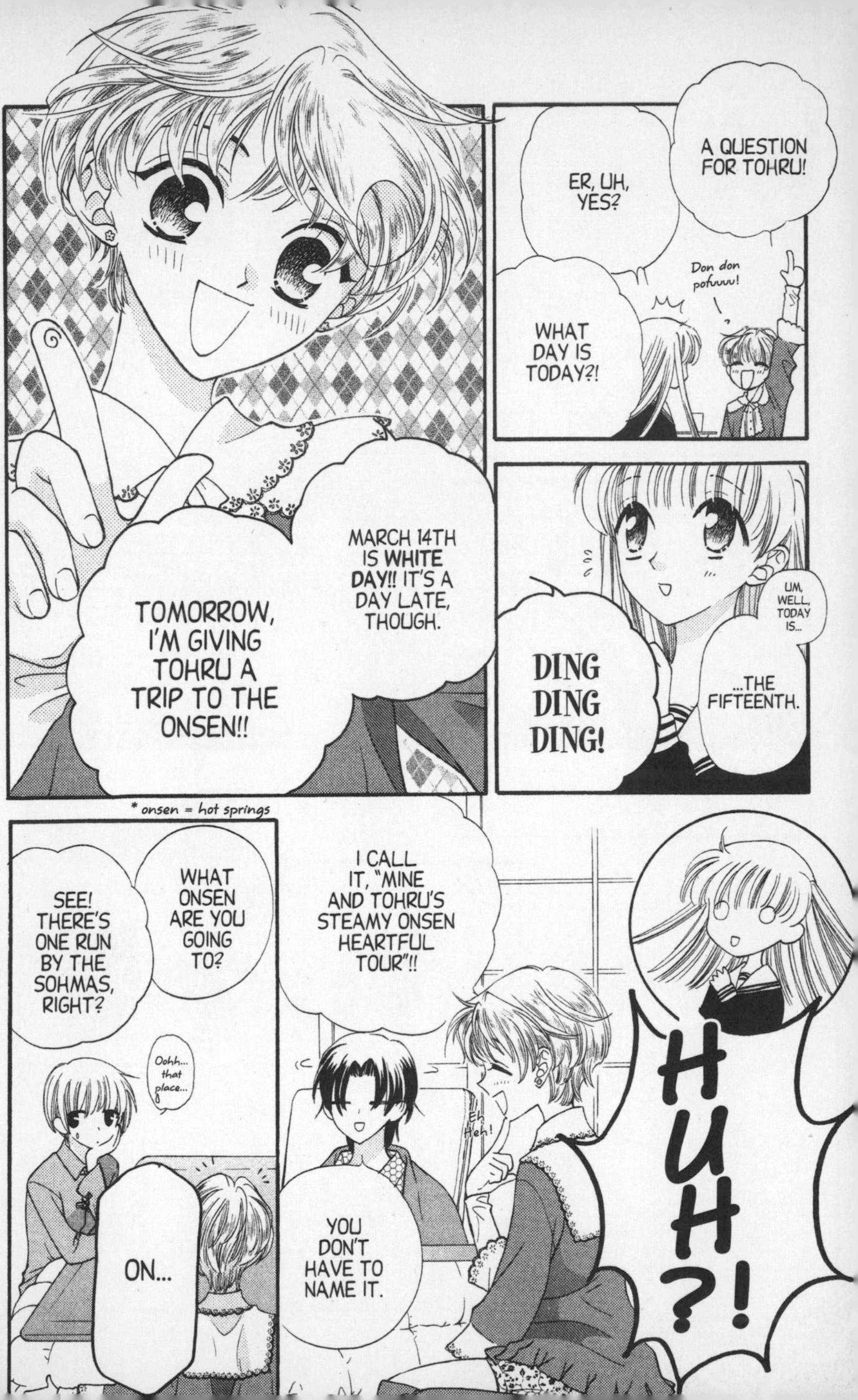
A QUESTION FOR TOHRU!
ER, UH, YES?
Don don pofuuuu!
WHAT DAY IS TODAY?!
UM, WELL, TODAY IS...
...THE FIFTEENTH.
DING DING DING!
MARCH 14TH IS WHITE DAY!! IT'S A DAY LATE, THOUGH.
TOMORROW, I'M GIVING TOHRU A TRIP TO THE ONSEN!!
HUH?!
I CALL IT, "MINE AND TOHRU'S STEAMY ONSEN HEARTFUL TOUR"!!
Eh Heh!
YOU DON'T HAVE TO NAME IT.
WHAT ONSEN ARE YOU GOING TO?
SEE! THERE'S ONE RUN BY THE SOHMAS, RIGHT?
Oohh... that place...
ON...

* onsen = hot springs

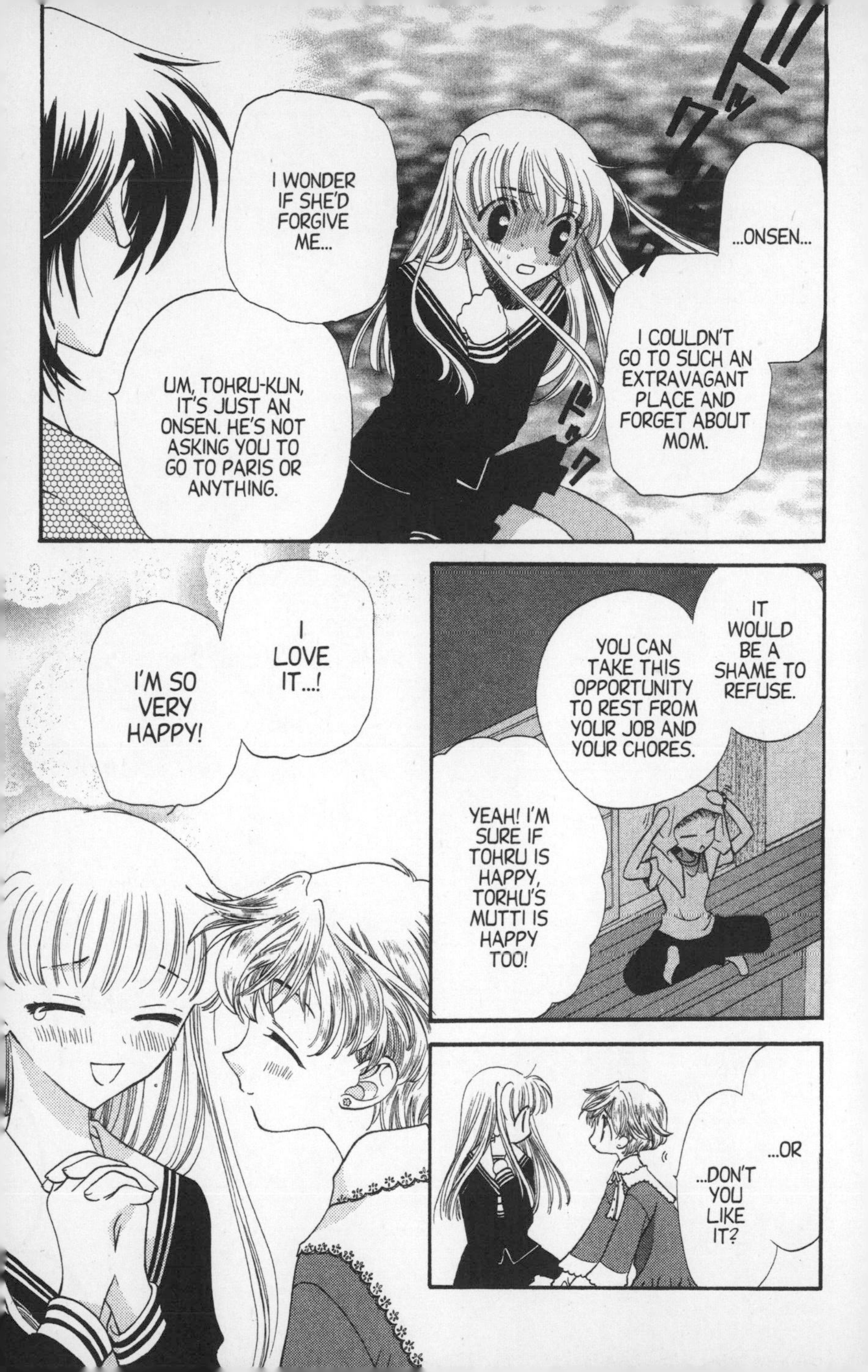
...ONSEN...
I COULDN'T GO TO SUCH AN EXTRAVAGANT PLACE AND FORGET ABOUT MOM.
I WONDER IF SHE'D FORGIVE ME...
UM, TOHRU-KUN, IT'S JUST AN ONSEN. HE'S NOT ASKING YOU TO GO TO PARIS OR ANYTHING.
IT WOULD BE A SHAME TO REFUSE.
YOU CAN TAKE THIS OPPORTUNITY TO REST FROM YOUR JOB AND YOUR CHORES.
YEAH! I'M SURE IF TOHRU IS HAPPY, TORHU'S MUTTI IS HAPPY TOO!
...OR
...DON'T YOU LIKE IT?
I LOVE IT...!
I'M SO VERY HAPPY!

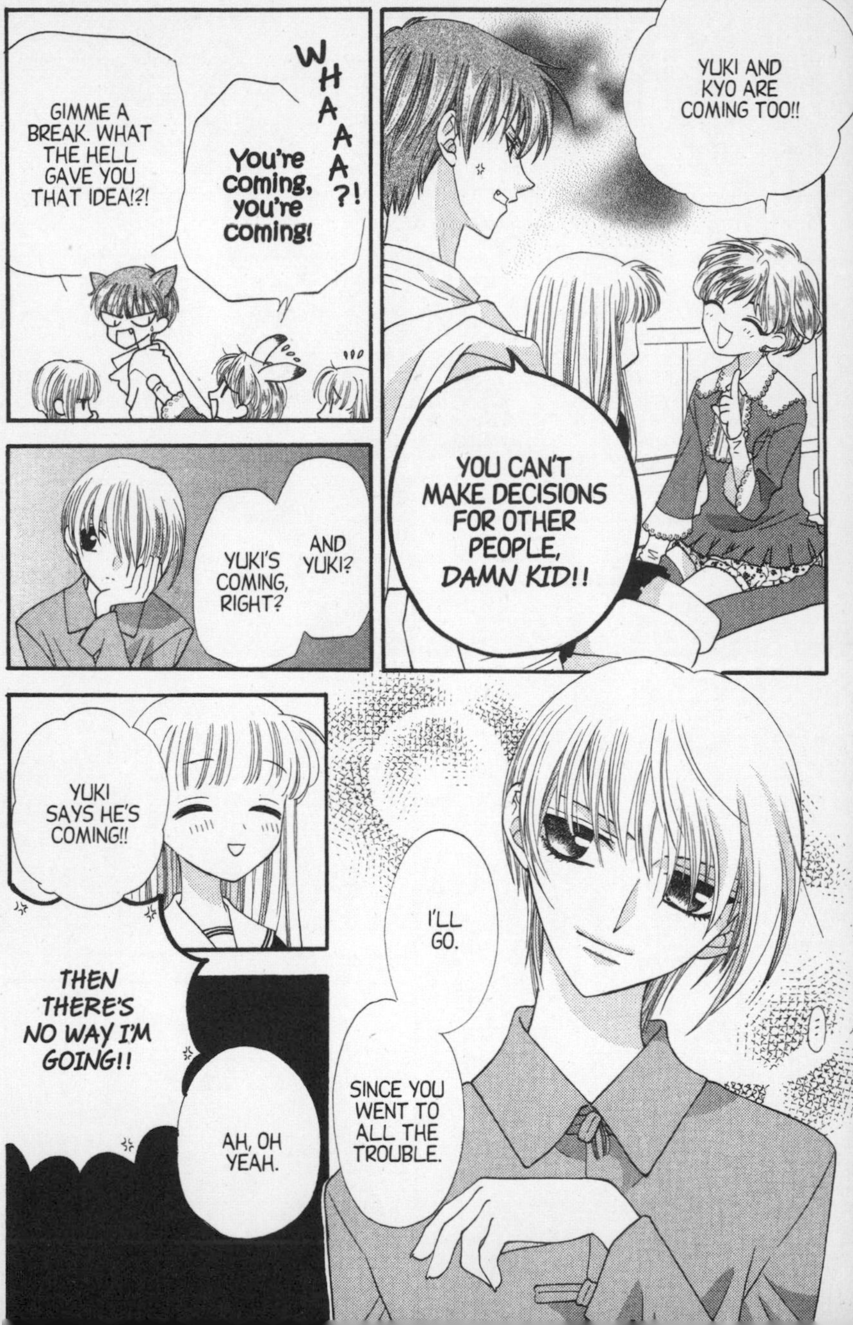
YUKI AND KYO ARE COMING TOO!!
YOU CAN'T MAKE DECISIONS FOR OTHER PEOPLE, DAMN KID!!
WHAAAA?!
You're coming, you're coming!
GIMME A BREAK. WHAT THE HELL GAVE YOU THAT IDEA!?!
AND YUKI?
YUKI'S COMING, RIGHT?
I'LL GO.
...
SINCE YOU WENT TO ALL THE TROUBLE.
YUKI SAYS HE'S COMING!!
THEN THERE'S NO WAY I'M GOING!!
AH, OH YEAH.

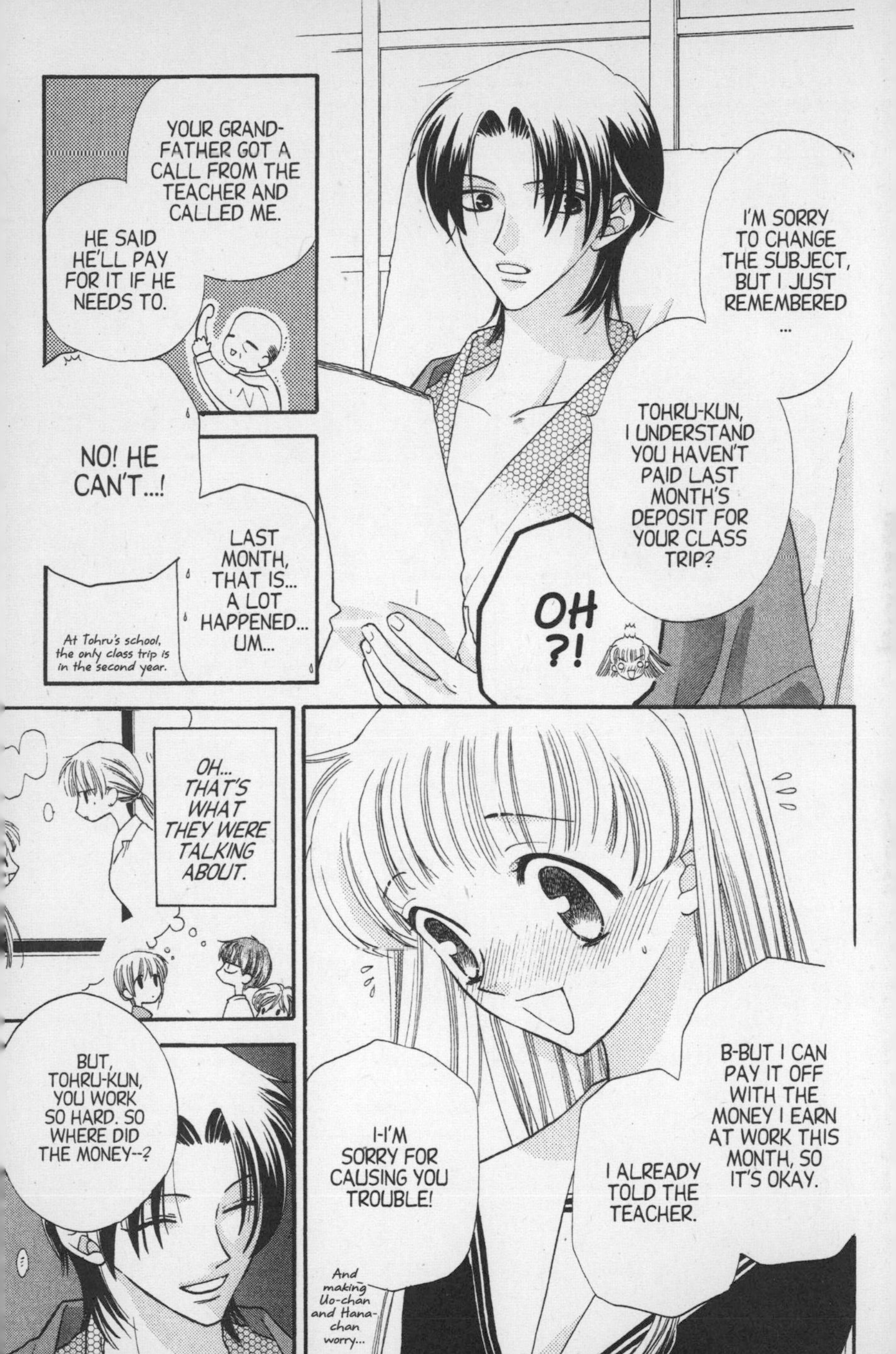
I'M SORRY TO CHANGE THE SUBJECT, BUT I JUST REMEMBERED ...
TOHRU-KUN, I UNDERSTAND YOU HAVEN'T PAID LAST MONTH'S DEPOSIT FOR YOUR CLASS TRIP?
OH ?!
YOUR GRAND-FATHER GOT A CALL FROM THE TEACHER AND CALLED ME.
HE SAID HE'LL PAY FOR IT IF HE NEEDS TO.
NO! HE CAN'T...!
LAST MONTH, THAT IS... A LOT HAPPENED... UM...
At Tohru's school, the only class trip is in the second year.
B-BUT I CAN PAY IT OFF WITH THE MONEY I EARN AT WORK THIS MONTH, SO IT'S OKAY.
I ALREADY TOLD THE TEACHER.
I-I'M SORRY FOR CAUSING YOU TROUBLE!
And making Uo-chan and Hana-chan worry...
OH... THAT'S WHAT THEY WERE TALKING ABOUT.
BUT, TOHRU-KUN, YOU WORK SO HARD. SO WHERE DID THE MONEY--?

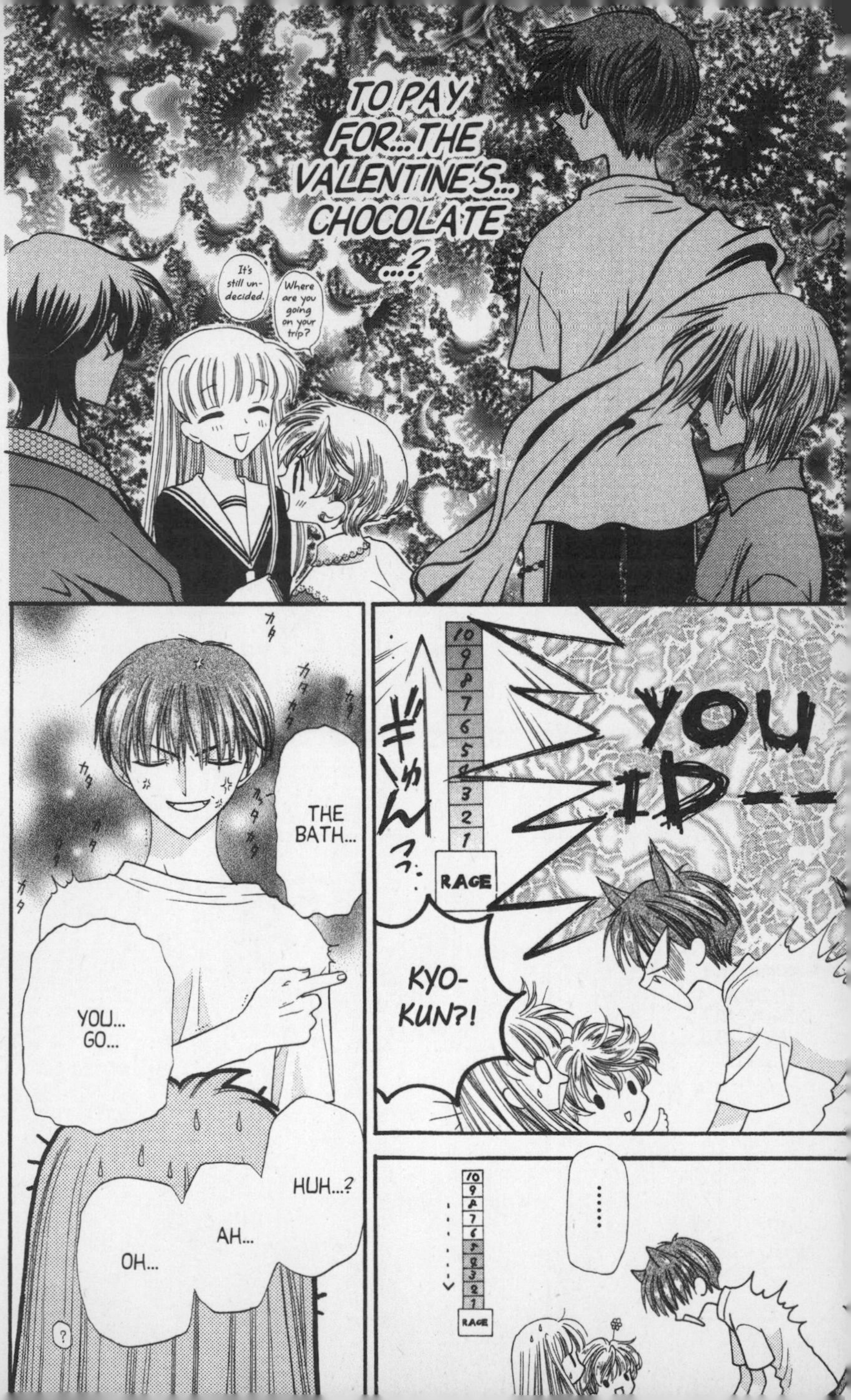
TO PAY FOR...THE VALENTINE'S... CHOCOLATE ...2
Where are you going on your trip?
It's still undecided.
YOU ID--
10 9 8 7 6 5 4 3 2 1
RAGE
KYO-KUN?!
......
10 9 8 7 6 5 4 3 2 1
RAGE
THE BATH...
YOU... GO...
HUH...?
AH...
OH...
?

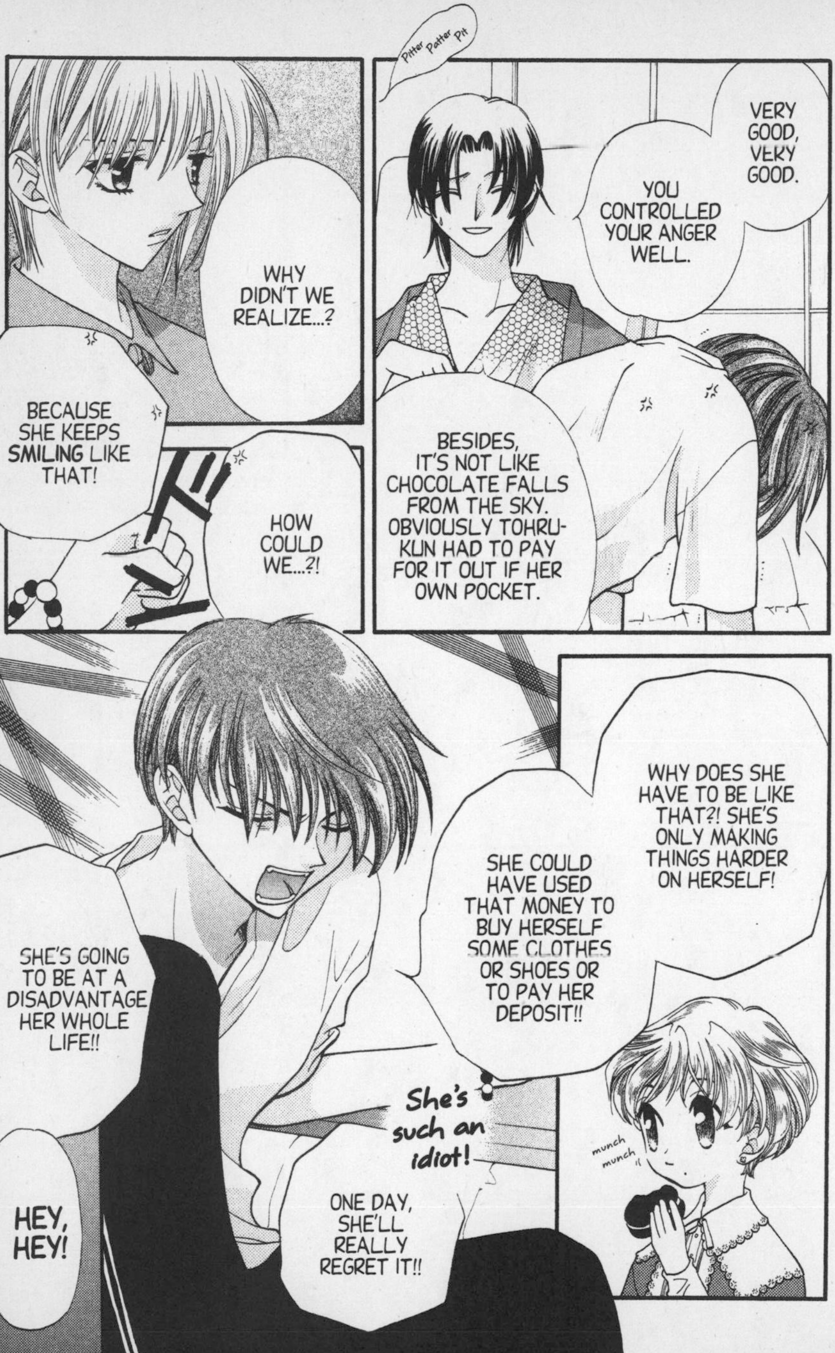
Pitter Patter Pit
VERY GOOD, VERY GOOD.
YOU CONTROLLED YOUR ANGER WELL.
BESIDES, IT'S NOT LIKE CHOCOLATE FALLS FROM THE SKY. OBVIOUSLY TOHRU-KUN HAD TO PAY FOR IT OUT IF HER OWN POCKET.
WHY DIDN'T WE REALIZE...?
HOW COULD WE...?!
BECAUSE SHE KEEPS SMILING LIKE THAT!
munch munch
WHY DOES SHE HAVE TO BE LIKE THAT?! SHE'S ONLY MAKING THINGS HARDER ON HERSELF!
SHE COULD HAVE USED THAT MONEY TO BUY HERSELF SOME CLOTHES OR SHOES OR TO PAY HER DEPOSIT!!
SHE'S GOING TO BE AT A DISADVANTAGE HER WHOLE LIFE!!
She's such an idiot!
ONE DAY, SHE'LL REALLY REGRET IT!!
HEY, HEY!

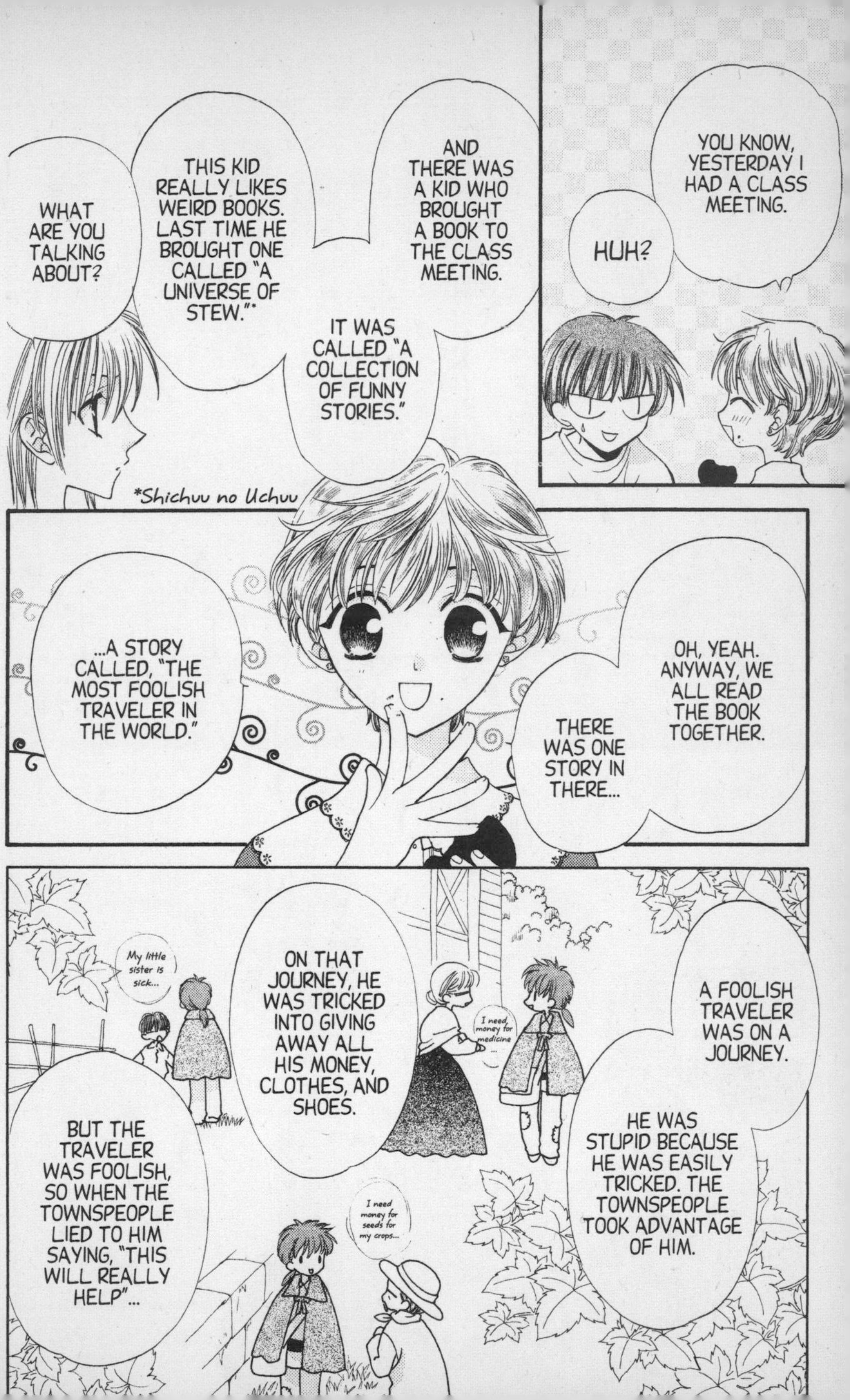
YOU KNOW, YESTERDAY I HAD A CLASS MEETING.
HUH?
AND THERE WAS A KID WHO BROUGHT A BOOK TO THE CLASS MEETING.
IT WAS CALLED "A COLLECTION OF FUNNY STORIES."
THIS KID REALLY LIKES WEIRD BOOKS. LAST TIME HE BROUGHT ONE CALLED "A UNIVERSE OF STEW."*
WHAT ARE YOU TALKING ABOUT?
*Shichuu no Uchuu
OH, YEAH. ANYWAY, WE ALL READ THE BOOK TOGETHER.
THERE WAS ONE STORY IN THERE...
...A STORY CALLED, "THE MOST FOOLISH TRAVELER IN THE WORLD."
A FOOLISH TRAVELER WAS ON A JOURNEY.
HE WAS STUPID BECAUSE HE WAS EASILY TRICKED. THE TOWNSPEOPLE TOOK ADVANTAGE OF HIM.
I need money for medicine...
ON THAT JOURNEY, HE WAS TRICKED INTO GIVING AWAY ALL HIS MONEY, CLOTHES, AND SHOES.
My little sister is sick...
I need money for seeds for my crops...
BUT THE TRAVELER WAS FOOLISH, SO WHEN THE TOWNSPEOPLE LIED TO HIM SAYING, "THIS WILL REALLY HELP"...

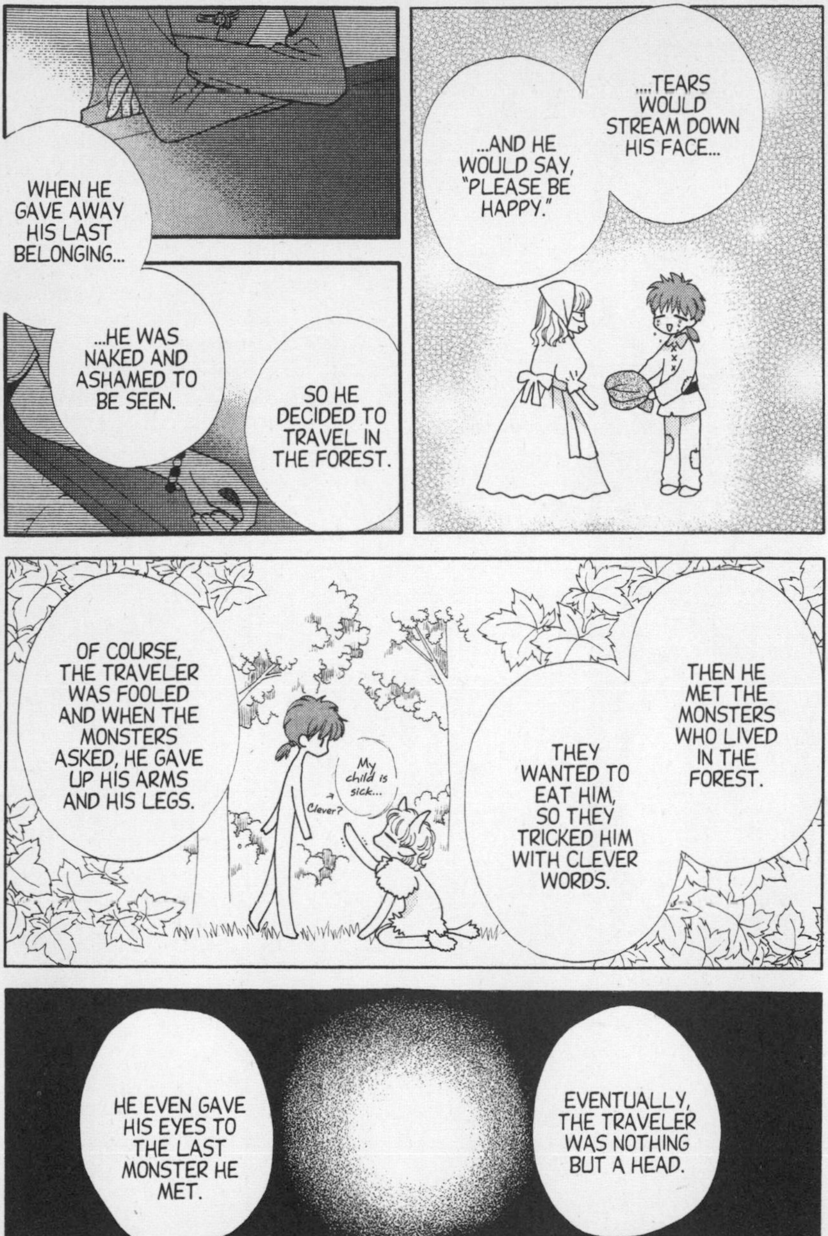
....TEARS WOULD STREAM DOWN HIS FACE...
...AND HE WOULD SAY, "PLEASE BE HAPPY."
WHEN HE GAVE AWAY HIS LAST BELONGING...
...HE WAS NAKED AND ASHAMED TO BE SEEN.
SO HE DECIDED TO TRAVEL IN THE FOREST.
THEN HE MET THE MONSTERS WHO LIVED IN THE FOREST.
THEY WANTED TO EAT HIM, SO THEY TRICKED HIM WITH CLEVER WORDS.
My child is sick...
Clever?
OF COURSE, THE TRAVELER WAS FOOLED AND WHEN THE MONSTERS ASKED, HE GAVE UP HIS ARMS AND HIS LEGS.
EVENTUALLY, THE TRAVELER WAS NOTHING BUT A HEAD.
HE EVEN GAVE HIS EYES TO THE LAST MONSTER HE MET.

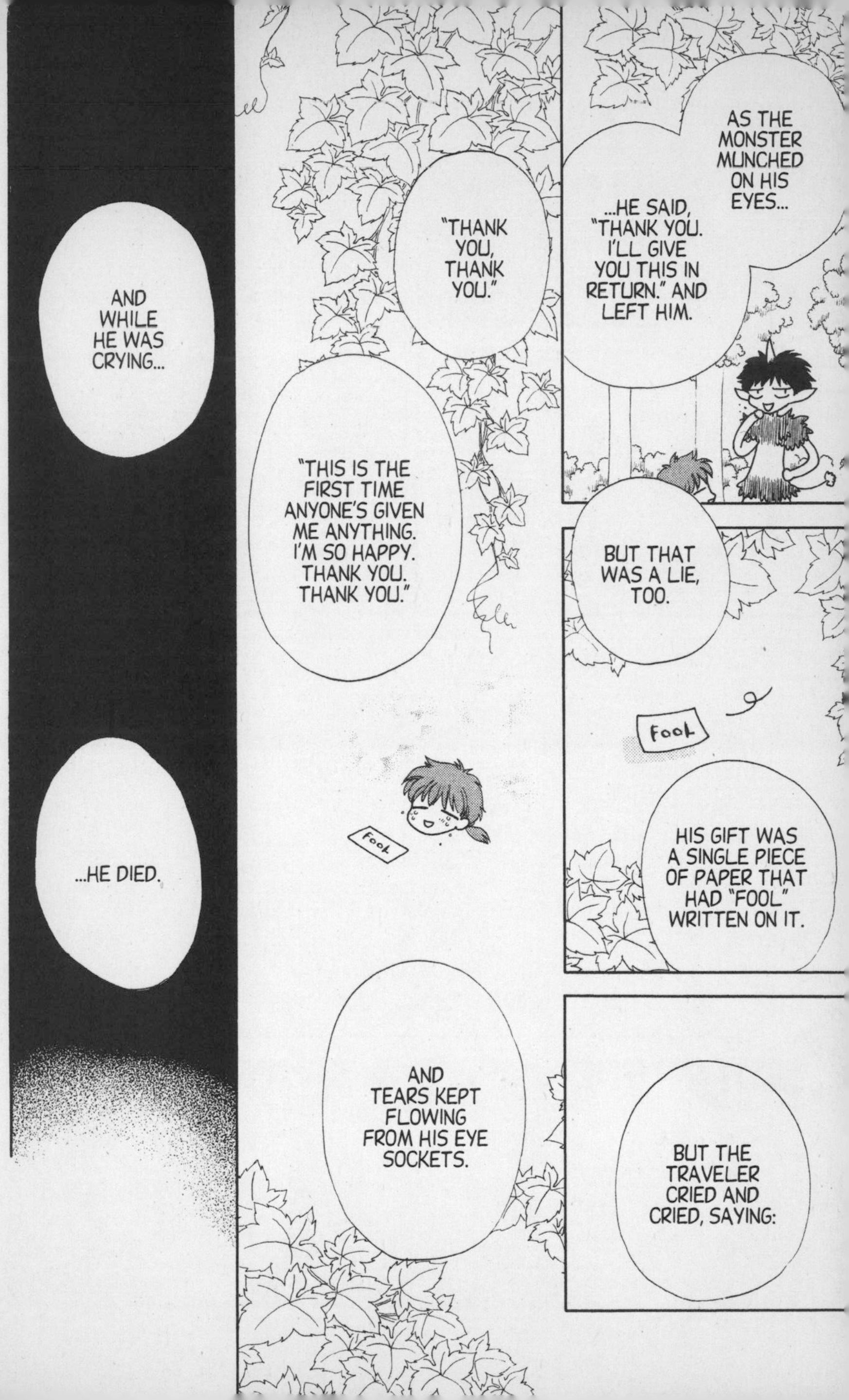
AS THE MONSTER MUNCHED ON HIS EYES...
...HE SAID, "THANK YOU. I'LL GIVE YOU THIS IN RETURN." AND LEFT HIM.
BUT THAT WAS A LIE, TOO.
Fool
HIS GIFT WAS A SINGLE PIECE OF PAPER THAT HAD "FOOL" WRITTEN ON IT.
BUT THE TRAVELER CRIED AND CRIED, SAYING:
"THANK YOU, THANK YOU."
"THIS IS THE FIRST TIME ANYONE'S GIVEN ME ANYTHING. I'M SO HAPPY. THANK YOU. THANK YOU."
Fool
AND TEARS KEPT FLOWING FROM HIS EYE SOCKETS.
AND WHILE HE WAS CRYING...
...HE DIED.

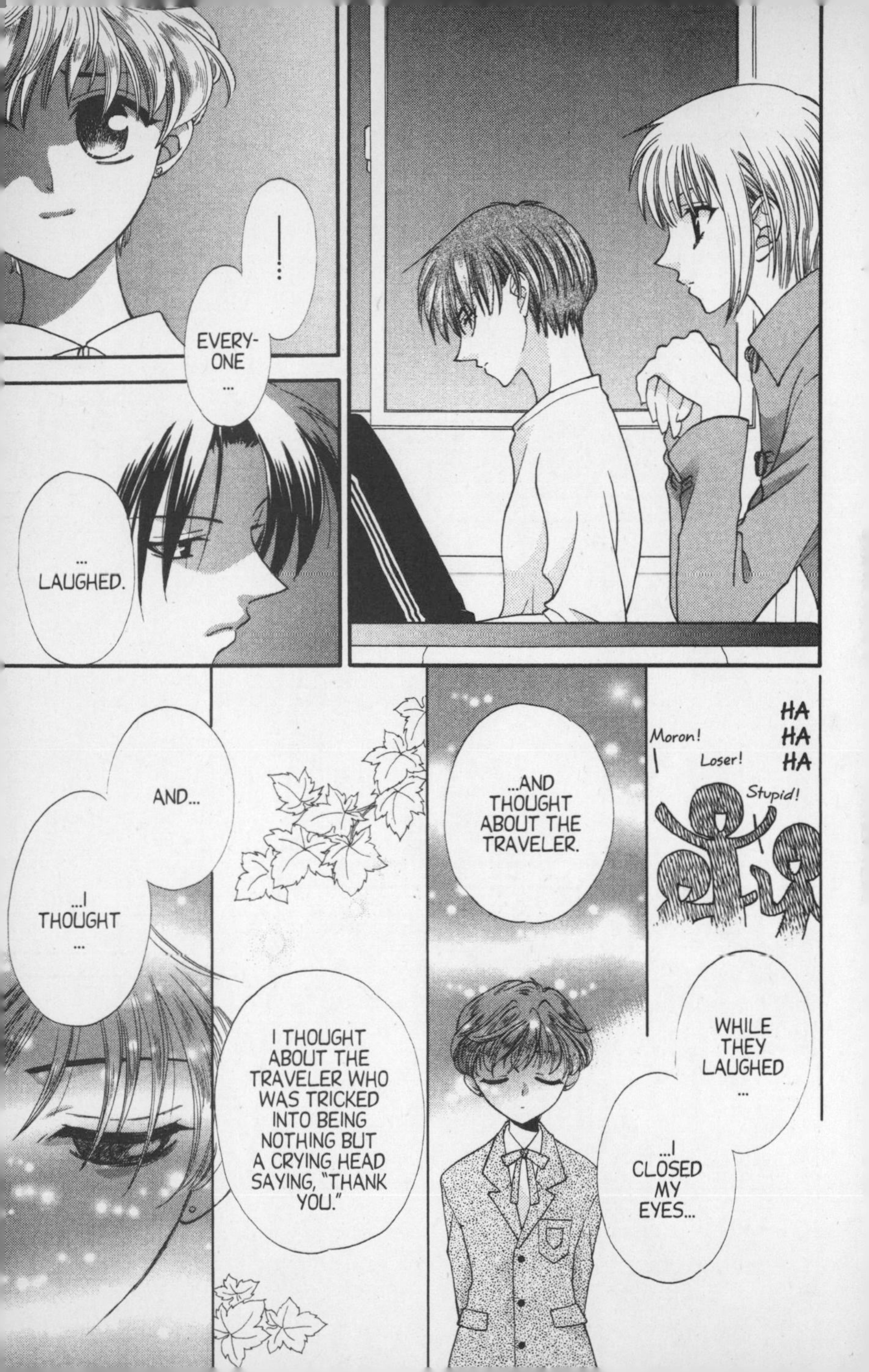
...
EVERY-ONE ...
... LAUGHED.
HA HA HA
Moron!
Loser!
Stupid!
WHILE THEY LAUGHED ...
...I CLOSED MY EYES...
...AND THOUGHT ABOUT THE TRAVELER.
AND...
...I THOUGHT ...
I THOUGHT ABOUT THE TRAVELER WHO WAS TRICKED INTO BEING NOTHING BUT A CRYING HEAD SAYING, "THANK YOU."

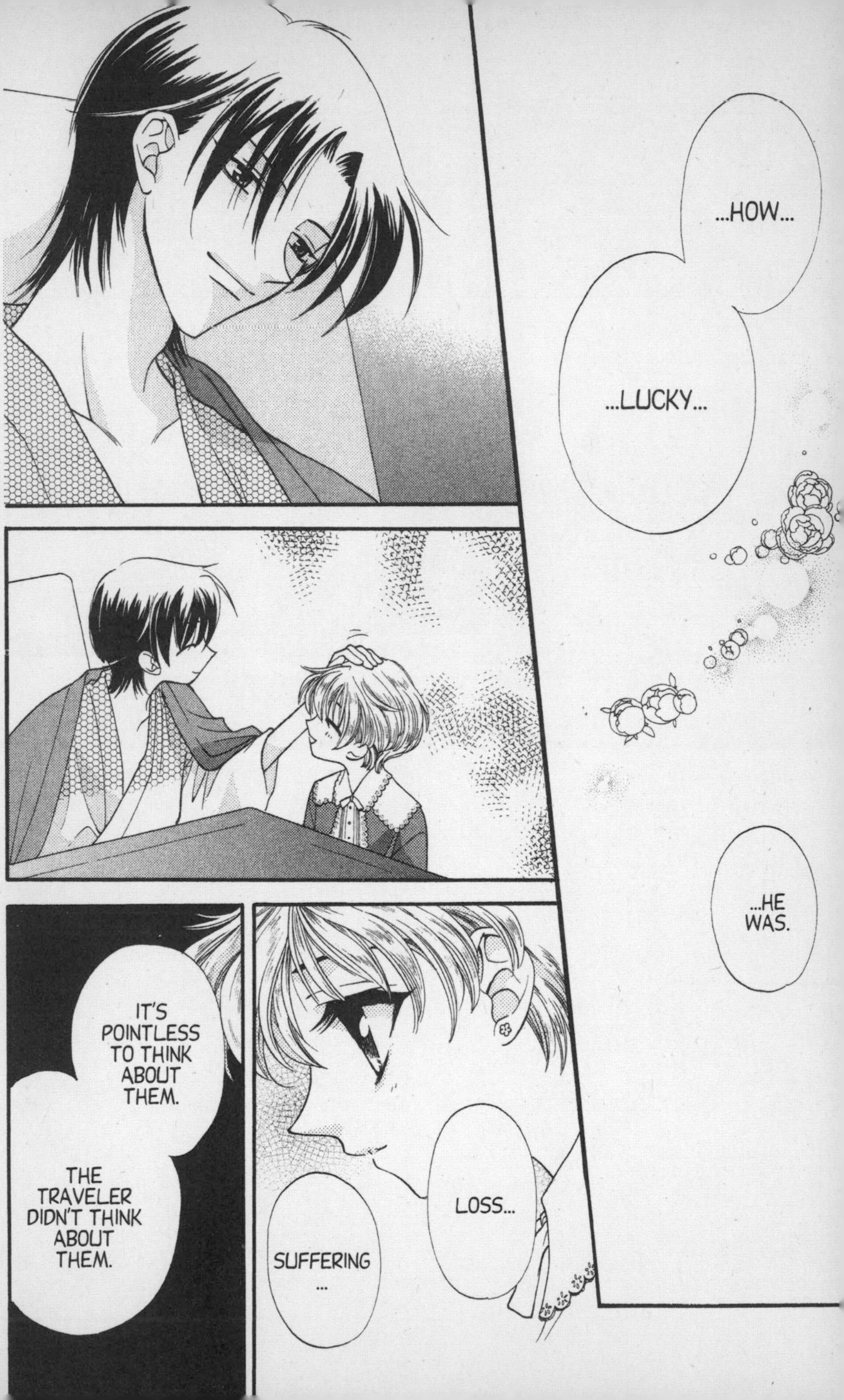
...HOW...
...LUCKY...
...HE WAS.
LOSS...
SUFFERING ...
IT'S POINTLESS TO THINK ABOUT THEM.
THE TRAVELER DIDN'T THINK ABOUT THEM.

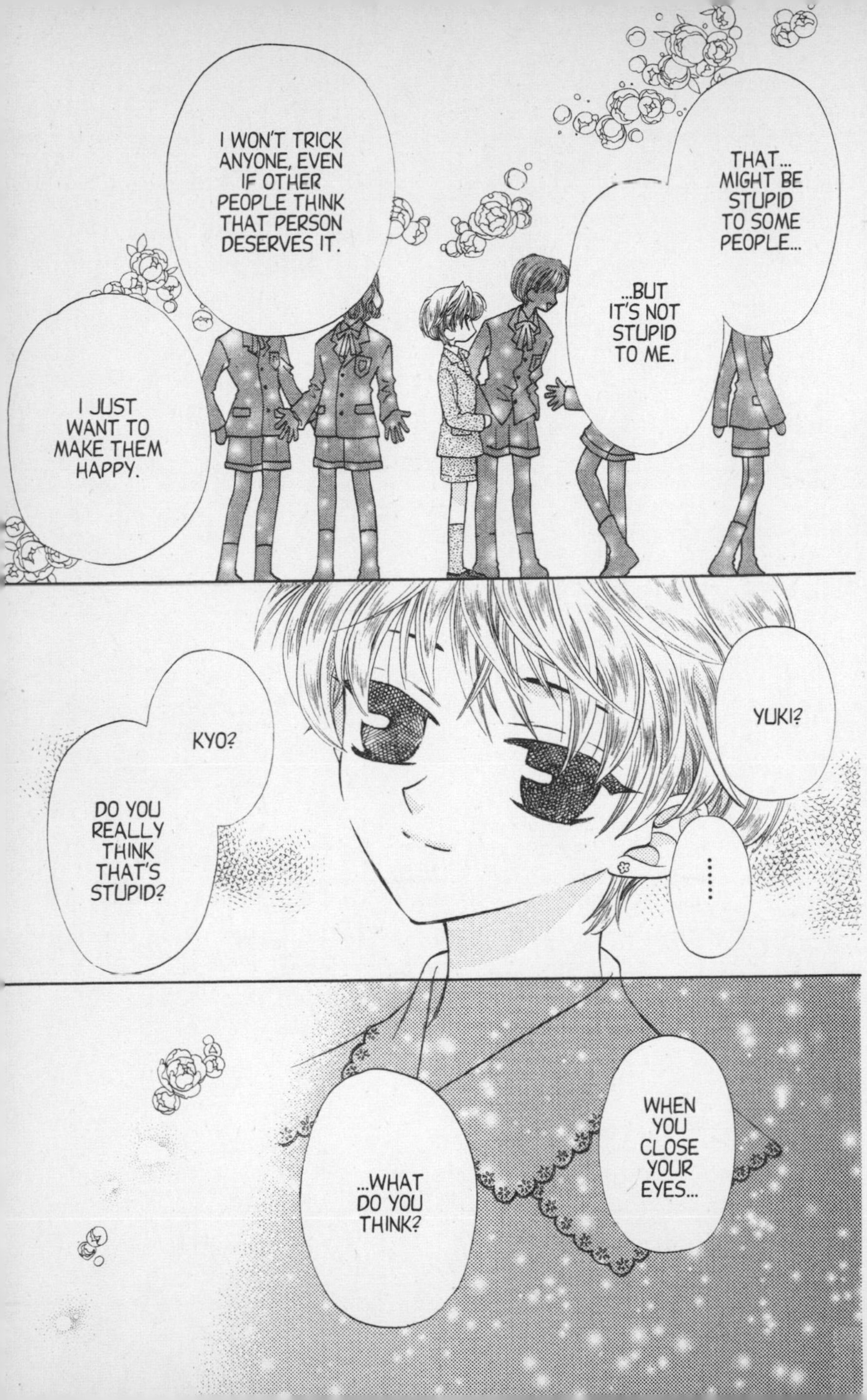
THAT... MIGHT BE STUPID TO SOME PEOPLE...
...BUT IT'S NOT STUPID TO ME.
I WON'T TRICK ANYONE, EVEN IF OTHER PEOPLE THINK THAT PERSON DESERVES IT.
I JUST WANT TO MAKE THEM HAPPY.
YUKI?
......
KYO?
DO YOU REALLY THINK THAT'S STUPID?
WHEN YOU CLOSE YOUR EYES...
...WHAT DO YOU THINK?

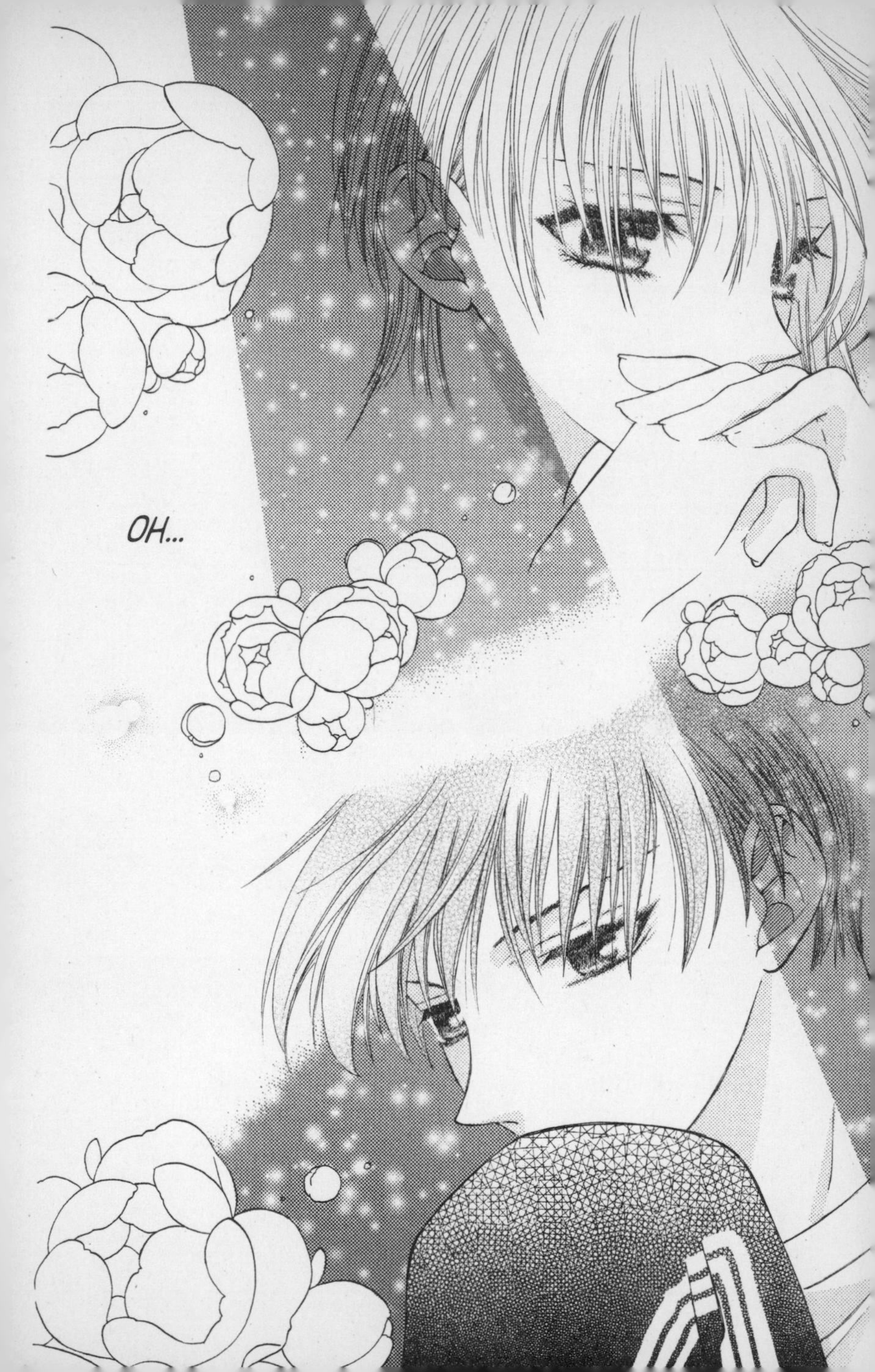
OH...

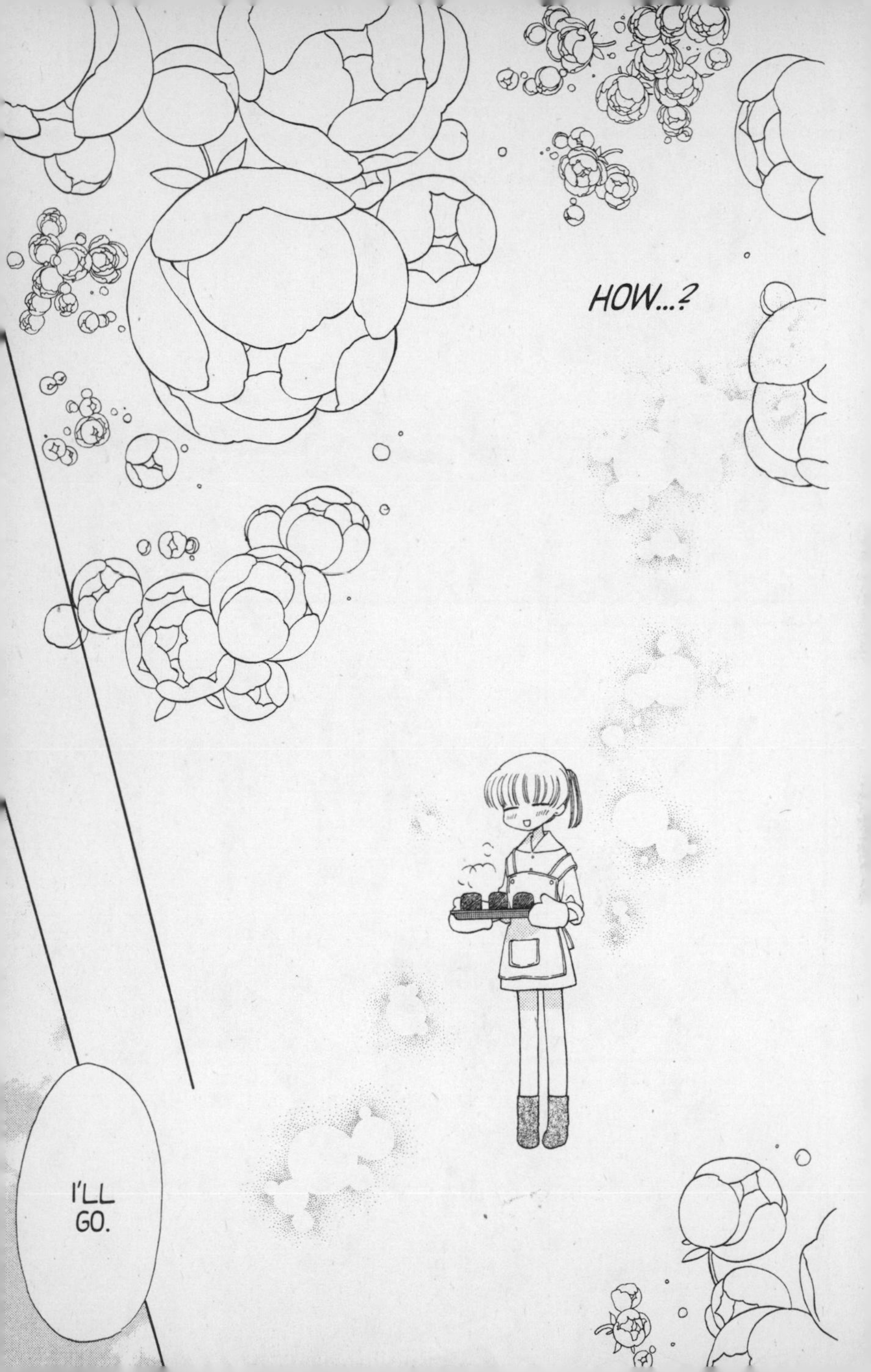
HOW...?
I'LL GO.

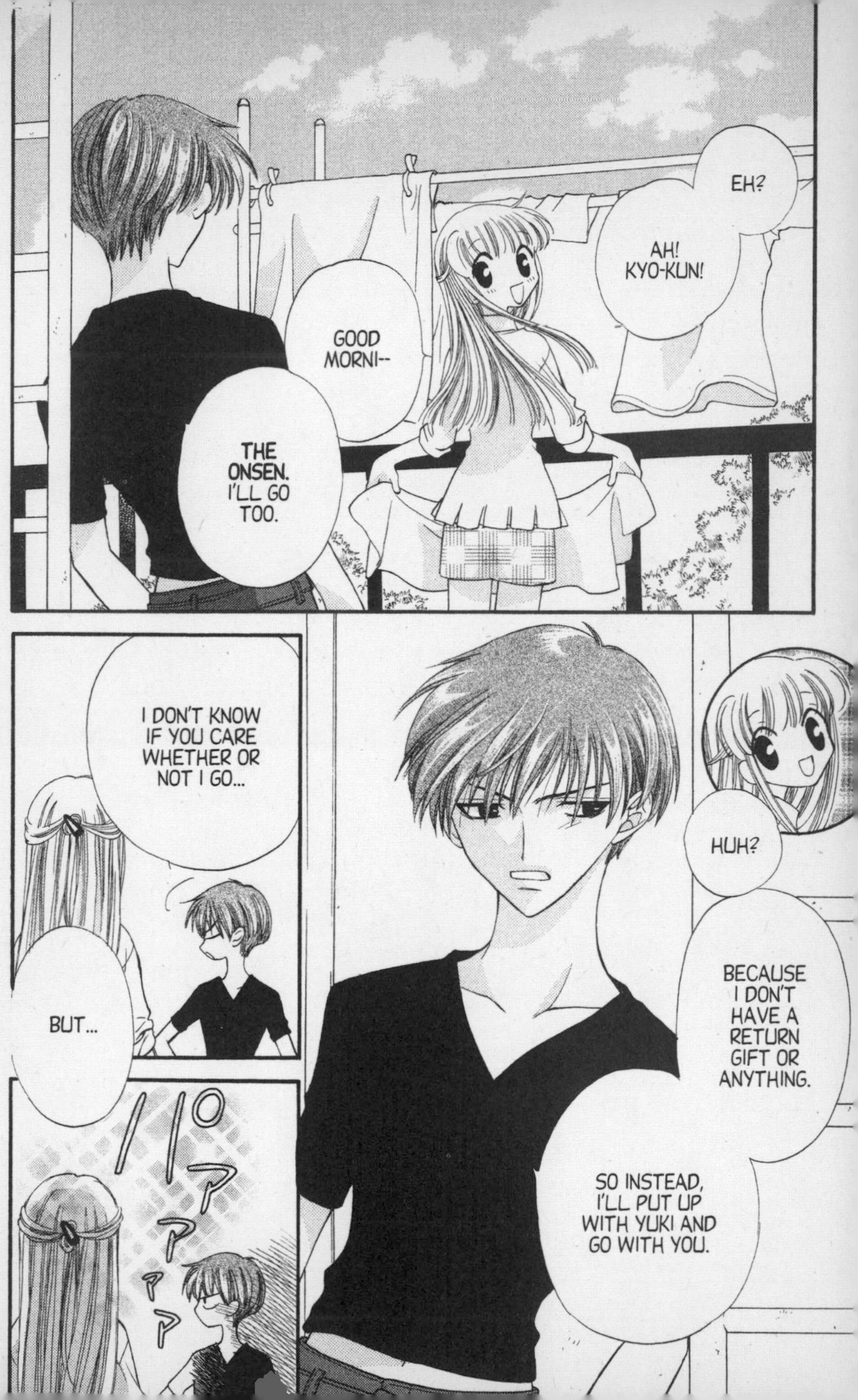
EH?
AH! KYO-KUN!
GOOD MORNI--
THE ONSEN. I'LL GO TOO.
HUH?
BECAUSE I DON'T HAVE A RETURN GIFT OR ANYTHING.
SO INSTEAD, I'LL PUT UP WITH YUKI AND GO WITH YOU.
I DON'T KNOW IF YOU CARE WHETHER OR NOT I GO...
BUT...

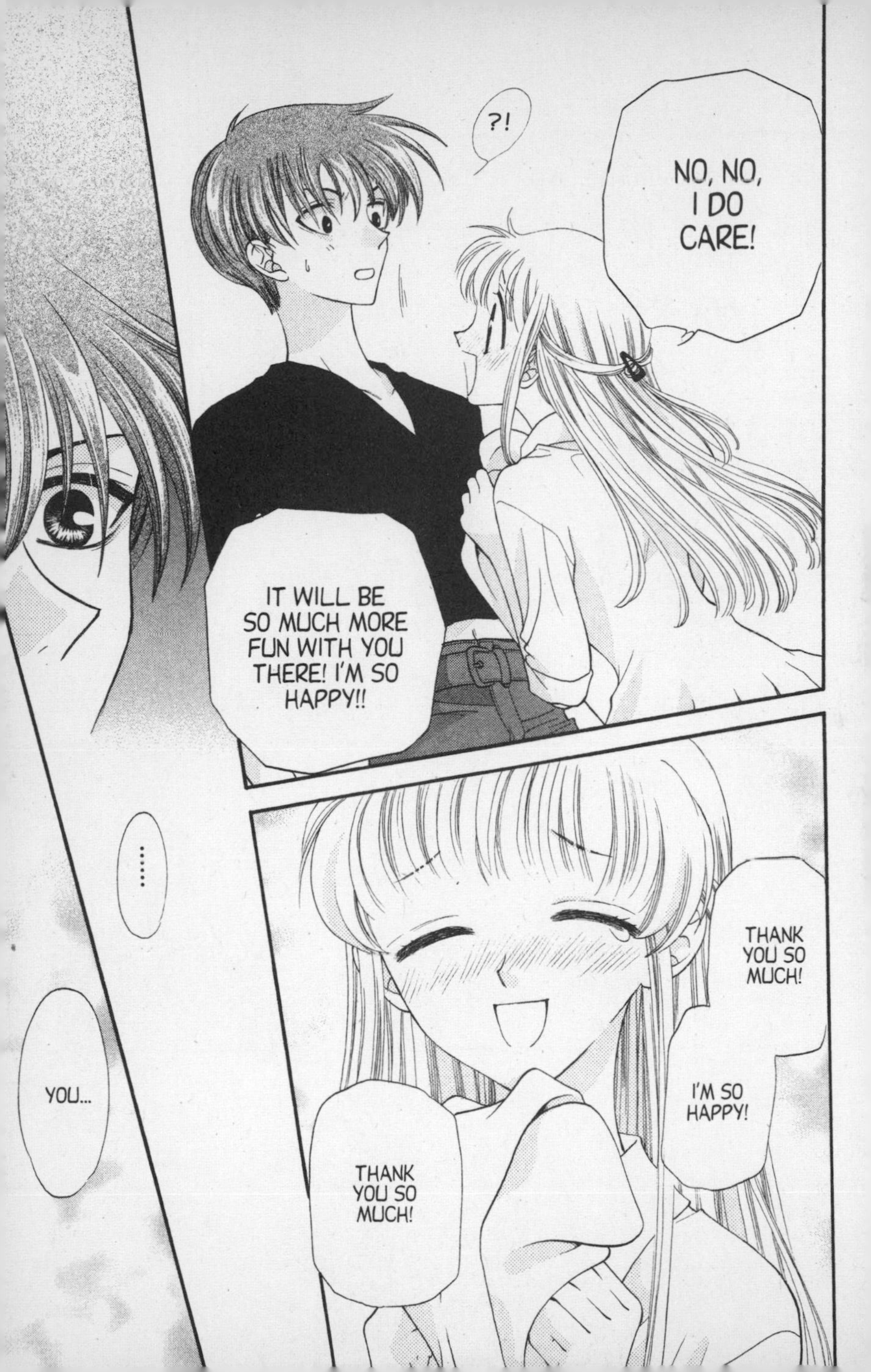
NO, NO, I DO CARE!
?!
IT WILL BE SO MUCH MORE FUN WITH YOU THERE! I'M SO HAPPY!!
THANK YOU SO MUCH!
I'M SO HAPPY!
THANK YOU SO MUCH!
......
YOU...

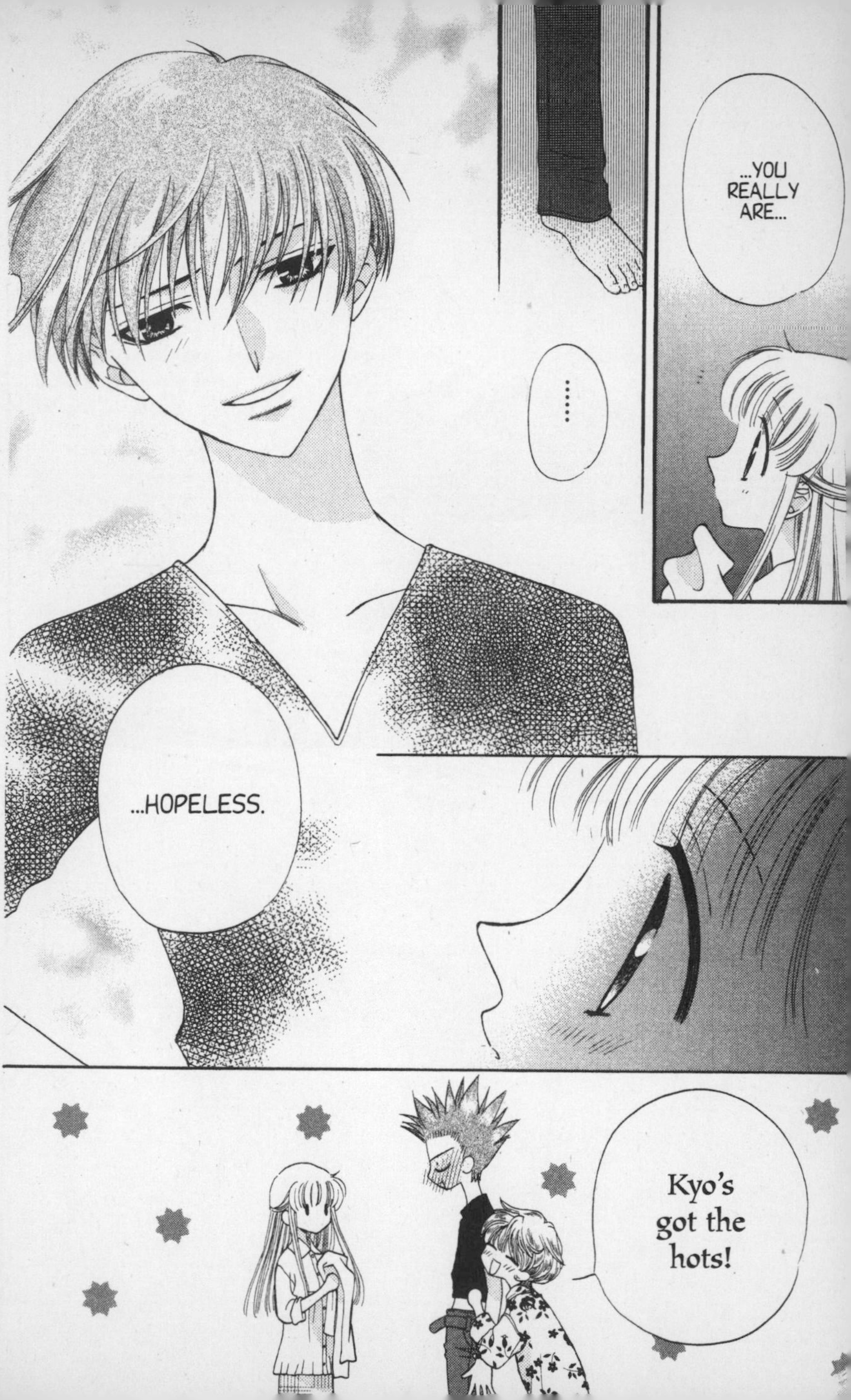
...YOU REALLY ARE...
......
...HOPELESS.
Kyo's got the hots!

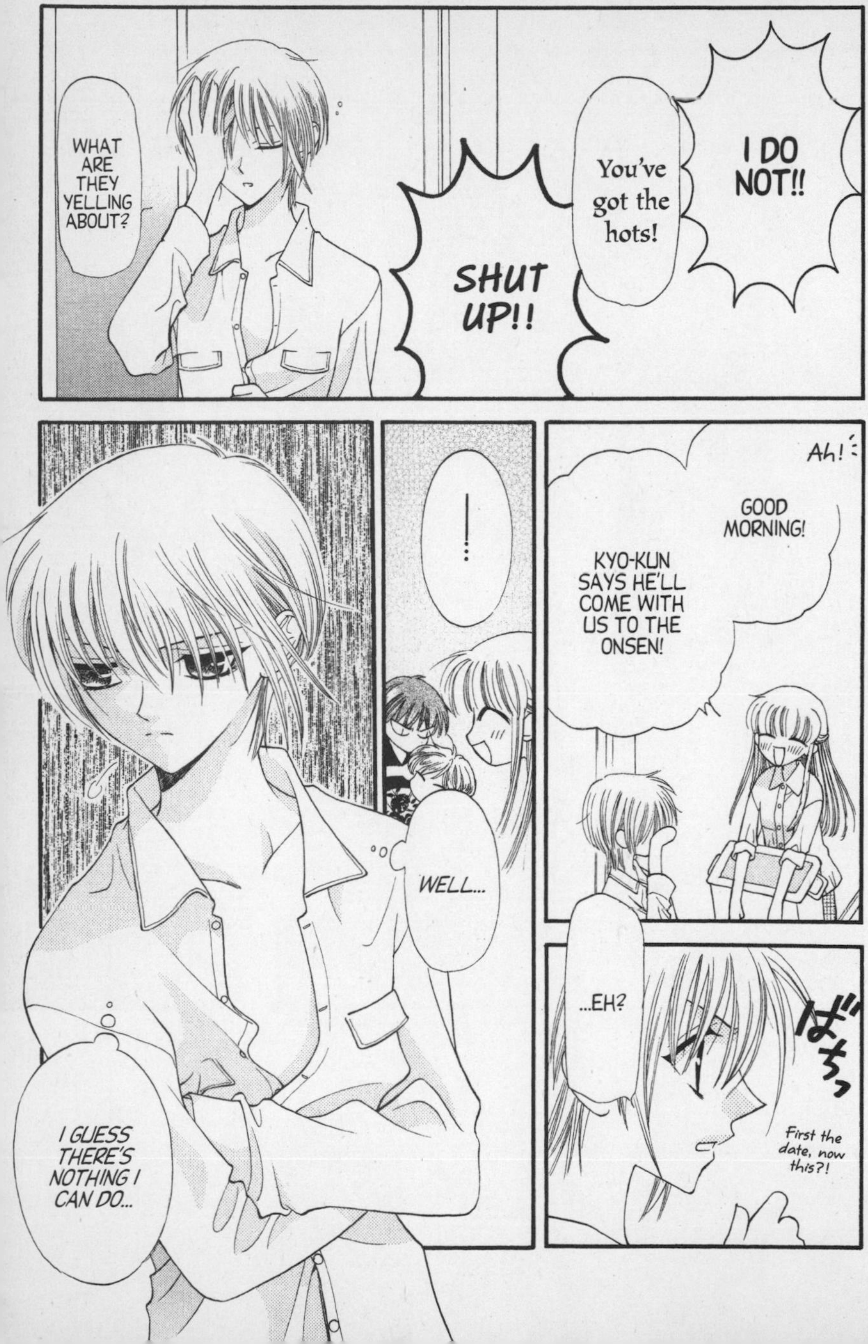
I DO NOT!!
You've got the hots!
SHUT UP!!
WHAT ARE THEY YELLING ABOUT?
Ah!
GOOD MORNING!
KYO-KUN SAYS HE'LL COME WITH US TO THE ONSEN!
...EH?
ばちっ
First the date, now this?!
—...
WELL...
I GUESS THERE'S NOTHING I CAN DO...

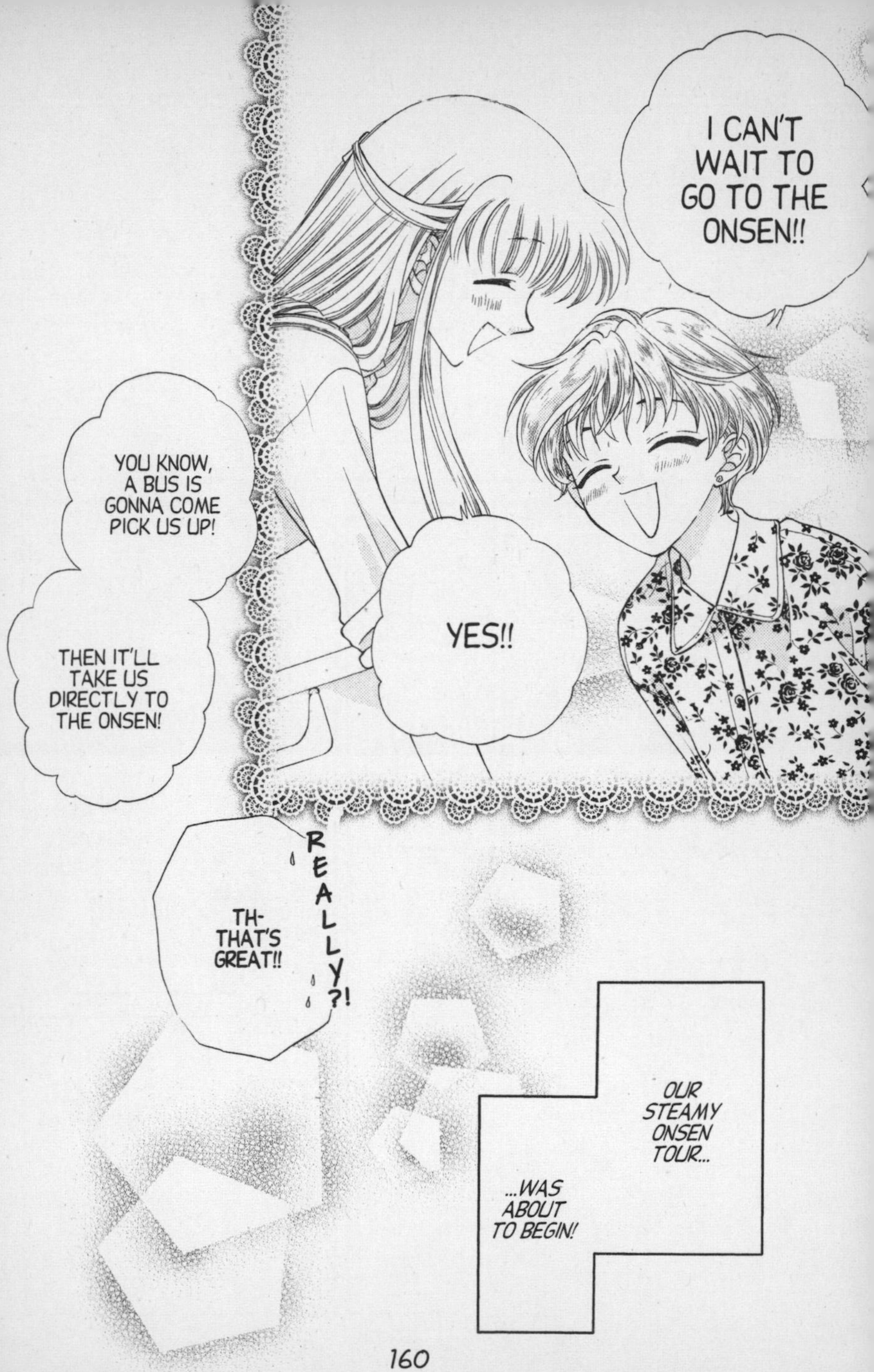
I CAN'T WAIT TO GO TO THE ONSEN!!
YES!!
YOU KNOW, A BUS IS GONNA COME PICK US UP!
THEN IT'LL TAKE US DIRECTLY TO THE ONSEN!
REALLY?!
TH- THAT'S GREAT!!
OUR STEAMY ONSEN TOUR...
...WAS ABOUT TO BEGIN!

Chapter 18

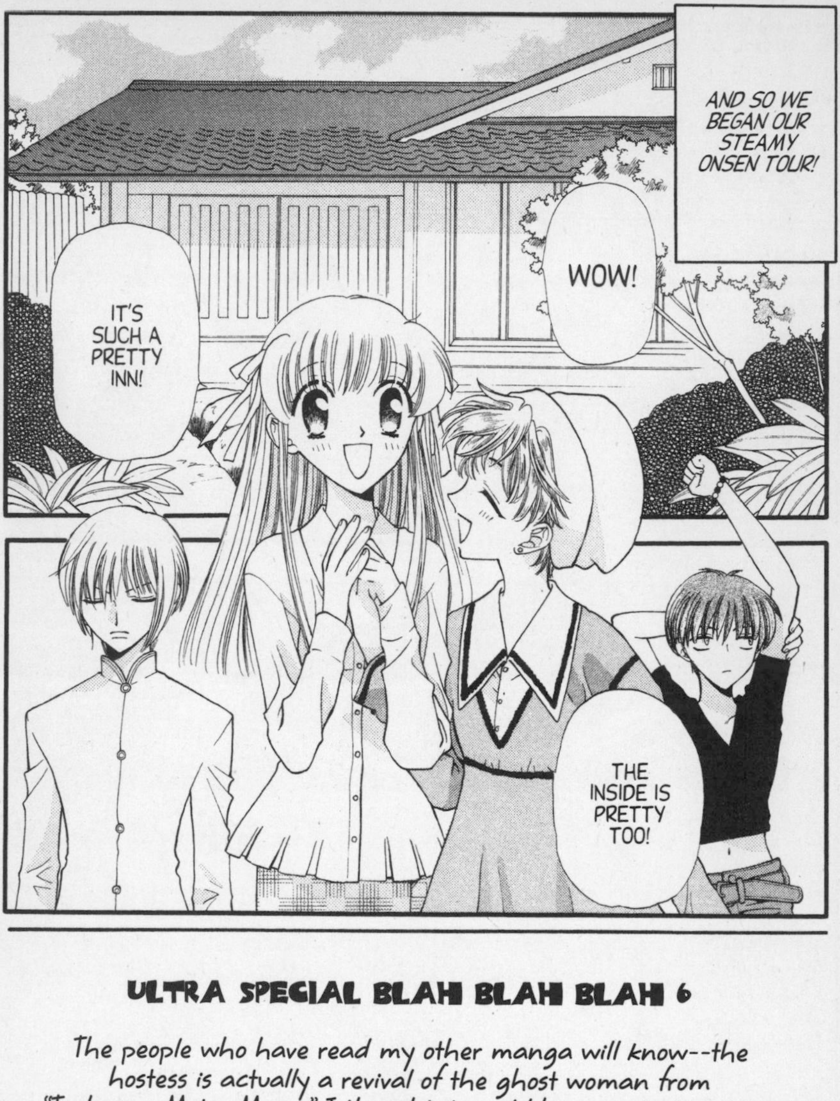
AND SO WE BEGAN OUR STEAMY ONSEN TOUR!
WOW!
IT'S SUCH A PRETTY INN!
THE INSIDE IS PRETTY TOO!

ULTRA SPECIAL BLAH BLAH BLAH 6

The people who have read my other manga will know--the hostess is actually a revival of the ghost woman from "Tsubasa o Motsu Mono." I thought it would be a waste to not use this character anymore...so I brought her back. It's very rare. Normally, I don't do that kind of thing.

I'LL BE BACK TO PICK YOU UP TOMORROW.
'KAY!!
......
I GET TO GO TO AN ONSEN FOR WHITE DAY.
AND ON TOP OF THAT, I GET TO RIDE IN A CHARTER BUS!
I feel like a princess ...
PRINCESS TOHRU!
OY. DON'T GET SO EXCITED. IT'S JUST AN ONSEN.

Fruits Basket 3 Part 6

Maybe because I said I really, really like King Of-san is why I get a lot of information about him and a lot of people saying, "I like him too♥!" So, I guess he really is popular! I think... I really must have been lucky to have him play Raimon. So I support him as a fan too. Anyway, since I started using the 'net, I've had the opportunity to meet a lot of people; for someone like me who spends all her time closed up inside working, it's kind of a sensational feeling. Maybe next I'll get a driver's license?! (Nah, that will never happen.) Someone as careless as me should not be allowed to drive. I'm sure I'd get into an accident. Oh no... Ah!!! I haven't talked about video games!! I'm almost done with Persona 2: Tsumi (AKA Persona 2: Eternal Punishment), and then I'll finish Ore no Shikabane (not available in the US).

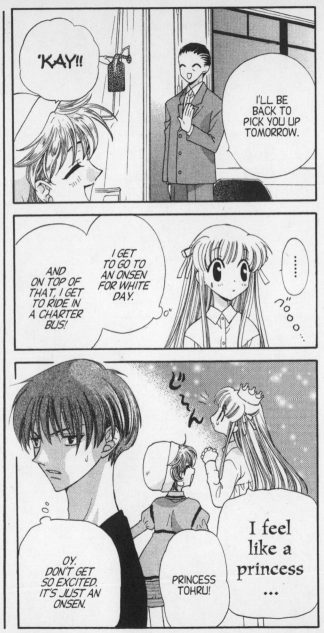

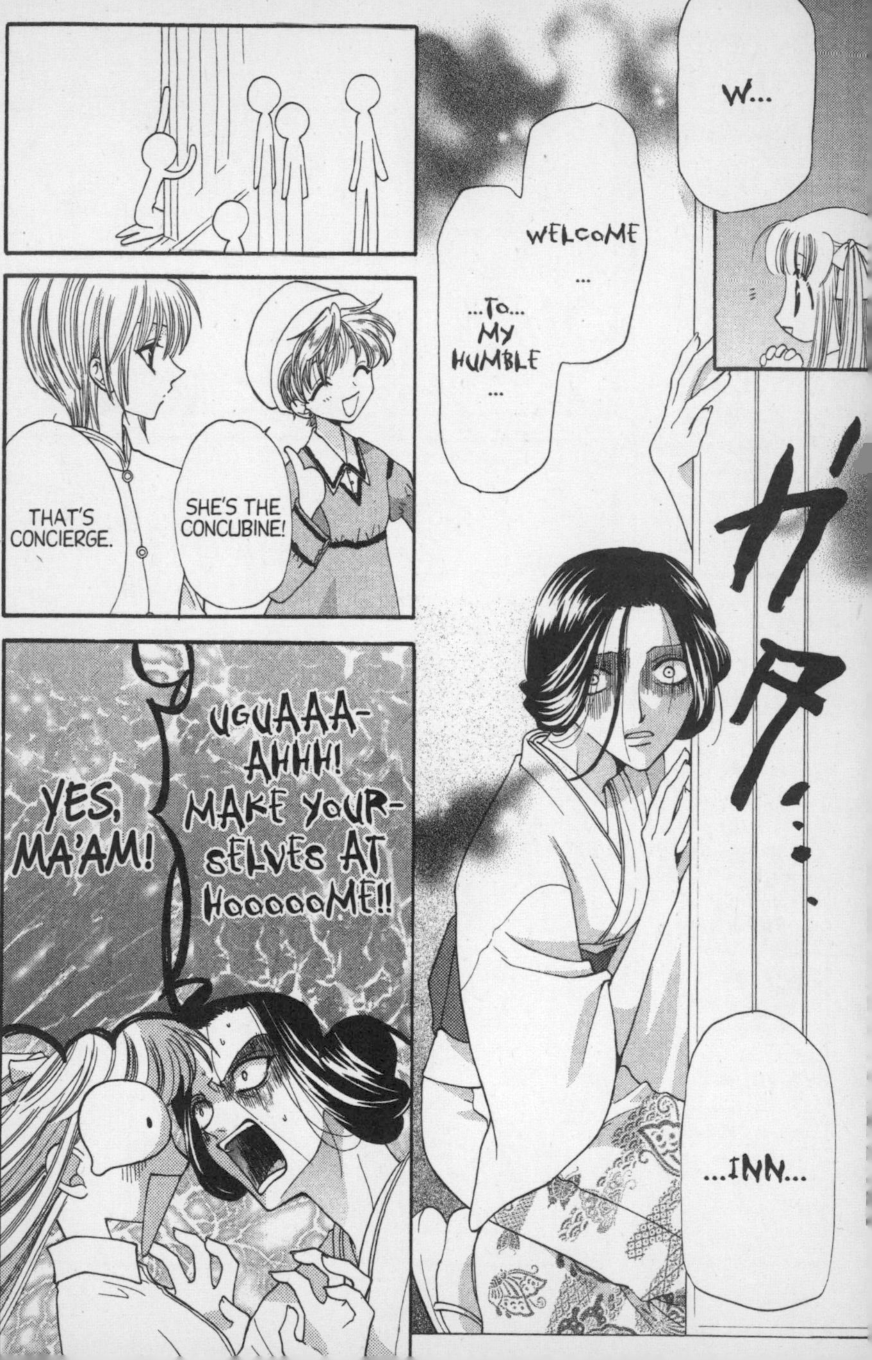
W...
WELCOME ... ...TO... MY HUMBLE ...
ガタ…
...INN...
SHE'S THE CONCUBINE!
THAT'S CONCIERGE.
UGUAAA-AHHH! MAKE YOUR-SELVES AT HoooooME!!
YES, MA'AM!

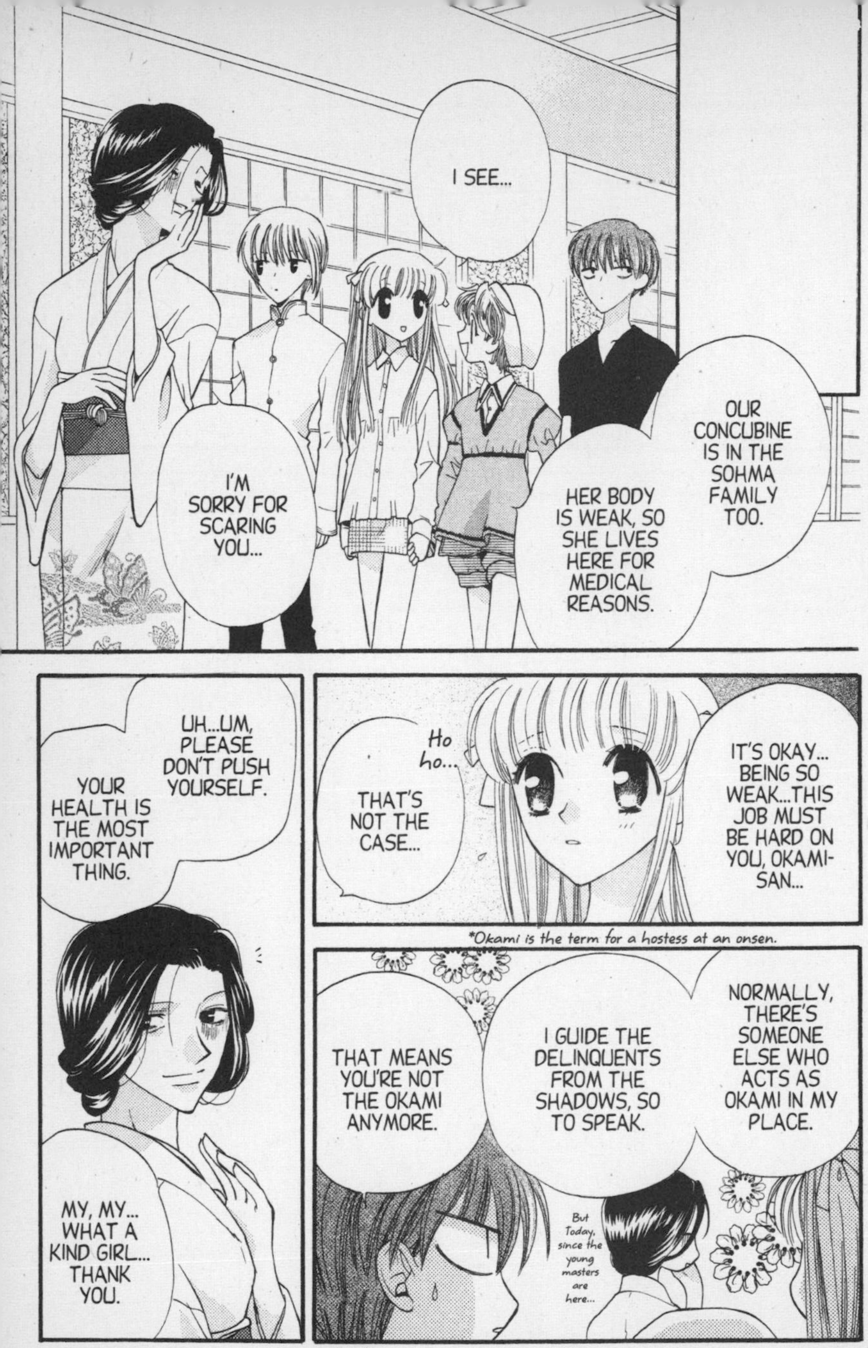
OUR CONCUBINE IS IN THE SOHMA FAMILY TOO.
HER BODY IS WEAK, SO SHE LIVES HERE FOR MEDICAL REASONS.
I SEE...
I'M SORRY FOR SCARING YOU...
IT'S OKAY... BEING SO WEAK...THIS JOB MUST BE HARD ON YOU, OKAMI-SAN...
Ho ho...
THAT'S NOT THE CASE...
NORMALLY, THERE'S SOMEONE ELSE WHO ACTS AS OKAMI IN MY PLACE.
I GUIDE THE DELINQUENTS FROM THE SHADOWS, SO TO SPEAK.
But Today, since the young masters are here...
THAT MEANS YOU'RE NOT THE OKAMI ANYMORE.
UH...UM, PLEASE DON'T PUSH YOURSELF.
YOUR HEALTH IS THE MOST IMPORTANT THING.
MY, MY... WHAT A KIND GIRL... THANK YOU.

*Okami is the term for a hostess at an onsen.

By the way, there are waitresses too.

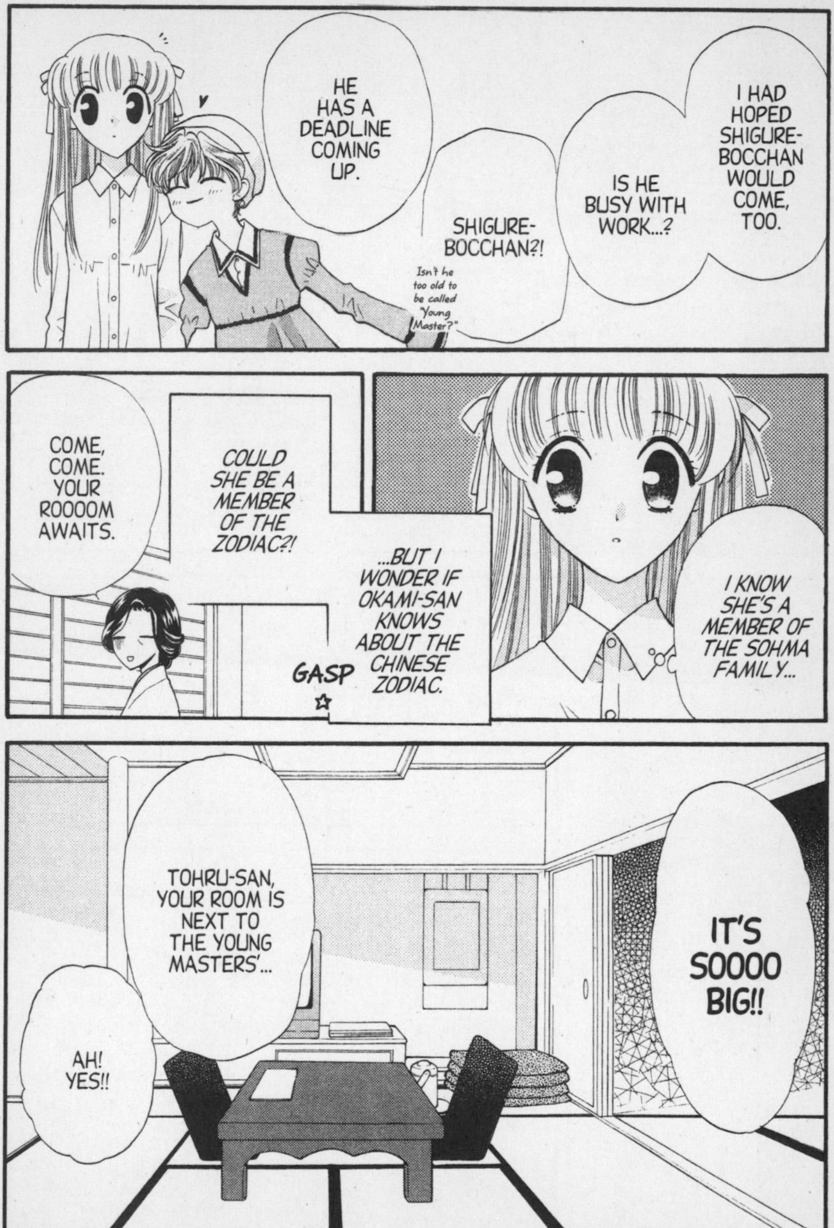
I HAD HOPED SHIGURE-BOCCHAN WOULD COME, TOO.
IS HE BUSY WITH WORK...?
SHIGURE-BOCCHAN?!
Isn't he too old to be called "Young Master?"
HE HAS A DEADLINE COMING UP.
I KNOW SHE'S A MEMBER OF THE SOHMA FAMILY...
...BUT I WONDER IF OKAMI-SAN KNOWS ABOUT THE CHINESE ZODIAC.
GASP
COULD SHE BE A MEMBER OF THE ZODIAC?!
COME, COME. YOUR ROOOOM AWAITS.
IT'S SOOOO BIG!!
TOHRU-SAN, YOUR ROOM IS NEXT TO THE YOUNG MASTERS'...
AH! YES!!

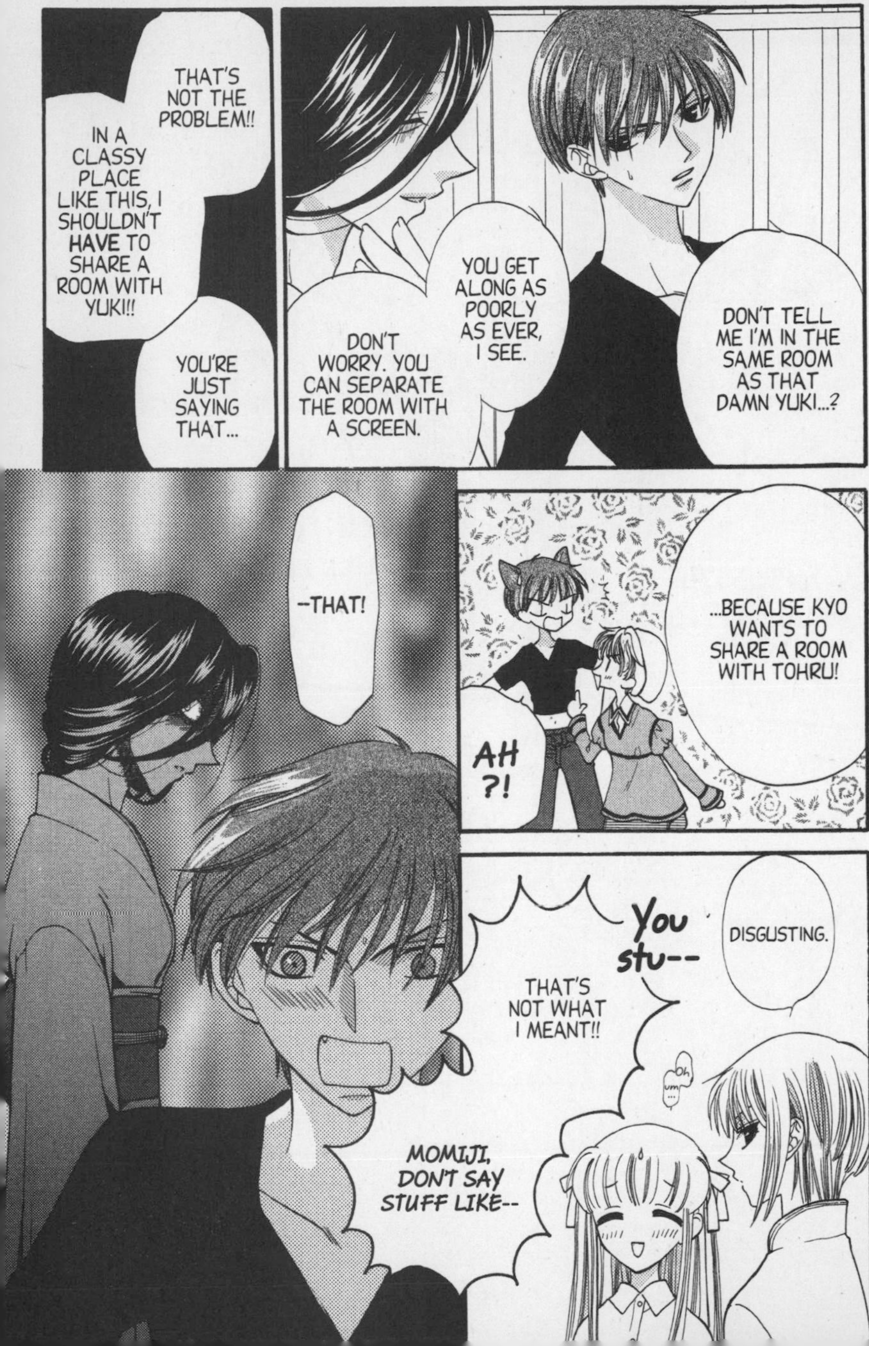

DON'T TELL ME I'M IN THE SAME ROOM AS THAT DAMN YUKI...?
YOU GET ALONG AS POORLY AS EVER, I SEE.
DON'T WORRY. YOU CAN SEPARATE THE ROOM WITH A SCREEN.
THAT'S NOT THE PROBLEM!!
IN A CLASSY PLACE LIKE THIS, I SHOULDN'T HAVE TO SHARE A ROOM WITH YUKI!!
YOU'RE JUST SAYING THAT...
...BECAUSE KYO WANTS TO SHARE A ROOM WITH TOHRU!
AH?!
DISGUSTING.
You stu--
THAT'S NOT WHAT I MEANT!!
Oh um...
MOMIJI, DON'T SAY STUFF LIKE--
--THAT!

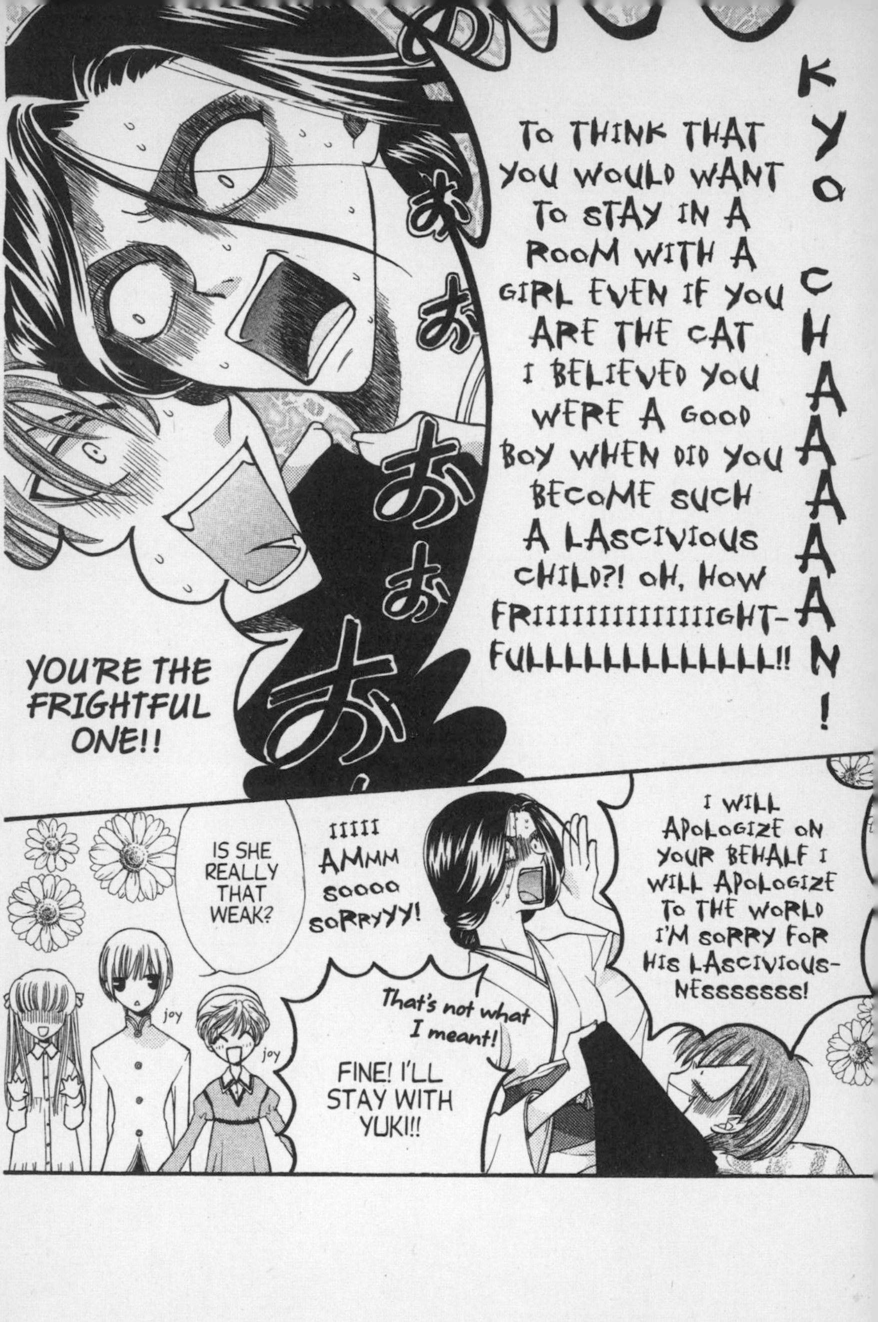
KYO CHAAAAAN!
TO THINK THAT YOU WOULD WANT TO STAY IN A ROOM WITH A GIRL EVEN IF YOU ARE THE CAT I BELIEVED YOU WERE A GOOD BOY WHEN DID YOU BECOME SUCH A LASCIVIOUS CHILD?! OH, HOW FRIIIIIIIIIIIIIIGHT-FULLLLLLLLLLLLLL!!
YOU'RE THE FRIGHTFUL ONE!!
I WILL APOLOGIZE ON YOUR BEHALF I WILL APOLOGIZE TO THE WORLD I'M SORRY FOR HIS LASCIVIOUS-NESSSSSSS!
That's not what I meant!
FINE! I'LL STAY WITH YUKI!!
IIIII AMMM SOOOO SORRYYY!
IS SHE REALLY THAT WEAK?
joy
joy

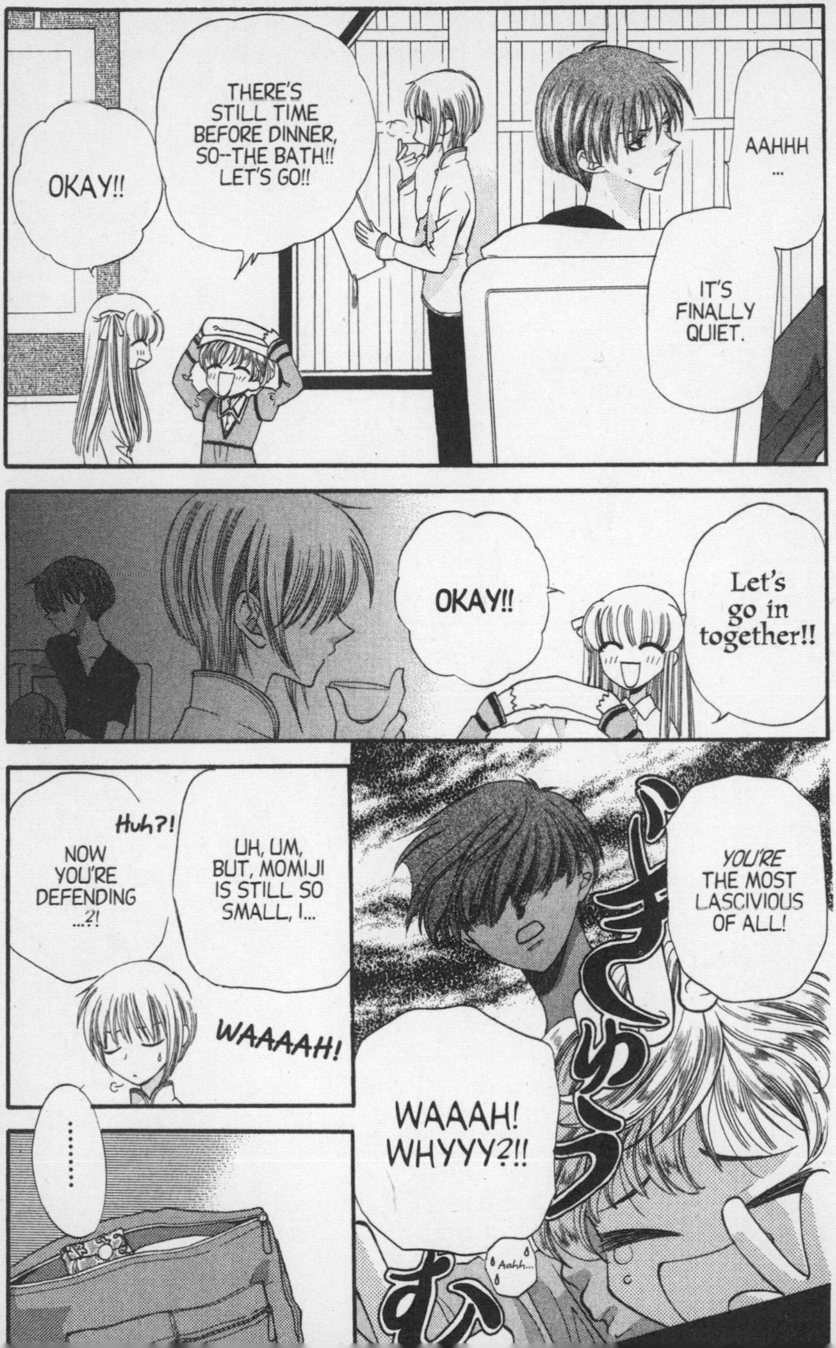
AAHHH ...
IT'S FINALLY QUIET.
THERE'S STILL TIME BEFORE DINNER, SO--THE BATH!! LET'S GO!!
OKAY!!
Let's go in together!!
OKAY!!
YOU'RE THE MOST LASCIVIOUS OF ALL!
WAAAH! WHYYY?!!
Aahh...
UH, UM, BUT, MOMIJI IS STILL SO SMALL, I...
Huh?!
NOW YOU'RE DEFENDING ...?!
WAAAAH!
......

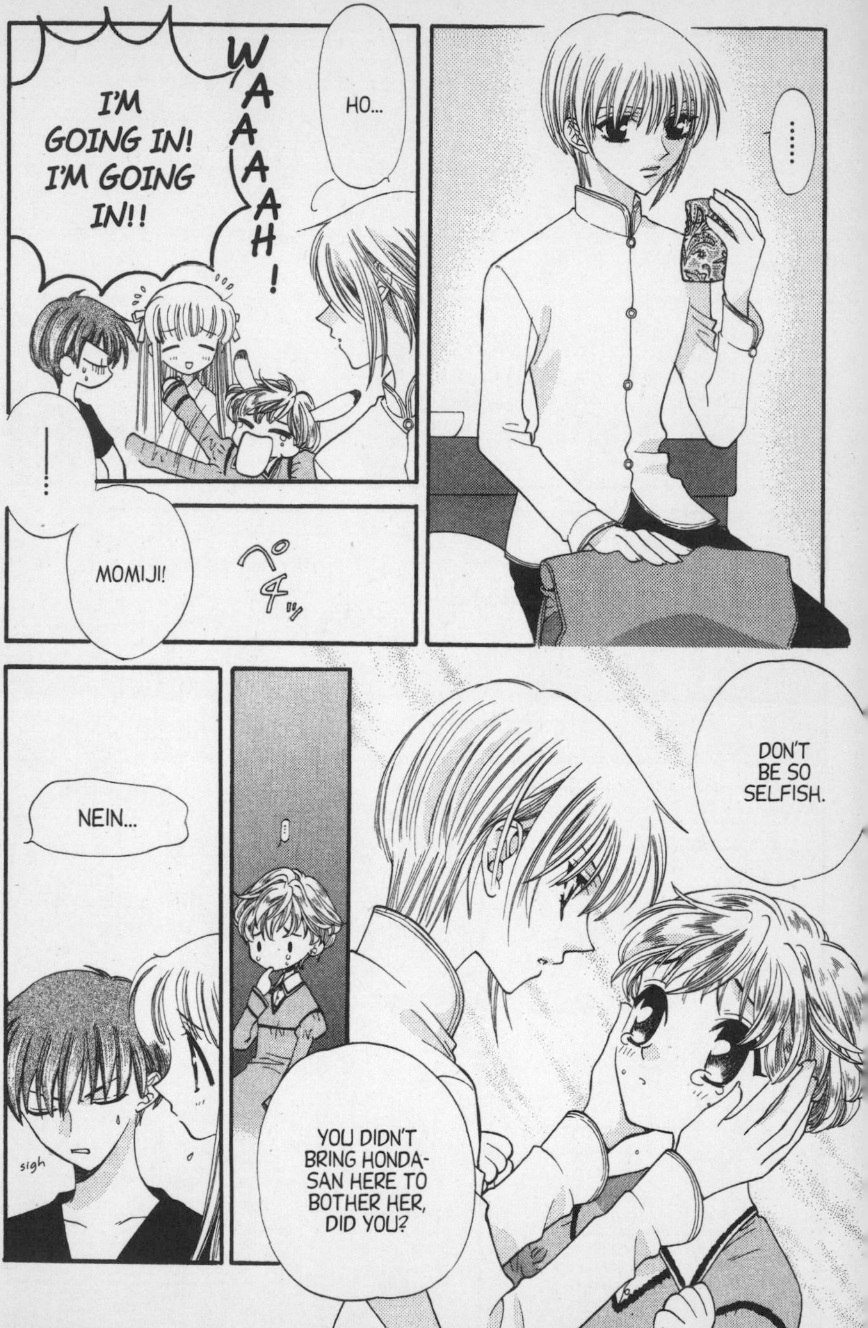
......
HO...
WAAAAAH!
I'M GOING IN! I'M GOING IN!!
...!
MOMIJI!
DON'T BE SO SELFISH.
YOU DIDN'T BRING HONDA-SAN HERE TO BOTHER HER, DID YOU?
...!
NEIN...
sigh

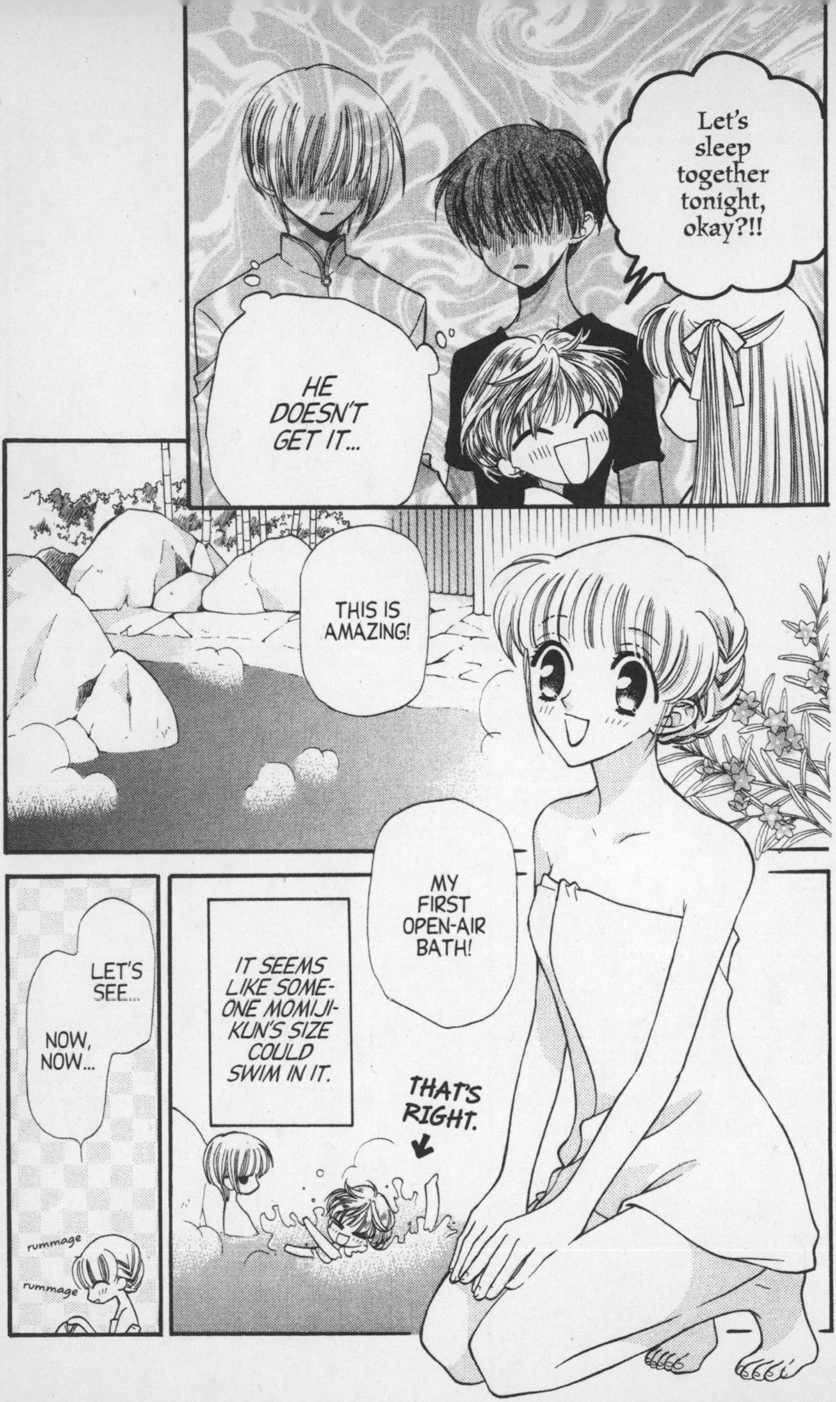
Let's sleep together tonight, okay?!!
HE DOESN'T GET IT...
THIS IS AMAZING!
MY FIRST OPEN-AIR BATH!
IT SEEMS LIKE SOME-ONE MOMIJI-KUN'S SIZE COULD SWIM IN IT.
THAT'S RIGHT.
LET'S SEE...
NOW, NOW...
rummage
rummage

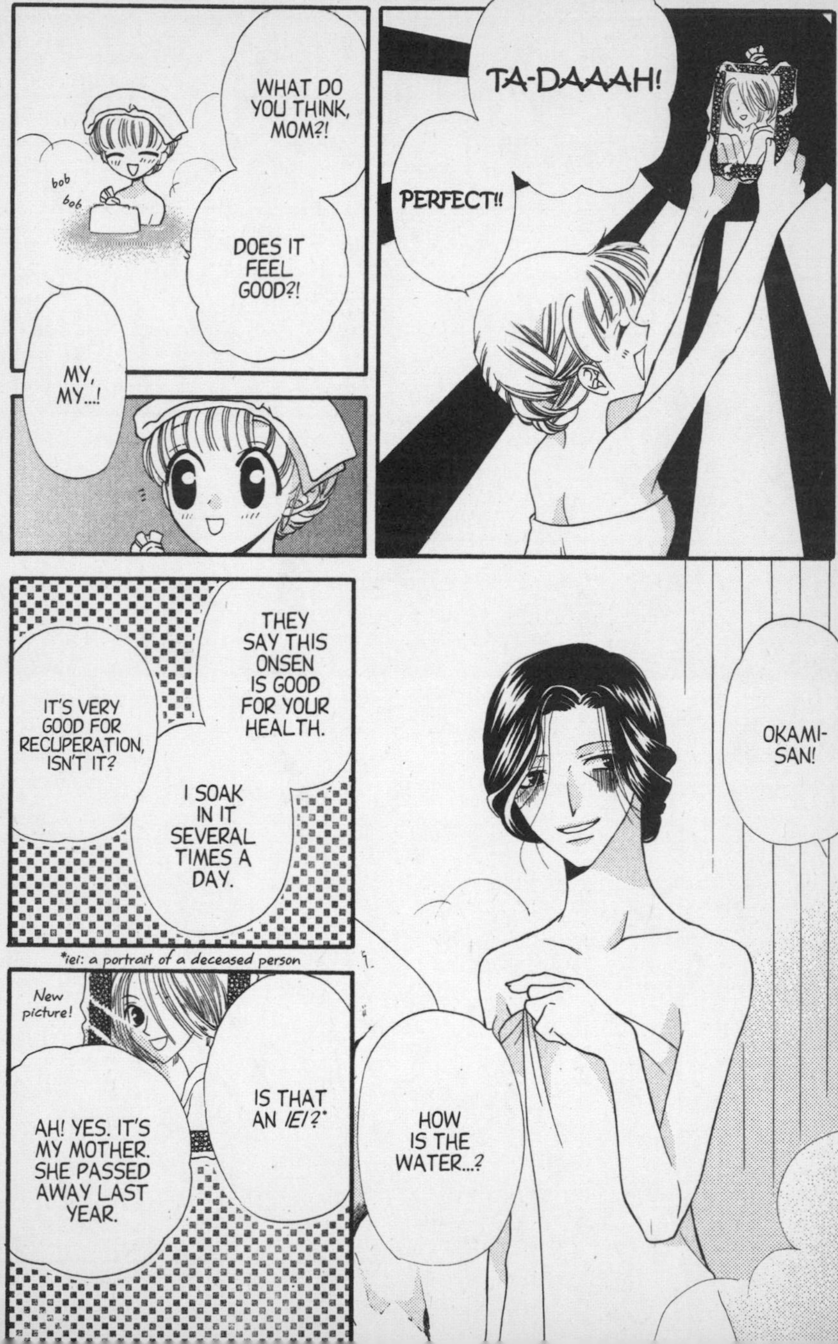
TA-DAAAH!
PERFECT!!
WHAT DO YOU THINK, MOM?!
DOES IT FEEL GOOD?!
bob bob
MY, MY...!
OKAMI-SAN!
HOW IS THE WATER...?
THEY SAY THIS ONSEN IS GOOD FOR YOUR HEALTH.
IT'S VERY GOOD FOR RECUPERATION, ISN'T IT?
I SOAK IN IT SEVERAL TIMES A DAY.
IS THAT AN *IEI*?*
New picture!
AH! YES. IT'S MY MOTHER. SHE PASSED AWAY LAST YEAR.

*iei: a portrait of a deceased person

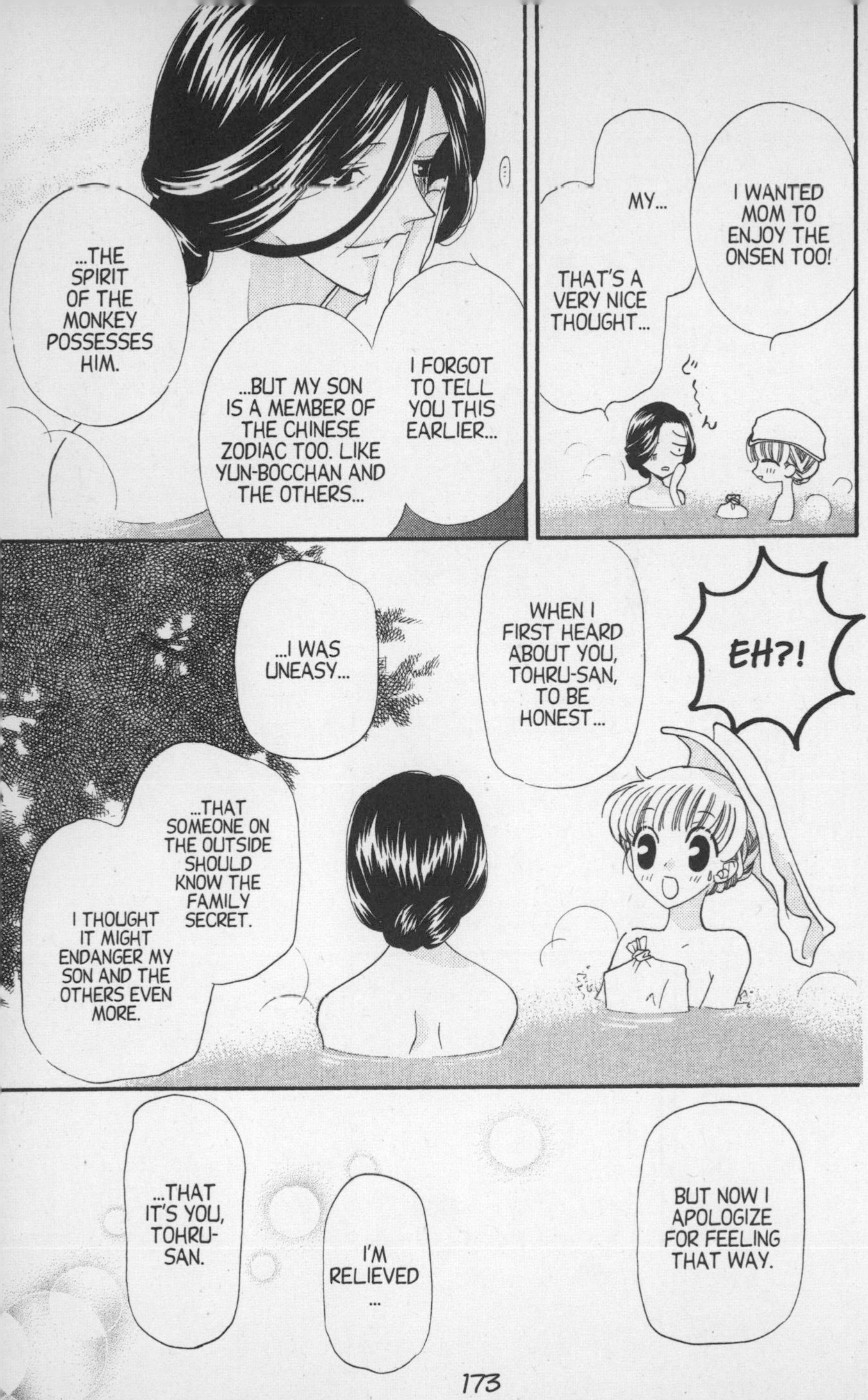
I WANTED MOM TO ENJOY THE ONSEN TOO!
MY...
THAT'S A VERY NICE THOUGHT...
I FORGOT TO TELL YOU THIS EARLIER...
...BUT MY SON IS A MEMBER OF THE CHINESE ZODIAC TOO. LIKE YUN-BOCCHAN AND THE OTHERS...
...THE SPIRIT OF THE MONKEY POSSESSES HIM.
EH?!
WHEN I FIRST HEARD ABOUT YOU, TOHRU-SAN, TO BE HONEST...
...I WAS UNEASY...
...THAT SOMEONE ON THE OUTSIDE SHOULD KNOW THE FAMILY SECRET.
I THOUGHT IT MIGHT ENDANGER MY SON AND THE OTHERS EVEN MORE.
BUT NOW I APOLOGIZE FOR FEELING THAT WAY.
I'M RELIEVED ...
...THAT IT'S YOU, TOHRU-SAN.

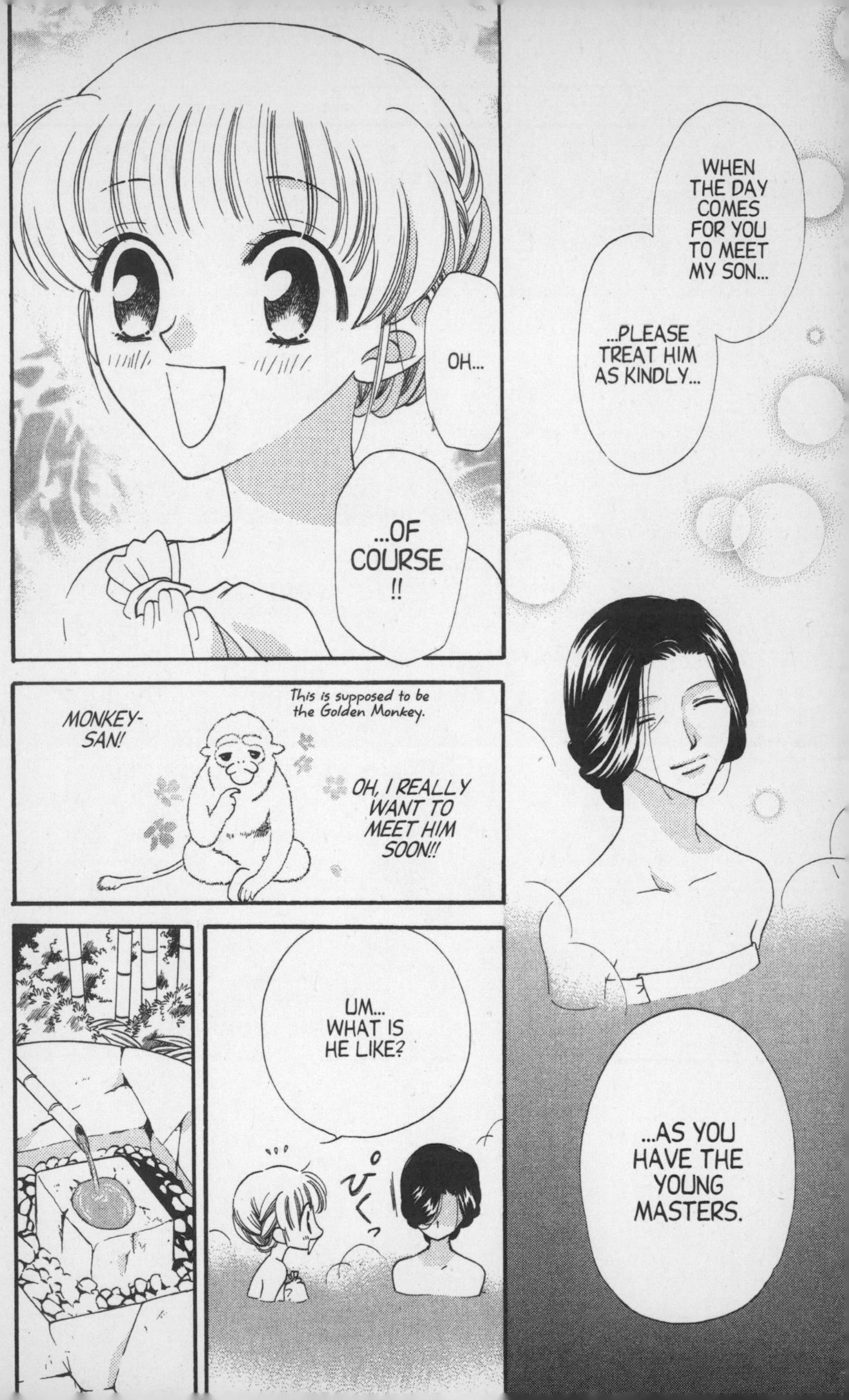
WHEN THE DAY COMES FOR YOU TO MEET MY SON...
...PLEASE TREAT HIM AS KINDLY...
...AS YOU HAVE THE YOUNG MASTERS.
OH...
...OF COURSE!!
This is supposed to be the Golden Monkey.
MONKEY-SAN!
OH, I REALLY WANT TO MEET HIM SOON!!
UM... WHAT IS HE LIKE?

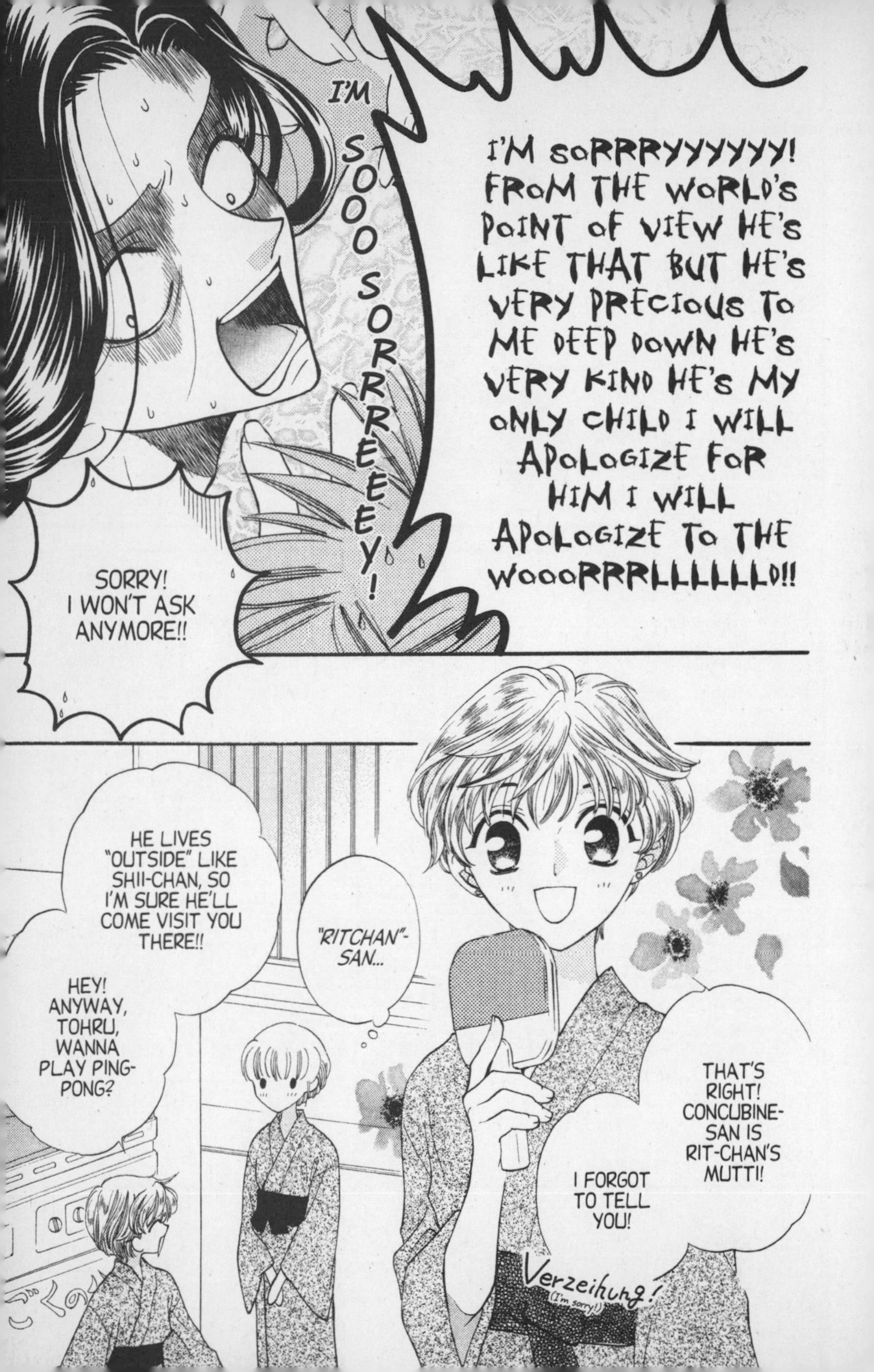
I'M SORRRYYYYYY! FROM THE WORLD'S POINT OF VIEW HE'S LIKE THAT BUT HE'S VERY PRECIOUS TO ME DEEP DOWN HE'S VERY KIND HE'S MY ONLY CHILD I WILL APOLOGIZE FOR HIM I WILL APOLOGIZE TO THE WOOORRRLLLLLLD!!
I'M SOOO SORRREEEY!
SORRY! I WON'T ASK ANYMORE!!
THAT'S RIGHT! CONCUBINE-SAN IS RIT-CHAN'S MUTTI!
I FORGOT TO TELL YOU!
Verzeihung! (I'm sorry!)
"RITCHAN"-SAN...
HE LIVES "OUTSIDE" LIKE SHII-CHAN, SO I'M SURE HE'LL COME VISIT YOU THERE!!
HEY! ANYWAY, TOHRU, WANNA PLAY PING-PONG?

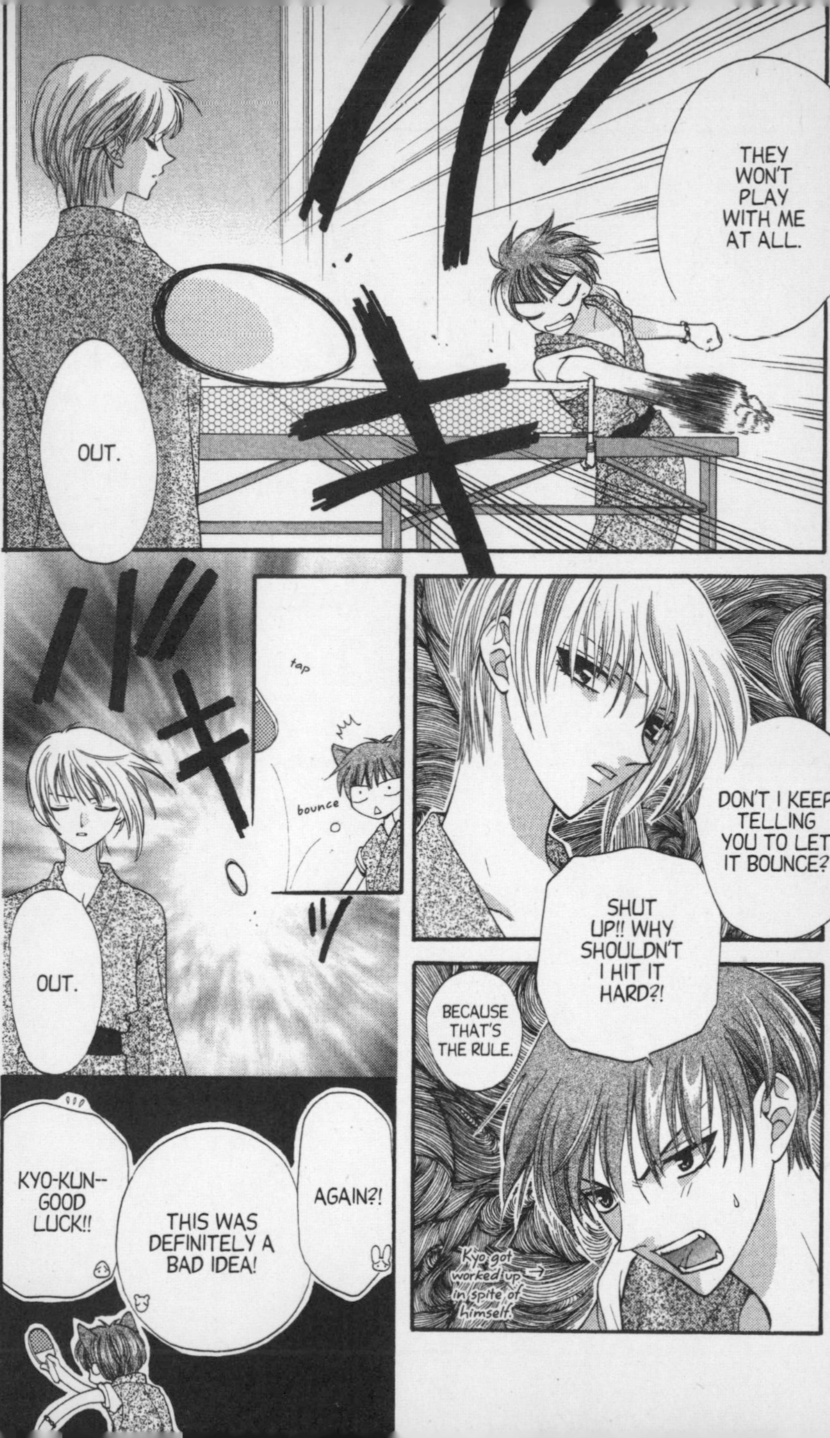
THEY WON'T PLAY WITH ME AT ALL.
OUT.
DON'T I KEEP TELLING YOU TO LET IT BOUNCE?
SHUT UP!! WHY SHOULDN'T I HIT IT HARD?!
BECAUSE THAT'S THE RULE.
Kyo got worked up in spite of himself. →
tap
bounce
OUT.
AGAIN?!
THIS WAS DEFINITELY A BAD IDEA!
KYO-KUN-- GOOD LUCK!!

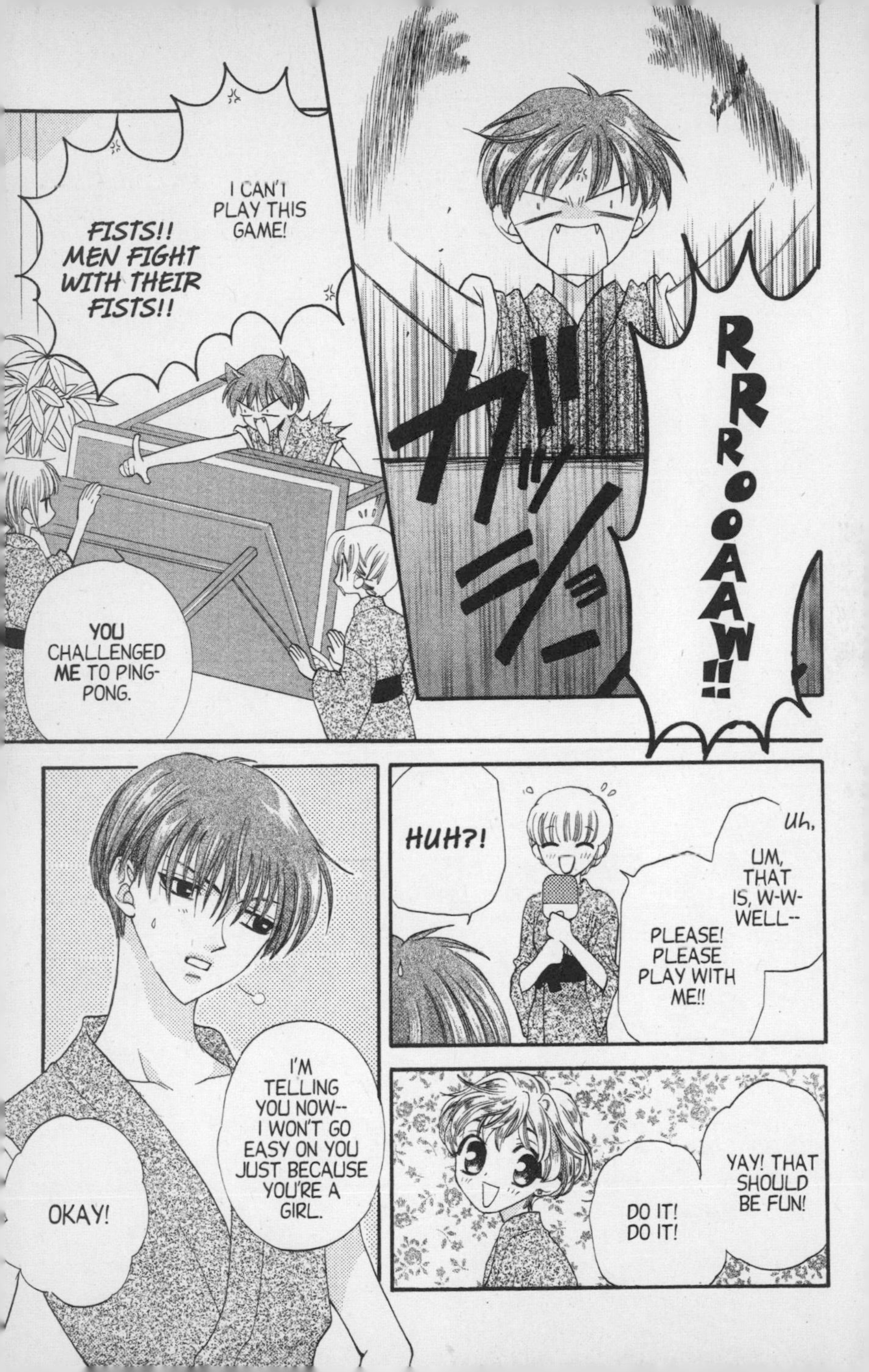
RRROOAAW!!
ガッシャーン
I CAN'T PLAY THIS GAME!
FISTS!! MEN FIGHT WITH THEIR FISTS!!
YOU CHALLENGED ME TO PING-PONG.
Uh,
UM, THAT IS, W-W-WELL--
HUH?!
PLEASE! PLEASE PLAY WITH ME!!
YAY! THAT SHOULD BE FUN!
DO IT! DO IT!
I'M TELLING YOU NOW-- I WON'T GO EASY ON YOU JUST BECAUSE YOU'RE A GIRL.
OKAY!

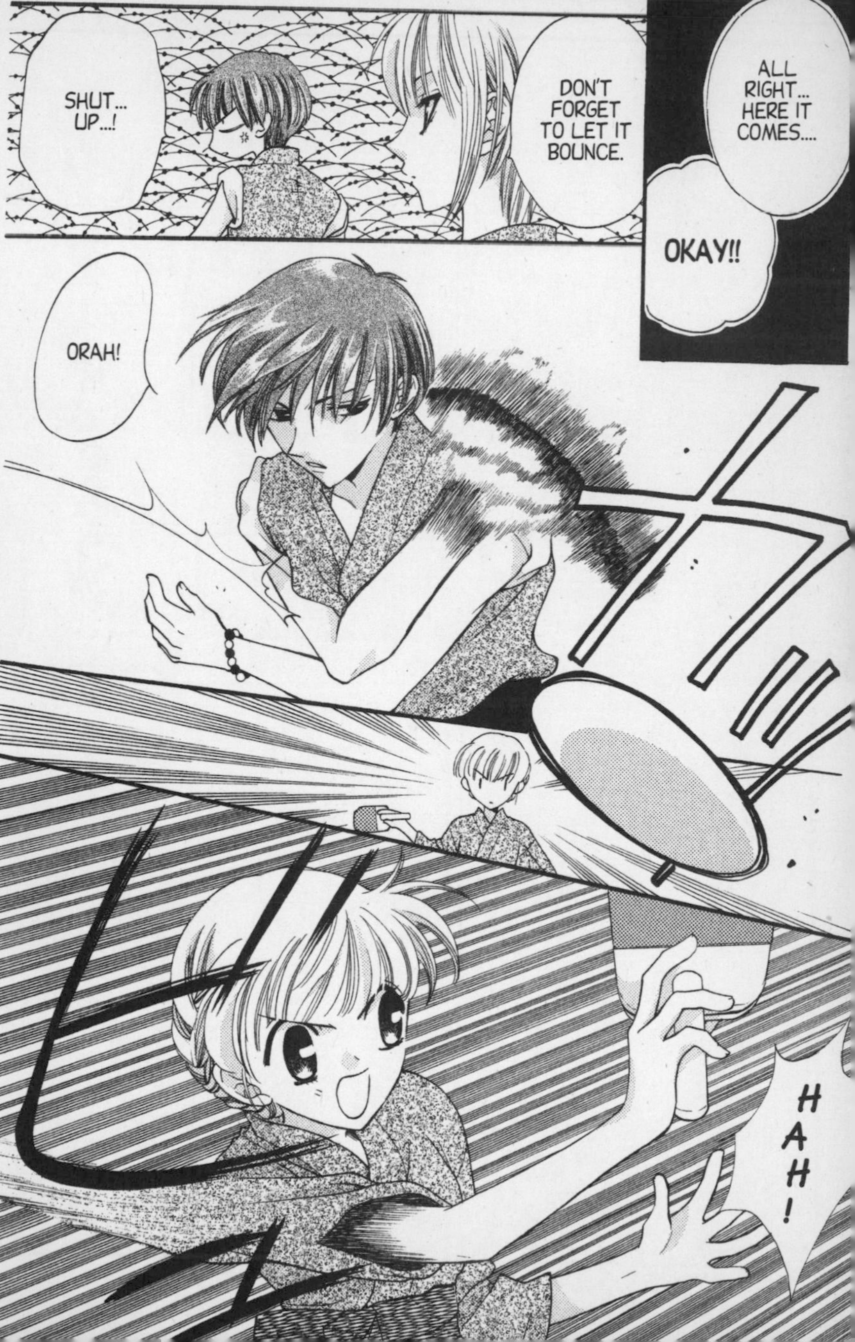
ALL RIGHT... HERE IT COMES....
OKAY!!
DON'T FORGET TO LET IT BOUNCE.
SHUT... UP...!
ORAH!
HAH!

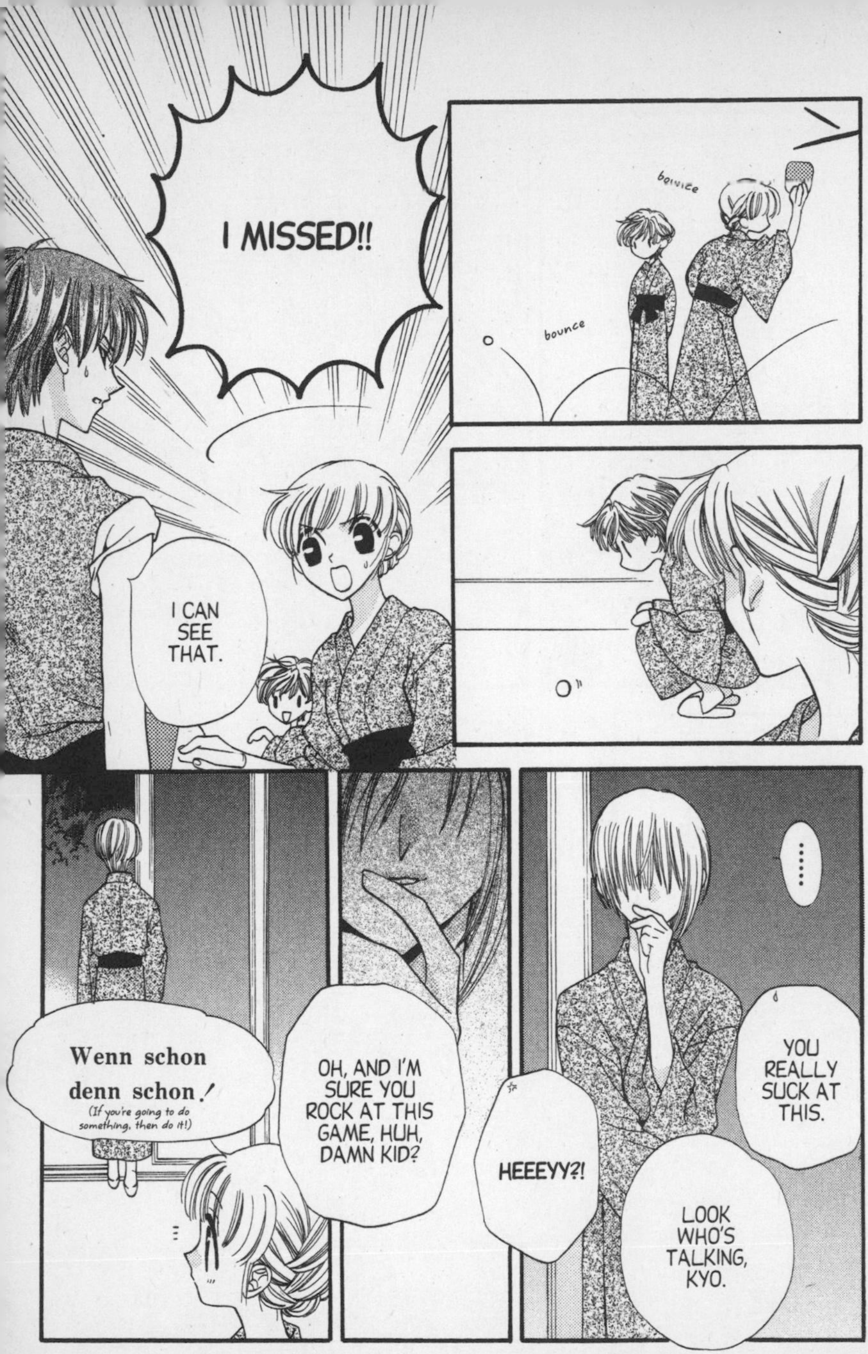
bounce
bounce
I MISSED!!
I CAN SEE THAT.
......
YOU REALLY SUCK AT THIS.
HEEEYY?!
LOOK WHO'S TALKING, KYO.
OH, AND I'M SURE YOU ROCK AT THIS GAME, HUH, DAMN KID?
Wenn schon denn schon!
(If you're going to do something, then do it!)

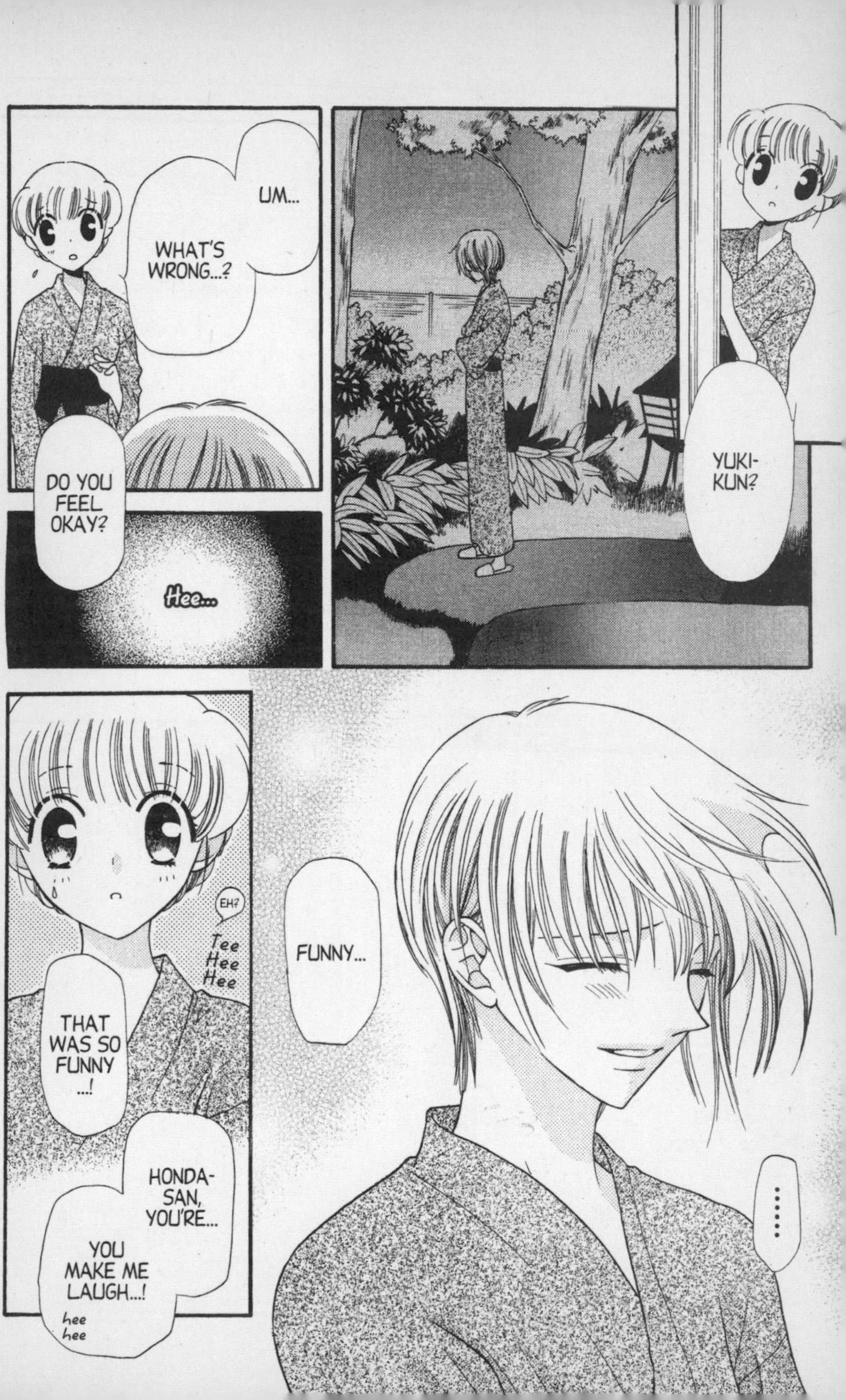
YUKI-KUN?
UM...
WHAT'S WRONG...?
DO YOU FEEL OKAY?
Hee...
FUNNY...
......
EH?
Tee Hee Hee
THAT WAS SO FUNNY...!
HONDA-SAN, YOU'RE...
YOU MAKE ME LAUGH...!
hee hee

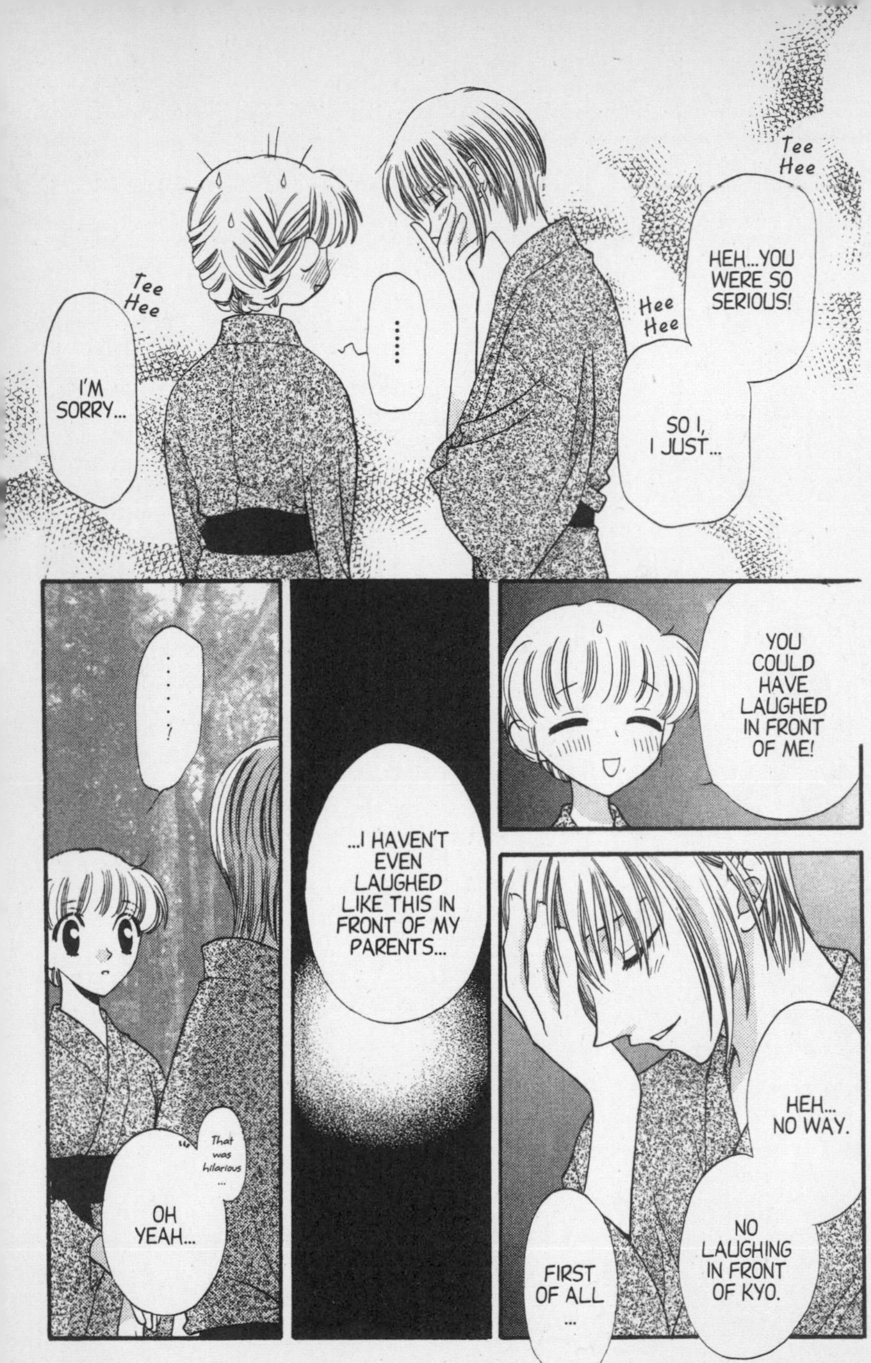
Tee Hee
HEH...YOU WERE SO SERIOUS!
Hee Hee
SO I, I JUST...
......
Tee Hee
I'M SORRY...
YOU COULD HAVE LAUGHED IN FRONT OF ME!
HEH... NO WAY.
NO LAUGHING IN FRONT OF KYO.
FIRST OF ALL ...
...I HAVEN'T EVEN LAUGHED LIKE THIS IN FRONT OF MY PARENTS...
......?
That was hilarious ...
OH YEAH...

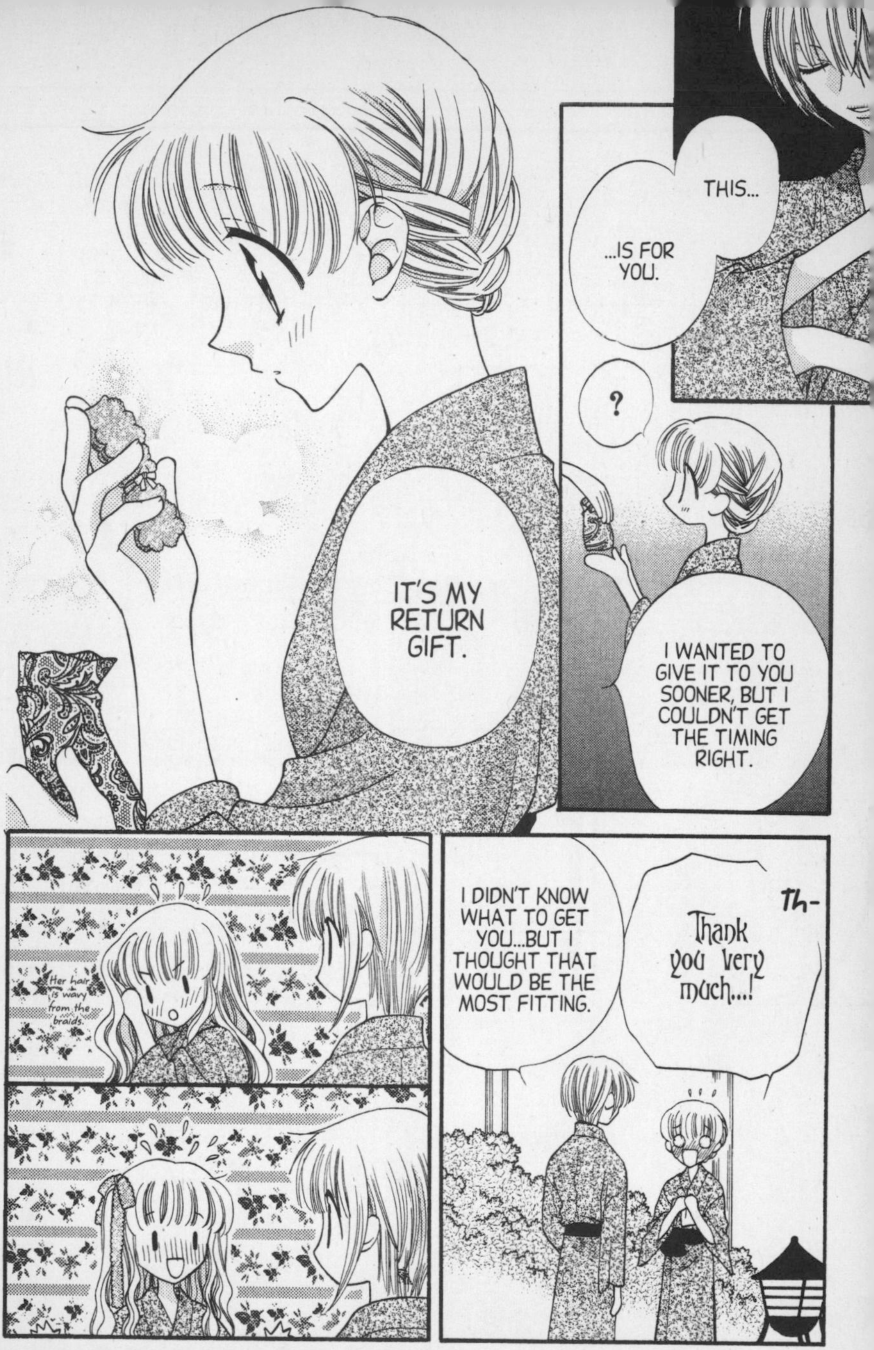
THIS...
...IS FOR YOU.
?
I WANTED TO GIVE IT TO YOU SOONER, BUT I COULDN'T GET THE TIMING RIGHT.
IT'S MY RETURN GIFT.
Th-
Thank you very much...!
I DIDN'T KNOW WHAT TO GET YOU...BUT I THOUGHT THAT WOULD BE THE MOST FITTING.
Her hair is wavy from the braids.

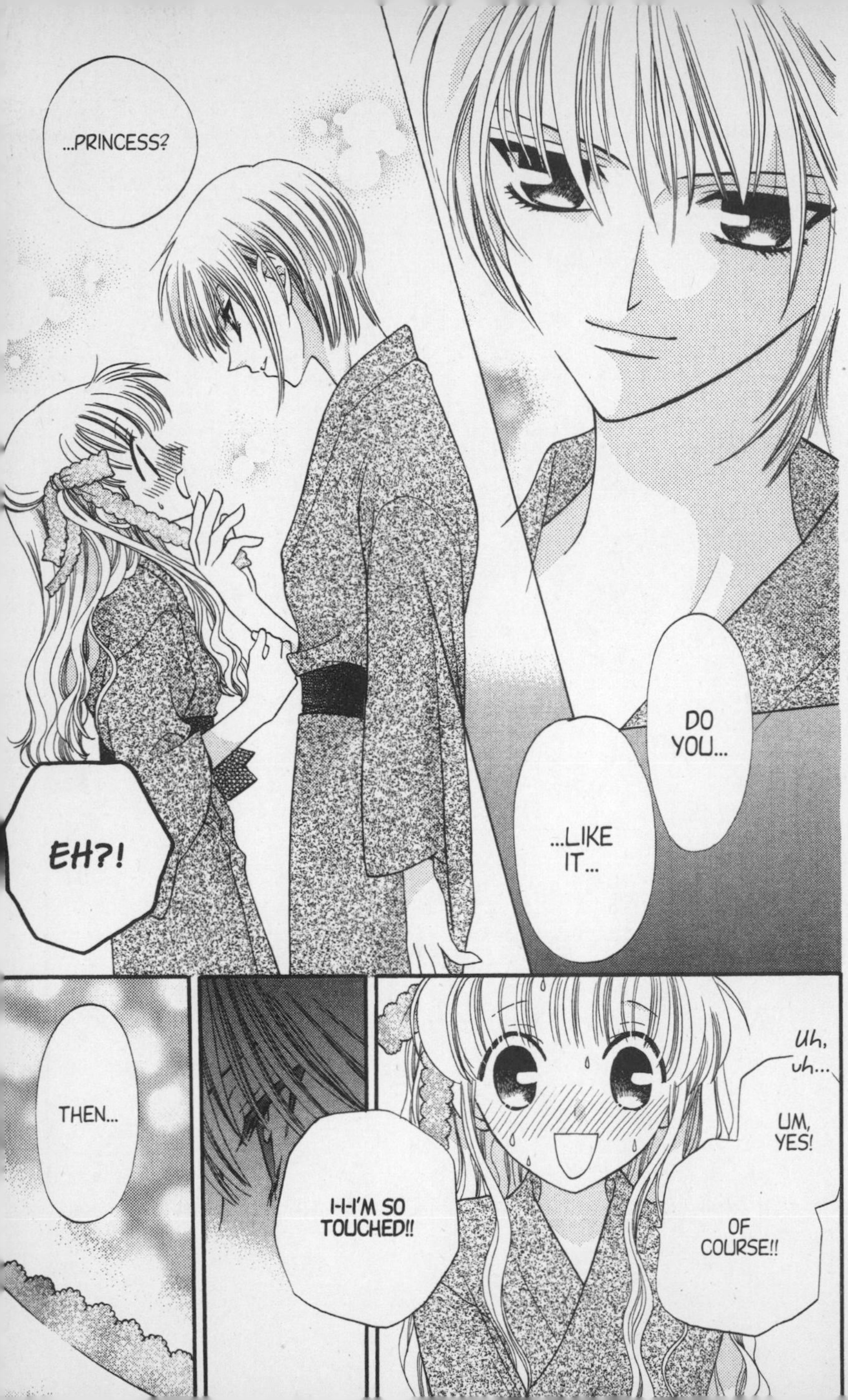
DO YOU...
...LIKE IT...
...PRINCESS?
EH?!
Uh, uh...
UM, YES!
OF COURSE!!
I-I-I'M SO TOUCHED!!
THEN...

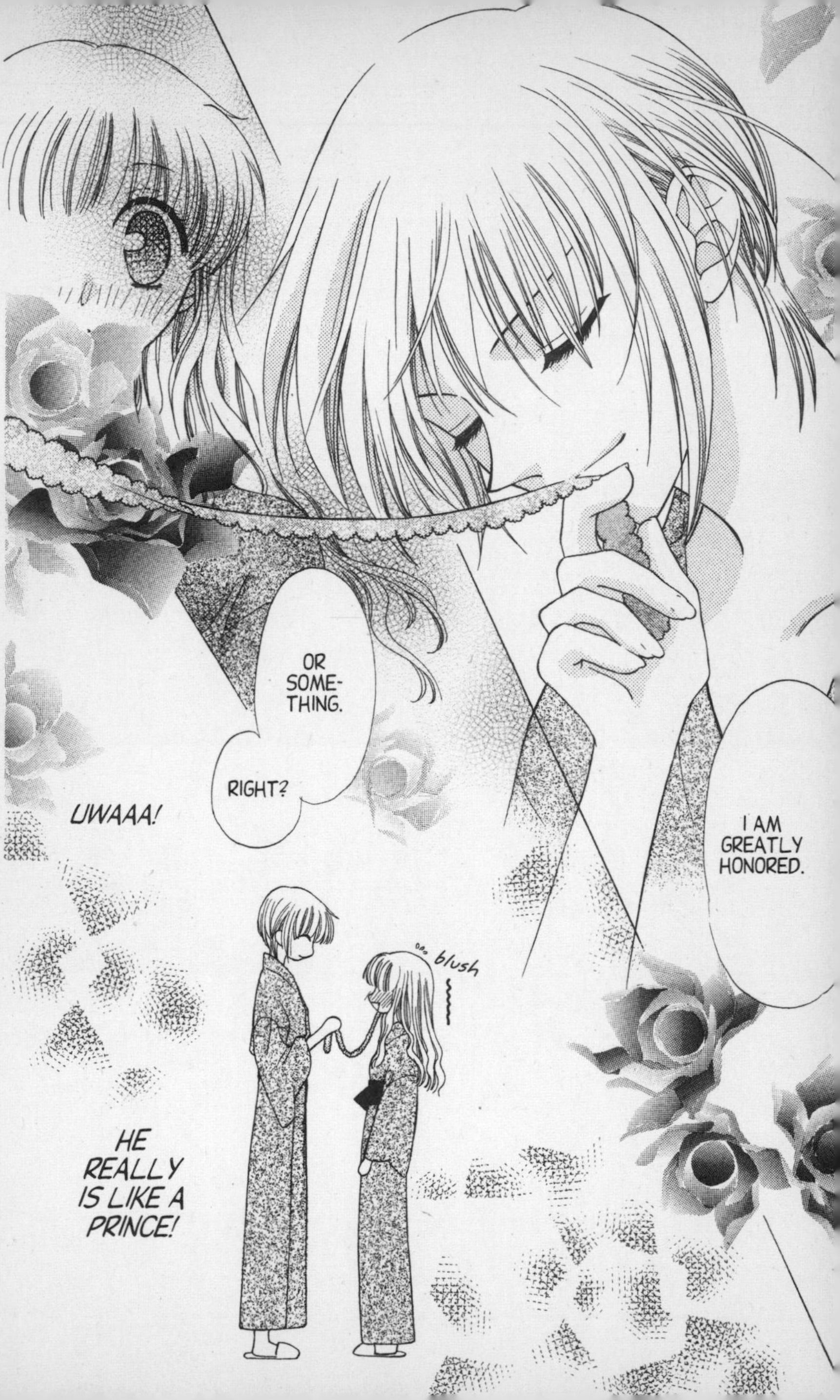
I AM GREATLY HONORED.
OR SOMETHING.
RIGHT?
UWAAA!
blush
HE REALLY IS LIKE A PRINCE!

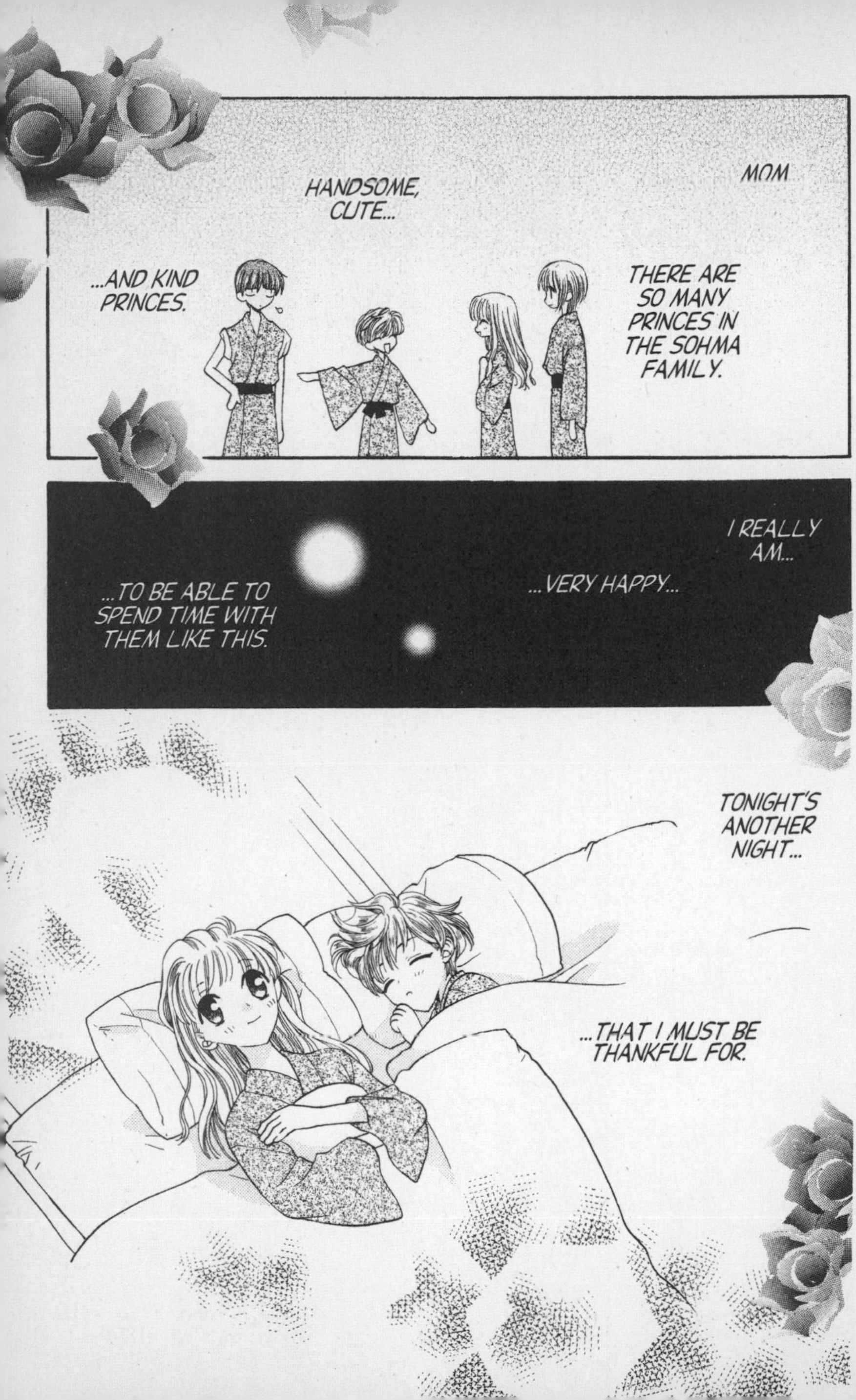
MOM...
THERE ARE SO MANY PRINCES IN THE SOHMA FAMILY.
HANDSOME, CUTE...
...AND KIND PRINCES.
I REALLY AM...
...VERY HAPPY...
...TO BE ABLE TO SPEND TIME WITH THEM LIKE THIS.
TONIGHT'S ANOTHER NIGHT...
...THAT I MUST BE THANKFUL FOR.

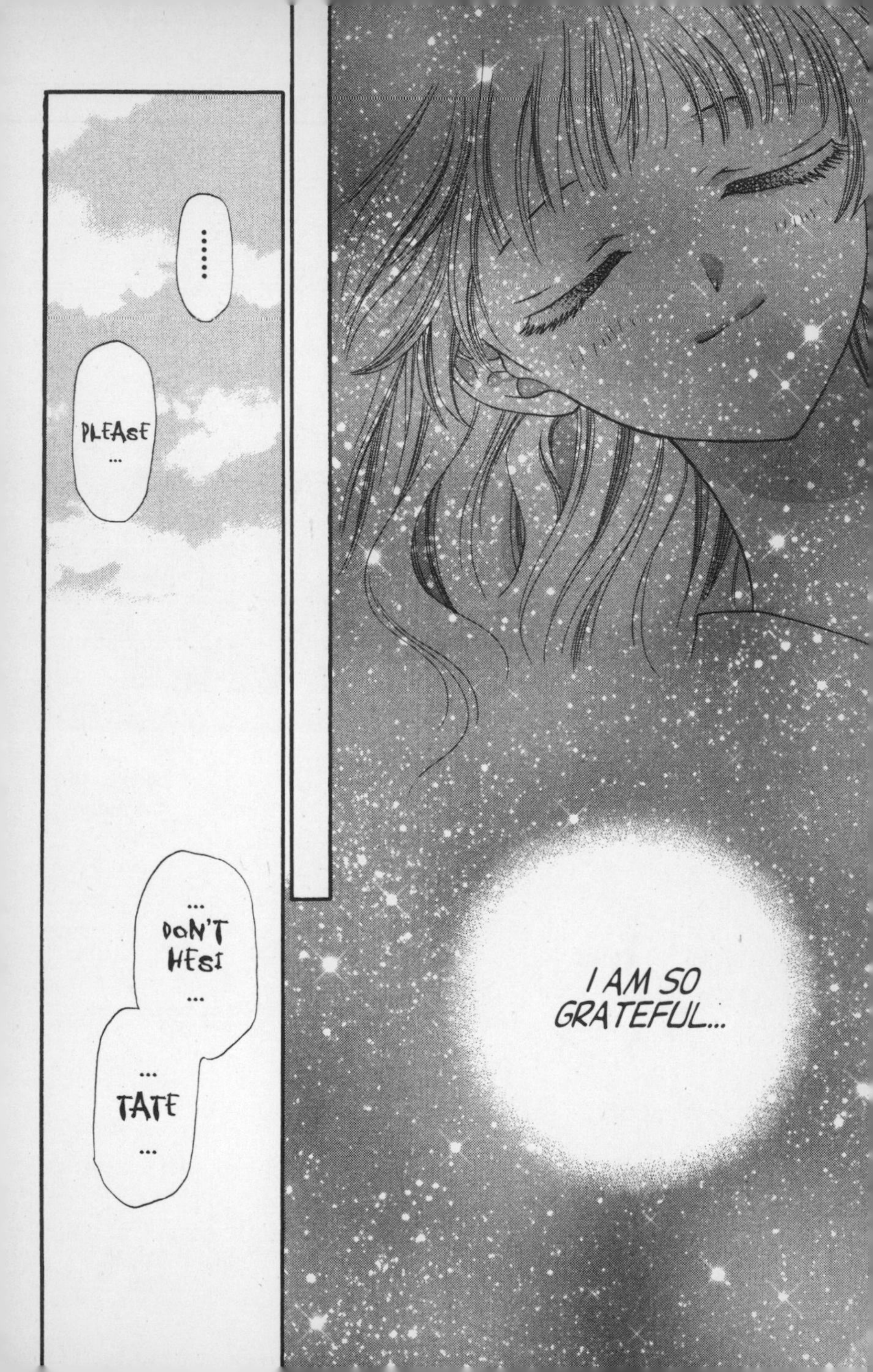
I AM SO GRATEFUL...
......
PLEASE ...
... DON'T HESI ...
... TATE ...

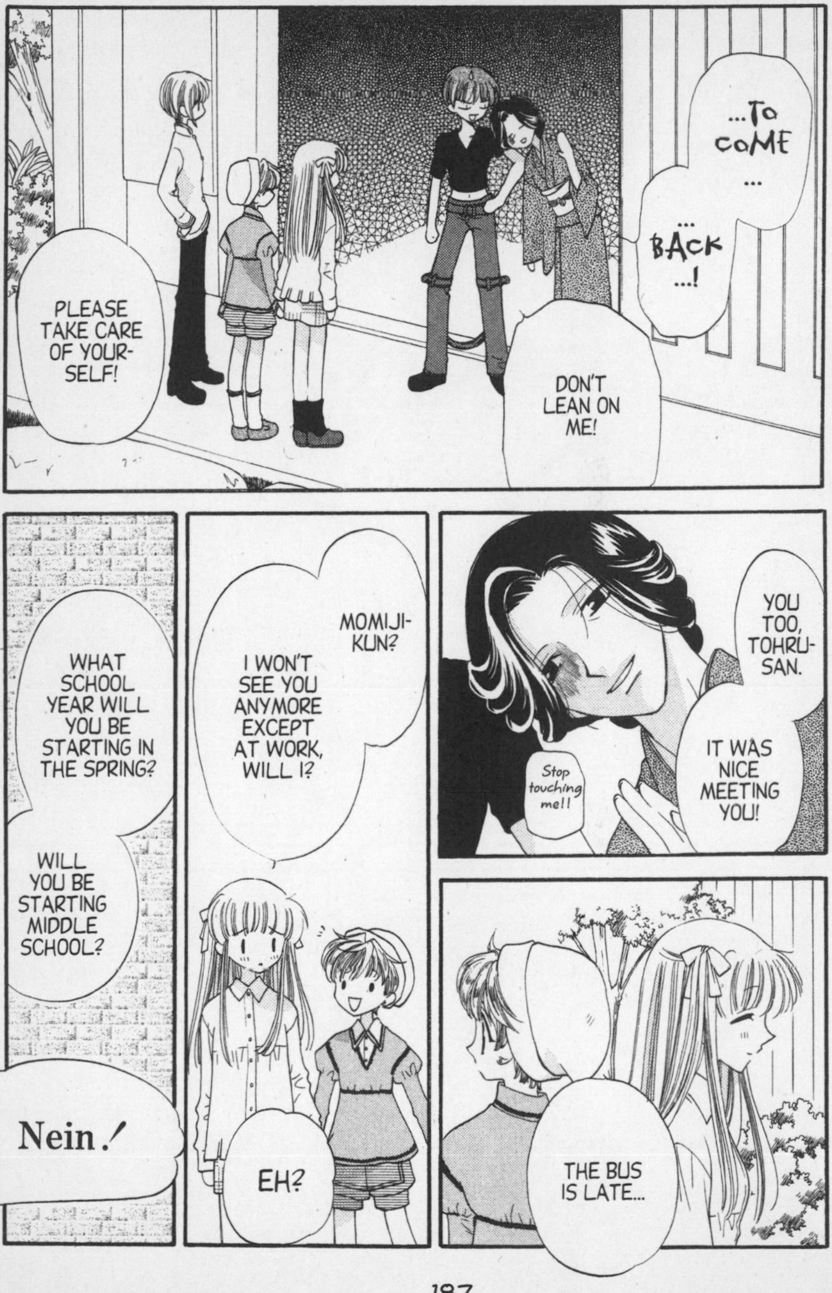
...To coME ...
... BACK ...!
DON'T LEAN ON ME!
PLEASE TAKE CARE OF YOUR-SELF!
YOU TOO, TOHRU-SAN.
IT WAS NICE MEETING YOU!
Stop touching me!!
THE BUS IS LATE...
MOMIJI-KUN?
I WON'T SEE YOU ANYMORE EXCEPT AT WORK, WILL I?
EH?
WHAT SCHOOL YEAR WILL YOU BE STARTING IN THE SPRING?
WILL YOU BE STARTING MIDDLE SCHOOL?
Nein!

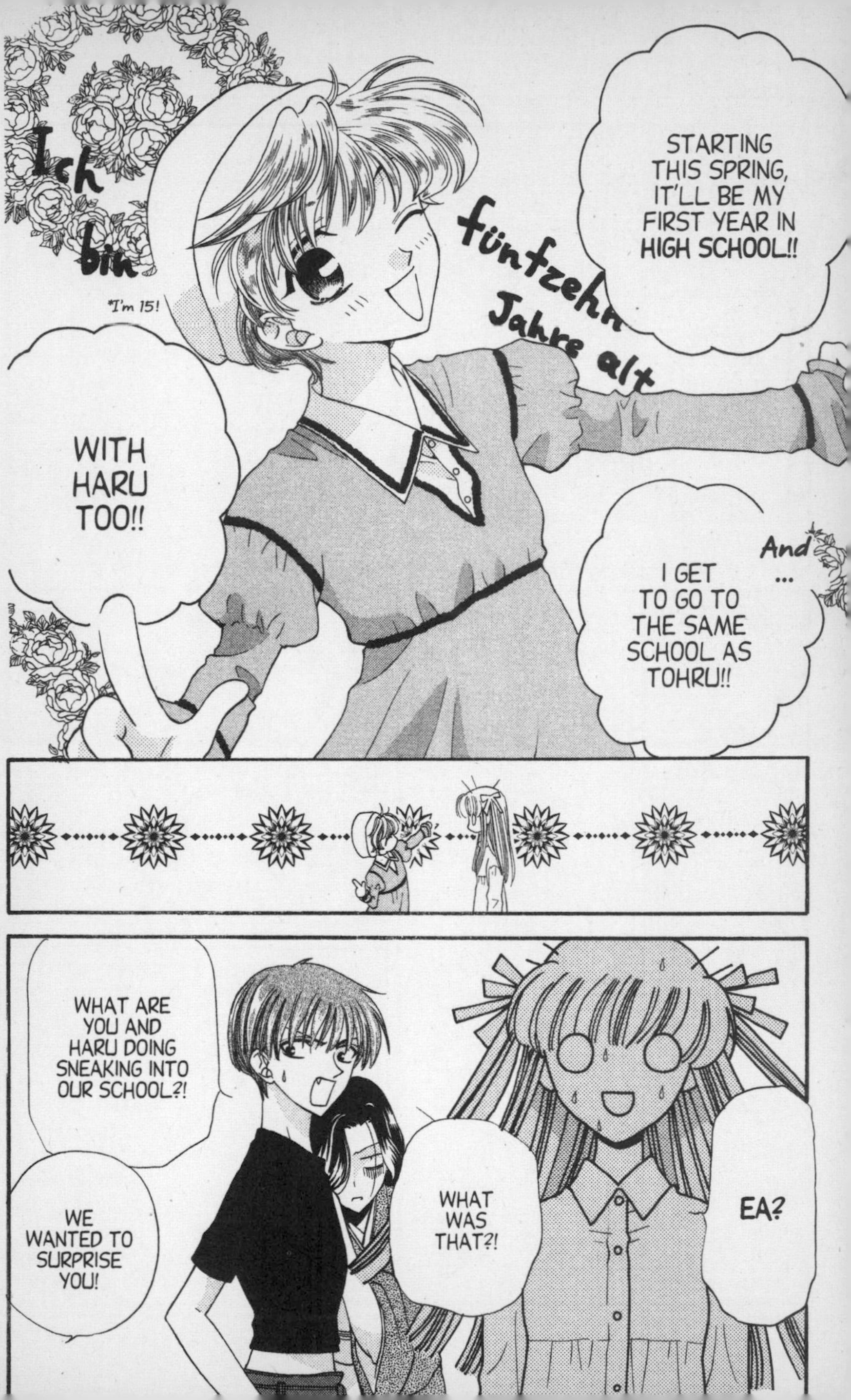
STARTING THIS SPRING, IT'LL BE MY FIRST YEAR IN HIGH SCHOOL!!
Ich bin fünfzehn Jahre alt
*I'm 15!
And ...
I GET TO GO TO THE SAME SCHOOL AS TOHRU!!
WITH HARU TOO!!
EA?
WHAT WAS THAT?!
WHAT ARE YOU AND HARU DOING SNEAKING INTO OUR SCHOOL?!
WE WANTED TO SURPRISE YOU!

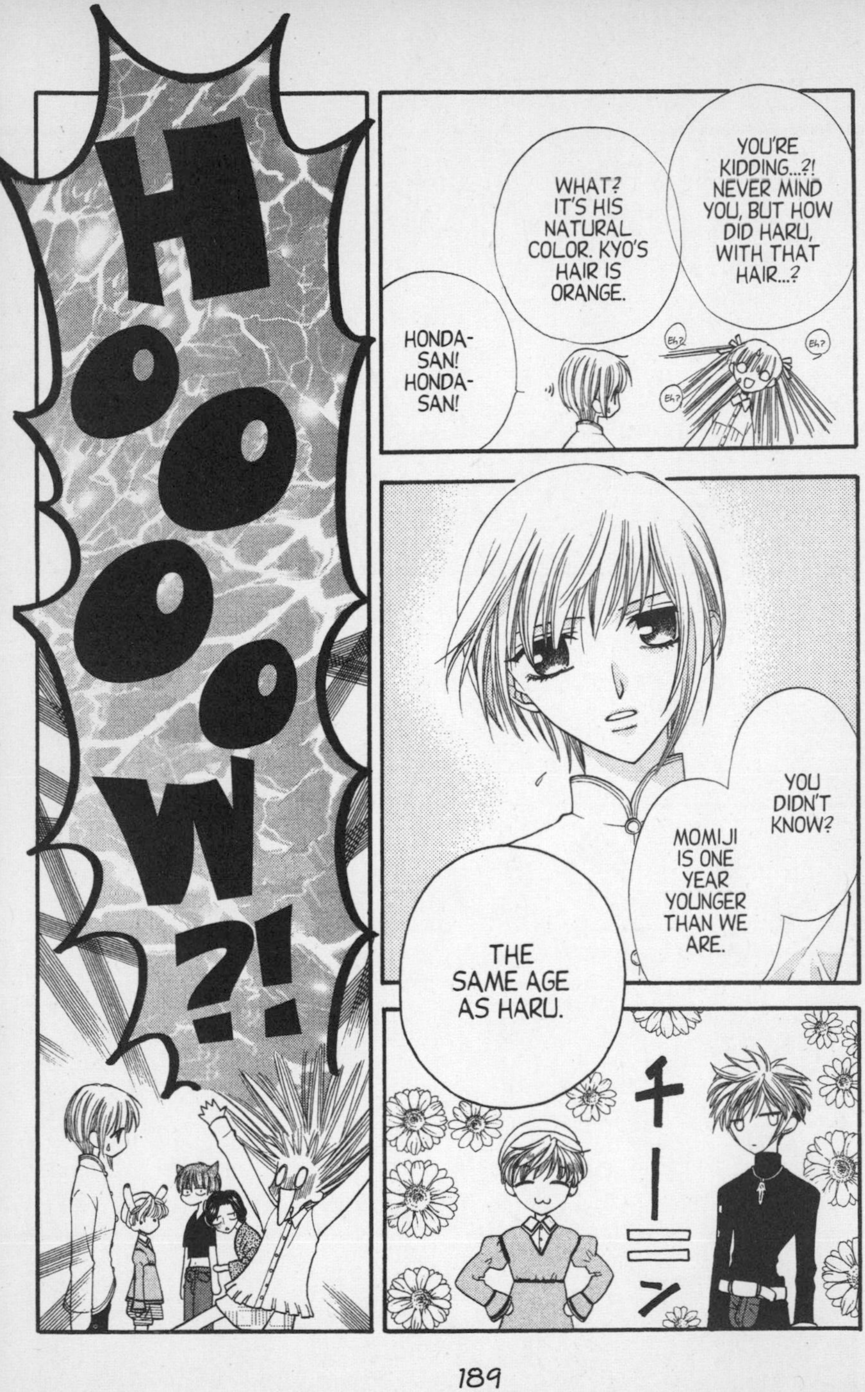
YOU'RE KIDDING...?! NEVER MIND YOU, BUT HOW DID HARU, WITH THAT HAIR...?
WHAT? IT'S HIS NATURAL COLOR. KYO'S HAIR IS ORANGE.
Eh?
Eh?
Eh?
HONDA-SAN! HONDA-SAN!
YOU DIDN'T KNOW?
MOMIJI IS ONE YEAR YOUNGER THAN WE ARE.
THE SAME AGE AS HARU.
チーン
HOOOOW?!

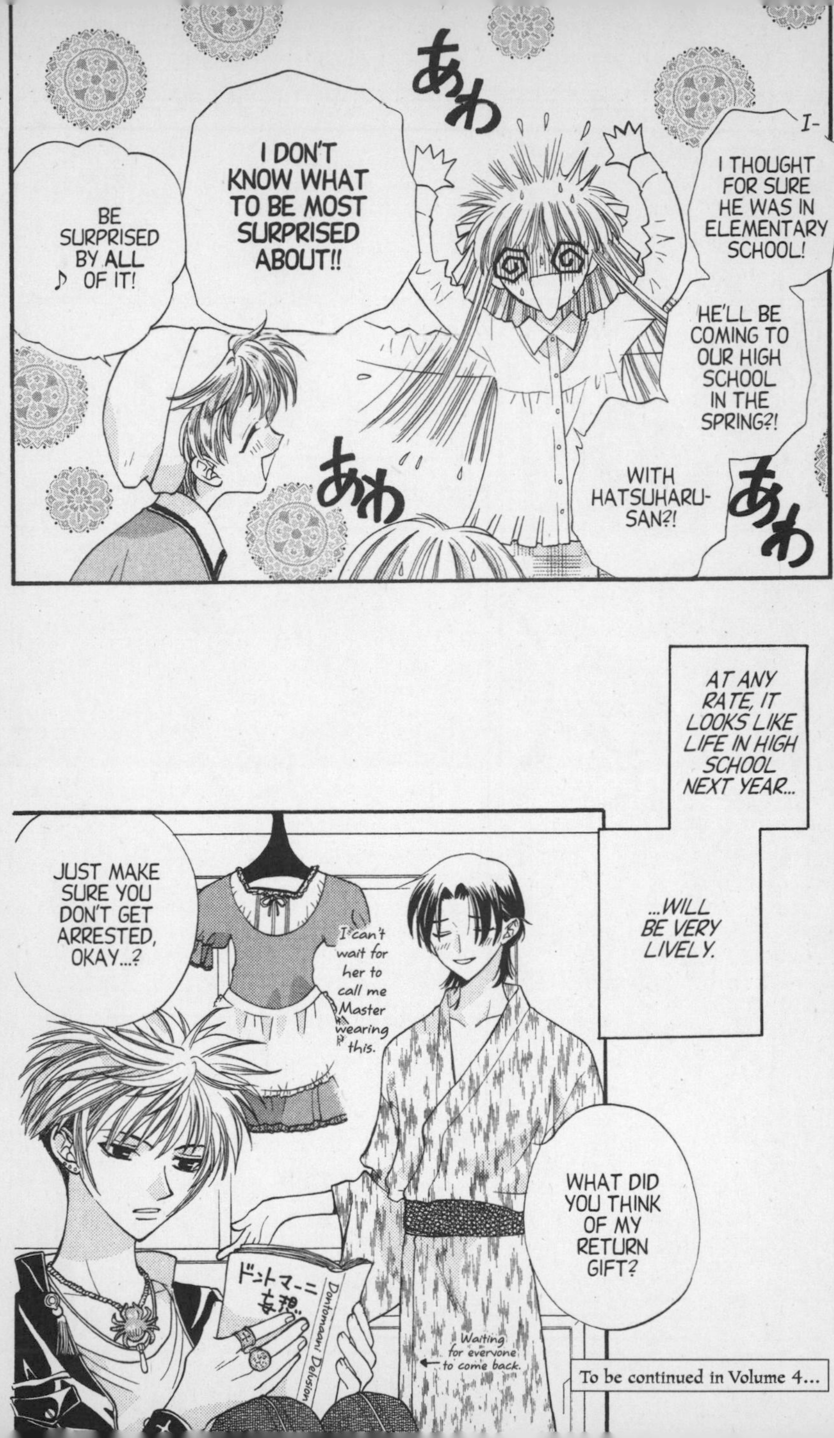
あゎ
I-
I THOUGHT FOR SURE HE WAS IN ELEMENTARY SCHOOL!
HE'LL BE COMING TO OUR HIGH SCHOOL IN THE SPRING?!
WITH HATSUHARU-SAN?!
あゎ
I DON'T KNOW WHAT TO BE MOST SURPRISED ABOUT!!
BE SURPRISED BY ALL ♪ OF IT!
あゎ
AT ANY RATE, IT LOOKS LIKE LIFE IN HIGH SCHOOL NEXT YEAR...
...WILL BE VERY LIVELY.
WHAT DID YOU THINK OF MY RETURN GIFT?
I can't wait for her to call me Master wearing this.
JUST MAKE SURE YOU DON'T GET ARRESTED, OKAY...?
ドントマーニ妄想
Dontomaani Delusion
Waiting for everyone to come back.

To be continued in Volume 4...

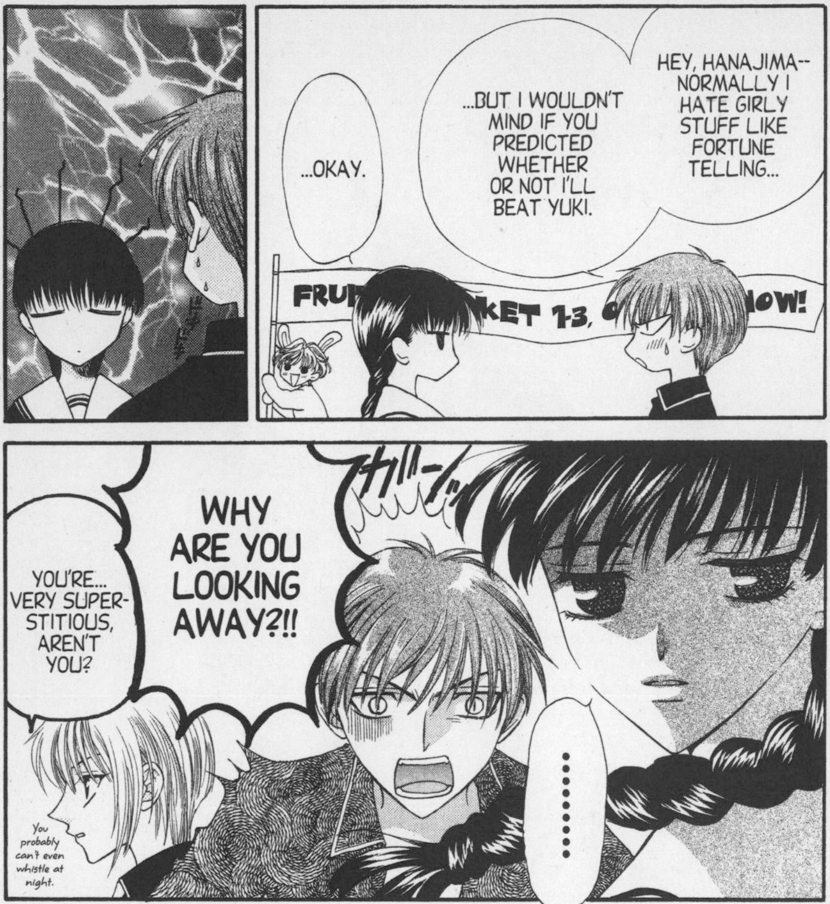
HEY, HANAJIMA--NORMALLY I HATE GIRLY STUFF LIKE FORTUNE TELLING...
...BUT I WOULDN'T MIND IF YOU PREDICTED WHETHER OR NOT I'LL BEAT YUKI.
...OKAY.
WHY ARE YOU LOOKING AWAY?!!
....
YOU'RE... VERY SUPER-STITIOUS, AREN'T YOU?
You probably can't even whistle at night.

Omake Theater, Part 3

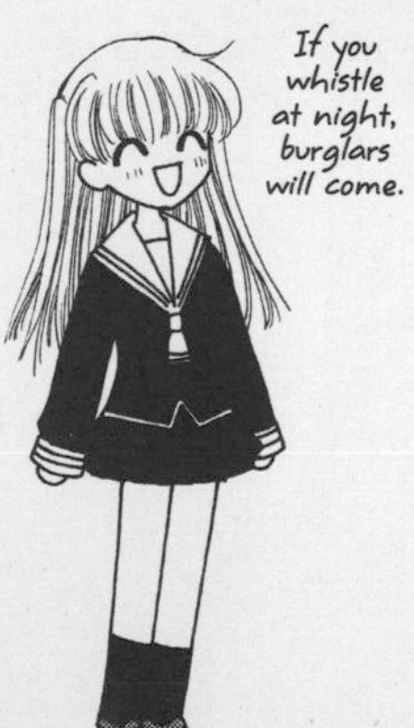
If you whistle at night, burglars will come.

Thank you so much!

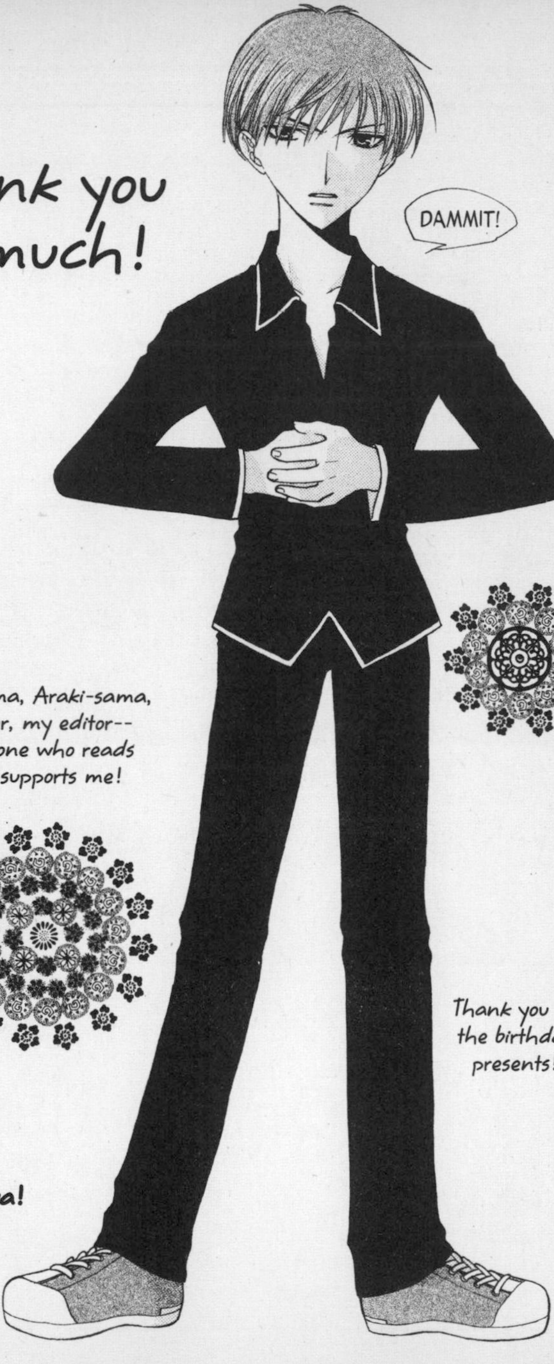
DAMMIT!

Harada-sama, Araki-sama,
my mother, my editor--
and everyone who reads
this and supports me!

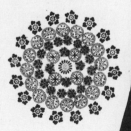

Thank you for
the birthday
presents!

Next time is
Gure-san!
This has been
Natsuki Takaya!

Next time in...

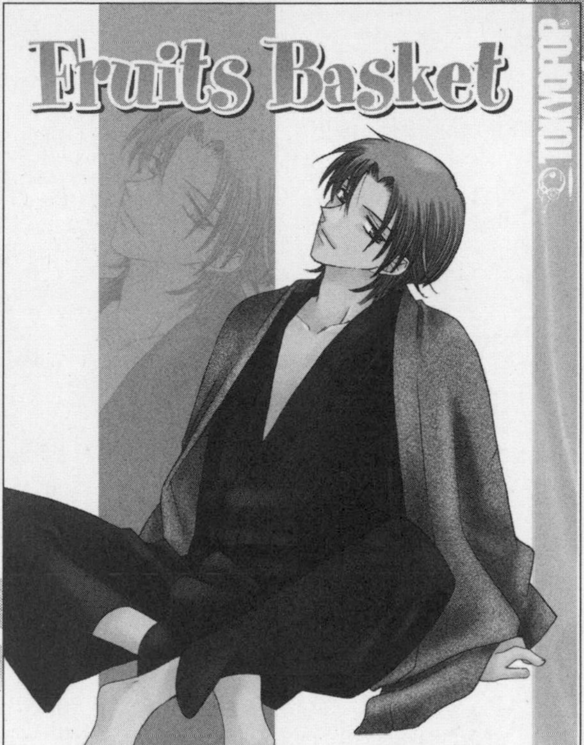
Fruits Basket
TOKYOPOP
4
Natsuki Takaya

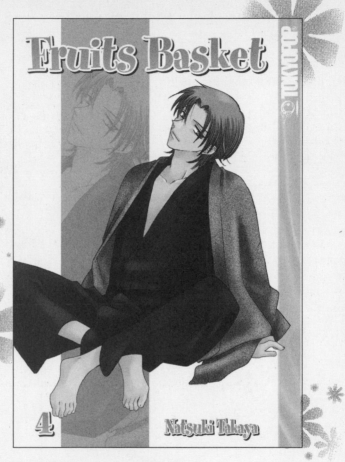

You Can't Choose Your Family...

When the infamous Akito makes an in-class appearance at the start of the school year, the Sohma family worries that his arrival will be an uncensored exercise of show-and-tell about Yuki's past. Meanwhile, when Ayame vows to rekindle his brother's lost friendship, he begins to realize that you can choose your friends but you can't choose your family—especially when they're acting like animals!

Fruits Basket Volume 4
Available August 2004

Interview with Takaya-sensei

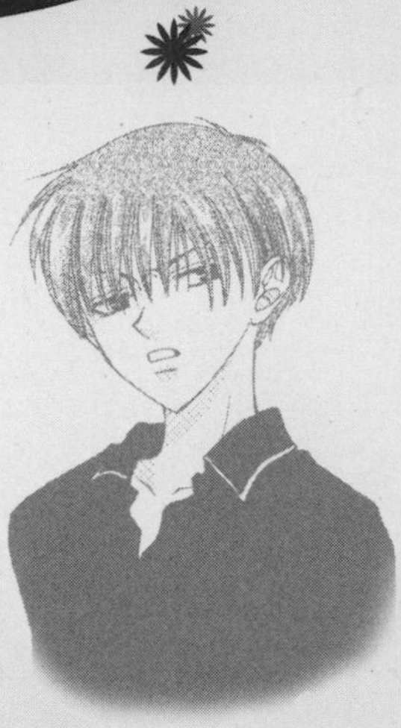

1) First, please tell us about yourself.

- Birthday: July 7
- Horoscope: Cancer
- Blood type: A
- Place of birth: Born in Shizuoka, raised in Tokyo
- Motto: I have about three, but… They're secret.
- Hobbies: Video Games
- Favorite color-Light colors, especially green and blue. Lately I've been into pastels.
- Favorite food: Abalone (because I rarely get to eat it). I love gum! I eat it so much they call me a gum monster. I don't like green peppers.

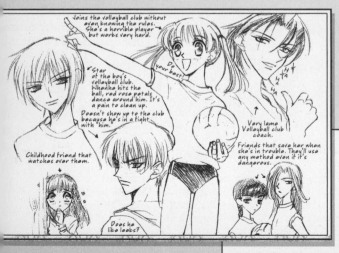

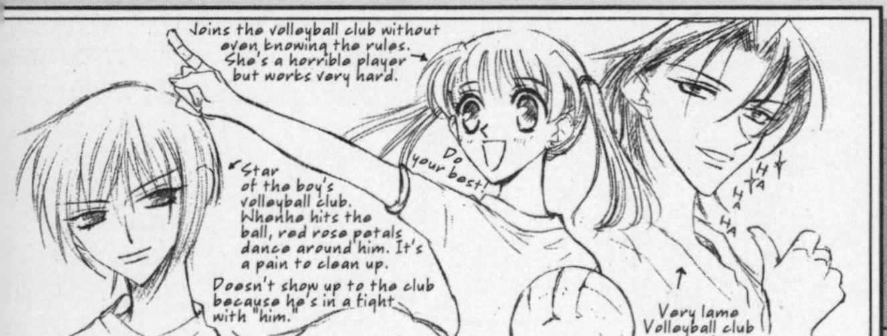
Joins the volleyball club without even knowing the rules. She's a horrible player but works very hard.
Do your best!
HA HA HA
Star of the boy's volleyball club. Whenhe hits the ball, red rose petals dance around him. It's a pain to clean up.
Doesn't show up to the club because he's in a fight with "him."
Very lame Volleyball club coach.
Friends that save her when she's in trouble. They'll use any method even if it's dangerous.
Childhood friend that watches over them.
Does he like looks?

SPORTS FURUBA

What if Fruits Basket was a sports manga? That was the idea behind these sketches. Yuki's dancing rose petals are amazing but what about Kyo being the son of a green grocer? Minagawa Motoko's family also runs a produce store… Why am I so obsessed with them?

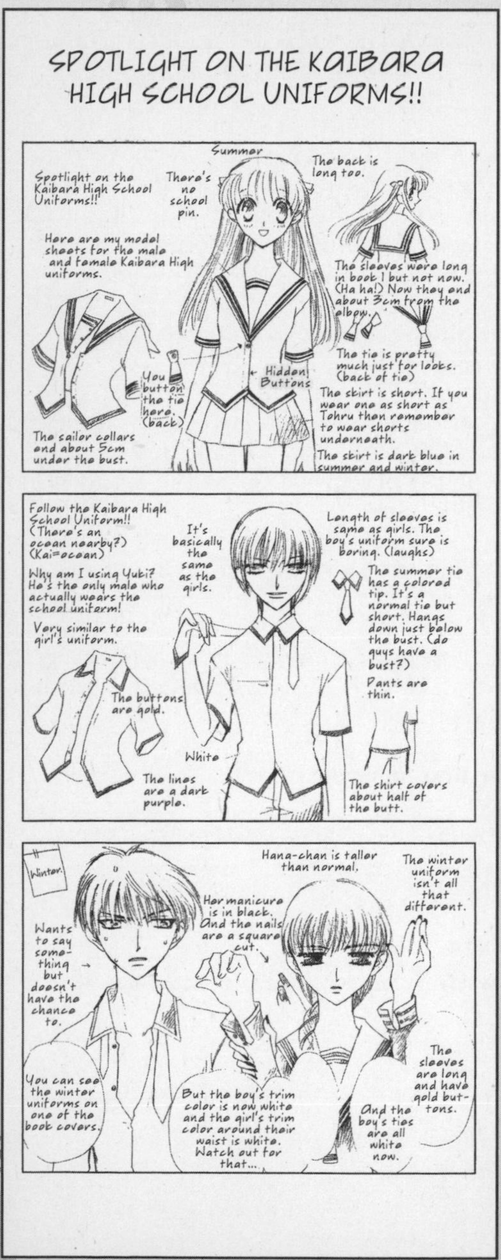
SPOTLIGHT ON THE KAIBARA HIGH SCHOOL UNIFORMS!!
The back is long too.
The sleeves were long in book 1 but not now. (Ha ha!) Now they end about 3cm from the elbow.
The tie is pretty much just for looks. (back of tie)
The skirt is short. If you wear one as short as Tohru then remember to wear shorts underneath.
The skirt is dark blue in summer and winter.
Summer
There's no school pin.
Spotlight on the Kaibara High School Uniforms!!
Here are my model sheets for the male and female Kaibara High uniforms.
Hidden Buttons
You button the tie here. (back)
The sailor collars end about 5cm under the bust.
Length of sleeves is same as girls. The boy's uniform sure is boring. (laughs)
The summer tie has a colored tip. It's a normal tie but short. Hangs down just below the bust. (do guys have a bust?)
Pants are thin.
The shirt covers about half of the butt.
It's basically the same as the girls.
White
Follow the Kaibara High School Uniform!! (There's an ocean nearby?) (Kai=ocean)
Why am I using Yuki? He's the only male who actually wears the school uniform!
Very similar to the girl's uniform.
The buttons are gold.
The lines are a dark purple.
The winter uniform isn't all that different.
Hana-chan is taller than normal.
Her manicure is in black. And the nails are a square cut.
The sleeves are long and have gold buttons.
And the boy's ties are all white now.
But the boy's trim color is now white and the girl's trim color around their waist is white. Watch out for that...
Winter.
Wants to say something but doesn't have the chance to.
You can see the winter uniforms on one of the book covers.

2) Tell us about your work schedule.

I don't write out a full script. Well, I'm just not able to do well, so I go straight from m notes (which only I can decipher to the rough draft. It's much easi to get the rough draft done righ off the bat, but the downside is, have to correct it over and over. but that's still easier for me. seems I'm the "draw it first the decide if it's good or not" type.

So getting back to the question. it takes me about 3-5 days fo the rough draft. Then I show to my editor and discuss it, cor rect problems, and when I get th OK I start the real drawings. Th sketches take about 2 and a ha days, then another 2 and a ha days to ink it. Then the tones an the rest take another 2 days or so

3) Tell us about your daily schedule.

I work all day long, stopping onl for meals. When I have a spar moment I take a bath or pla video games.

4) What tools and supplies do you use for your work?

Nothing particularly special. I paper, various brands of tone Zebra no Maru pens and a N cutter. And currency ink.

5) When did you start using your Macintosh for work? What do you use it for?

Around the final chapter of Genei Musou. I used it mainly for the color art. I've always been bad at coloring since I was a child. My mother once told me, "I'm not going to buy you any more coloring books!" That's how bad I was. Coloring with the Mac is so helpful. Plus it's so fun to use! Although I still can't do anything complicated with it.

6) When you're working on the plot or rough draft, do you ever get writer's block? How do you cope with that?

Yes, that does happen… My biggest problem is working out how to fit the story into the allotted pages. When I'm stuck I take a break. Sometimes I'll talk it over with my editor, other times I play a video game and get my head away from the problem. That usually helps.

7) When did you decide you wanted to be a manga-ka? What made you decide to pursue that career?

Around first grade, I think. At that time my sister wanted to become a manga-ka too, and that influenced me. I don't know… I just really wanted to become one for some reason.

8) What kind of work was your first manga?

It was a Sci-Fi comedy with a female duo… I think. I was in grade school so I don't remember too well.

See more Questions with Takaya-sensei in volume 4!

Fans Basket

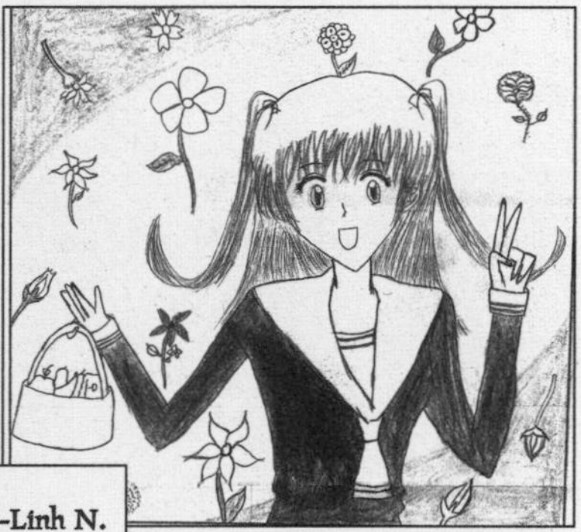

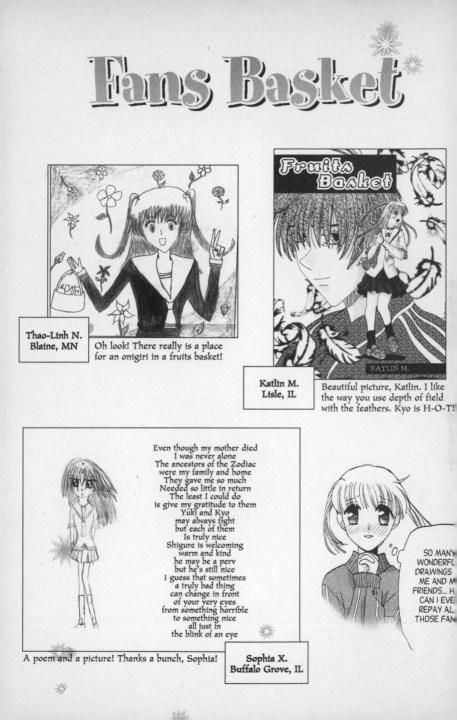

Thao-Linh N.
Blaine, MN

Oh look! There really is a place for an onigiri in a fruits basket!

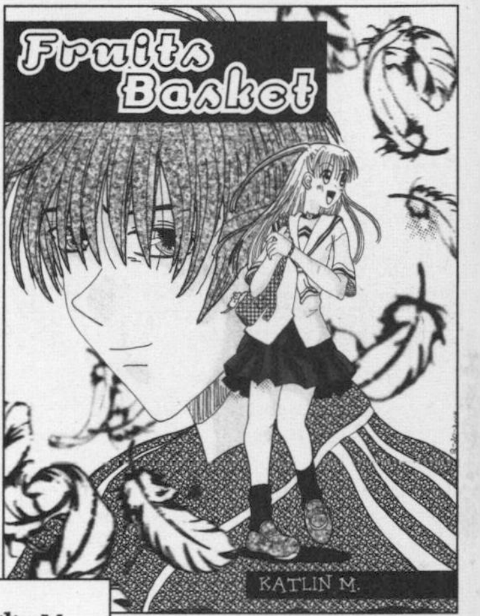
Fruits Basket
KATLIN M.

Katlin M.
Lisle, IL

Beautiful picture, Katlin. I like the way you use depth of field with the feathers. Kyo is H-O-T!

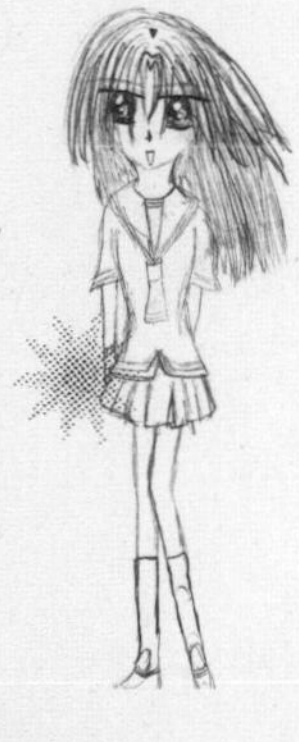

Even though my mother died
I was never alone
The ancestors of the Zodiac
were my family and home
They gave me so much
Needed so little in return
The least I could do
is give my gratitude to them
Yuki and Kyo
may always fight
but each of them
Is truly nice
Shigure is welcoming
warm and kind
he may be a perv
but he's still nice
I guess that sometimes
a truly bad thing
can change in front
of your very eyes
from something horrible
to something nice
all just in
the blink of an eye

A poem and a picture! Thanks a bunch, Sophia!

Sophia X.
Buffalo Grove, IL

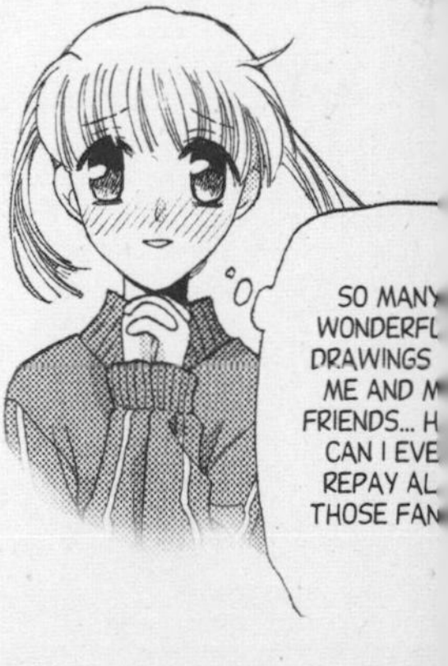

Do you want to share your love for Fruits Basket with fans around the world? "Fans Basket" is taking submissions of fan art, poetry, cosplay photos, or any other Furuaba fun you'd like to share!

How to submit:

1)Send your work via regular mail (NOT e-mail) to:

"Fans Basket"
c/o TOKYOPOP
5900 Wilshire Blvd.
Suite 2000
Los Angeles, CA 90036

2) All work should be in black and white and no larger than 8.5" x 11". (And try not to fold it too many times!)

3) Anything you send will not be returned. If you want to keep your original, it's fine to send us a copy.

4) Please include your full name, age, city and state for us to print with your work. If you'd rather us use a pen name, please include that too.

5) IMPORTANT: If you're under the age of 18, you must have your parent's permission in order for us to print your work. Any submissions without a signed note of parental consent cannot be used.

6) For full details, please check out our website.http://www.tokyopop.com/aboutus/fanart.php

Disclaimer: Anything you send to us becomes the exclusive property of TOKYOPOP Inc. and, as we said before, will not be returned to you. We will have the right to print, reproduce, distribute, or modify the artwork for use in future volumes of Fruits Basket or on the web royalty-free.

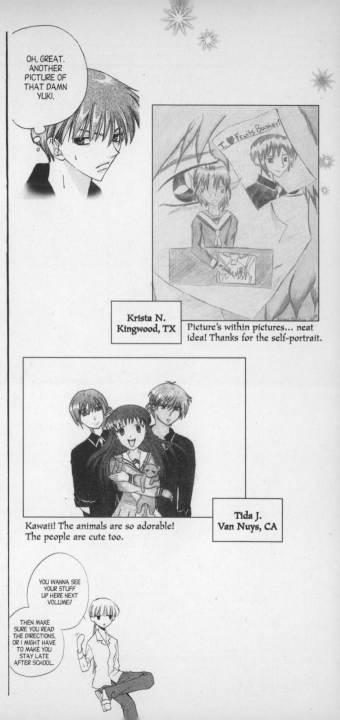

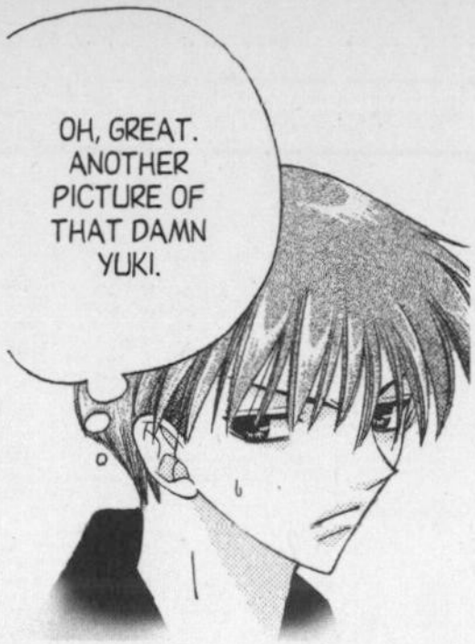
OH, GREAT. ANOTHER PICTURE OF THAT DAMN YUKI.

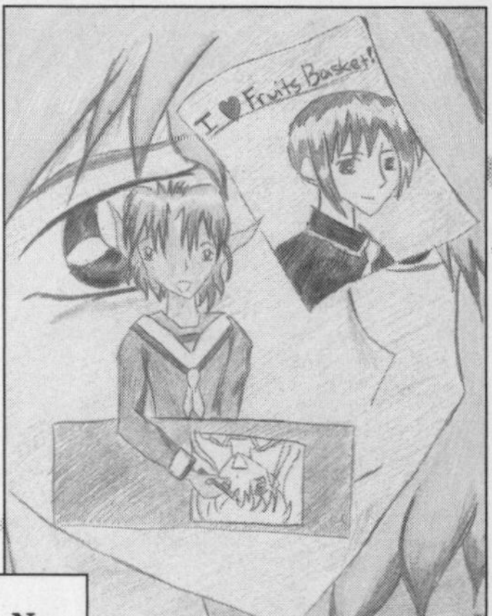
I ♥ Fruits Basket!

Krista N.
Kingwood, TX

Picture's within pictures... neat idea! Thanks for the self-portrait.

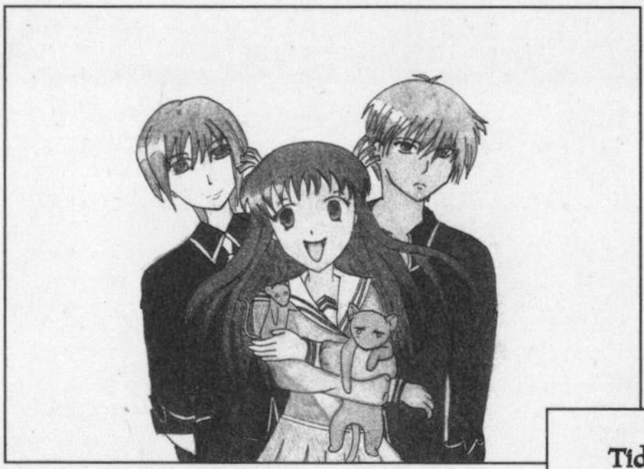

Tida J.
Van Nuys, CA

Kawaii! The animals are so adorable! The people are cute too.

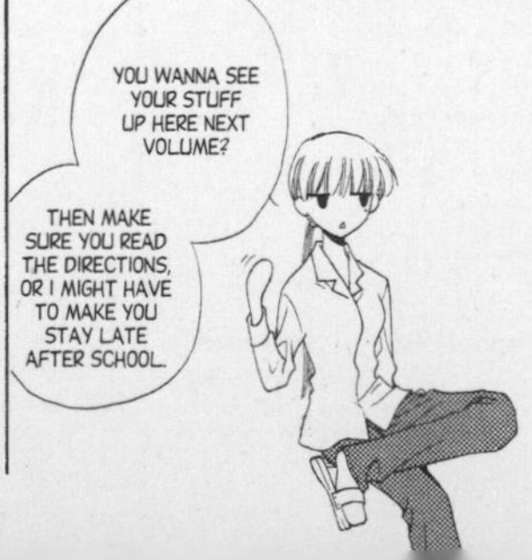
YOU WANNA SEE YOUR STUFF UP HERE NEXT VOLUME?
THEN MAKE SURE YOU READ THE DIRECTIONS, OR I MIGHT HAVE TO MAKE YOU STAY LATE AFTER SCHOOL.

SOUND EFFECT INDEX

THE FOLLOWING IS A LIST OF THE SOUND EFFECTS USED IN FRUITS BASKET. EACH SOUND IS LABELED BY PAGE AND PANEL NUMBER, SEPARATED BY A PERIOD. THE FIRST DESCRIPTION IS THE PHONETIC READING OF THE JAPANESE, AND IS FOLLOWED BY THE EQUIVALENT ENGLISH SOUND OR A DESCRIPTION.

23.2	gakuh: stagger
26.2	dopyuun: zoom
27.1	ze: wheeze x3
27.3	piku: twitch
27.4	suku: rise
27.5	suta suta: stride
28.2	kyuu: tug
28.3	shyuru shyuru: wiggle
28.4	dota dota: (approaching footsteps)
28.5a	batan!: crash
28.5b	bishi: twang
28.5c	zusa: skid
29.3	gaba: surge
29.4	doku doku: dribble (blood)
31.1	goshi goshi: rub rub
31.5	peko peko: bow
32.6	gyaa gyaa: bicker
33.3	Gan!: whack
33.5	gishi: snap
34.1	zun: (fanfare)
34.4	doh!: kick
35.3	su: slip
36.1	giri giri: struggle
38.1-2	gogogogo: thunder
42.2	za!: (drama!)
42.4	gakii: snap
43.1	muka: (anger)
43.3	buchi: snap
43.4	Goh!: wham
43.5	doka baki: whack, bam
45.3	Zuru: slump
45.6	su: fall
46.4	suku: rise
46.5	ga: grab
48.5	ji: stare
49.2	Gyuu: hug
49.3a	bon: poof

9.1, 9.2	zawa zawa: chatter
10.1	Sucha: strap
10.2	gyu: squeeze
10.3	za!: (drama!)
10.4	don!: (impact!)
10.5	charin charin: ring ring
12.2	Sha: slide
12.3	fu: fume x2
13.5	gyaa: bicker
14.1	Ki: anger
14.2	za!: (strike a pose!)
14.3	zuppo: shoop
14.4	Agaaa: gag

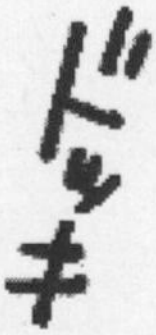
ドッキ

DOKI-DOKI

ONE OF THE MOST COMMON SOUND EFFECTS IN MANGA, "DOKI-DOKI" IS THE SOUND OF A POUNDING HEARTBEAT. IT'S USED TO INDICATE A TENSE, EMOTIONAL SITUATION.

15.3	kara kara: rattle (sliding door)
16.2	Biku: wince
17.3	Zudoon!: (meanacing fanfare)
18.1	Mera: burn
18.4	Zugogoon: (meanacing fanfare)
21.4	Gaiin: wham
21.5	zuru zuru: slide
22.1a	zawa zawa: chatter
22.1b	hero hero: wobble
22.2	don!: (impact!)
22.3	zawa zawa: chatter
23.1a	paan: (starting gun)
23.1b	zaa...: chatter (cut off)

132.2	zawa zawa: chatter
133.1	zawa zawa: chatter
133.2	gata: clatter
138.1	patata: pitter patter
138.3	guu: clench
141.3	koro: turn

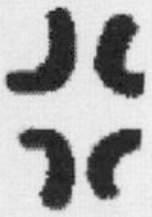

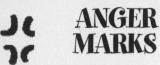

ANGER MARKS

THESE LITTLE "PLUS SIGNS" ARE MEANT TO REPRESENT A THROBBING VEIN. OVER THE YEARS, THESE HAVE BECOME A VISUAL SHORTCUT IN MANGA FOR ANGER. IN THE FRUITS BASKET ANIME, SHIGURE POKES FUN AT HIS EASY GOING PERSONALITY BY HOLDING AN ANGER MARK IN FRONT OF HIS FACE TO SHOW HIS RANGE.

143.1	doku doku (pounding heartbeat)
146.2	gyuun: shoom
146.3	kata kata: (surpressing anger)
147.3	don: bam
156.4	paaa: brighten
159.3	bachi: snap
163.2	gororo: vroom
163.3	jiiin: stare
164.2	gata: clatter
168.1	aaaa: moaning
169.3	gyuumu: (the grab of doom!)
170.3	pecha: grab
173.1	jiiin: stare
174.4	piku: bright
176.1	baki!: whack
176.5	baki!: whack
177.1	gashyon: upheave!
178.3	kah: smack
178.5	byu: swing
189.3	chiin: ching!
190.1	awa awa: panic
191.2	doki doki: (heartbeat)
191.3	gaan: shock

49.3b	Bari Biri Bori: (ripping clothes)
51.1	pi:shing
54.1	bon: poof
54.2	doki doki: (heartbeat)
54.4	jiiin: stare
55.1	gacha: click
56.1	giri giri: struggle
58.2	wata wata: flap flap
58.4	gashyon: shock
59.3	gacha: click
66.1	gaba: jolt
67.3	Ka: blush
67.4	bon: poof
73.5	Goh!: slam
74.4	zawa zawa: chatter
74.3	kya: grab
76.6	Zudoon!: horror

ZAWA-ZAWA

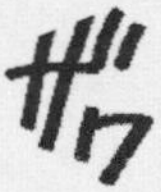

THE SOUND OF A CROWD. IF YOU SEE "ZAWA"S IN A CLASSROOM, IT PROBABLY MEANS THAT CLASS HASN'T STARTED YET. EITHER THAT, OR A TEACHER CAN'T CONTROL HIS OR HER STUDENTS!

77.1	gata: clatter
77.5	shuu: shoop
78.1	ban!: bam!
79.4-5	Hyuoooo:wind
81.1-2	do-do-do-do: stomp stomp...
83.2	kaa: blush
83.4	zugogogogo: (menacing presence)
84.1	gyo: irk
84.3	shiku shiku: sob sob
90.3	pata pata: stomp stomp
91.5	kasa: step
98.2	gotsu: smack
102.3	butsu: click
103.1	gara: rattle
104.5	pon: pat
106.3	gara: rattle
106.5	butsu: click
106.7	chari: (remove)
110.3	Pishan!: Slam!
113.5	kah: tink
124.5	gusa: poke
125.6	chiki chiki: click click
129.1	pori pori: scratch scratch
132.1	kiin kon kan kon: (school bells)

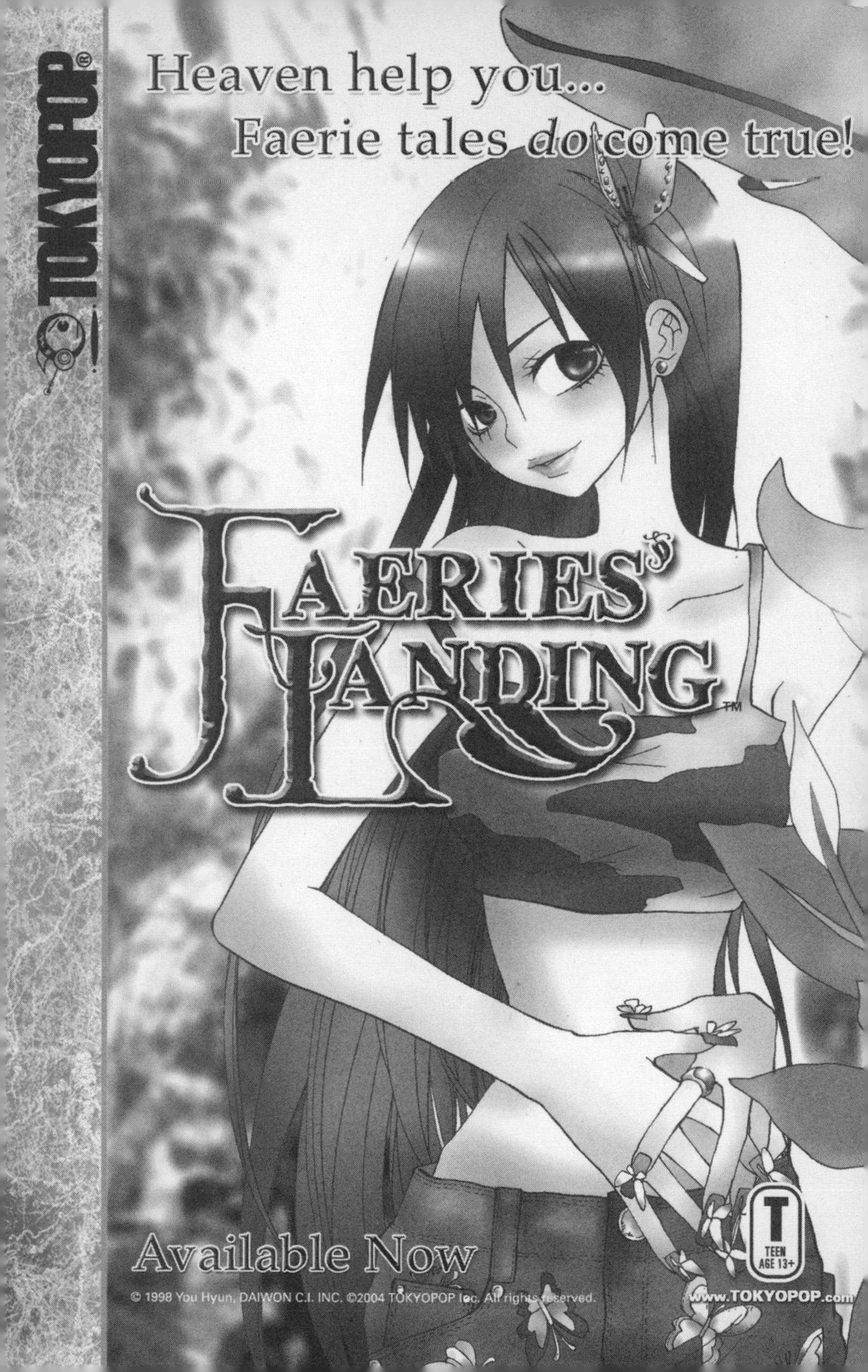

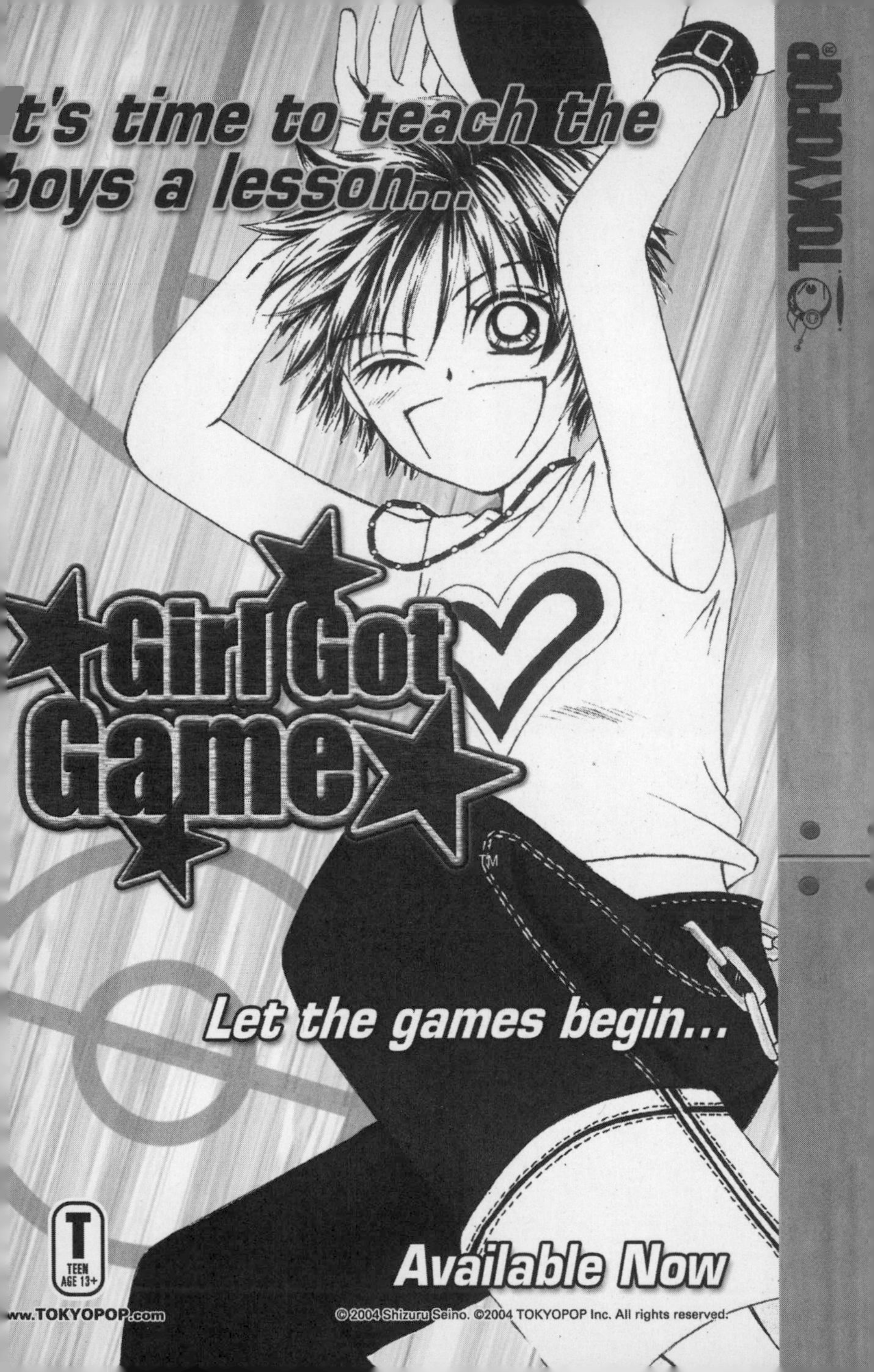
t's time to teach the
boys a lesson...
TOKYOPOP
Girl Got Game
TM
Let the games begin...
T TEEN AGE 13+
Available Now
www.TOKYOPOP.com
© 2004 Shizuru Seino. ©2004 TOKYOPOP Inc. All rights reserved.

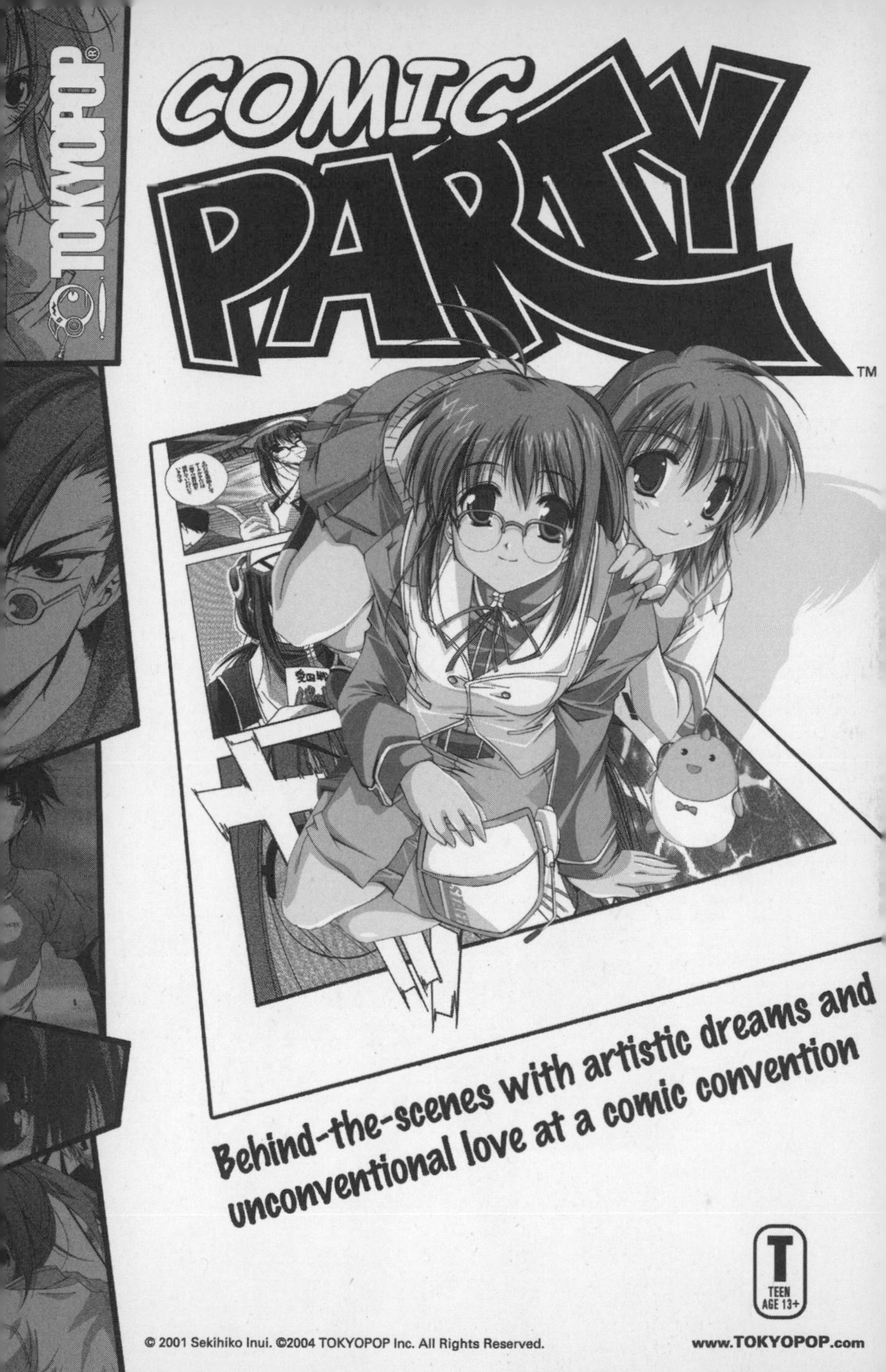
TOKYOPOP®
COMIC PARTY™
Behind-the-scenes with artistic dreams and
unconventional love at a comic convention
T
TEEN
AGE 13+

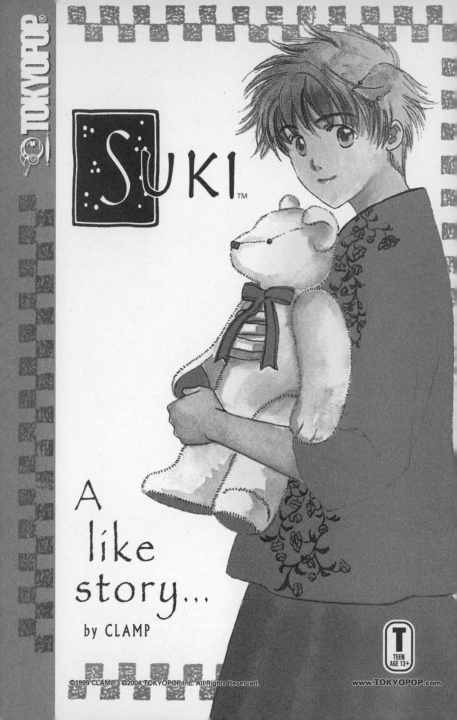

ALSO AVAILABLE FROM  TOKYOPOP®

**For more
information visit
www.TOKYOPOP.com**

03.30.04T

ALSO AVAILABLE FROM TOKYOPOP®

MANGA

.HACK//LEGEND OF THE TWILIGHT
@LARGE
ABENOBASHI: MAGICAL SHOPPING ARCADE
A.I. LOVE YOU
AI YORI AOSHI
ANGELIC LAYER
ARM OF KANNON
BABY BIRTH
BATTLE ROYALE
BATTLE VIXENS
BRAIN POWERED
BRIGADOON
B'TX
CANDIDATE FOR GODDESS, THE
CARDCAPTOR SAKURA
CARDCAPTOR SAKURA - MASTER OF THE CLOW
CHOBITS
CHRONICLES OF THE CURSED SWORD
CLAMP SCHOOL DETECTIVES
CLOVER
COMIC PARTY
CONFIDENTIAL CONFESSIONS
CORRECTOR YUI
COWBOY BEBOP
COWBOY BEBOP: SHOOTING STAR
CRAZY LOVE STORY
CRESCENT MOON
CROSS
CULDCEPT
CYBORG 009
D•N•ANGEL
DEMON DIARY
DEMON ORORON, THE
DEUS VITAE
DIABOLO
DIGIMON
DIGIMON TAMERS
DIGIMON ZERO TWO
DOLL
DRAGON HUNTER
DRAGON KNIGHTS
DRAGON VOICE
DREAM SAGA
DUKLYON: CLAMP SCHOOL DEFENDERS
EERIE QUEERIE!
ERICA SAKURAZAWA: COLLECTED WORKS
ET CETERA
ETERNITY
EVIL'S RETURN
FAERIES' LANDING
FAKE
FLCL
FLOWER OF THE DEEP SLEEP
FORBIDDEN DANCE
FRUITS BASKET
G GUNDAM

GATEKEEPERS
GETBACKERS
GIRL GOT GAME
GIRLS' EDUCATIONAL CHARTER
GRAVITATION
GTO
GUNDAM BLUE DESTINY
GUNDAM SEED ASTRAY
GUNDAM WING
GUNDAM WING: BATTLEFIELD OF PACIFISTS
GUNDAM WING: ENDLESS WALTZ
GUNDAM WING: THE LAST OUTPOST (G-UNIT)
GUYS' GUIDE TO GIRLS
HANDS OFF!
HAPPY MANIA
HARLEM BEAT
HONEY MUSTARD
I.N.V.U.
IMMORTAL RAIN
INITIAL D
INSTANT TEEN: JUST ADD NUTS
ISLAND
JING: KING OF BANDITS
JING: KING OF BANDITS - TWILIGHT TALES
JULINE
KARE KANO
KILL ME, KISS ME
KINDAICHI CASE FILES, THE
KING OF HELL
KODOCHA: SANA'S STAGE
LAMENT OF THE LAMB
LEGAL DRUG
LEGEND OF CHUN HYANG, THE
LES BIJOUX
LOVE HINA
LUPIN III
LUPIN III: WORLD'S MOST WANTED
MAGIC KNIGHT RAYEARTH I
MAGIC KNIGHT RAYEARTH II
MAHOROMATIC: AUTOMATIC MAIDEN
MAN OF MANY FACES
MARMALADE BOY
MARS
MARS: HORSE WITH NO NAME
MINK
MIRACLE GIRLS
MIYUKI-CHAN IN WONDERLAND
MODEL
MY LOVE
NECK AND NECK
ONE
ONE I LOVE, THE
PARADISE KISS
PARASYTE
PASSION FRUIT
PEACH GIRL
PEACH GIRL: CHANGE OF HEART
PET SHOP OF HORRORS

03.30.04T

STOP!

This is the back of the book.
You wouldn't want to spoil a great ending!

This book is printed "manga-style," in the authentic Japanese right-to-left format. Since none of the artwork has been flipped or altered, readers get to experience the story just as the creator intended. You've been asking for it, so TOKYOPOP® delivered: authentic, hot-off-the-press, and far more fun!

DIRECTIONS

If this is your first time reading manga-style, here's a quick guide to help you understand how it works.

It's easy... just start in the top right panel and follow the numbers. Have fun, and look for more 100% authentic manga from TOKYOPOP®!